TO BE A WOMAN

TO BE A WOMAN

The life of Jill Craigie

CARL ROLLYSON

A catalogue record for this book is available from the British Library.

ISBN 1 85410 935 9

1 3 5 7 9 10 8 6 4 2
2005 2007 2009 2008 2006

Text design by James Campus

Typeset by SX Composing DTP, Rayleigh, Essex

Printed and bound in Great Britain by MPG Books, Bodmin

'When You Are Old' by W.B. Yeats
reproduced by kind permission of A.P. Watt Ltd
on behalf of Michael B. Yeats

To Lisa

Contents

Acknowledgements

This biography would not have been possible without the full and cheerful co-operation of Michael Foot and Julie Hamilton. They withstood countless hours of interviews, telephone calls, e-mails and faxes. They supplied letters and many other kinds of documents. They put no restrictions on my work; indeed, they encouraged others to respond to my questions. Like many of my interviewees, they have checked my manuscript for errors and misinterpretations. But as Michael said to me at the beginning of this enterprise: 'This is your book.' Both Michael and Julie wanted a candid biography, and I've done my best to write one.

I am grateful to Michael Holroyd, Jane Marcus, Kenneth Morgan, Patricia Romero and June Purvis, for providing me with copies of Jill Craigie's correspondence. I thank Philip Kemp and Charles Drazin for supplying transcripts and tape recordings of their interviews.

Unless otherwise specified in footnotes, all quotations in the text are from my interviews with June Aberdeen, Leo Abse, Ian Aitkin, Tony Benn, Cornelia Bessie, Michael Bessie, Melvyn Bragg, Alan Brien, Brian Brivati, James Callaghan, the late Yvonne Clench, Jill Craigie, Peter Cuming, Stevan Dedijer, Barbara Dell, Margaret Drabble, Charles Drazin, Sarah Easen, Faith Evans, Tommy Evans, Anne Foot, Michael Foot, the late Paul Foot, Sir Denis Forman, Moni (Cameron) Forman, Alan Fox, Megan Fox, Vesna Gamulin, Geoffrey Goodman, Margit Goodman, Julie Hamilton, Tom Hancock, Cate Haste, Denis Healey, Chris Highet, Sue Highet, Quintin Hoare, Patricia Hollis, Michael Holroyd, Ted Honderich, Brian Jones, Gillian (Gilly) Jones (née Short), Mervyn Jones, Philip Kemp, Bruce Kent, Glenys Kinnock, Neil Kinnock, Celine La Freniere, Jason Lehel, Jillian Lehel, David Leigh, Midge Mackenzie, the late William MacQuitty, Branka Magas, Kay Mander, Jane Marcus, Fiona Millar, Alison Morgan, Owain Morgan, Kenneth Morgan, Ronald Neame, Pauline Neville, Mary Noble, Philip

Oakes, Ursula Owen, Richard Pankhurst, Rita Pankhurst, Elizabeth (Lizzie) Parker, Lord Paul, John Penrose, Duro Pulitika, Mira Pulitika, June Purvis, Damon Randall, Esther Randall, Laura Randall, Nigel Rees, Anne Robinson, Sheila Rowbotham, Bonnie Scott, Kathy Seery, Mark Seddon, Milton Shulman, Jon Snow, Madeleine Snow, Jenny Stringer, Peter Thorburn, Elizabeth West, Barbara Winslow, Sally Vincent, Francis Wheen, Maxine Willett and Terry Witts. To these generous people I owe much of what I know about Jill Craigie.

Many libraries and archives have also contributed to my research, providing articles, transcripts, letters and other items that form the tissue of my narrative: the BBC, the British Council, the British Library, the British Film Institute (Michael Balcon Papers, Jill Craigie's screenplays), the Colindale Newspaper Library, the Durham University Library (Malcolm Macdonald Papers), the Imperial War Museum (transcripts of Jill Craigie interviews), the Open University Library (Jennie Lee Collection), McFarlin Library (Special Collections) and the University of Tulsa (Rebecca West Papers).

My work on Jill Craigie's film career was facilitated by Shona Barrett at the British Film Institute. She spearheaded the effort to make available to me videocassette copies of Jill's work. Sue Sutton tracked down documents and made many phone calls on my behalf. Amanda Day went through the entire *Tribune* archive to retrieve Jill's articles.

I would also like to thank Francis King, Pauline Neville, Sarah Easen, Mandy Jenkins in Glenys Kinnock's office, Beverly Tempest in Neil Kinnock's office, P.A. Heffernan (Open University Library), Elizabeth Allan (Lord Paul's office), Paul Cotgrove (British Council), Michael Paige (BBC), Janette Martin (Labour History and Archives Centre), Tracey Chapman and Karen Harper (Anne Robinson's office), and at the British Film Institute, Gavin Beattie, Fleur Buckley, Kathleen Dickson, Janet Moat and Katrina Stokes.

Writing biographies is a very expensive proposition, and I have been fortunate to receive travel funding and payment for other expenses from the PSC-CUNY research award program administered by my colleagues at the City University of New York. I have been heartened by their support. Patricia Barba at the Research Foundation of the City University of New York facilitated the administration of my PSC-CUNY grant and made the whole process clear and convenient. I also owe a debt of gratitude to my colleagues at Baruch College and the Dean's office for awards of reassigned time, which reduced my teaching load during the research for this biography.

I am grateful for the expert guidance of Piers Burnett and Natasha Martin, my editors at Aurum Press, and for the unfailing good advice of Gloria Ferris and Rivers Scott at Scott Ferris Associates.

Prologue

'British Filmmaker and Socialist Dies at 85', *The New York Times* announced on 18 December 1999. The obituary called Jill Craigie a feminist and observed that her 'half-century marriage to Labour Party Leader Michael Foot put her at the heart of the country's leftist politics'. Craigie's life unfolded in overlapping phases: the child of a broken home and a neglectful mother who sent her to boarding schools that resembled those places of confinement in Charlotte Brontë's novels; the young abandoned wife of an alcoholic, Claude Begbie-Clench; the frustrated junior partner in a second unhappy marriage to screenwriter Jeffrey Dell; the struggling young journalist, playwright and screenwriter. She did not find her métier until she decided to direct documentaries, emerging in a male-dominated film industry as the first woman filmmaker to attract national attention.

In 1944, Craigie encountered the survivors of the suffragette generation who had gathered at the statue of their great leader, Emmeline Pankhurst. Craigie had been drawn to this meeting after reading Sylvia Pankhurst's stirring book *The Suffragette Movement*. Now just past thirty, Craigie charmed and energized the survivors of a struggle she regarded as central to the history of modern Britain. Craigie befriended and interviewed these women, then sought funding for a film that ultimately could not be made in wartime London, at a time when Sylvia Pankhurst and her sister Christabel had become estranged and the movement itself split into factions, each one demanding loyalty from Craigie, who could not appease them all. Instead, she produced *Out of Chaos* (1944), perhaps the first documentary about modern art, featuring the sculptor Henry Moore and painters Graham Sutherland, Stanley Spencer and Paul Nash. Craigie put the famous art historian Kenneth Clark on camera for the first time, directing him in a style that he would later use for *Civilization*, his groundbreaking television series.

By 1945, Craigie had met Michael Foot during his successful campaign for a parliamentary seat in Plymouth, the setting for Craigie's masterpiece, *The Way We Live*, her exhilarating account of the rebuilding of postwar Britain. This film exemplified her outspoken socialism and a concern for the aesthetics of modern life with a determination to tell the story of the modern women's movement. In this documentary, Craigie captured Michael Foot's rousing speech to the people of Plymouth. He not only epitomized the spirit of the British Labour Party in the historic election that would determine how postwar Britain was to be rebuilt, he also became, during the making of the film, the love of Jill Craigie's life. The ebullient Craigie's impact on Foot was electric: 'I did not think I was going to win, and my father and family did not think so, but Jill did.' Craigie and Foot turned out to be an intriguing political team. In *Diaries of a Cabinet Minister* (1975), Foot's Labour party contemporary Richard Crossman wrote that Craigie fought for her husband like a tiger; she was not merely interested in politics, she was a politician herself.

But Craigie was more than that: she had a gift for delighting Foot's Labour colleagues, many of whom, like the great leader of the Labour left, Aneurin Bevan, the founder of the National Health Service and Foot's hero, were captivated by this petite and beautiful woman who had the aura of a film star (several obituaries referred to her as an ex-actress). Julie Hamilton, Craigie's daughter by her first husband, marvelled at how her mother seemed to magnetize men, yet she remained not only loyal to her husband but also a source of vitality, bringing to her parties the raffish world of actors and writers from the stage and screen who became a staple of the Foot/Craigie parties. An invitation to their home meant you could be dining with actresses like Peggy Ashcroft, writers such as Harold Pinter, the comedian Spike Milligan and, in later years, even rock star Pete Townshend – not to mention an assortment of architects, painters and professionals of all kinds who were there as much for Craigie as for Foot. Indeed, as newsman Jon Snow observed, at home Jill was in command and would set the terms of discussion.

To Julie, her mother was an awesome presence, demanding and sometimes hypercritical but also as much as a friend as a parent. Indeed, mother and daughter were world-class gossips, sometimes occasioning Foot's caution, when he thought Jill and Julie had been a little too forthcoming. This gift for gossip, however, was an invaluable political tool, for it served Craigie well in her collecting of political intelligence. Craigie knew that in order to secure secrets she also had to supply them. Foot's parliamentary colleagues like Leo Abse were often amazed at the sources of Craigie's political rumours, which could also produce the most amazing speculations about what she thought was happening behind-the-scenes. Whether rightly identified or not, very little escaped her radar.

A forceful presence in the debate about Britain's quality of life and its place in the world, Craigie began in the 1950s to campaign for unilateral nuclear disarmament. She also wrote screenplays for the actors Gregory Peck and Peter Finch, articles and newspaper columns about the film industry, architecture and broader political and culture issues, as well as working on her crowning achievement, *Daughters of Dissent*, a magisterial history of the drive for women's rights nearly completed at the time of her death. Craigie's six decades of involvement with women's issues provide a virtual barometer of changes in social and political attitudes both in Great Britain and in the world at large. She tried to integrate her feminism into every aspect of her life. Even as she was involved in the air-raid alert system in wartime London, she was seeking financing for her film on the suffragettes. Later she turned their story into a radio documentary, broadcast in 1950 as *The Woman's Rebellion*. In 1951, she pushed the issue of equal pay for equal work in her feminist documentary, *To Be a Woman* (1951). That same decade she protested against the threat of nuclear war in public speeches that included an impassioned warning against the dangers of radiation. Citing such risks as birth defects, she spoke as a mother and feminist, making the issue of nuclear proliferation a woman's issue. At the same time, of course, she campaigned fiercely within the Labour Party for a whole range of issues including public housing, which she thought should be organically tied to human communities so that the classes intermingled in a setting reminiscent of the traditional village green. She had an aesthetic aspiration to make people's lives vivid and rewarding. Inspired by her friend, the cultural commentator and historian of cities, Lewis Mumford, and Aneurin Bevan (another Mumford admirer), Craigie portrayed the need for town planning in her documentary, *The Way We Live*. Here she featured the 'Plymouth Plan', designed to rebuild the city and to draw all classes of the community together. Craigie was part of a generation of political women, including Michael Foot's close friend and Labour Party colleague Barbara Castle, who called themselves 'William Morris Socialists', a term meant to emphasize that improved living conditions and an appreciation of aesthetics were equally important in building a better world.

Town planning at the end of the war was a cutting-edge art and a sign of progressive thinking. Never again would architects and urban planners offer such an exciting opportunity to remould society. Town planning was not the dull and retrograde subject that Craigie attacked in postwar years, when she accused architects of abandoning their dreams of creating an affordable and beautiful world. Her outstanding television documentary *Who Are the Vandals?* (1967) is an excoriating assault on urban planners who had ruined both the cities and the countryside. Like Morris, that Victorian domestic polymath, Craigie argued for the appreciation of the need to craft pattern and colour into the forms and structures of everyday life. This conviction underlined both her professional and home lives throughout her life.

The 1970s proved to be a crisis period in which Jill Craigie had to re-evaluate not only what it meant to be a woman but also a marriage to which she had sacrificed so much for her husband's political career. While her ideas were ahead of her time, she was still locked in the traditional patriarchal institution of marriage, and one whose tenets had been formed in the early twentieth century. She was acutely aware of the choice she had made, but she had to wonder how much of her own potential she had surrendered. Because of her dedication to her marriage she struggled to fulfil her feminist ideals, although she remained committed to them all her life.

In the 1970s, energized by the women's movement, Craigie began her epic book about the drive for female enfranchisement, beginning in the middle of the nineteenth century and climaxing with the great suffragette agitation directly preceding the First World War. Her impressively documented study relies on a deep reading of secondary sources as well as on the copious primary evidence she collected from the 1940s until her death, which formed an impressive library sought out by scholars. Craigie's book is also a disguised autobiography: *Daughters of Dissent* explores the complex interaction of women's issues, the demands of the labour movement and the development of modern political parties and their constituencies from the perspective of a woman who had access to Cabinet Ministers and Prime Ministers and campaigned alongside her husband in his quest for high office. In 1975, through the intervention of Foot, then Secretary of State for Employment in the Harold Wilson government (1964–70), Craigie obtained new records about the treatment of suffragettes in British prisons, records previously sequestered under the Official Secrets Act which made for damning reading.

Also in the 1970s, Craigie became actively involved in the early development of Virago Press. Indeed, Craigie, who brought back into print a good deal of the texts now important to the discipline of women's studies, first suggested many of this feminist publisher's titles. Countless scholars in the field can testify to Craigie's encouragement of their work as well as to her critical, demanding judgment that women's studies must produce new data and give due credit both to militants such as Emmeline Pankhurst and to gradualists or more reform-minded figures such as Millicent Fawcett. And indeed, *Daughters of Dissent* explores the conflicting but also complementary roles of these two great figures and their families. The stories of the Pankhursts and the Fawcetts form the spine of Craigie's book.

In the 1980s and 1990s, Craigie became increasingly involved in a study of Yugoslavia after her husband visited the country, demanding to speak out in defence of the Yugoslav dissident, Milovan Djilas, one of the greatest commentators on Marxism and the history of Communism. During his visit, Foot fell in love with the country, especially Dubrovnik, a beautifully compact historic town on the Adriatic coast, which became his and Craigie's favourite holiday spot, even rivalling Venice in their affections. For the last fifteen years of her life, Craigie travelled to Dubrovnik at least once each year. Inspired by her friendship with the great feminist and writer Rebecca West, author of *Black Lamb and Grey Falcon* – still the greatest book ever written about Yugoslavia – Craigie would resume her career as a documentary filmmaker. *Two Hours from London* (1994) is a stinging indictment of the West's failure to intervene in the Balkan wars. Jill Craigie died in 1999, just two chapters short of completing her masterpiece, *Daughters of Dissent*. This work, along with all her documentaries, articles and writings, constitutes the legacy of a writer, filmmaker and political activist who throughout her life kept enlarging the scope of what it meant to be a twentieth-century woman.

On Her Own

(1911–28)

Men and women never struggle so hard as when they struggle alone, without witness, counsellor, or confidant; unencouraged, unadvised, and unpitied.

Charlotte Brontë, *Shirley*

Jill's Craigie's childhood and, indeed, much of her early life must remain a mystery to the biographer because it is undocumented, and Jill herself preserved no trace of her first twenty-five years. This does not mean, of course, that this period meant nothing to her. Her extreme reticence suggests memories too painful to confide even to her family or closest friends. A biographer can only infer from a handful of anecdotes and public records the circumstances and events that surely helped to shape her character

Jill's third husband, Michael Foot, heard very little about her childhood. 'Jill never wanted to talk about her upbringing at all,' he declared. She was even vague about her birthplace. Several obituaries said Derbyshire, but her birth certificate lists London. She always gave a birth date of 7 March 1914, and her obituaries dutifully repeated this fiction. The correct year is 1911. Shaving three years off her age signalled the struggle of a woman to re-invent herself – as she did when she called herself Jill and jettisoned Noreen Joan, the legal name she affixed only to important documents. A guarded interview subject, Jill would curtail discussion of her childhood and adolescence with the comment: 'My early life is a rather dismal, sordid affair.'[1]

Jill's Scottish father, Arthur Charles Craigie, listed on her birth certificate as a 'theatre box office clerk', did not die in World War I, as her obituaries reported. There is no record of his war service. In 1933, when Jill married Claude Begbie-Clench, her first husband, an assistant producer for director Alfred Hitchcock, her marriage certificate identified Arthur Charles Craigie as a merchant. In 1938, when she married her second husband, screenwriter and playwright Jeffrey Dell, her father is described as a man 'of independent means'. He had married Jill's mother, Sonia Elkind, in the Fulham Registry Office on 10 May 1910. He was twenty-five. Sonia put her age as nineteen, although she was actually fifteen.* The daughter of a schoolmaster, Leo Elkind, Sonia had come from Russia – when and under what circumstances is not known, for Jill did not leave a single record regarding her mother in her papers.

Jill seems to have invented the story about her father dying in World War I during an interview with journalist David Leigh for a biography of Michael Foot. She apparently wanted to deflect questions about him. If Jill had any memory of her father, she kept it to herself. If she had any contact with him after her parents divorced in 1920, Jill told no one in her remaining family.†️ If she felt the lack of a father, she never admitted it to anyone interviewed for this biography. 'Not much there. She didn't talk much about her Scotch ancestry,' Michael insisted. Jill's Russian ancestry through her mother Sonia meant little more. When it snowed, really snowed in the country, Jill would say, 'My Russian soul is beating there.' She often referred to her Russian soul, her daughter Julie Hamilton recalled.

Jill's birth certificate records her parents' residence as 17 Dancer Road, Fulham, then one of the rapidly developing middle-class outer areas of the city, full of streets with two- and three-storey houses usually occupied by two families.[2] But Jill never acknowledged this home – if it was a home – or any other family abode. 'I had no home ever,' she asserted.

Jill had a brother, Arthur Ivan Craigie, born on 17 September 1914, about whom almost nothing is known. Sonia gave him away to a policeman in Bexhill (in east Sussex, not far from Hastings), Jill told Julie. Later, somehow, Ivan ended up in Kenya or Tanganyika, imprisoned for a crime that apparently included fraud. 'So I understand,' Julie said, who met Ivan only once, when he visited Britain with his wife and two children.

Arthur Charles Craigie filed a divorce petition on 26 March 1920, naming as co-respondent J. Marchant, the pseudonym of Eric MacManus, whom Sonia married after her divorce from Arthur on 22 August 1923. In all likelihood Jill lived with Sonia and her lover by the end of the war in those 'sordid' circumstances she refused to describe. But MacManus, a cotton planter, spent much of his time in the Sudan while Sonia travelled all over the

* Sonia's death certificate states she was born 4 October 1894. Arthur's birth certificate verifies his age and states he was the son of a grocer, also named Arthur Charles Craigie, from Beckenham.

† When Jill married Michael Foot in 1949, she did not list her father as deceased. There is a blank in the box for his profession. The only death certificate for an Arthur Craigie (no middle name listed) is dated 22 October 1963 in Ilford, South Essex. His age corresponds to that of Arthur Charles Craigie.

continent, engaging in love affairs, according to Jill, who herself remained in boarding schools, even during the holidays. 'I can only remember spending two or three holidays with my mother, and she was apt to send me away in the middle of the holidays back to school, to be alone.'

'Jill's mother was *terrible*,' Michael maintained:

> a dreadful woman. Jill never knew when she was finishing the term whether she was going to be taken off or not, or if she had to stay there. She had a real hatred of her mother. How Jill got her ideas and her temperament and her fighting spirit and her moral outlook out of such an upbringing is extraordinary. It was all done on her own. It was reading books, you know, at a much earlier age than most people – no, no I never heard Jill say one single good word for her mother.

Jill's mother was '*awful*', Julie affirmed:

> Her mother would write to her at boarding school and say, 'This Christmas we're going to spend it together in St Moritz.' At the end of term Jill would get a letter saying, 'Sorry, darling, can't make it. See you in the summer.' So she would go to the lavatory and sit down for a cry. Sometimes she would spend the holidays alone at school; sometimes she was farmed out to other children's families.

One day when the same kind of 'sorry, darling' letter arrived, Jill went to the lavatory and discovered she could not cry. 'I realized it was a hurt too many.' She said to herself: 'I don't love my mother anymore.' Jill told this story many times. When her friend Moni Forman heard it some time after they met in 1969, the account had acquired a matter-of-fact quality: 'She didn't say it asking for pity. She certainly didn't want it. She never complained.'

Jill's loathing of her mother never lessened, yet in 1968 she provided Sonia with a convenient home during her last years. 'She was the first occupant of our top floor flat,' Michael recollected. Jill left no photographs of her mother, but Julie remembered a handsome older woman standing under five feet tall, with big round eyes, high cheekbones and a large, sensuous mouth. 'She must have been very beautiful when young,' Julie speculated. 'She dressed well, stylishly, and had exquisite taste in furnishings.'

Jill took her close friend Jenny Stringer upstairs to meet Sonia. 'She said hello to me and I said hello back. And then we came downstairs again,' Jenny remembered. Michael and Julie agreed that Sonia was 'wrapped up in herself'. If she had any convictions – any political opinions – they remained unspoken. Jill called her mother's politics 'reactionary'. Jill did her best to keep Sonia away from Michael, who could not remember a single sustained conversation with his mother-in-law. Sonia was trouble; she liked to 'stir things up' – to use

Julie's expression. Kathy Seery, Jill's housekeeper, found Sonia a friendly, smartly dressed woman, yet it was 'clear enough' that she and Jill 'did not get on well. I can never remember her coming down for a meal. She might have a coffee with Jill.' Did they talk? 'Only just,' Kathy emphasized.

The quality of Jill's schooling depended, she said, on the fluctuations of the MacManus Sudan dividends.[3] To Mervyn Jones, Michael Foot's friend and biographer, she offered sketchy, grim details, mentioning that she had attended thirteen different boarding schools. Other accounts mention twelve. How many there were in truth is impossible to determine, since Jill left no pertinent records and many of these institutions no longer exist.

In the story Jill told about her early education, three schools stand out. Two of them were Belgian convents: St Ursuline's in Limbourgh and Sacré Coeur in Brussels. In later life Jill owned a copy of Antonia White's *Frost in May* (1933), a classic novel about a convent school. White evokes a hermetic world in which young girls pray to Jesus, 'wounded on the cross for me, help me to become crucified to self for love of Thee'. In this regime of 'rigid virtue' a nun announces to a new arrival: 'We do not encourage particular friendships among little girls.' To encourage their spiritual discipline, girls receive good conduct ribbons and 'exemptions' and 'permissions'. Sonia Orwell, the wife of George Orwell and a friend of Jill's, attended the convent school on which White's novel was based and would in later life spit on the street if she saw a nun.[4]

In this restrictive milieu, inquisitive natures are 'properly gloved and veiled'. An incipient romanticism that drives the girls in *Frost in May* to read Shelley is ruthlessly rooted out. The will has to be broken and 're-set in God's own way'. War breaks out between the aesthetic and the religious sensibility. The 'literary romantics' are transformed into 'soldiers of Christ'. But imaginative young girls like Jill respond powerfully to art, not to catechism. When one of them reads, 'Too late have I known thee, too late have I loved thee, O Beauty ever ancient and ever new,' she 'felt she did understand, not with her eyes or her brain, but with some faculty she did not even know she possessed'. In her copy of *William Morris* (1994) by Fiona McCarthy, Jill underlined this passage: '[T]hings worked on Morris's imagination just as words did: as a child he was absorbing the visual and verbal with the same degree of intensity.' This imagination, his biographer points out, had virtually nothing to do with his family or his environment: 'The Morrises could not connect.' Jill understood an aesthetic temper akin to her own, one that segregated the self from a conforming world. Jill's favourite essay, Michael noted, was Oscar Wilde's 'The Critic as Artist'. Very early on, before she read Wilde, Jill sought a credo that Nanda in *Frost in May* articulates: 'It was just the thing itself. I don't want poetry and pictures and things to be messages from God. I don't mind their being that as well, if you like, but not only that. Oh, I can't explain. I want them to be complete in themselves.'

In the 'wonderfully definite' world of the convent school, as described by Antonia White, a Protestant student is a 'poor, inquiring heathen' who rebels against rote learning that never explains what is euphemistically referred to as the 'irregular motions of the flesh'. Margit Kaffka, author of *The Ant Heap* (1917), a memorable novel based on her convent school experience, wrote about 'three years, stunted, day dreaming with sick fantasies, physically weak. There I could never see bright sunshine, flowers in the meadows or even a living dog. I must have been quite different from other children.'

Like White and Kaffka, Jill had a literary sensibility: 'I used to write. I was very unhappy... I wrote poems, very realistic poems, not fantasy ones. I was good at school.' But why send Jill to a convent school? They were cheap, Jill figured out later – and a 'cheap way of guarding adolescents', Kaffka suggests. Jill also felt what Charlotte Franklin, Kaffka's translator, has expressed: 'convents were useful places for unwanted girls.'[5] Jill ran away from one of them. She wrote to historian David Mitchell on 9 December 1986 about another: 'I used to squirt perfume on the nuns for the fun of seeing them look scared and hastily cross themselves.' In a similar act of revenge, Sonia Orwell told a nun: 'I'm so bored I wish I'd been birth-controlled so as not to exist.' Jill also told Mitchell that the nuns were 'most obsessed with making us little girls cover our knees when sewing, difficult to do when the sewing was on our laps'. Yet the nuns were 'not at all prudish about drumming into us our duty to indulge our future husbands in bed, very different from some English boarding schools I went to... where, if we were taught to believe anything, it was that sexual matters did not exist.'

Although Jill called the nuns 'insensitive' because they made English girls 'recite an anti-British poem about the burning of Joan of Arc', the line '*Ceux sont les anglais qui voulent voir mourir une femme,*'* she told an interviewer:

> had a tremendous effect upon me, because it never occurred to me there was another point of view... this made me very critical of my previous teachers – I felt they should have warned me. And this gave me great doubts about authority. It sowed the seeds in my mind that authority cannot be trusted, which I suppose was a sort of way towards Socialism, really... I was a rebel, and this fed my rebellious instinct.

* The English are the ones who wanted to see a woman die.

Reading remained a route to another world: 'The English girls there had to attend Mass, but they didn't have to say the prayers so that they could read books from the library, and I thought I'd discovered Dickens!'

Other than a 'great Tory sort of empire-building school', which Jill did not even deign to name, only a school at Harrow-on-the-Hill (also unnamed) made much of an impression:

> a very snobby school because we little girls learned the public school boys' ties, like little boys learn the names of aeroplanes and cars. And I remember that one of my school friends, when we were away at the seaside – there was a boy I rather fancied – and they said well he's only Wrekin, which was a despicable public school that was very cheap, and we were only concerned with schools like Winchester or Harrow or Rugby, or Eton of course. Some of my friends at school … were the sisters of Harrow boys and I think my mother thought I'd marry a rich man by mixing with these sort of people.

June Aberdeen, one of Jill's schoolfriends who had a brother at Harrow, remembered seventy-four years later a bright and good-looking Jill Craigie. June concentrated on having a good time, and Jill attracted her because she was such fun. Jill got invited to stay a few times with June and her parents. June also remembered that Jill always seemed to be getting into trouble. She had a tendency to 'fall out with the authorities', as June put it. After so many years, June still recalled that Jill seemed 'unsettled'.[6]

Jill's stepfather Eric MacManus visited her once at boarding school. As she later confided to her daughter, during an outing her stepfather bought Jill a bathing costume and then made a sexual advance towards her.

Since Jill kept virtually no records of her life before marrying Michael Foot, it is rather significant that she kept a book, a collection of Byron's poetry, which her principal gave to 'Joan Craigie' as an award for excellent scholarship. This presentation copy, signed by a 'S.D. Petty', led a Borough of Harrow librarian to identify Jill's school as 'Southlands', promoted in its literature as 'A School for the Daughters of Gentlemen'. Here is a description of Southlands *c.*1929:

> High situation, giving an uninterrupted view for twenty miles. All the important living rooms and class-rooms face south. Tennis Courts and large field for Games.
>
> Music, Art, and French are special features of the School. Careful attention is given to Physical Culture. There is a large and fully equipped Gymnasium, and the department is under the care of a Resident Mistress… There are also Domestic Science and Secretarial Courses. (*Telephone*: Byron 1191).[7]

The school had been in operation for nearly thirty years when Jill, aged sixteen (already calling herself Jill, June Aberdeen said), arrived in 1927 or perhaps 1928. It prided itself on an 'awareness of good aesthetic values. Particular stress is laid on the writing of good English and the speaking of verse.' Photographs portray a well-appointed institution, with manicured grounds, an entrance hall and dining room that seem poised halfway between high Victorian and arts-and-crafts.

Did Jill have S.D. Petty in mind when she mentioned the 'wonderful schoolmistress' who took an interest in her?

> I was wallowing in Byron and Shelley and Keats, largely to find out about sex, to tell you the truth! We knew nothing whatever about it, but I knew they wrote a lot about love, and I thought I might learn something in this way. And I enjoyed the poetry. And then suddenly this schoolmistress said: 'I think you've had enough of that.' And she put into my hands Bernard Shaw's *Intelligent Woman's Guide to Socialism*. And it was absolutely like a douche of cold water, it was wonderful. And that's what I think turned me into a Socialist.

Shaw first published his revolutionary book in June 1928, and it had been reprinted twice that same month and again in October, with a cheaper 'popular edition' (five shillings) appearing in May 1929. The voting age for women had just been lowered from thirty to twenty-one, and they now shared the same residence qualifications with men. Five million more women now appeared on the electoral register, prompting Shaw's biographer, Michael Holroyd, to remark that Shaw's book had been 'perfectly timed'.[8]

Shaw's first two paragraphs establish a direct, conversational tone and an exhilarating appeal to the independent mind:

> It would be easy, dear madam, to refer you to the many books on modern Socialism which have been published since it became a respectable constitutional question in this country in the eighteen-eighties. But I strongly advise you not to read a line of them until you and your friends have discussed for yourself how wealth should be distributed in a respectable civilised country, and arrived at the best conclusion you can.
>
>   For Socialism is nothing but an opinion held by some people on that point. Their opinion is not necessarily better than your opinion or anyone else's. How much should you have and how much should your neighbours have? What is your own answer?

In effect, Shaw said: 'You can understand economic principles. You can understand how government works. You can understand how business works. There is no reason why you cannot understand these things.' Businessmen and politicians had no better understanding of such matters – indeed, they had ceased to think about them.

Of course Shaw gives his own answers, but at each stage of his argument he asks the intelligent woman to make her own calculations and to act as her own authority. Chapter titles reveal his straightforward approach: 'What Capital Is', 'The Runaway Car of Capitalism', 'Sham Socialism'. There is hardly a topic in this almost 500-page book that is not given a chapter – including 'Communism', 'Laisser-Faire', 'Eugenics', 'The Industrial Revolution', 'Women in the Labour Market', 'Trade Union Capitalism', 'Nationalization', 'Party Politics'. While male experts have obfuscated concepts (often confusing themselves), Shaw reiterates that the intelligent woman can comprehend socialism and capitalism in terms of her daily experience.

Shaw's capsule indictment of capitalism is as uncompromising and as relentless as the economic system he opposes:

> Capitalism, in its ceaseless search for investment, its absolute necessity for finding hungry men to eat its spare bread before it goes stale, breaks through every barrier, rushes every frontier, swallows every religion, levels every institution that obstructs it, and sets up any code of morals that facilitates it, as soullessly as it sets up banks and lays cables. And you must approve and conform, or be ruined, and perhaps imprisoned and executed.

Yet Shaw does not advocate immediate revolution or even the subversion of capitalist institutions as such. He argues that socialism can only prosper and rule because of the industrial and business base capitalism has developed: 'We must build up Capitalism before we can turn it into Socialism. But meanwhile we must learn how to control it instead of letting it demoralize us, slaughter us, and half ruin us, as we have hitherto done in our ignorance.'

Shaw's hold over Jill increased with his linking of the aesthetic and the political in his invocation of William Morris, who was to become one of her guiding lights: 'Under Marx and Engels, Morris and Hyndman, Socialism was a middle class movement caused by the revolt of the consciences of educated and humane men and women against the injustice and cruelty of Capitalism, and also (this was a very important factor with Morris) against its brutal disregard of beauty and the daily human happiness of doing fine work for its own sake.'

Shaw also struck home with Jill when he commented on the 'virtual exclusion of women from certain occupations'. He likened the plight of Western women to that of women in India who are 'mostly in purdah and do not go out'. The problem here, however, was not capitalism but men: 'I dare not tell you, even if I knew, how many members of the Labour Party believe that the proper place for women is in purdah.'* Yet, in Shaw's view, 'it is fundamental in Socialism that idleness shall not be tolerated on any terms'. Shaw's call to action replaced Sonia Craigie's inert advice. As Jill said later:

> the only thing I ever learned from my mother when I saw her was to marry a rich man. It was rather typical of the sort of mores of that period – there was no other hope for women. She didn't say have a career, or anything like that. She just used to say, marry a rich man, that's all. I rather resolved to marry a poor one as a matter of fact, because I didn't think her life was up to much!

Jill told an interviewer when describing the profound impact of Shaw's book on her sensibility, 'I wasn't a feminist… I didn't know anything about it'. *The Intelligent Woman's Guide* served as a sort of repository for feelings she could only act on much later when she found a focus for her life. Shaw's books, essays and plays would form an essential part of the education of a young woman who much later described her teenage self as 'generally sort of rebellious in my spirit, but not in my actions'. When Michael Holroyd began his monumental biography of Shaw, he found in Jill a woman well versed in his subject's plays and essays who, according to her husband, rarely missed attending a new production of the playwright's work.

It took years for Jill to assimilate Shaw and to act upon his principles. At the age of sixteen or seventeen she had no sense of direction. 'She was fighting against her mother,' Michael reiterated. As Carl Jung observes:

> Anything, so long as it is not like Mother!… This kind of daughter knows what she does *not* want, but is usually completely at sea as to what she would choose as her own fate. All her instincts are concentrated on the mother in the negative form of resistance and are therefore of no use to her in building her own life.[9]

Jill played the piano well, but not well enough to become a professional. Jill loved to dance, but she doubted the strength of her talent. Apparently, S.D. Petty, her Southlands mentor, suggested Jill sit for the Oxford entrance exam. She passed, but her mother, Jill told Mervyn Jones, 'could not or would not pay the fees'. Jill never got over it. 'She thought she missed something great by not going to the university,' Michael reported. 'She thought she should have done.' Of this period Jill said:

---

* Jill left behind an unidentified magazine profile in which she is quoted: 'There is a sort of purdah atmosphere about being a politician's wife, isn't there? You walk carefully six paces behind, and you don't quite know where to look.'

I was always having ideas, and I didn't quite know. I didn't have any guidance. What it must be to be in a family like the Longfords, where you're brought up with historians who are talking about it. Perhaps I wasn't brainy enough to think things out. I was an emotional mess…

Shoved into the adult world with no resources or skills, Jill would have to make her own way.

2

The Death of the Heart
(1928–36)

I decided to see what would happen if I started from zero with nothing but my personality to stand on. London is a city of sudden and violent contrasts. You can step from the comfort and security of existence into destitution within a few minutes. I would arrive in London with nothing but my personality between me and starvation.

In Darkest London (1926) by Mrs Cecil Chesterton, Jill Craigie's library

In the tribal city of London,* Jill, now approaching eighteen, took a 'humble, boring, office job'.[1] The vagueness about her age and about her work is Jill's. How long the job, or jobs, lasted, she did not say. Instead she evoked the horror:

> I was alone in London without a family, without a background of any sort… and though I say it myself when I look at the photos, I wasn't bad looking – and one is a prey to every man. Men have a different attitude to a girl without a background, without mothers. I couldn't go anywhere without being followed, accosted, specially by married men, old men, fat men, men that one wouldn't dream of looking at. I was often very hungry and would accept meals, and they thought they could take any liberty. So I was quite suicidal.

Where was Jill's mother? No one seems to know. Where are the photographs Jill mentions? Scarcely any seem to exist from before 1940.

Jill did not exaggerate the predatory, isolating nature of the city for women.† When Francis King was asked if he could think of a novel about an

---

* 'The streets of the City are thronged at morning, evening and noonday; in the morning, by countless tribes of men of all sorts and conditions, but all in black, all in tall hats, and all hurrying to their respective offices or places of business; in the evening, by the same men returning; and at noonday, by the same men swarming, like ants, out to lunch, at their particular club, restaurant…', Darlington's London and Environs (1902).

† 'It is generally supposed that London is, or was, a male city… Single women were certainly vulnerable to every kind of attention and even molestation,' Peter Ackroyd, London: The Biography (2001). He is describing late seventeenth-century London, but it might as well be London in 1929.

adolescent on her own in London around 1930, the novelist promptly suggested Elizabeth Bowen's *The Death of the Heart* (1938). Portia, the novel's heroine, is the offspring of adultery and a broken marriage. Like Jill, she has been partly educated abroad and feels 'exiled not only from her own country but from *normal, cheerful* family life'. Only sixteen, Portia has yet to experience what awaits her: 'a woman's checked, puzzled life, a life to which the intelligence only gives a further distorted pattern'. The desperate Portia cries out: 'I've got nowhere to be.' She asks, 'But what can I go by?' Jill remembered: 'All women, all young girls, were conscious of the fact that there was very little one could do. There was typing. It's a terrible thing to have no roots and no values. You have to work out everything for yourself, and for a very long time life seemed to be quite purposeless.'

Like Portia, who keeps a diary, Jill turned to writing. But her manuscripts attracted no publisher and Jill kept none of this early work. What little family Jill did find in London reacted to her earnest adolescent beauty with alarm. 'I discovered I had some cousins,' she told Julie. Two young men about Jill's age – and their mother and father – were all delighted with Jill. This incipient sense of having a family faded when one of her male cousins said,

'You can't come to the house anymore.'

'Why is that?'

'Because my father has expressed an improper desire for you. So mother won't have you in the house.'

Jill did not know what love was, she later told her daughter. She had never been loved. 'She told me this story many, many times,' Julie stressed.

Jill knew nothing about sex, either. In Bayswater she tried to buy Marie Stopes' *Married Love* (1918), but a reproachful shopgirl rebuffed her.* She entered a London still cast in the long and deep shadow of the Victorian period. Novelist Storm Jameson, describing her dreary time in 1919 at a London advertising agency, declared:

> I was dying of discontent with myself. And with London. This – these endless cold streets smelling of mud, sweat, petrol, these cafés and restaurants I could not afford to enter, these people with their flattened voices and faces, seeming to be nothing and nowhere, like shadows in water...[2]

In 1929 the only difference for Jill would have been less mud – the result of electrifying the trams and discarding horse-drawn vehicles.

---

*Simon Hoggart and David Leigh, *Michael Foot: A Portrait* (1981). Marie Stopes (1880–1950) was a pioneer birth-control campaigner. Jill's friend Jennie Lee (see Chapter 11) had a father who 'wordlessly placed on her bookshelves a copy of Marie Stopes when Jennie was seventeen'. See Patricia Hollis, *Jennie Lee: A Life* (1997).

Not much more can be gleaned from these lean years, the period between 1929 and 1932, when the voting age for women was reduced from thirty to twenty-one, Labour formed its first shaky, cautious government, followed almost immediately by the US stock market crash, the rise of Fascism in Germany and a worldwide depression that caused mass unemployment. How Jill made do in these three crucial years is a mystery; it is a time of turmoil that she obliterated by changing her birth date from 1911 to 1914, so that she could say she began her first significant job when she was eighteen, not twenty-one.

In early 1932 *Betty's Paper* – 'for silly young women, like me,' Jill told an interviewer – hired her for £2 10s a week. The paper sponsored beauty contests, a 'sweethearts competition' (send in pictures of your boyfriend), provided fashion notes and displayed ads for products such as Dr Cassell's Tablets, a sure remedy for weak nerves, anaemia, loss of appetite, insomnia, indigestion, headaches, nervous breakdowns and miscellaneous pains. Ads also extolled wrinkle ointments and La-Mar Reducing Soap from La-Mar Laboratories: 'Wash away Fat and Years of Age.' Each issue serialized novels such as 'How She Was Tempted', 'Born to Be Bad', 'The Girl Who Cheated Men', 'How Girls Lose Love', 'When Love is Ruthless', 'Why Men Wanted Her' and 'Sinner in Silk'.

Jill had two jobs on the paper. As 'Professor Philastro' she wrote horoscopes. Readers would fill out a coupon, specifying 'name, address, sex, date, month, year of birth, day of week, before or after sunset (if known)', and send it into the professor in order to receive a 'detailed outline of your future prospects – your chance of success – your luck in love – where and how to find good fortune'. Unfortunately, the professor's reports were not published, although Jill provided this description: 'I learned to write the kind of things that might apply to everybody. I got an amazing number of letters saying, how true. I used to say: "you're optimistic and pessimistic in turns!"'

Using the name Betty, Jill also became – just on the verge of her twenty-second birthday – an agony aunt:

> If you've a beauty problem that worries you – or if there's some personal or intimate subject you want to confide to a pal, write to Betty, c/o 'Betty's Paper', 196, Gray's Inn Road, London, W.C.1. If you don't want your reply to appear in print, or want your answer quickly, enclose a stamped self-addressed envelope with your letter.

Jill dispensed cures for freckles, pimples, weight gain, thin legs, dark hair in unwanted places, conflicts with parents and boyfriends, and broken hearts. 'Betty' explained how to meet boys (learning to dance well helped), to make a

BETTY'S PAPER 33

A SK BETTY

"We have quarrelled..."

Betty Gives Some Frank Advice to a Reader Whose Boy is Jealous, and Has Quarrelled With Her.

SO LONELY (Burton-on-Trent) writes : " When I first met my boy, he used to come to see me every night. Now he seems tired of me, and we have quarrelled; but I know he is jealous when he sees me with other boys."

As you love your boy very much, and he seems so jealous of other boys, I think that things will come right between you. I do hope so, dear. But if, as you suggest, he has grown tired of your friendship, it would be better to go out with your other friends, and try to forget him. Why don't you meet him, and have a talk with him? It would be better to know definitely if he does not wish to see you any more, although it may hurt at the time.

LUCK.—After reading your letter carefully, I believe that the cause of the trouble is over-heated blood, and I feel sure that if you will try taking some effervescent salts each morning, you will soon notice a difference. They are very cooling and refreshing. Failing this effecting a cure, you should see a doctor, as the trouble is probably something quite simple which he could easily put right.

IF you've a beauty problem that worries you—or if there's some personal or intimate subject you want to confide to a pal, write to Betty, c/o "Betty's Paper," 196, Gray's Inn Road, London, W.C.1 If you don't want your reply to appear in print, or want your answer quickly, enclose a stamped, self-addressed envelope with your letter.

You seem to have tried most things for your freckles, *JUST SEVENTEEN.* Try to keep out of the sun, and use equal parts of witch hazel and peroxide of hydrogen. Cream your face every night, dear, and use coloured powders with vanishing cream as a basis. Do not worry about them ; men often consider freckles most attractive.

PUZZLED writes : *"When I am introducing my girl friends to men, I always get in a muddle. Can you help me over this ? "*

It is quite simple, dear. Always introduce the man to the girl first, not the girl to the man. Turn to the girl and say, " May I introduce Mr. ——? " and then turn to the man and say, " Miss ——."

GLADYS (Paisley).—Glad you enjoy the Real Life Stories so much. Thanks for all the good wishes, my dear.

F.G. (Morpeth).—I hope you will recognise your reply, as you forgot to give a pen name. I believe this is the lotion to which you refer. It is very good indeed for making the skin soft and smooth. Half an ounce of tincture of benzoin, 2oz. of rosewater, 20 drops of spirits of camphor, and ½oz. of glycerine. This should be shaken well, and applied to the skin after washing.

WORRIED (Birmingham). —To keep your hair light, dissolve camomile leaves in the rinsing water, when you wash your hair. You can get them at any chemists. Massage your legs with olive oil to make them fatter ; but with the present long fashions, dear, there is very little cause for you to worry about them.

short figure look taller ('Wear your frocks long, and avoid jumpers and skirts, costumes and anything that cuts the figure'), to enhance eyebrows and eyelashes (vaseline or olive oil regularly applied), and to develop the chest with deep-breathing exercises while singing ('you've probably noticed how developed people's chests are who sing a lot'). Indeed, faithful readers could assemble a Betty kit: hydrogen peroxide, cold cream, olive oil and vaseline. Should Jill be credited as the first advice columnist to recommend six glasses of water a day? The column showed considerable concern for catering to the male ego:

> You also ask what to talk about when you're out with a boy. Just be natural, dear, and interested in *his* conversation. Find out the things that interest *him*, and learn all you can about them... I think that as long as your boy doesn't neglect you, you mustn't interfere with his friendship with his pal. There is nothing a boy hates more than not to be able to have his own friends and he may feel that he isn't old enough to take a girl's friendship seriously... Learn to be a good listener – men love talking to someone who seems to hang on their very words, you know... Try to put the boy at his ease straight away (because he'll be nervous too, remember) by some laughing

remarks and keep things going once you've got a start… This may be 1932, my dear, but I think you should let your boy friend take you out sometimes without offering to go fifty-fifty. You may earn as much as he does, but it is the man's privilege to pay, you know. Perhaps, sometimes, you could make him little presents of cigarettes, if you feel you've got to do something. But you must offer these very discreetly, for the average boy is very proud of his independence and ability to pay his way, and you must be careful not to hurt his feelings.

Being 'Betty' evidently lasted about a year, and during that time life changed for Jill Craigie. When she confided to an interviewer that at eighteen 'nothing was important to me. Life seemed absolutely not worth living', he asked, 'How long did this last?' 'Until you fall in love,' Jill replied. 'But I don't want to go into that side.'

'Then she met my father,' Julie explained. 'He was extremely attractive and good looking and a lot of fun.' Was Claude Begbie-Clench Jill's first serious beau? Jill apparently never said. She once described herself as a slow developer to her friend, the writer Alan Brien, telling him: 'I was extraordinary. I didn't have my first period until I was eighteen.' Julie once heard her mother say that sex with Claude was the best she ever had.

Jill's obituaries identified Claude as a sculptor, though he never made a living from his art. But his aesthetic sensibility would have appealed to a young woman absorbed in reading William Morris and John Ruskin. Claude's sister, Yvonne, thought Jill first met Claude at Elstree Studios, where he worked for Alfred Hitchcock as an assistant producer. Why Jill was at Elstree is not clear. Certainly she was not employed there. Jill provided exactly one sentence on the subject: 'Gradually I wanted to become a film writer.'

Claude liked film work, according to Yvonne, and was good at it, although he never achieved any prominence in the cinema world. He was also an alcoholic. The drinking began, Yvonne said, when he began working at Elstree. Jill apparently did not understand the extent of his addiction until after they were married. His oblivious parents would never know what a hard time Jill had coping with his disease.

Claude's conservative and wealthy family lived north of London in Leamington Spa. His father, an engineer-inventor (he helped to develop the tank), had charge of the Lockheed factory. He married his first cousin, who claimed direct descent from William Shakespeare. Julie remembered their well-appointed house, filled with 'beautiful things'. Yvonne said that her parents did not know what to make of Jill: 'She was rather intellectual, you see. I don't think they had a lot of contact with her. They were old fashioned, and Jill represented another world to them.' They had their most extended view of Jill when she came to stay with them during her engagement to their son. They liked her well enough, and though they doubted that their son was mature enough to begin a family of his own, they evidently did not object to the marriage.

The wedding was 'solemnized at the Church of All Souls' in the parish of St Marylebone, 'according to the Rites and Ceremonies of the Established Church'. Claude is listed on the marriage certificate as Claude Shakespeare Clench, twenty-three, residing at 76 Great Portland Street. A month shy of her twenty-second birthday on 4 February 1933, Jill gave her age as twenty. Only recently, after Yvonne's death, did Julie discover a wedding photograph of her parents among her aunt's possessions. In the picture, apparently taken outside the church, the groom stands a good head taller than the five-foot-two Jill. Despite the formal wedding pose, the couple look relaxed, half-smiling, arm-in-arm. Jill is dressed in a cloche hat and two-piece wool jersey dress, carrying a clutch bag and wearing light-coloured gloves with scalloped edges. Claude is in conventional formal wear, with spats and a carnation in his buttonhole.

Another photograph seems to tell a different story. Jill is standing with Sidney – the husband of Claude's Aunt Maudie, née Clench. In view of Maudie's role in their subsequent break up, it is tempting to read a good deal into this photograph: Jill looks defensive – judging by the way she holds her arms close to her body in an introverted, rigid stance. Compared to the wedding picture, she looks deflated as Claude's uncle towers over her in top hat, morning coat, wing collar and watch chain. The shine on his shoes – indeed on the shoes of everyone in these two photographs – suggests a highly polished and proper atmosphere that may have been offputting and perhaps a bit overwhelming for Jill. She still seems alone. 'I don't even remember her mother being at the wedding,' Yvonne said.

Claude's parents furnished the young couple's home and provided a dog. Jill made an awkward wife and became pregnant almost immediately. Her daughter Julie, born 11 August 1934, was named by Aunt Maudie (Jill wanted to call her daughter Angela). Jill did not know how to cook – not even an egg. She knew nothing about homemaking and resented not having the chance to learn. In this pre-Dr Spock era she followed current advice that dictated ignoring an infant's cries – and sticking to rigid four-hour feeding schedules. Meanwhile, Claude did not come home with his pay packet. Jill tried to catch him at the studio, but he would already be at the pub. Sometimes out of sheer loneliness she visited Yvonne, then studying art at the Slade in London.

Marriage did not alleviate Jill's loneliness. A child had not helped to rectify life with Claude. She felt desperate. Although Jill remained fond of the warm and charming Claude, according to Yvonne, who believed the couple would not have separated if her family had not interfered in the marriage, Yvonne also admitted that Jill was 'keen on men' and 'susceptible, perhaps because of her loneliness'. At the very least, Jill turned to other men for solace and became rather careless, in one dramatic instance, about keeping her liaisons discreet.

On a visit to Jill and Claude with Claude's mother, Aunt Maudie spotted a letter on the mantelpiece addressed to Jill from Jeffrey Dell, a twice-married screenwriter she had met on a movie set during one of her failed efforts to head Claude away from the pub. Jeffrey wrote her letters and pursued her hotly. He was 'kind and understanding', Julie remembered her mother saying much later. While Aunt Maudie stood reading the letter, Jill was upstairs in her bath and Julie downstairs in her pram. When Jill came down from her bath, the letter and her baby were gone.

In a panic, Jill wanted Julie back at whatever price. She cared passionately about her child. But how could she negotiate with this rich, self-confidant clan? She had hardly begun to assert herself as an individual. She had only one protector, Jeffrey Dell, a trained solicitor. Claude's family did not allow Jill to see Julie until she signed an agreement stipulating that she would divorce Claude and marry Jeffrey and that Julie would spend seven months with Jill and five months with them. What Jeffrey made of Maudie's terrible ultimatum is not known. He was still married when he met Jill. Yvonne understood Jill's despair. 'I don't think he was the person Jill wanted.' And if she did want him, she did not want him this way. As Elizabeth Bowen observes in *The Death of the Heart*: 'The wish to lead out one's lover must be a tribal feeling; the wish to be seen as loved is part of one's self-respect.'

3

At Sea

(1936–9)

A love affair induces abandon; marriage induces reticence. It should be the other way round.

Jill Craigie, *Odd Reflections*

Jill and Jeffrey did not marry until 15 July 1938.* What hopes she had for this marriage are not clear. Certainly her new husband's successful quest to become a writer would have appealed to her. Born in 1899, Jeffrey attended the Berkhamsted School, Herts, along with Graham Greene. During World War I he served as a pilot in the Royal Flying Corps. An indifferent student with an aesthetic bent, he enrolled at the Brighton College of Art. His father then persuaded him to become an articled clerk in his law firm. Jeffrey found legal detail tiresome and working for the prosecution disturbing, because he was 'innately sympathetic to the underdog'.

Like Jill, he turned to writing for 'solace and satisfaction' and determined to pursue a writer's career when *Punch* accepted three of his pieces.[1] Jeffrey's first great success came in 1931 and 1932 with his stage and screen adaptations of C.S. Forester's novel *Payment Deferred*. The next year Jeffrey turned the play into a film, a riveting thriller with an electrifying performance by Charles Laughton as a guilty murderer. Other successes included the same formula: courtroom scenes, cross-examinations and the plight of individuals caught up in legal machinery. By 1938 Jeffrey was a well-established playwright and screenwriter.

In Jill's estimation, Jeffrey reached the peak of his powers with *Nobody*

*Claude filed his divorce petition on 26 June 1936 (Decree Nisi 29 April 1937; Decree Absolute 1 November 1937), and Jeffrey's wife Eileen filed hers on 18 June 1936 (Decree Nisi 20 April 1937; Decree Absolute 1 November 1937). On the marriage certificate Jeffrey listed his full name as John Edward Flowers Dell. The thirty-nine-year-old Jeffrey married Jill, who reduced her age by one year, to twenty-six, in the Kensington register office. His profession is listed as solicitor; the space for Jill's profession is left blank.

Ordered Wolves (1939), which included this dedication: 'For Jill, who bore it with fortitude.' In what she called 'the most brilliant book about the film industry', the wolves, which reproduce at an alarming rate, have been ordered by nobody knows who for a film nobody has yet written or can even remember wanting to write and at a steadily multiplying cost no one wishes to contemplate.

When Jill met Jeffrey in 1934 or 1935, the rapid opening of new studios and cinemas created a 'buoyant sense of achievement to British studios and a conviction that they had a great future', writes film historian Ernest Betts.[2] By the time Jill married Jeffrey, British film production had sagged, the studios were losing thousands of pounds, and the voice of the independent film producer with 'ideas of his own was seldom heard'.

Jeffrey was charming and fun. His friend William MacQuitty treasured Jeffrey's 'puckish sense of humour' – an endearing trait that in the beginning may have bridged the age gap between Jeffrey and Jill. Jeffrey also offered her entry into a fantasy world that appealed because it induces a mass make-believe for which no one need take responsibility. As one film-maker in *Nobody Ordered Wolves* puts it: 'We don't make statements anybody's likely to check up. All we do is "suggest" and the Great British Public fill in the blanks for themselves. They love doing it. It's a national pastime.'

At the time of her marriage to Jeffrey, Jill had not done much more than publish short, unsigned journalism. 'I could usually get pieces in the papers, but I couldn't earn enough to keep myself until the war came out,' Jill told an interviewer. Jeffrey offered opportunities in the film industry and could serve as a kind of mentor. But Jill had yet to find her own vocation. She had tried acting, making a brief appearance as Tania, a Russian circus performer in *Makeup* (1937), a film Jeffrey Dell scripted, but which seems lost or in the remote reaches of the Pathé vaults in Paris. There is no evidence, however, that she seriously considered acting as a career. None of her family even knew about this role.

The downturn in film production in 1937 may be one reason why husband and wife decided to collaborate on a play; another was surely Jill's desire to create work that had both entertainment value and ethical fibre – a combination that could more easily be melded on the London stage. Jill is cited as lead author of *The Judge*, perhaps because Jeffrey wanted to acknowledge her worthy aims and to build up her career.

In *The Judge*, Blake, a man on trial for murder, can be proven innocent – but only at the cost of revealing that the trial judge's wife, Jane, has committed adultery in the hotel where the murder occurred. Jane confesses the truth to her husband, who insists she testify. At the last minute, however, the murdered man's mother reveals crucial facts exonerating Blake so that Jane does not have to appear in court.

The *Times* reviewer (27 September 1938) noted: 'the murder story thus told has in the cross-examination of witnesses, the slow piecing together of evidence, and the solution of a mystery, all and perhaps more than all the suspense and narrative power that a court setting might be expected to give it'. *The Judge* reflects an earnest desire to make melodrama do the work of morality and social commentary.

Only a typescript of the play survives, at the British Library, and it contains no clue as to Jill's contribution. What she brought to this theatre piece can be discerned in a general sense. As Barbara Dell, Jeffrey's last wife, put it, Jeffrey was good at satire and at drawing the bones of a character. But he often needed a collaborator to fill in the emotion and to put some flesh on the body, so to speak. Certain lines reflect Jill's interest in the differences between women and men. 'Your sex has an awful lot to answer for,' says Roger, the husband of Jane's sister Betty. Betty wonders aloud what it must have been like for women during the Stone Age: 'I should have adored seeing Roger off by the eight-thirty with a large club under his arm.' Roger rejoins: 'Yes – with odds about fifty to one that I didn't come back in the evening!' Betty counters: 'Oh, but someone much bigger and stronger would have come in your place, darling. It must have been such fun for the women wondering what would turn up!' Betty's point would vex and amuse Jill later: women do not live in a world where the man has to compete for a woman's affection and loyalty – unless the woman is especially adroit at setting the terms of competition.

Fidelity – a major theme in Jill's later diaries – is explored in scenes about the Macintyres' apparently perfect marriage. They have been married for ten years and are a 'unique couple', says the judge's friend Sir Henry Amory. Amory is compassionate when he discovers Jane's adultery: 'Lord forbid I should judge anyone, especially anyone as attractive as Jane, and married to someone so much older than herself.' The judge is just as forgiving. Jill would later write in a small notebook titled *Odd Reflections*: 'Infidelity is not necessarily incompatible with loyalty.'

And what of Jill and Jeffrey? 'Jeffrey was very much older than I,' Jill told an interviewer. She felt the weight of his experience and his talk about the war disenchanted her. It seemed like ancient history: 'Well, you know how it is with young people today, if you talk about the last war...'. But more than an age difference bothered Jill. Many years later, Jill confided to her daughter that

she and Jeffrey were sexually incompatible. Jill may have already begun affairs
with other men. Later she admitted:

> If you are very attractive… you get so involved. They absorb so much of your time
> emotionally… Fending off men. Men who felt they had broken their hearts. Yet they
> get somebody else pretty quickly. At the time you are convinced that you did
> something terrible. You've said, yes, you might, and then, you don't want to, and
> then they get mad.

Jill's motivations in this period remain occluded. That she was finding life
with Jeffrey a scramble, however, is clear: 'We weren't very well off because
he was paying vast sums of alimony,' Jill explained to an interviewer. Jeffrey
took the world as he found it, and the world, in this period, was primarily the
British film studio, a realm Ernest Betts describes as 'intellectually sterile' and
with a 'fixation about money'. Jill complained: 'I got very browned off because
he had this immense talent and wonderful notices, but he'd just make any old
stories and any old scripts in order to make money.' As Jill wrote later in *Odd
Reflections*: 'Integrity was always my test of a man, but it has to go all the way
through.'

Discussing the politics of this interwar period, Jill revealed a temperament
that was passive and not yet ready to be awakened to a cause:

> My main politics was pacifism, anti-war plays. There were a lot of slogans: nobody
> wins a war, everyone loses. We all felt we'd lost the first world war, what we knew
> of it… I would have been among the crowds who cheered Chamberlain. I thought
> that Czechoslovakia had been betrayed, there's no doubt about that. I thought it was
> a dirty trick that they'd done on Czechoslovakia, but even that was better than war.
> I was naive politically, really. I didn't have anyone to talk to about politics, even
> when I fell in love… I didn't meet intelligent people that one had discussions with,
> that you might have met at university, so I was at sea, mentally.

If Jill was at sea, her daughter certainly felt the shock waves. Only five years
old in 1939, Julie plunged from her mother's catch-as-catch-can life into her
five-month stays with the stolid conservatism of her Begbie-Clench relatives –
chiefly Aunt Maudie and her grandparents. Julie cannot remember any visits
with her father. He did not send gifts; he provided no child support.

Life with Jill and Jeffy – as Julie called him – proved peripatetic: 'We kept
living in different places,' Julie remembered. Jeffy was 'around, but not all the
time'. She adored this tall man who seemed a hundred feet high to her. 'He
was the only father I had.' Like her, he loved animals and taught her the
names of trees. Jill remained, in her own words, in a 'confused state'. Jeffrey

could seem quite remote – especially to a young woman like Jill who saw every day how desirable other men found her. Was she thinking of Jeffrey when she wrote in *Odd Reflections*, 'Marriage is a confidence trick the old play on the young'?

Jill left remarkably little commentary on Jeffrey. She did not even have a copy of *Nobody Ordered Wolves* among her small collection of film books when she died. She preserved only three of Jeffrey's letters (all undated) written on movie sets. His tone is bantering but also worried:

> What a very nice letter! But a little disturbing – 'the most exciting conversation I've ever had.' What do I make of that one?? I tried to think what was the most exciting conversation I'd had in my life and decided that it took place in a car going up the hill to [?] village & the girl with whom it took place was curiously enough not unlike you! And then I decided that there was a still more exciting one which occurred on the [?] set, although it was about banalities it was very rich indeed in promise and if ever silences could be inoffensively described as 'pregnant' those were! And then I decided there was a still more exciting one which occurred in a flat at St. John's Wood on the floor! And at that point I started remembering about fourteen hundred others and was working myself up into a rare state of sexy nostalgia… I feel there are matters at home requiring my urgent attention!!

Jeffrey wrote to reassure Jill: 'I am sorry you should suffer on account of *Wolves* when it was only for you and on account of your sweetness that it ever came to be made [had Alexander Korda, the target of Jeffrey's satire, made it difficult for Jill to find subsequent script writing work?]. But I know it won't be long before they'll say "Does your husband write too?"' On the set Jeffrey remained bored and days went by waiting for sunshine. 'I need you terribly. Without you my mind goes flat. Just now my heart leapt. I heard a laugh, downstairs, just like yours! For one moment I thought you were here.'

But Jill was otherwise occupied. Her marriage to Jeffrey had introduced her to a new range of friends in the theatre and film world. She had formed a friendship with the actress Dorothy (Dot) Hyson, and apparently through her with Malcolm MacDonald, the son of the first Labour Prime Minister. These associations would lead her by the beginning of the war to enjoy an essentially independent life while remaining married to Jeffrey. He did not give up on Jill even if she strayed, but he remained a screenwriter scurrying for jobs, and this rather frenetic existence only exacerbated Jill's frustration with the marriage. If she did not strike out on her own and leave Jeffrey, it may have been because she had not yet found her proper role.

4

Free
(1939–43)

I wanted to be free.

Jill Craigie

'After Munich, I began to think about politics. Munich shook me. I was pro-Chamberlain, which is awful to think of now,' Jill admitted to an interviewer. 'The war changed everything.' Like millions of others, she felt the force of a public spirit and energy that dispelled her diffuse pre-war phase. Jeffrey Dell tried to join up but his duodenal ulcer disqualified him from military service.[1] Jill and Jeffrey carried on with their troubled marriage during the Blitz, the intense nightly bombing raids of London beginning on 7 September 1940 and lasting – in its most concentrated phase for fifty-seven consecutive nights – to 31 October, then continuing sporadically until May 1941. As many as 1500 aircraft attacked the city's homes, factories, businesses, public buildings and dockyards. On the night of 29 December, German bombs created a firestorm destroying several historic churches. St Paul's Cathedral barely escaped destruction. Incendiaries damaged Buckingham Palace, Westminster Abbey and the House of Commons. By the end of 1940 German air raids had killed 15,000 British civilians.

Amidst this turmoil Jill and Jeffrey hired a secretary, seventeen-year-old Barbara Poxon, who would later become Barbara Dell, Jeffrey's fourth and final wife. Her voice broke down sixty years later when she recalled arriving at work late because of the bombing. Jill and Jeffrey told her: 'We thought all of south London was burning.' 'It was,' Barbara said, adding later, 'We were friends whatever happened.' By the end of May 1941, 375,000 Londoners were homeless – including Jill and Jeffrey Dell. The 'nice little house' on Rutland Street in Kensington had been bombed – on the same day (7 September 1940) the dockyards had been hit, Barbara thought. Julie remembered that Jill and Jeffrey moved temporarily to Buckinghamshire and lived in a house in the woods with the actress Googie Withers.

In Jill's accounts of the war years she jumps over her marriage to Jeffrey Dell. She tidied up her biography in a few breezy remarks: 'I left my husband... I met Malcolm MacDonald, who is a friend of mine, and he gave me his house in Hampstead while he was High Commissioner in Canada... It was really a very happy period. I was free.' Jill neglected to mention that she moved into Malcolm's Hampstead home, Frognal Lodge, with Jeffrey Dell. Until Churchill appointed Malcolm High Commissioner of Canada in the spring of 1941, he was 'around quite a bit'.

After Jeffrey Dell died, his widow Barbara found Malcolm MacDonald's love letters to Jill in Jeffrey's papers. To Barbara, who vividly remembered the war years when one felt the next day might be one's last, when any sort of pettiness was out of the question, preserving these letters seemed unfair to everyone – to Jeffrey, to Malcolm and to Jill. 'You'll hate me,' she confessed, 'but I destroyed the letters.'

Malcolm MacDonald (1901–81), the son of Labour Party leader and prime minister (James) Ramsay MacDonald (1867–1937), had nothing in common with the stuffy, inhibited English schoolboys of his generation.[2] He remained exuberantly youthful and unaffected. Celebrating an electoral victory over Randolph Churchill in Scotland, he walked the length of a long hotel lounge on his hands (a feat he often repeated). Looking on, Churchill said, 'I would rather be able to do that than win Ross and Cromarty.' Malcolm, a distinguished diplomat who served in Ireland, Canada and in Asia and Africa, has an honoured place in helping to bring the British Empire to a peaceful end. Or as he put it in *Constant Surprise*, his unpublished autobiography, 'I did not make but unmade a piece of history.'[3]

A press report during the war had Jill writing a biography of Ramsay MacDonald. No scrap of such a work survives in her papers, but William MacQuitty, who first met Jill in 1943, remembered her working on the book, and it is obvious why she would have found such a project inspiring. The story of Malcolm's parents, for example, furnished a democratic and socially responsible vision of family absent from Jill's upbringing. Shortly after Malcolm's birth, his mother Margaret helped to organize the Barmaids' Committee to investigate the exploitation and degradation of young women. Concerned as well with the plight of women at home in the so-called cottage or sweated industries, she spent part of her honeymoon in Boston inspecting rooms where women were licensed to work. The home, Margaret maintained, should be a 'paradise' – one founded on democratic principles, in which the cockney charwoman and a young nursemaid sat down with the family to eat. Of course, the MacDonald children met important political figures, including a Scottish coalminer, Keir Hardie, their 'most endearing' visitor and the first Labour MP. Margaret thought it a disgrace that women did not have the vote. Not a militant suffragette, she nevertheless brought her three-year-old daughter Ishbel to the 'first large demonstration for women's suffrage'. Malcolm attended Bedales school near Petersfield in Hampshire, an extraordinary institution for its time, affording him a rare co-educational milieu enlivened by the principles of William Morris, Jill's own inspiration. Bedales should certainly be given credit for Malcolm's lifelong belief that art ought to inform every level and realm of existence and for his remarkable ease with women:

> We accepted them as a matter of course as fellow human beings with many interesting sides to their characters, among which 'a pair of sparkling eyes and a pair of ruby lips' were no doubt attractive items but of no more importance than a pleasing personality, a sense of humour… Co-education encouraged a natural relationship between members of the opposite sexes during their growing-up years.

Jill could not have met many men who could write:

> Some of my most intimate boon companions have been women whose feminine natures were complementary to my masculine one, whose reactions to all sorts of human affairs were therefore to some extent interestingly different from mine, and who have taught me by their attitudes many valuable things about the world.

This was not mere sentiment. In December 1938 as a Cabinet minister he put women for the first time in important staff positions at the Colonial and Dominions offices.

Malcolm pursued and collected 'beautiful objects – china, painting and books – as well as beautiful people, to have about him,' his biographer Clyde Sanger writes. Or as Malcolm exults in *Constant Surprise*: 'I liked Beauty, I loved Beauty, I worshipped Beauty.' Sanger observes that Malcolm 'kept an idealized picture of most young women'. He did not lose his virginity until he was twenty-seven, when he became devoted to Dorothy Dickson (1893–1995), a star of the London stage and a film actress, and through her to a glamorous cast that included Noel Coward, Laurence Olivier and Vivien Leigh. Besides Dorothy's 'breathtaking beauty', Malcolm admired her 'excellent taste and creditable knowledge of literature, music and painting' and her 'racy' talk laced with wit. Dorothy and her friends represented a world of fun and sexual adventure that relieved the 'demanding slavery of statecraft'.

Malcolm's affair lasted seven years, ending in 1936. Then, perhaps in 1939, he fell in love with Dorothy's daughter, Dot Hyson (1914–96), also an actress and also married. A theatre devotee, Malcolm may have met Jill in Dot's company at the beginning of the war. In 1942 Denis Forman (later Director of the British Film Institute) met Dot and Jill, who had become an inseparable pair, in a nightclub, along with Anthony Quayle, who was 'crazy about Dot'. On the nightclub circuit Jill 'illuminated the scene,' Denis remembered. 'She was a very good complement to Dot, because Dot was rather placid and very English. Jill would chatter away and be very amusing and daring. Dot sat looking quite beautiful and occasionally saying "Yes."' Jill never had any money and was always asking for fivers, unless Dot paid Jill's share. Denis thought Jill small and plucky and irresistible.

In *Constant Surprise*, Malcolm writes that he and 'Diana' (an amalgam of Jill and Dot) took 'our pleasure in contemplating artistic beauty, such as the gallery filled with Constable's paintings in the Victoria and Albert Museum, or (if we could escape for long enough) the regal apartments in Hampton Court Palace. For the present people were inclined to sweep aside all avoidable cares, and to enjoy to the utmost every moment of their day by day existences – lest it should turn out to be their last.'

As Minister of Health, Malcolm supervised care of civilians. Under his administration, thousands of children and the elderly were evacuated from cities targeted for attacks. He managed air-raid shelters, including an underground network of eighty-two stations offering shelter to as many as 145,000 people a night. He visited the underground and bombed sites, dealing with sanitation problems, overcrowding (as many as 1800 people would cram into an underground station), access to drinking water and poorly lit, leaking and improperly ventilated shelters.

As an ARP (Air Raid Precaution) warden in Hampstead, Jill witnessed how Londoners reacted to the Blitz: 'We used to go to battle headquarters, as we grandly called it.' Summoned to help at many different locations, she learned the names of all the roads. She checked to make sure blinds were pulled during blackouts. During the war, Hampstead had become, she noted

a wonderful democratic place, because a lot of ladies, the judges' wives, who'd never done anything but arrange flowers, were suddenly needed. There was no feminism during the war, because all women were needed... And they used to say, 'I don't know what I'll do when there's no ARP'. This was the best time in their lives because they were working, they were all needed. 'No, Mrs Jones, you can't have Saturday night off, we need you very badly, you must be there between seven and eleven.' 'Oh, very well then,' and they'd go off absolutely delighted.

The anti-aircraft guns were on the Heath, so the racket was absolutely terrific. Well, when you went out the next day, you talked to everybody. Everybody talked to everybody. 'Could you get any sleep last night at all? Did you go down to the shelter?'… It was fiendishly exciting, I'm sorry to say. Sometimes we would stand on Parliament Hill and we would watch the burning of the East End, and you knew these people were suffering terribly… It was awful, riveting. My little daughter, when she was here, I sent her away for a while like lots of people, she used to say, 'May I stay up and watch the flashes please, Mummy?'

In *Constant Surprise*, Malcolm wrote: 'Whilst in Canada, two of my closest friends stayed in my house in Hampstead, and they looked after my belongings there with scrupulous and indeed loving care.' A wartime letter (10 April 1941) to Dot Hyson tells a somewhat different story: 'They are so incredibly and incurably inefficient, those charming and dear Dells, that I have an awful feeling that if we have to depend too much on them to look after us, they will lose us.' Another letter refers to 'the Dellys', as though they were a comedy team.

Barbara, acting as the couple's secretary and baby-minder, saw in Jill a woman out of touch with her husband and no longer observing her marriage vows. A 'scatter-brained' Jill tore up the bills when they arrived. Barbara had to ask Jeffrey for her salary. After Barbara's first six weeks, the furious Jeffrey learned that Jill had still paid her nothing. Jill entertained large dinner parties of theatre people – at the last minute sending Barbara out for flowers. 'Oh, that table looks exquisite,' Jill told Barbara when Barbara returned with the centrepiece, and then Jill forgot to pay her for the flowers. Jill, always in a rush, seemed to Barbara an 'absentee mother'. Julie, often in Barbara's care, resented her distracted mother's disappearances and found comfort in Jeffrey Dell's Sussex farm – mainly a refuge from the city and a place to keep his beloved animals. 'Jeffrey was a private person,' Barbara says. He did not care much for parties.

Julie described her impression of Jeffrey and Jill at Frognal Lodge:

Jeffrey was, in my childish eyes, very tall and big compared to my little mother. He had a loud voice, too, and was sometimes very, very short tempered. If I put my head round the door of the room he was working in (not that I knew about his work at that time), he would hurl books at me and scream at me to get out. Frightening to a little girl. He used sarcasm, which always confused and frightened me… I grew up hating the sound of a typewriter. When she and Jeffrey were both working, that meant two typewriters in different parts of the house going at once. I remember very clearly the feeling of being shut out and lonely, a feeling of abandonment, too.

Watching Julie spread strictly rationed butter on her toast at breakfast, Jeffrey said, 'Stop pushing it into the toast to conceal how much you're taking.' He could switch from harsh reproval to loving solicitude in a second. These mood swings profoundly disturbed Julie, who adored her stepfather.*

Julie's war revolved around Gilly Short, whose father worked with Jill in the ARP. The girls met at Julie's sixth birthday party. Jill had asked Gilly's father whether he had any children, and he told her he had a four-year-old daughter and a brand new baby. Jill invited other children, but they were not Julie's friends, and to Julie they seemed part of a 'forced' atmosphere. Gilly lived just over the road, and there was a gate, just at the bottom of the garden, which opened onto Frognal. 'So Mummy could stand at the window and watch me leaving your house and into the garden gate, where I was safe,' Gilly recalled, reminiscing with her friend

Jill regarded Gilly's father, one of nine children who never finished his schooling, as a 'natural leader' who took charge during the war and 'broke down the class barriers'. After the war, the class system returned 'in a big way', Jill remarked. 'I'm no longer invited to anyone's home except yours,' Mr Short told her. But Gilly and Julie do not remember their parents meeting or comparing notes. Jill always called Gilly's father Mr Short and the families did not socialize. And what did Mr Short think of Jill? 'Very beautiful,' Gilly commented quietly. 'I think she was out of his league as a woman. Jill was such a woman of the world, so full of ideas. I think he would have been swept off his feet by her.' Very fond of Julie, he called her right up to the end the 'light of my life'. When she phoned and he answered, he would say to Gilly: 'Here is the light of your life.' A shy girl who had few friends and craved her mother's affection and encouragement, Julie, like her mother before her, hated being sent away to boarding school. 'Judy't was a child of the blitz,' Jill pointed out in a letter (26 May 1994) to biographer Mervyn Jones. During the war many children were sent for their safety out of London, and Julie's school, Long Dene, near Slough, remained accessible by train. It comforted Jill to know that Julie had plenty of fruit, vegetables, yoghurt and 'other goodies' in a period of food rationing.

Jill also believed in the permissive principles of a school 'run on the same lines as Bertrand Russell's Dartington Hall'. Students could choose from a wide range of subjects but still seemed able to qualify for entrance to university. Julie had a horse at school – a gift from Malcolm MacDonald. She liked to spend her time at the stables rather than at lessons. Only later did she

* This portrait of Jeffrey astounds Barbara Dell, who emphasizes what a quiet and even-tempered man her husband was. She could remember only two quarrels with him in their long marriage.

† Jill called Julie 'Judy', and Julie never understood why. Usually Julie signed her letters Julie, the name she prefers.

realize that Jill feared for her safety. 'Only with hindsight,' Julie pointed out, 'have we learnt that generally the little ones who remained in London with their parents throughout the blitz, though they lost their homes and slept in underground shelters, fared very much better – if they survived.'

Jill kept Julie's letters. Some are illustrated (one depicts a sad child all alone standing next to what is apparently a schoolhouse). The letters, often bordered with hugs and kisses, reflect a child's anxiety and eagerness to please:

> Dear Mummy,
>   I hope you will soon see me. You must see me on Saturday please because you promised. I have no idea what the surprise is I hope you are having a nice time. I am learning to read better.
>   Love from
>   Judy
>   x x x x x x x x x x x x x x x
>   o o o o o o o o o o o o o o o

Julie called it 'hateful' not spending holidays with her mother. Other than quite delightful Christmases, she spent her holidays with the Begbie-Clench clan. 'I was sent down in a train with a label around my neck in the guard's van' with the dogs and signal flags. She would then wait at the station for the chauffeur to pick her up. She stayed in a big country house with a house-keeper, servants and a gardener. Gilly sometimes accompanied her, and remembered Julie's formal, conservative relatives: 'We were made to appear dot on the time for meals, dressed, clean.' Everything looked like a period room in a museum. The rigid daily routine included a trip to the lavatory after breakfast, 'until I had been successful,' Julie recalled:

> Then I'd have to call for inspection, and so on. Every detail – changing my knickers every other day – whereas my mother, at that stage in her life, took her clothes off and dropped them on the floor. Her room was extremely untidy. She got better as she got older. Meals came out or they didn't. The ashtrays were never empty. The house was a mess. It was slaphappy.

During the summer holidays Julie went to stay with her Aunt Maudie, who had moved from Leamington Spa to Lee on Solent in Hampshire (between Portsmouth and Southampton). Gilly sometimes accompanied her, and the girls enjoyed the sea and a dinghy. As long as they showed up promptly for meals in clean clothes, no questions were asked about what they did. Portly, old fashioned and stern, Maudie nevertheless seemed to Julie the nicest member of the family, a welcome change from her cruel, sarcastic grandfather (who once made a pass at Jill and later, gun in hand, disowned Julie for returning from a theatre performance at midnight). Jill had little to say about Maudie, except that she remained the most decent member of the family.

Jill apparently never commented on this sharing-the-holidays arrangement that had been stipulated by her first husband's family. Julie never wanted to leave her mother, and Jill just said that she had to go. Like her mother, Jill was peripatetic, a restless woman in a man's world who did not always have time for her child. Reflecting on the parallels between Sonia and Jill, Julie thought her mother, whatever her shortcomings, had bettered Sonia's poor performance. Indeed, so successful had Jill been in forming a bond with her daughter – in spite of Jill's frequent absences – that Julie would come to resent the presence of anyone who claimed a large share of her mother's affections.

Gilly described the difference between her world and Julie's as one of 'chalk and cheese. I came from a large, very supportive family. I attended the local state primary school in Hampstead, and all my family voted Conservative.' At Malcolm MacDonald's house, which Jill occupied throughout the war, she held wonderful, glamorous parties that included film stars and other celebrities. Julie and Gilly hid at the top of the stairs and watched and watched. 'It was like an old movie,' Gilly recalled. 'All these people in evening dress, the grand piano and your mother playing. Everyone was beautiful and beautifully dressed.' Jill seemed reluctant to play for company; she was not 'particularly good at it,' Julie said. But to Gilly, 'Jill looked *stunning* doing it. I don't remember my mother ever having a party.'

General De Gaulle took a house next door to Frognal Lodge, and the girls, who could see over their wall into his sloping garden, used to watch him walk his invalid daughter Anne. They would spy on him and shout '*Bonjour*' and duck down below the wall. One of Jill's most poignant memories was of watching the General – this very tall man – taking such delicate care of his daughter – his favourite child – during the supreme trial of his life.[4] But even the De Gaulle residence had its comic moments: a servant, speaking in a mixture of French and English, would run out of the house and declare, 'the *poulet* has escaped'.[5]

Julie and Gilly wrote up plays and entertained her mother's glamorous guests at dinner parties in the conservatory. The girls enjoyed making entrances through swinging double doors. 'All these people were forced to watch these obnoxious girls,' said Gilly who also saw Jeffrey Dell, a 'tall handsome man. There was always something slightly blank about Jeffrey. He put up a kind of barrier and seemed preoccupied. I remember him being a very unhappy man.'

Jill was always at the typewriter, Julie said. Day after day Jill would give the girls half a crown to have a lunch of baked beans on toast at Hampstead cafés. Between 1940 and 1942 she wrote short scripts for British Council documentaries. These films fostered patriotic action, offered practical advice for coping with a wartime economy and featured the people, professions and institutions contributing to the war effort.[6] To Jill, this work lacked an aesthetic element, a way of making a story and a work of art out of people's lives. The documentaries were 'inhuman', 'boring' and focused too much on 'machinery and the way machinery works'. Her script for *Looking Through Glass* (1943) had to concentrate on the product, whereas she wanted to focus on the 'boffin [technical expert] who set up his own laboratory and published all the secrets. I would have made a film about him, not about glass, if I'd had the chance. That's why I left. I was fed up working for the British Council, it didn't get anywhere and I thought some of the films were pretty silly.'

Jill never explained why – with her marriage in disarray – she now decided to work with Jeffrey on a screenplay for *The Flemish Farm* (1943), which also marked his directorial debut. In fact, she never said anything about what her working life with him meant to her career in film. Jeffrey Dell gave her an entrance to the film world that eluded other women of her generation. It is also curious that when an interviewer mentioned *The Flemish Farm*, Jill did not take the opportunity to comment that it reflected her film aesthetic – not merely in making the visual element tell the story, but also in subtly integrating music into the narrative pace of the film. The film's composer, Ralph Vaughan Williams, would become another one of her admirers and supply music for her documentaries, and the film's conductor, Muir Matthieson, would work on Jill's other films and become one of her suitors.

The Flemish Farm screenplay was derived from an item Jeffrey spotted in *The Times* reporting that the flag of the Belgian Air Force, secretly buried by the Belgians when they retreated from the German advance, had been recovered and brought to England for a ceremony. Jill and Jeffrey (the film credit reads Jill and Jeffrey Dell) built their story on essentially one sentence in the news item stating that a Belgian officer (Duclos in the film) had risked his life returning to German-occupied Belgium to bring back the buried flag. The Exhibitor's Campaign Sheet, on file at the British Film Institute, accurately articulates the film's message about 'freedom, justice, the right of every man in every country to live out his life in peace with his neighbour'.

Jill and Jeffrey are also making a statement about how to live and about what the defining characteristics of an everyday hero ought to be. When Duclos first arrives at the farm, where he is searching for the buried Belgian flag, he encounters a man stooping over a tractor that will not start. A menacing German soldier is threatening to shoot the man for contriving the mechanical breakdown. But the malfunction is no ruse, the man tells Duclos, who carefully examines the vehicle and shows the man how to fix it. Duclos may be the film's hero, but he is also a mechanic, an ordinary man who works with his hands and is attuned to the farm's everyday rhythms. He is William Morris's idea of a man whose hand and eye and mind perceive and act upon the order and form of the world – a central idea in Jill's subsequent work.

Although reviews in *News Chronicle* (8 July 1943) and the *Daily Worker* (2 August 1943) complain of the film's slowness and lack of fluent dialogue, most assessments are positive, praising 'the intelligent and artful treatment, the exquisite attention to detail, the perfection of minor characters ... without the blaring of patriotic music or noises "off"' (*Reynolds News*, 8 August 1943), and noting with gratitude, 'no machine made situations of comic relief and synthetic love interest that destroy nine films out of 10' (*Daily Telegraph*, 9 August 1943). 'Nor are the people in the occupied country represented as all heroic secret heroes and the Germans as all nitwits, as they have been in practically every film of the kind we have yet seen,' the reviewer adds. Only one critic mentions Jill specifically, noting that in her 'grim determination to create an authentic atmosphere and to avoid any hint of melodramatics, Mrs Dell has underplayed everything severely' (*What's On*, 12 August 1943).

After writing *The Flemish Farm*, the couple spent more and more time apart as they worked on separate film projects. Although they could not build a home together, they both desperately wanted a home and family in their own separate fashions. Jill would later say that Jeffrey did not want her to have a child.* The circumstances suggest that it was actually Jill who was not ready to care for another child, and perhaps both husband and wife acknowledged that fact. As Jill said many years later, 'I wanted to be free.'

---

* Jeffrey had a son, Richard, by his first marriage, and two daughters with his last wife, Barbara.

Out of Chaos
(1942–3)

Jack: You always want to argue about things.
Algernon: That is exactly what things were originally made for.

Oscar Wilde, The Importance of Being Earnest

Jill Craigie's career did not suddenly shift from her role as scriptwriter for British Council films to writer/director of her own documentaries, although she made it seem so: 'I was quite persuasive... I could write so that people could see what it would look like on the screen.' Of her decision to write and direct her first documentary, *Out of Chaos*, she said: 'Mr [Thomas] Bentley was an old film director, and he thought I had a visual sense.'*

An independent director or producer – or anyone, really – who knows anything about the making of a film will wonder how a thirty-two-year-old woman, in 1943, in the midst of a war, got the funding, assembled a crew, found the artists and located a company willing to distribute a documentary lasting a little less than thirty minutes. Even though the war did open up certain opportunities for women, the studios, the British Council and the Ministry of Information did not suddenly employ a cadre of women directors.

Jill gave various incomplete explanations of how she got to do the film. She said she went to J. Arthur Rank (1888–1972), the movie mogul, and convinced him of the film's timeliness. She said she had the good fortune to work for a remarkably generous producer, Filippo Del Giudice (1892–1961). She said she pitched her idea to Kenneth Clark (1903–83), director of the National Gallery, who surprisingly put his faith in this neophyte director. All true, but how did Jill make these contacts?

During the making of *The Flemish Farm*, associate producer William (Liam)

---

* *Halliwell's Who's Who in the Movies* (1999) gives only approximate dates for Bentley (c.1880–195?). A prolific director, his notable films include *Hobson's Choice* (1931) and *The Old Curiosity Shop* (1935).

MacQuitty used to drive over to Hampstead to pick up Jeffrey Dell, who had been asked to direct the film by Sidney Box (1907–83). That is how Liam met Jill, an ardent woman, who used her big eyes, he remembered, to charm men. Liam saw nothing amiss between husband and wife, although he noted that they had a sort of friendly rivalry as writers. Jill watched a jolly Jeffrey depart for the studio each day, and she became, Liam suggested, jealous. She wanted to write and *direct*, and to a receptive Liam she confided her idea of making a film about art and wartime artists. She had met an impressive array of artists through her friendship with Malcolm MacDonald, who had taken her to galleries and collected art and artists like Stanley Spencer, who had often dined with MacDonald and his friends at restaurants and nightclubs.

Jill's next film, *Out of Chaos*, arose out of the powerful yearning of wartime Britain to preserve and perpetuate its art. Public figures such as the great economist John Maynard Keynes (1883–1946) and Kenneth Clark worked tirelessly to ensure that 'culture' should not be put aside for the duration: in the act of fighting to save Britain, 'English culture must not be sacrificed.'[1] Clark became the primary force behind the War Artists' Scheme, which Peter Stansky and William Abrahams term the 'most extensive patronage scheme for British artists that has ever existed', producing almost 6000 works of art distributed to museums across the country.

Virtually every museum, cinema, theatre and concert hall closed at the start of the war, except the National Gallery, which sponsored one-hour afternoon chamber music concerts (admission price one shilling). For five days a week, from 10 October 1939 to 10 April 1946, the museum presented concerts attended by as many as 1750 people each. *Out of Chaos* sought to capitalize on this burgeoning interest in the arts.

The story of a people coming together through art seemed to Jill the fulfilment of William Morris's socialist dream. He developed his vision in a series of lectures to artists and craftsman in London, Birmingham, Oxford and many other parts of England between 1877 and 1896. 'I thought you can't have a Socialist society unless the socialists themselves study their Morris and Ruskin… Read his lectures and other writings, he is very, very modern,' Jill emphasized to an interviewer.

Morris (1834–96) was an architect, designer, printer, poet, novelist and social reformer, a man who made his own furniture, wallpaper, textiles, ceramics and stained glass, as well as many other kinds of everyday hand-crafted objects inspired by a profound reverence for the artisans of the Middle Ages. He seemed supremely important to Jill during the war, when, as documentary film-maker Humphrey Jennings wrote, London had again become a big village in which barriers and partitions and prejudices were breaking down.* London had its museums, Morris acknowledged, but art (an appreciation of form) had become so divorced from the common experience of people that it needed help:

> People need some preliminary instruction before they can get all the good possible to be got from the prodigious treasures of art possessed by the country in that form: there also one sees things in a piecemeal way: nor can I deny that there is something melancholy in a museum, such a tale of violence, destruction and carelessness, as its treasured scraps tell us.[2]

In *Out of Chaos* Jill set out to cure precisely this sense of alienation from works of art, this inability to 'read' art because it exists only in the fragmentary form of a museum.

In the age of industry and urban expansion, Morris lamented, men looked upon art as 'at best trifling'. Yet what we know of past civilizations, Morris countered, is through their art. And even in the most oppressive eras, 'daily labour was sweetened by the daily creation of Art'. In short, '*all* people shared in art'.

How could a documentary film put art at the centre of a just and democratic society? What would be the equivalent, in filmic terms, of a William Morris lecture? Script the give and take of ideas into dialogue as Oscar Wilde (1854–1900) had done in 'The Critic as Artist'? 'What is the use of art-criticism?' Ernest asks Gilbert, his interlocutor in Wilde's most famous essay.[3] 'Criticism is creative,' Gilbert answers. The critic shapes the work of art just as the artist shapes the world into the work of art. The 'meaning of any beautiful created thing is, at least, as much in the soul of him who looks at it, as it was in his soul who wrought it'.

The artist's mandate is to extricate form out of chaos, Gilbert concludes: 'Life is terribly deficient in form.' In Alan Reeve's *Picture Post* article announcing the release of *Out of Chaos*, Jill observed: 'With mass production, industrial design and town planning, the artist is becoming increasingly important and useful to society. He has been neglected too long, and we can't live full lives if we continue to ignore him. If we question the look of a

---

* 'London – to look at it – has settled down to a big village-like existence. Most of the damage demolished and cleared up. Endless allotments – beds of potatoes, onions, lettuces – in parks, in the new open spaces from bombing, tomatoes climbing up ruins – trees and shrubs overgrowing evacuated and empty houses and gardens – in some places shells of eighteenth century cottages with black blank windows and Rousseau-like forests enveloping them, straying out over the road – no railings – climbing in windows. Elsewhere the utmost tidiness and care in lines of planting on AA gunsites, aerodromes, firestations. The parks and squares open to all – all railings gone, shelters overgrown', Humphrey Jennings to Cicely Jennings, 28 July 1942. Quoted in Stansky and Abrahams.

painting, we will also question the look of other things, our houses and our towns.' The *Picture Post* article called *Out of Chaos* 'the first serious effort … to guide the public's wartime interest in art into something which may be permanent'. Liam MacQuitty, an astute businessman, world traveller and superb photographer, took Jill's idea to Sydney Box, a producer almost as remarkable as MacQuitty. 'He had this effortless confidence, beyond belief,' Liam recalled. Like Liam, this entrepreneur had established his own documentary film company, Verity Films, in the autumn of 1940. By 1943 it had become the largest producer of documentary films in the country, working in conjunction with both the Ministry of Information and the studios. Like Liam, Sydney did not discount women's talents. Indeed, his sister Betty got the job of supervising film units, some of which were comprised of women directors and camera operators.

To fund Jill's documentary, Sydney worked through Filippo Del Giudice, senior producer for J. Arthur Rank, then at the height of his power in British films. Del, an extravagant Italian (exiled from fascist Italy), eagerly encouraged 'ze new tal-ents' – as Jill would say, mimicking his tendency to divide English words in two.[4]

Liam and Sydney knew that they only had to sell Del on the idea of the film, and then Jill could do what she wanted under the imprimatur of Del's company, 'Two Cities' (named for London and Rome). Del never seemed to visit a set while in production. He never interfered with directors or writers or the producers he engaged to work for him, saying, 'We all know that if you have a very good Director it is useless to interfere with his work. If you interfered it would be like looking over the shoulder of Picasso or Augustus John whilst they are doing their work. Anybody really great could not stand being watched in such a way.'[5] Although Del earned good money and critical acclaim for J. Arthur Rank with films such as Laurence Olivier's *Henry V* (1944), he also spent it lavishly on himself and film projects. In this case, however, Liam and Sydney figured that the film could be done on location (thus taking up only a week of precious studio time and space) and for the modest sum of £7,000. Nevertheless, as Liam pointed out: 'Del was taking a risk with an untried woman director… and a subject that lacked mass appeal. The British Council and the Arts Council, from whom we hoped for more backing, both turned the project down.' As Laurence Olivier later said about Del: 'I know no one else in British films so kind, generous, imaginative and courageous.'[6] Olivier's valedictory is not merely an expression of gratitude, it is a lament for a dream of film, a lament for a vision of a future British film industry that dwindled after the war years – and along with it the career of Jill Craigie.

Through Del, Jill had access to J. Arthur Rank, who entered the British film industry in the mid-1930s and infused it with new life. Rank could be remarkably generous in giving producers and directors the freedom to develop their projects without studio interference. On the other hand, as a businessman he exercised rigid control over finances and budgets through his alter ego, the notoriously malicious accountant John Davis (1906–93).

Rank's father had amassed his fortune in the flour-milling business, and his equally successful son wanted to expand the family's fortune and spread its Methodist precepts by creating profit-making pictures with uplifting ideas and sound moral messages. You cannot spread the word if you do not have the funding for it, but the blessing of the funding derives, of course, from spreading the word. So any film with moral or idealistic pretensions would appeal to Rank but would also be chargeable to Davis's box office/entertainment value ledger. Films like Jill's, in other words, incited wars over J. Arthur Rank's soul. Producing Jill's film in the realm of Rank proved propitious because at this stage Del's gains overcame his losses, and Rank's 'evangelical side', notes film historian Geoffrey Macnab, 'warmed to the Italian'. Or, as Jill liked to say, 'There was methodism in his madness.'[7]

Jill also called Rank a 'benevolent dictator', and she found an ingenious way of making a pitch to him: 'Would you consider replacing the second feature film with British documentaries on things of social importance, in view of the war situation?'[8] The second feature was often a 'quota quickie', a film produced mainly to fill the quota of British films mandated by a law aimed at reducing the overwhelming presence of Hollywood product in British cinemas. Since the second feature amounted to an add-on that audiences tolerated, and because of low entertainment expectations, Rank could afford to soothe his conscience without risking very much money. This was one of the few times Jill actually spoke to Rank. 'I'm a very small cog in this,' Jill instructed Charles Drazin, 'don't build me up as something too big, because I'm very small!'[9]

Unlike the principal documentary film-makers of the period who relied on government funding or were employed by private companies to make films for non-theatrical venues, Jill had to deal with very negative market conditions. That Del proved susceptible to her ideas made her career possible, but his isolation as a producer ultimately contributed to her undoing. As Drazin points out, Del was 'routinely ridiculed. His attempts to be innovative were dismissed in the trade magazines as fantastic nonsense. He was laughed at not because he was impractical but because he was trying to give exhibitors what in the main they did not want: Art.' This view of a film industry crushed in the vice of distributors and exhibitors is, in part, derived from the probing interview with Jill that Drazin conducted while preparing his study *The Finest Years: British Cinema of the 1940s*. The style and aplomb with which she out-manoeuvred those who sought to obstruct her had seldom been recognized except by Drazin and Macnab.

In his autobiography, *A Life to Remember*, Liam observes: 'Jill was small, dark, pretty and determined – very determined. Her script was to answer those questions that arose in the minds of the public when they saw their money being spent on artists whose work they regarded with suspicion or ridicule.' Men responded to her eager, ingenuous manner, Liam remembered. She recalled how she went to visit Kenneth Clark to explain which war artists she wanted to film. 'I know nothing about films,' she told him, 'but I'm sure I can manage somehow.' She got his backing.

Liam found Jill a relief from the tetchy egos of male directors. 'She was wonderful with people.' She had to be, for she was quite aware, as she said decades later, that her virtually all-male crew, eventually numbering forty, initially looked on her as no more than a 'girl'. As Liam observed: 'She was able to stroke the male ego with enormous effect.' A female interviewer once pressed Jill on this subject:

Interviewer: You did tell me once that you weren't above using the fact that you were a woman for getting a film underway.
Jill: I think that when women enter public life of any sort… they should not lose their charm. I am conscious of the fact that when there are debates in the House of Commons about women voting… the anti-suffragettes frequently say this… repeat it over and over 'Women will lose their charm and will become aggressive.' Well, men don't… lose their charm. But women… sometimes become – the politicians – too aggressive, a bit too tub-thumping, and remembering all these things that I had read, I was not above exercising an occasional womanly wile.
Interviewer: In what way?
Jill: Well – I might flatter a fellow perhaps to get a film going. I might say… 'If you don't do it, nobody else will.' Which was true, incidentally. I tried not to get into fierce arguments, or pour scorn on… a man who said to me, 'Why do you do this?' or 'Why don't you do this?' and though it was the most ghastly idea I had ever heard, I would never let him know. I'd say, 'Well, that's a marvellous idea, BUT'… and find some way round it. It was very difficult to be absolutely straightforward then, I think, if you wanted to do something, if you had a sufficient passion to. I really had a passion to translate my visions into actions and so I was prepared to – not go very far, mind you, don't get the wrong idea, but I did what I could to get my own way.

The word sex is never uttered in this interview, but it provides the obvious subtext. The circumspect Liam ventured only the comment, 'I imagine most men found her attractive. But that did not mean they got anywhere.' Of his own relationship with Jill, he remarked, 'I was the other half', meaning she did the writing and directing, and he engaged the cameraman and crew and dealt with the other mechanics and business of film-making.

According to Jill, Clark 'left it to me to persuade the war artists to appear in the film'. Of those she had in mind, only John Piper refused. 'And rightly so,' Jill added, 'I was not only young and naïve, but had no experience in directing a film.' Alan Reeve's *Picture Post* article reports that Jill had to 'overcome the nervousness and suspicion of the artists, none of whom were anxious to star in the movies. But once having gained faith in her as a sympathetic director, they responded intelligently.' Jill, on the other hand, remembered that the artists 'seemed most eager to be filmed and only wanted to know when, where and how'.[10] Liam suggested: 'It was a time of heightened adrenalin. All the artists were totally dedicated to capturing their response to war and showing what it felt like to be in a country that was at war. They all drew upon their deepest reserves.'[11]

Liam recalled that he and Jill first set out with cameraman Pennington 'Penny' Richards and a loader-clapper boy, Leslie Hughes, to film Paul Nash (1889–1946), then a renowned artist in the tradition of William Blake who identified with the surrealists. Primarily a landscape painter, Nash had produced extraordinary images of a countryside devastated by World War I. In World War II he produced his masterpiece, *Totes Meer* (*Dead Sea*, 1940–41, now at the Tate Britain), a symbolic – almost allegorical – vision of a landscape strewn with shot-down German planes – waves and waves of them with wings overlapping in a concentrated complex of bent metal that evokes the German onrush of bombers over Britain and the aftermath of the country's heroic defence. Nash took Jill and her crew back to the aircraft dump that had inspired his vision, and Liam vividly described the scene shot for the film: 'Engines had smashed through air-frames already riddled with bullets and grotesquely melted seats nestled in the wreckage so that you half expected to see human fragments amid the horror.' Jill and her crew then shot Graham Sutherland (1903–80) at the Imperial Chemical Limestone Quarries at Hindlow, Buxton. The artist had come into his own in the 1930s with a series of oil paintings that depicted landscapes of 'semi-abstract patterns of haunting and monstrous shapes',[12] almost as if he had been anticipating a holocaust. Jill liked to tell the story of photographing Sutherland doing an odd sketch every now and again. Dissatisfied, he crumpled it up and threw it out on the pavement. Liam picked it up, stretched it out, and Sutherland said: 'That's fifteen quid it will cost you.'[13]

Liam remembered Sutherland as 'dapper and forceful'; Jill called him 'rather vain'. He wanted to be filmed wearing a helmet (he was), 'doing important things' and 'involved in the war,' she confided in her scrapbook. She also recalled that she had tried to film Sutherland drawing in a Cornish tin mine. But the conditions proved too daunting, and she watched in dismay as he tore up his 'marvellous' pictures. She did not get on with him that well, although they shared a devotion to socialist politics.

Stanley Spencer (1891–1959), easily the most flamboyant artist to be filmed, has been called 'one of the most original figures in 20th-cent. British art'.[14] Like Paul Nash, he created distinguished works of art during both world wars, concentrating in the former on the lives of ordinary soldiers – as in *The Dug-Out* – and in the latter on war workers, focusing on the Clyde shipbuilders. Stanley was so spectacularly odd that Jill chided biographer Fiona McCarthy in a book review, 'She even denies that he was eccentric.'[15] Jill contended the artist was 'quite mad'. She remembered travelling with him, third class in a train carriage, and him announcing to the mothers and children, 'all my painting is masturbation. I masturbate, and masturbate, and masturbate.' He did his sketches on toilet paper and would say, 'My lavatory paper is worth more than your cameras.' Jill noted in her scrapbook: 'Toilet paper not so soft or absorbent as it became after the war.' She found him 'always outrageous. He liked dirt, and he wore dirty pyjamas, and he smelled quite badly. He approved of dirt for its own sake.' Such comments, however, reflect amusement, not disapproval. Jill's film captures the extraordinary intensity and joy Spencer took from his work in the shipyards. Indeed, of all the artists in *Out of Chaos*, he is the one who embodies the idea of the worker – not because of the way he is dressed or because of what he is doing but because of his air of preoccupation with his task. He seems at one with the industrial environment. As Fiona McCarthy observes, the 'lives of ordinary working people interested him immensely'.[16] Another Spencer biographer reports that 'he lived entirely among the shipyard people', who had no idea he was a famous artist – in part because he did not seek out prominent or educated figures.[17] William Morris's spirit comes alive in Spencer's paintings of shipbuilders and in his statement about the men and equipment he depicted: 'Everything I see is manifestly religious and sexual... it is not that coils of rope suggest haloes it is just that all these men, hawsers, strings, as in all forms have a hallowing effect of their own... it is part of their nature.'[18]

The film focuses not so much on the finished product as on Stanley in situ: he excitedly draws the workers' different positions and attitudes. Liam remembers that the artist was 'immensely popular' among the shipbuilders. Watching Stanley sketch in 'rapid bursts on a roll of strong white toilet paper' made Liam think of 'papyrus scrolls of ancient scribes'. Liam asked him why he used toilet paper. 'Because it is cheap and doesn't end. It gives me continuity, and if I don't like the sketch I don't have to waste the paper!' Stanley grinned. 'Stanley was very appealing,' Liam wrote in *A Life to Remember*.

Yet the star in Jill's film and in her memory of making it remained Henry Moore (1898–1986). Like the other artists in *Out of Chaos*, he had a considerable reputation among his fellow artists and the critics but was not yet the world figure he would become after the war. The son of a Yorkshire miner, Moore had a tactile and earthy sensibility that made his work in stone or wood sensuous and palpable. His abstractions of the human figure contain a 'vital force and vigour' that derived from his absorption in the swelling, rhythmic bodies in the frescoes of Masaccio (1401–28), one of the key figures of the Renaissance, and from the pent-up energy and monumental presence of the human form in Meso-American and Sumerian sculpture.[19] Recalling Moore's reputation before the war, Jill later said, 'His curious sculptures with their famous holes could enrage even some well-known collectors of Post-Impressionists.'

Jill later wrote that her crew 'expected they might encounter a weird fellow talking about art in incomprehensible language'.[20] They soon thought differently of this 'down-to-earth' Yorkshireman. 'He alone spent hours with me in advance to ensure that I had the right ideas. A more engaging teacher it would have been impossible to find.' In fact, Moore had been a teacher of art, and he paid Jill and her crew the sublime William Morris compliment of treating them as fellow artists.

Henry and Jill walked together hand in hand in the underground tube/ tomb. They shared what Moore called a 'morbid curiosity & a strange, subdued excitement',[21] observing the scene that had stirred some of his greatest art: the sight of a sea of figures swaddled together, rolling over and pitching against each other, slumbering in exhausted, fitful sleep and collapsing into stillness – in the dim light looking to Jill like 'rows of Egyptian mummies'. Moore watched, making notes and brief sketches, catching the anxiety just behind the 'bonhomie' of these plucky individuals. 'He could hardly suppress his anger at what was happening to these people,' Jill remembered. 'Two women restlessly asleep clutched at their blankets as if they were both in the grip of a nightmare. He proposed to recreate this impression for the benefit of our film.'

Moore was the only artist who discussed with Jill the nature of film as an artistic medium:

> He had already told me that he considered the reclining figure most appropriate to the hard, heavy qualities of stone and bronze, more true to the materials than portrayals of actions, such as running or wrestling. That being so, I asked him whether he agreed that to be true to the medium of cinematic film, movies should move. 'Of course,' he replied, as if he had already given some thought to the matter.

Film would become, in Moore's hands, another way of presenting his portfolio.

In Moore's studio the army of technicians trampled about examining Moore's work. Jill observed their puzzled faces, imagining them trying to

> reconcile so much rubbish with so commonsensical a man. They were in for a big surprise. We focused the camera on a blank sheet of white paper and called for action. Henry then took a white wax crayon and seemed to scribble all over it. As the white upon white was invisible he appeared to have no way of seeing precisely what he was doing. He gave the impression he might just as well have been blindfolded. He then washed the paper all over with a brush filled with a dark water-colour. Naturally the water could not take on the wax, the colour could only fill in the spaces left by the artist. Magically, a powerful impression of two women restlessly asleep in the Underground appeared, the whole creating an atmosphere of oppression beyond the scope of a photograph. The execution of the work was so beautifully timed and adapted to a medium devised for action – it was shot in one take – that Henry's conquest of the film unit was complete.

During a break in filming, Jill asked Moore about his interest in three-dimensional form. He explained it by recollecting how he used to ease the pain of his mother's lumbago: 'He demonstrated the movement first by rubbing his own hip, then mine. To have Henry Moore rub one's hip is not an experience anyone would be likely to forget. To rub one's hand over a Moore sculpture, which he liked people to do, is often reminiscent of stroking a hip.' But why the small heads and holes, she asked. He replied that these elements evoke an aura of dignity and mystery.

Jill's memoir of working with Moore is of a piece with her film. Writing forty-three years after the release of *Out of Chaos*, Jill echoed the words of Eric Newton, the critic featured in her film: 'As with most of the greatest artists and composers, [Moore's] work was widely denounced until it became more familiar. People do not know what they like so much as like what they know.' Moore taught Jill and her crew something new and fresh and creative to like, and he did so through understanding the terms and conditions of film work:

> He made only one request: the filming of his sculpture must be left to the last. Lighting interiors was then more complicated than it is today, requiring many more lamps, each with its own name, complete with gauzes and other paraphernalia. When the lighting cameraman gave instructions to a team of electricians, he used technical terms beyond the comprehension of laymen. When the time came, Henry took the cameraman aside and quietly told him just how to light the sculpture, not merely by suggesting where a shadow should fall and whether the correct depth of shade had been achieved, but by using all the right technical terms.

Everyone left the studio certain of Moore's genius. Although Jill gives all the credit to Moore, he obviously responded to a sensitive and perceptive filmmaker who created the conditions in which he could educate and edify his audience.

In *A Life to Remember*, Liam describes Moore as a 'strong, quiet man with a simple, natural way of explaining what he was doing'. Similarly, magazine editor Tom Hopkinson, who frequently lunched with Moore during this period, noted: 'I had never met anyone so calm, so certain of himself and of what he was doing, and so generous towards the work of everybody else.'[22] Although Moore did many of his sketches in the Hampstead tube station, Liam remembers that scenes were shot in Holborn for the film. Liam also mentions Moore's 'charming wife', Irina, whom Jill liked very much – so much that she resisted the very powerful temptation to act on her erotic attraction to the artist. To the end of her life, she was both proud that she had respected his marriage and regretful that she had not made love to Moore. Jill kept in her *Out of Chaos* scrapbook photographs of herself, Henry, Irina and the distinguished photographer Lee Miller seated around a table and clearly enjoying each other's company.

Out of Chaos begins with a portentous trumpet solo, a shot of what looks like cave drawings of animals and a human figure, upon which is superimposed a brief statement: 'Soon after man learned to walk on two legs he wanted to draw. At first he drew on the wall of his cave, and no doubt when his neighbours saw what he'd done, they argued about it. The kind of argument they had has gone on ever since.'[23] Shots of people entering the National Gallery on a Saturday afternoon are accompanied by a voiceover female narrator asking: 'Who are these people? Part of an "arty minority"?' Men and women in uniform are shown gazing at paintings. 'Do they often come here?'

the narrator asks. A shot of a young man in glasses prompts the narrator to say he is the type you would expect to find in a gallery. Three men with their backs turned to the camera suggest a group of businessman. The narrator recalls how artists, housewives and institutions of various kinds 'packed up' their treasures in anticipation of war. Kenneth Clark then appears, explaining his programme to employ artists to record the war. He seems stiff, moving his hands uncomfortably.

Clark eventually learned, like others a generation later, how to 'be himself' on screen, but Jill could not endow him with that experience beforehand. Liam remembered Clark's nervousness and that Jill suggested he sit on the edge of his desk. Liam photographed Clark and asked him for an autograph. 'From your most incompetent and overpaid stand-in,' Clark wrote.[24] In her scrapbook Jill only remembered how eager and helpful Clark remained throughout the filming.

Mercifully, after a minute or so the camera cuts to scenes with the artists out in the field. Stanley Spencer is shown working at the shipyard and in his studio, and the narrator concludes: 'Some of us can interpret these compositions for ourselves, but it is usually a help to hear what a perceptive critic like Eric Newton has to say about them.' Newton's rather gloomy voice-over interpretation emphasizes how carefully and repeatedly the artist has watched shipyard scene until his art, like that of the workers, 'turns the chaos of metal into a pattern and so intensifying its meaning'.

The film's tempo abruptly changes with a newsreel-like narration: 'September 1940, the Battle of Britain, when so many of us were jolted out of our old way of living. And our old way of thinking.' Scenes of downed planes with Nazi insignia shift to a medium shot of Paul Nash sketching the sea of wreckage juxtaposed against a close-up of his pre-war surrealistic landscapes. Shots of the sea are transposed onto Nash's painting. Different shades of light from dusk to twilight reveal not only the different times at which Nash painted, but also how this complex pattern of light is filtered into the painting's final composition. Surveying the scene, the narrator comments, 'It seemed to him that the wreckage heaved itself up and down in a great tide flooding the fields.' The heaving up of the metal reminds Newton of the 'last agony of the German air fleet'.

Then, as shots appear from Humphrey Jennings' wartime classic *Fires Were Started*, the narrator recounts how firemen felt called upon to paint the 'astonishing scene they had taken part in'. Their art is shown, and the narrator describes exhibitions of their work seen all over the world, which stimulated many who had never been to an art gallery to develop the habit of attending other shows.

Henry Moore then appears walking among the shelterers in the underground. In his studio, amidst close-ups of his miniature figures, Moore, the only artist to speak in the film, works on paper. He describes how he uses the white crayon to capture the parts of the figure that are going to 'catch the light… It's more or less feeling the form without seeing it.' He then shows how he uses a grey watercolour to cover the entire sheet of paper and then blots it with newspaper to complete just the first stage of the work. It is a magical yet unpretentious performance.

Describing Moore's painting of two people sleeping, Newton declares:

> A great rolling movement runs across the drawing, like a broad Atlantic swell or like the rocking lilt of a lullaby. The rhythm is just but only just broken by the lines of the listless tired fingers. Deep shadows brood over the picture, and out of the shadows emerge two heads sunk in uneasy sleep. There are no sharp details – only the mouths and nostrils of the sleepers stand out in sharp relief, the slow breathing of exhaustion, an unnatural sleep troubled by memories of fear. It's an oasis of tranquility.

As these words are spoken, images of actual sleepers briefly replace Moore's composition, reinforcing the nexus between the artist's observation and his imagination, between the people he observes and himself.

The Blitz brought the artist and the man in the street closer together, the narrator recapitulates, crediting artist Dennis Matthews with an organizing capacity that led to discovering an unused gallery in Bond Street, where the work of Civil Defence Artists was shown. Jill and Dennis had spent much time together in their ARP 'battle headquarters… linked by phone to other areas and from where we could be called out to cope with casualties etc. of the Blitz,' Jill recalled in her scrapbook. In the film, shots of enthusiastic painters bringing in their work, and an up-tempo musical score introduce a brief speech by the Home Secretary, who predicts, 'This bond between the artist and the man in the street will outlast the war.' The narrator adds that all over the country such activities have inspired amateur and professional painters, and the Home Secretary's speech ends with his conviction that the artist is valuable for bringing colour and imagination to everyday life.

Out of Chaos then comes full circle to the opening shots of the National Gallery to find out what viewers there think about the art. Their opinions (which Jill actually heard in galleries) are a compendium of typical responses to modern art.

'What interesting tone value.'

'I can't explain what I mean, but I know what I like.'

'I don't know what I like until I've worked it out.'

'If this is painting, my small son's a genius.'

'What would happen if they all got together?' the narrator asks. Gathered together around a painting, they are disputing its merits, one commenting on the artist's reputation, another urging the others to 'just look at it', another saying 'people can't always see what they're looking at'. One sees a rhythm in the painting, another does not. The debate continues, although one debater argues that 'it's no use arguing about art'. The narrator breaks in to say, 'they will never get anywhere that way. We better get Eric Newton himself.' Newton appears on camera for the first time, striding with his hands behind his back and sounding like a schoolmaster: 'What's all the trouble about?' He looks at the painting: 'Oh, Graham Sutherland. Yes, it's pretty good.' 'Good!' says one outraged viewer, who does not believe Sutherland has ever seen a limestone quarry, the subject of the painting.

Then off camera Newton comments on a scene showing Graham Sutherland observing men, shapes, landscape and machinery in visually appealing progression. The artist stores up, simplifies and make sketches – 'short hand notes' – that he takes back to his studio to shape the raw material into the finished work of art, Newton concludes. 'Now he knows what he wants.' Trying his best to smile, Newton is shown looking at one of the viewers and saying, 'very different from the real quarry as prose is very different from poetry'. Centering on the painting again, a shot removes the painting's dark sky to show 'how all the drama is gone'. Arrows point towards the swirling rhythm of the painting and the oppressiveness of nature that engulfs the pale quarry buildings. Everything by man in the painting is blocked out in white to show the clash between the man-made geometrical forms and the curvilinear natural structures.

One of the gallery spectators asks Newton whether Sutherland's art is 'beautiful'. Newton replies by suggesting that if we do not understand a work of art, we call it ugly, and reserve the term beautiful for what we think we know. To the scoffer in his group, Newton points out that 'you don't earn much of a living by pulling people's legs'. When another notes that Turner and Constable do not need to be explained, Newton points out that in their time these artists were greeted with the same misunderstanding and bafflement as contemporary artists encounter. He cites one critic, for example, dismissing a Constable: 'Did Mr Constable ever see anything like this in nature?' But now, the critic emphasizes, these artists have taught us to see through their eyes. Then a museum guard speaks to the critic: 'May I butt in, sir? An old lady in the gallery the other day looking at the Henry Moore's came to me and said "They're positively disgusting, an insult to the human form. If I had my way, I'd rip them out of their frames."' Newton treats the comment as an 'old story' and a typical response to the new, adding: 'Sooner or later everyone begins to suffer from a sort of hardening of the aesthetic arteries. It will happen to me one day. People say, "I know what I like." But they really mean is "I like what I know."' Another sceptic still wonders, 'What's the point of it all?' To simply increase the enjoyment of life, to learn to read in another way, the critic rejoins as the camera pans across several paintings and the narrator exhorts the audience to look at pictures 'again and again'. To keep looking is to begin to appreciate the art of painting, 'which is part of the art of living'. Against this varied display of paintings of common objects (a shoe), grand landscapes, voluptuous reclining nudes and beach scenes, the full orchestra brings the film to a triumphal, resounding conclusion.

Although *Out of Chaos* cost the Rank organization only £7,000 (easily ten times that amount in today's currency), Rank's accountant, John Davis, who arranged for theatre bookings, did not think the money could be recouped. 'Del and John Davis were at each other's throats,' Jill remembered, and Davis convinced Rank that her film was 'absolute rubbish'. Del did his best for Jill, but he sent her a discouraging letter on 6 October 1944: 'It would be a very good thing if the British Council were to buy the film. I do not think they can afford the money we have spent, but it is very difficult to get any substantial amount of money from the Exhibitors and this last point deters me from planning any production of shorts for the future.' He sent Jill into the studio for publicity shots and played up her role as a woman director in charge of a forty-man crew. (Jill noted in her scrapbook that the only other woman on the production was the continuity girl.) She disliked posing for the cameras and would be quite scornful in later years about the sepia glamour shots.

Reviewers, invited to private screenings, liked the film – with reservations. *The Times* (7 December 1944) was typical, noting that the film did not fit into 'any obvious category', being not merely a portrayal of the artists but a work of interpretation itself. The final paragraph still seems a fair summary judgement: '*Out of Chaos* is not, in the event, quite as exciting a film as it promised to be. Its treatment of its most interesting subject is a shade too pedestrian and imitative of the orthodox documentary, but at least it is a film well worth making, and it is to be hoped that it will be widely shown.' Ernest Betts saw the film's historic importance, writing in the *Sunday Express* (10 December 1944): 'It tries something new and advances the cause of the cinema as an intelligent medium. It is so good. In fact, it isn't being shown anywhere! No release has been set, but it will be and the sooner the better.'

Slowly, Liam reports in *A Life to Remember*, the film made it into art houses, but 'it received no general distribution and thus, after all the hard work, all the hopes and fears, all the wonderful notices, remained on the distributor's shelves'. Even worse, according to Jill, 'they tore up the negative'. But this was the 'first film about modern art,' she added, and 'there were various prints around the place and people took negatives from the prints... and today if anybody wants any stuff about Henry Moore... they have to use the bit that I did in his studio, and they charge £7,000 for it.'

Jill showed remarkably little bitterness about her film's poor distribution. She also never really said what it meant to her to make *Out of Chaos*. In retrospect, she called her work amateurish, and yet she was clearly proud of her achievement and eager to work on an even more ambitious project. However, film historian Charles Drazin believes that John Davis's opposition to *Out of Chaos* damaged her career:

> *Out of Chaos* would have announced the arrival of a gifted and sensitive film-maker had any company been willing to distribute it... The distributors were reluctant to show films they did not consider to be 'popular entertainment'. Their lack of support is a major reason why Craigie, who was a fine film-maker, is so little known as such today.

Revelation
(1940–44)

How many young girls about to take up a career realise what they owe to the gaol-birds of their grandmothers' era?

Jill Craigie, 'Honourable Gaol-birds', *Radio Times*, 9 March 1951

During her duties as an air-raid warden in the Blitz, Jill sat for hours waiting for the siren to signal the approach of enemy aircraft. 'These long vigils gave me an ideal chance to make good some of the gaps in my lamentable education,' she wrote in a brief unpublished memoir.[1] Looking for an edifying tome, she happened upon *The Suffragette Movement* (1931) by Sylvia Pankhurst (1882–1960), daughter of the suffragette leader Emmeline Pankhurst. Jill had not even heard the name before and did not know the history behind it. But she became immediately absorbed in the book's 609 pages, which she called in her memoir, 'not so much a history of the movement as a deeply subjective autobiography originally conceived under the more appropriate title, *The Inheritance*'. As Jill observed, Sylvia invited readers to 'share her own feelings about her upbringing, her family, her loves and hates, her political opinions, her suffering during the suffragette campaign, and to consider life during the nineteenth and early twentieth centuries from her own point of view'. Suddenly an enormous vista opened up to Jill Craigie. Her life, women's lives, now took on a new significance: 'Before reading the book it had not occurred to me to question the situation between the sexes, least of all had I thought that it might be changed, though it was evident that men on the whole lived a far more agreeable and exciting life.'

The colourful writing, 'packed with information on every page, enlivened by a highly developed visual imagination, presented the social scene through the eyes of an artist', Jill discovered. In other words, Sylvia Pankhurst took her place beside Bernard Shaw, William Morris and Oscar Wilde in the formation of Jill Craigie's aesthetic and political education. She cited this passage from *The Suffragette Movement* to prove her point:

> I remember many years later, as a young girl, entering on Votes for Women propaganda in London, encountering [Henry] Hyndman [a socialist leader and author] at the house of Dora Montefiore. 'Women should learn to have influence as they have in France instead of trying to get votes,' Hyndman shouted at me in a fierce tirade, menacing me with his lion-like front. He always seemed to me like an old fashioned china mantelpiece ornament – the head and chest disproportionately large and prominent for the lower limbs, and everything from the back view small and unfinished. Socialists in those days usually affected tweeds and a red tie, but Hyndman always had a dusty black frock-coat and a top hat.

Through Sylvia, Jill could *see* history. Sylvia documented history through the movement of her characters. Jill did not say it, but Sylvia was cinematic. Jill did say that 'in all that has been written about the Marxist, Henry Meyers Hyndman, no one has portrayed him so vividly as Sylvia Pankhurst. It is difficult not to think of him resembling a piece of Staffordshire pottery, the kind of ornament she obviously had in mind. He, incidentally, was one of a majority of Marxists deeply opposed to votes for women.'

After reading Sylvia, Jill felt 'as if a heavy gauze had been lifted from my mind to reveal the social system from an entirely fresh perspective'. Now women's lives seemed to her hampered with 'artificial restrictions imposed upon my sex, socially, economically, and politically'. No wonder 'so many normally law-abiding women of all ages, some of them distinguished with no complaint about their own lot, went to such extreme lengths and brought so much obloquy and suffering upon themselves in their desire for the parliamentary vote,' she realized. They had identified the political problem: 'So long as the legislators depended only on men for their seats in Parliament they had little incentive to repeal the discriminatory legislation.'

Jill's outrage over the subjugation of women ignited her 'unbounded' admiration for the courageous suffragettes, and for Sylvia:

> I was convinced that she was the real heroine and martyr of the movement – the only true Socialist. In short, she had turned me into a feminist, or so I believed at the time, just as I thought that Bernard Shaw had turned me into a socialist. Now I wonder whether, perhaps, we are not so much influenced by books as that we find books which crystallize our latent predilections.

Jill began to search for a way to tell her version of the suffragette saga. In her Hampstead study is a folder marked 'unpublished stories written at my request in 1940', although some of the accounts are dated as early as June 1929 and as late as August 1943, suggesting that Jill was doing her own interviews and acquiring written material already produced for other purposes. Barbara Dell remembered that when she first met her in 1941, Jill was already obsessed with the suffragettes and was writing a play about them called *White Saturday* – apparently, Barbara believed, a reference to a kind of anthem the suffragettes sang.[2]

In her memoir Jill sharpens the drama of her encounter with the suffragettes by vaulting from her reading of *The Suffragette Movement* to 'some time later' – the year was probably 1943 – when she spotted a newspaper announcement that the 'former suffragettes would assemble in Westminster Gardens at 3 P.M., July 14, to lay their bouquets at the base of Mrs Pankhurst's statue for their annual commemoration of the anniversary of her birth, 1858'. Emmeline Pankhurst, leader of the WSPU (Women's Social and Political Union) militant campaign (1905–14), had died in 1928. Rebecca West, who began her career writing about the suffragettes, had called her the 'embodiment of an idea': women deserved to be treated as full citizens, which meant not only voting, but also participating in all the tasks of building and maintaining a free, open and democratic society.[3] Mrs Pankhurst's statue, in Victoria Gardens adjacent to the House of Commons, had been unveiled on 6 March 1930 before thousands, with a trumpet fanfare and a proclamation by former Conservative Prime Minister Stanley Baldwin (1867–1947): 'I say with no fear of contradiction that whatever view posterity may take, Mrs Pankhurst has won for herself a niche in the Temple of Fame which will last for all time.' Millions listened to the broadcast of his speech, while Sylvia, Emmeline's estranged daughter, remained sidelined in the crowds, representing a split among the suffragettes that would deepen into a fissure reaching into Jill Craigie's life.

Jill concentrates on her solitary pilgrimage to Westminster Gardens in her memoir, where 'I resolved to pay my own tribute as a gesture of gratitude for all that they had done to enable my generation to live a fuller life by means of the vote.' Jill revered the nobility of these women, yet saw their poignancy, since most women of Jill's generation doubted that getting the vote had done much for them. Jill had her own doubts, she admitted, after hearing MP Dr Edith Somerskill at a Trafalgar Square meeting held to protest against the Government's intention to provide less compensation to female victims of air-raids than male victims. 'As if it were more distressing for a man than a woman to lose a leg – a monstrous injustice.'

Jill's pilgrimage had a 'double motive':

I had just started what I hoped might become a splendid career in the film industry. 'Movies must move,' the technicians were fond of saying in those days. The suffragette movement certainly moved in every sense of the word. In response to the Government's increasingly severe attempts to suppress the agitation, the suffragette campaign escalated gradually from peaceful persuasion to mild but perfectly legal militancy, to infuriating militancy, to semi-anarchy, finally to revolutionary tactics in a series of spectacular scenes the like of which had never before been enacted any-where in the world, nor have been repeated. Indeed, the subject as conceived for the screen would be primarily one of spectacle mingled with politics, yet offering plenty of scope for emotion, romance, comedy, violence, suspense, despair and tragedy. The lengths to which the Government went and some individual politicians to deny women their democratic rights, would also provide some very good parts for men.

Jill's enthusiasm reads like a pitch that might be made to a movie producer – except that Jill was in no hurry. Some day she might make a great film about the women's cause; it would take years, however, to fulfil her dream. The male-dominated film industry, including the distributors, would not welcome the subject. Jill also foresaw problems with the British Board of Censors. In any case, feminism was treated as a dirty word.

What to do? She decided on making it a starring vehicle. 'Indulging in a ridiculous fantasy, as I often did at the time, I considered which of the most famous film stars might be suitable for the three leading parts, those of Mrs Pankhurst and her eldest daughter, Christabel, both of whom were conveniently beautiful and elegant and that of the more interesting Sylvia.' What actresses would not want to appear as such striking heroines? The trip to Westminster Gardens, then, constituted the first stage of writing the treatment, the idea of the film that could be turned into a full script. 'Such was the foolish dream of my youth,' Jill sighed.

When Jill arrived – a little late – a crowd of elderly woman were already gathered around Mrs Pankhurst's statue:

wearing hats and gloves, clutching bunches of flowers, chatting with animation among themselves and looking like aunts and grannies up from the country. I approached slowly wondering what to say. Suddenly, they caught sight of me, fell silent and stared and stared. I felt like an intruder. Evidently, they were as curious to see a young thing approaching, also clutching a bunch of flowers, as I was to see them. But I felt rather intimidated. A tall woman dressed in a cream coloured costume came forward to greet me. When she drew near I saw a brooch designed as a portcullis on the lapel of her linen jacket and knowing its significance from Sylvia's description, I blurted out: 'That's your prison badge.' 'Oh yes, we're all gaol-birds here,' came the proud reply.

Jill thought 'a more unlikely crowd of gaol-birds could hardly be imagined'. They thought Jill the relative of a suffragette, but she explained that, after reading Sylvia Pankhurst's book, she had come to express her appreciation for what they had done for her generation. Jill flattered and engaged these veterans with questions about the movement. She met all of its stars: Emmeline Pethick-Lawrence (treasurer of the WSPU until Mrs Pankhurst broke with her in 1912), Annie Kenney (a WSPU working-class stalwart who interrupted one of Prime Minister Asquith's speeches to ask if he was prepared to grant votes for women) and many others, including Sylvia herself.

Conversation continued after the flower-laying ceremony, and finding the suffragettes so receptive and charming, Jill asked the question that had been troubling her. Did the women now believe that their activism and suffering had been worth it? They spontaneously affirmed it was. But Jill wondered what the vote had done for women:

> One woman suggested in the kindliest manner that if I really wanted to know more about the movement, I would have to do some homework, read *Hansard*, and compare the debates in the House of Commons held before women could vote with those which came afterwards. Another added: 'Before we could vote, any mention of the word "baby" in the House of Commons or "midwife" was a cue for ribald laughter.'

Emmeline Pethick-Lawrence handed Jill her card and invited her to tea, a gesture Jill did not find surprising, since she had read about this friendly woman in *The Suffragette Movement*. This meeting began a lifelong engagement with the suffragettes and the suffragette story, a story Jill would write again and again as a stage play, a radio drama, a pictorial biography, a play with music and a work of history – not to mention her newspaper articles and reviews that drew on her memories, her collector's eye and her prodigious scholarship. Finding the right form for this story – for Jill's story – would become an endless quest, one that could never seem complete until, like an individual life, it is over.

In August 1943 Jill began assembling her materials and focusing on the film to be. She worked like an oral historian, interviewing suffragettes and encouraging them to write down their reminiscences. She spoke with Lillian Lenton, 'a famous suffragette', as Jill labelled her in a note on Lenton's testimony. Lenton was one 'who had food pumped into her lungs while being forcibly fed. Typically, she does not mention the horror she suffered in prison.' Women did not wish to speak of this torture because, in many respects, the aggressive procedure felt like a rape. 'It is a violation of oneself even to write or speak of it,' said Ada Cecile Wright, arrested and incarcerated half a dozen times and one of the suffragettes Jill interviewed. Lenton was arrested several times for setting fire to buildings such as the Kew Gardens tea pavilion and a house at Hampton. She described the ruses suffragettes adopted to elude policeman attempting to arrest them under the 'cat and mouse' act, the infamous law that released women after forcible feeding, gave them a certain number of days to recover their health and then re-arrested them, only to begin the torture all over again. The more histrionic and athletic suffragettes assumed disguises, used other women dressed as themselves as decoys, and, in Lenton's case, jumped fences and whatever else was in the way when the police were in hot pursuit.

Grace Roe, one of Mrs Pankhurst's chief organizers, who was later to become Jill's close friend, described her adventures on the run from the police, when the Actresses Franchise League provided her with an old woman's clothes. Although suffragettes admitted their activities were thrilling, Grace emphasized the despair she felt in hiding and the extraordinary isolation a woman could feel, cut off completely from family and society. One of the most committed suffragettes, Grace nevertheless acknowledged how hard it was to maintain her militancy:

> I took a sheet of paper which I headed: 'For and Against'. The 'Against' was completely filled. There was no word on the other side but 'Loyalty.' I got up and paced the room in great pain and agony of mind. I sank into a very comfortable armchair in front of the fire. Suddenly I became relaxed and felt myself almost in another world. When I came to myself once more it seemed that my mind was made up. Nothing could stop me going on, whatever happened.

When mounted police 'closed in' to break up a suffragette demonstration, Grace shouted to the women, 'Come on.' She had ridden horseback in southern Ireland and the horses did not terrify her. 'Never have I seen a man look so white as the officer on horseback who had pulled his steed right up. I was under the very hoofs of the horse as I was lifted bodily and arrested off my feet by the police,' Grace remembered.

Jill became utterly absorbed in the stories of women like Ada Cecile Wright, who noted that 'every moment of the day and much of the night was taken up with working for the Vote: speaking at meetings, working at by-elections, interrupting Liberal Cabinet Ministers, clerical work at [WSPU] headquarters, chalking pavements,* advertising meetings and selling the paper 'Votes for

---

* The suffragettes used chalk to write their Votes for Women propaganda.

Women' at street corners.' For 'women of culture and refinement and of
sheltered upbringing, the throwing of a stone, even as a protest, in order to
break a window, required an enormous amount of moral courage'. Their acts
of violence were often prefaced by agonizing moments of 'nervous tension and
hesitation', emphasized Wright, one of Mrs Pankhurst's lifelong friends.

Charlotte ('Charlie') Marsh, who had climbed onto the roof of a house with
an axe and loosened slates which she hurled at Asquith's car, breaking
windows, remembered another incident when she told Christabel Pankhurst
that she was afraid that her hammer might '"hang in the window when I break
it and then I shan't be able to smash any more." She looked at me, then at the
hammer, and said: "Couldn't you take two?"' The practicality of the suffragettes, their humour and their sense of spectacle leapt out of their
reminiscences. Flora Drummond, who could organize suffragette demonstrations as well as any general, marched up to 10 Downing Street, pressed a
button she thought was a bell but which opened the door, allowing her to
enter the seat of Government – momentarily, as she was immediately ushered
out. At a Hyde Park procession in 1908 she dressed in a peak cap and a
uniform and rode in on a white charger. Another imprisoned suffragette,
made to work on cut-out pieces of male prisoners' pants, sewed together the
wrong edges, held her 'oddities high above my head and called out to the
wardress at the other end of the hall: "IS THIS RIGHT?"'

Jill repeatedly heard about how quick Christabel was on her feet. At one
demonstration a man called out to her, 'Don't you want to be married?' She
asked the man to stand up, took a good look at him, and then replied: 'The
answer is in the negative.' Picking up a head of cabbage that had been thrown
at her, Christabel said: 'I'm afraid some gentleman has lost his head.' E.M.
White, another suffragette, told Jill that while writing her leading articles for
Votes for Women, Christabel would 'become so oblivious of anything else
around her that she forgot all about creature comforts. One cold winter's
morning Miss Kerr went in her room to find her literally blue with cold. The
office was icy and the fire dead out.'

It is one thing to read such stories; it is another to hear the participants tell
them to you and to feel, as Jill did, that she was becoming not merely a
repository of history, but a conduit through which these stories could move
her film along and move her audience to remember and act upon the
inspiration of these women. As with *Out of Chaos*, plans for the Votes for
Women film developed out of a missionary impulse. As Jill told a reporter
doing a feature on *Out of Chaos*, she hoped to 'tell the story of town planning
in Britain [*The Way We Live*], and expose obstacles in the way of its

enlightened achievement. After that may come a feature film on the suffragette movement.'[4]

By January 1944, Jill had in hand letters between Emmeline and Christabel Pankhurst, courtesy of Helen Archdale, who also supplied her own reminiscence of her suffragette days. Archdale, a close friend of Emmeline Pankhurst and a confidant of her daughter Adela, became a key source and facilitator of Jill's project. Jill's correspondence with the suffragettes and with librarians and historians indicates that by early June of 1944 she had already secured records of important speeches, events and publications, and had enlisted participants for her film. Immediately she encountered an obstacle: on 7 June, Emmeline Pethick-Lawrence wrote to Jill: 'I should have told you something which I quite forgot at the moment and that is that Christabel may make difficulties.' Since she had become honoured as a Dame of the British Empire, Christabel had become 'very conventional'. She had repudiated her radical past by becoming an extreme religious fundamentalist, preaching that 'all political and social work is completely futile' in the light of Christ's imminent second coming. She had resorted to the law to prevent Dame Ethel Smythe from publishing Emmeline Pankhurst's letters to Smythe. Jill should therefore settle the question of Christabel 'at once' to avoid later complications. As for herself, Emmeline Pethick-Lawrence remained enthusiastic about Jill's film and was writing on Jill's behalf to Sylvia Pankhurst, whom Jill would see next.

During the next four months, Jill tried to negotiate between different factions. She assured Sylvia that the film would be historically accurate and strike a balance between Sylvia's role and her mother's. But Jill found herself ricocheting between two daughters who had very different notions of their mother's legacy. Christabel sent a telegram from Los Angeles (where she then lived), asking Jill to convene a committee composed of Annie Kenney, Flora Drummond, Charlotte Marsh and others to consider 'PRESENTATIONS MOTHER AND MOVEMENT'. But Annie Kenney kept putting off Jill's entreaties for a meeting. 'Why all this hurry?' she asked. Jill explained that she had to move the project along in order to gain her film company's funding. Then Sylvia raised objections to the depiction of historical figures like Lloyd George. Jill answered that her film company saw no problems with libel. Jill wanted Sylvia's permission to make a public announcement about the project. Sylvia objected and asked to see an outline of the film, noting that she still had legal concerns, including 'certain stipulations on my account'.

While Jill was still trying to meet with Annie Kenney, Sylvia was demanding a meeting with Del Giudice, Jill's producer at 'Two Cities'. But to Jill such a meeting did not make sense without an appealing script she could pitch to him. Jill did her best to hold on to her allies, but in mid-July she wrote to Sylvia:

> I have embarked on this subject in a spirit of enthusiasm and admiration for everyone who has done so much to win for women their present position. I am doing my best to go about it in the most honest way possible, so as to cause no offence. It is not easy. If now my energy has got to be spent in breaking down an uncongenial atmosphere, I can't help wondering whether it wouldn't be better to try and tackle the thing from an entirely different angle, or even make another film first. It is help and co-operation I need. I realise there is no earthly reason why I should expect it; but equally I could find no reason why it should be withheld. If it is that you personally don't wish to be represented on the screen do please say so. As for any other living person, I wouldn't dream of putting them on the screen without seeking their co-operation first.
>
>   I hope, however, we will be able to get together on this.

Sylvia accused Jill of misleading her by establishing the impression that the film project was much further along than now appeared to be the case. Jill had Malcolm Macdonald write to Christabel about Jill's work and career. But Christabel kept bucking Jill back to the aloof Annie Kenney. Other suffragettes were more helpful, sharing memories and documents, but then in early August Helen Archdale and Annie Kenney became fixated on a phrase Jill used in a letter to Christabel. There was potentially another planned film on the Suffragettes – a biography of Mrs Pankhurst – which Daphne du Maurier had been asked to write. Jill's letter commented that this other film was in 'abeyance' and that Jill had Mrs Archdale's full 'support'. In fact, Daphne du Maurier had approached Mrs Archdale who had lent her some books and other materials. Jill tried to straighten out the misunderstanding, writing on 16 August to Mrs Archdale:

> I did not realise at that period [early June] just quite how deeply implicated you were in the other project as the position had not been made clear to me. All you had told me was that there was a suggestion for another film on the life of Mrs Pankhurst and that you saw no reason why there shouldn't be two. When I asked what was happening to the other you told me Daphne du Maurier had three children to look after at present and that was taking up all her time. My secretary [Barbara Dell] interpreted your help as support, though, of course, when one starts analysing the word its meaning becomes somewhat elastic.

Helen Archdale, finding herself in the crossfire between Christabel, Sylvia and Annie Kenney, who would not see Jill unless Jill supplied a script approved by her studio, was backing away from Jill. Unfortunately, Jill had opened up Mrs Archdale's escape route by making too much of what Mrs Archdale had told her and Barbara about du Maurier. But there had been no deliberate attempt to mislead anyone. How could there have been when Jill had circulated her letter to Christabel to all concerned with making the film? On the defensive, Jill noted:

> In working on documentaries I have had to deal with all kinds of people, local authorities, the personnel of St Paul's, the glass industry, artists etc, and this is the first time my methods have ever been criticised. I have generally managed to fulfill my obligations to my employers too, which in the film industry is something far more difficult.

She was sorry if she had 'ruffled' Mrs Archdale.

Jill then felt obliged to reply to rumours that had begun circulating about her motivations: 'I do hope Annie Kenney won't let me down. I am completely held up for the sake of seeing her. It also prevents me from working on anything else in a paid capacity. So far, I am, of course, considerably out of pocket. Not that I care in the least. I mention it only, so that you can answer those people who have jumped to the conclusions that I am being paid by the Pethick-Lawrences.'

In the rivalry between suffragettes, Jill had become factionalized. In a letter to Mrs Archdale, Jill objected to Annie Kenney's behaviour and observed that 'in the face of all these difficulties I'm beginning to realise just what a foolhardy thing I am proposing to do. But then when I begin to think of the great job they all did in the past the thing seems to become worth while again.' She closed by reporting that Charlotte Marsh and her husband were 'extremely keen' about her film and by asking Mrs Archdale to 'please try and get Annie Kenney to come soon'.

Jill had become very close to Emmeline Pethick-Lawrence and her husband Frederick. 'My dear Jill,' she wrote, on 15 August. 'I recognise in every letter and interview your courage, tact and persistence.' She understood why Jill had taken on Helen Archdale as an advisor, 'though I knew her to be "difficult"'. That may be the reason for your decision for you have a clear combination of inspiration with practical common sense to lead you through the maze of suffragette politics.' She went on to allude to 'vested interests & political strife & personal vanities' that had to be 'placated before the artist or historian set to work'. Professing 'great confidence' in Jill's work, she concluded, 'Yours is a great undertaking... I shall always be glad to see you, my dear Jill & talk over matters with you.'

Evidently Mrs Archdale took Jill's clarifications in good spirit, since by 8 September she had coaxed Annie Kenney to write a statement that she would co-operate with the film-maker if 'Two Cities' announced they were considering the film proposal. To Mrs Archdale, Kenney wrote: 'Now I know that you will be behind her to guide and direct I feel a little more reconciled to the idea.' Two days later, however, Mrs Archdale wrote, 'I am sorry to report a further refusal from Annie Kenney. She seems utterly unreasonable about the whole affair.' This meant that Jill would not get the Christabel side of the story (represented by Kenney).

On 14 September, Sylvia demanded to be made the film's chief advisor: 'I do not think a film about the Suffragette movement can possibly be a success without one who took an active part in the Movement having a considerable share in the production.' By 'active part', Sylvia meant artistic control: 'As I have written the history of the Movement it was of course quite natural that I should present the Movement also in another medium.' Only war had prevented Sylvia from doing so, and with a war on she was not sure this was the 'best time to produce a Suffragette film'.

Four days later Jill replied to Sylvia, noting she had taken on Mrs Archdale as 'my official advisor', which was the only way she could get any help at all from Annie Kenney, 'as that particular group [a reference to Christabel and her friends] are all very sold on the Daphne du Maurier idea'. The obstacle of war did not hold, Jill explained, because it would take at least a year to produce the film. At any rate, Jill was shelving the film for the present and working instead on 'a film about post-war planning'. So if Sylvia wanted to do her film, she should go ahead, because 'with the best intentions in the world, I would be completely incapable of writing about it in anybody else's way.'*

Emmeline Pethick-Lawrence disagreed with Sylvia, declaring that now was the 'very moment for such a film, which deals with the same ideological issues of democracy & freedom as the present conflict & presents the contrasts as well as the similarities in the methods adopted to win the war. And that is not the only advantage of this present moment. For it can be made plain that *now* more than ever, men & women must unite to create peace in the world.'

In time, the role that Sylvia played in thwarting this film would assume epic proportions in Jill's mind. Sylvia's book, which had so inspired Jill, began to trouble her, especially since it continued to dominate the portrayal of the suffragettes – to the detriment of Mrs Pankhurst and Christabel – in works of history, literature and film. Jill could not find any peace among the suffragettes.

---

* Sylvia never did make a suffragette film and Jill never took her intention to do so seriously.

The Way We Live
(1944–6)

Film producers began to recognize that the real life of the people was more exciting than bedroom farces in historical fancy dress. Publishers suddenly discovered that they could sell vast numbers of books on political and sociological topics... Community life, so far from being disrupted by bombs and blackouts, was being richly renewed... Men and women became true neighbours, even comrades, and England caught a glimpse of what a co-operative Commonwealth might be.

Michael Foot, *Aneurin Bevin: A Biography, Volume 1: 1897–1945*

When Jill was not reading Sylvia on the suffragettes, she was reading Lewis Mumford. 'I'd read ... everything Lewis Mumford had written. I like to get one author and read everything that he's written on – usually it was "he" then... I read nearly all the books of the architects... I was interested in the arts, and home-making, I suppose not having a home – I was very interested ... in the creation of homes.' Indeed, the arts and home-making were inseparable in the minds of both Jill Craigie and Lewis Mumford (1895–1990). Like William Morris, Mumford was an 'encyclopaedist', to use Michael Foot's term, 'who seeks to embrace and relate all forms of knowledge; a popular philosopher, if you like, who does not care a fig for demarcation disputes with scientists, archaeologists, biologists and the rest'.[1] Biographer, literary critic, architectural historian, an anthropologist of sorts and an urbanist, Mumford was a synthesizer who helped Jill fuse her feminism, her socialism and her desire to make a home. Jill met Mumford on his trips to England, and he inscribed several of his books to her, acknowledging in one of them, *The Culture of the Cities* (1938), her film about the postwar reconstruction of Plymouth, *The Way We Live,* and the affinity he felt for its director. In her album about the making of the film, Jill placed a photograph that had been taken of the two of them in Plymouth.

In her copy of *The Culture of the Cities*, Jill underlined Mumford's description of pre-modern Europe providing a 'daily education of the senses'. Echoing William Morris, Mumford evoked a vision of the 'craftsman who had walked through fields and woods on holiday [and] came back to his stone-carving or his wood-working with a rich harvest of impressions'. Mumford wrote prose deeply appealing to socialist sensibilities: 'Common men thought and felt in images more than in the verbal abstractions used by scholars: esthetic [sic] discipline might lack a name, but its fruits were everywhere visible. Did not the citizens of Florence vote as to the type of column that was to be used on the Cathedral?'*

Almost in the same breath as she spoke of Lewis Mumford, Jill mentioned to an interviewer reading Sylvia Pankhurst and 'then I saw architecture from the feminine point of view'. Jill sensed the feminine implicit in Mumford and later elaborated in *The City in History* (1961), which contains proto-feminist passages from his earlier books. For example, he adopts a feminine view of architecture that Jill embodies in *The Way We Live*. In her film Jill uses women as a kind of community chorus to enact and comment on the consequences of male-inspired designs, even as the film itself expresses a feminist temperament. Mumford, in other words, strengthened – although he did not initiate – Jill's thinking. Retrospectively, she underlined the following passage because it validated her film:

> Woman's presence made itself felt in every part of the village: not least in its physical structures, with their protective enclosures, whose fuller symbolic meanings psychoanalysis has now tardily brought to light. Security, receptivity, enclosure, nurture – these functions belong to woman; they take structural expression in every part of the village, in the house the oven, byre and the bin, the cistern, the storage pit, the granary… the moats and inner spaces, from the atrium to the cloister. House, village, eventually the city itself, are woman writ large.

In a characteristic Mumford mannerism, he anticipates the reader's gasp at this sweeping generalization by nonchalantly referring to the 'original bowl described in Greek myth, which was modelled on Aphrodite's breast'.

After her heartbreaking experience with the suffragettes and the limited distribution of *Out of Chaos*, the resilience, persistence and ingenuity Jill now exhibited was extraordinary. She realized that the best way to deal with her

---

* Mumford had far greater influence in Britain, especially among the new Labour Party ministers in 1945, than he did in his native United States. In the spring of 1946, government authorities invited him to consult on the rebuilding of London. At a dinner in his honour he met the leading British architects and then toured other British cities, meeting with government ministers and planners. 'Imagine anyone in similar circles in the United States begging for the opportunity of consulting me,' he wrote to his wife. See Donald L. Miller, *Lewis Mumford: A Life* (1989).

interest in women, architecture, art and home-making would be to capitalize on public determination to rebuild the country. The British Council had sponsored two films in 1942, *New Towns for Old* and *When We Build Again,* to explore the 'opportunities that now exist for replanning towns after the war', and efforts to clear slums, rehouse people and build new towns.[2] Both architects and people who needed new housing were interviewed. But Jill had – of necessity – to do something flashier and more ambitious, for Del had told her that Rank would not be willing to fund any more short documentaries: 'It is a great pity,' he wrote to her on 6 October 1944, 'but such is the business! Moreover, I am dependent upon the leader of the Industry with whom lies the decision of investing money in productions.'

Jill began visiting the blitzed cities: Hull, Coventry, Durham, Liverpool and Leeds. She chose Plymouth because it was so picturesque. Those in charge of reconstructing the city wanted to capitalize on its dramatic location, half surrounded by water on the rugged coast of England's south-western peninsula with the barren uplands of Dartmoor just a few miles inland. A film could take advantage of superb natural visuals, including stunning cliffs and two harbours.[3] The city also had a Hoe, a piece of high ground that formed a platform or promenade by the sea, which Jill would turn into a spectacular open-air stage. Plymouth, a great port city, had a historic backdrop perfectly suited for a film about a wartime nation, since it was the home of Sir Francis Drake (1540–96), the first Englishman to circumnavigate the world and one of the leading actors in the defeat of the Spanish Armada. Still one of the Royal Navy's principal bases, the city had suffered grievously from German air raids that damaged not only the port installations but also large areas of civilian housing and public commerce.

Plymouth also had a city plan inspired, in part, by two of Jill's architectural heroes, Mumford and Charles Reilly (1874–1948), the former being quoted in *A Plan for Plymouth*, a book sold in bookshops as part of the effort to arouse public support for the rebuilding scheme:

> Perhaps in no direction has planning advanced more rapidly in recent years, than in the conception of the City as a human Community. Mr Lewis Mumford has said that city planning and house planning have been and still are too mechanical: 'we forget the human spirit and the changes of the human spirit to which everything should be adjusted, and we tinker too much with mere structures… The City must be planned for a community life… and not as a mere repository of industry.'

One of the plan's authors, Patrick Abercrombie, had been the student of Sir Charles Reilly (1874–1948), whom Jill called 'a great man' and the 'father of town planning', and whom she met, Michael Foot said, at a London theatre or film fête. Reilly had almost singlehandedly created the Liverpool School of Architecture in the early decades of the century – at a time when most architects shied away from an academic career. He shifted the architect's focus away from the individual buildings towards consideration of the larger questions such as how culture and buildings could complement one another. He encouraged his colleagues to forge more direct connections with the public by writing for popular publications such as *Country Life* and the *Manchester Guardian*. He addressed ordinary people, not just his peers or his clients. Most importantly, for Jill, Reilly insisted that architecture could thrive only in an atmosphere of healthy criticism. No style and no architect – including himself – was sacrosanct. Reilly, in short, suited Jill right down to the ground.[4]

Reilly's celebration of community suffuses the Plymouth plan, although it did not – Jill recognized – go nearly as far as Reilly in implementing the 'village green' concept, in which houses were arranged around greens 'as in pre-Industrial Revolution England, and the greens themselves arranged like the petals of a flower round a community building, the modern equivalent of the village inn'.[5] Jill praised Reilly's plan in a later interview:

> We should build round a green, mixed developments where the people looked at each other instead of everyone keeping themselves to themselves … you should leave great gaps for organized developments because you can't cater for the diversity of human need all in one go … if people all face each other, the children can play in safety on the green … their backs are facing the roads, and that is where your tradesmen come. He says if you keep yourself to yourself, you don't all talk to each other, you don't create neighbours, your children don't mix.

The village green, moreover, promoted 'mixed development', a natural socialist society, Jill thought:

> because they're all dependent upon one another. Like in the Cotswold town, where you see the lawyer living next to the ironmonger, or the blacksmith as he was in those days … the squire and the vicar might live separately, but the rest of the classes were all jumbled up together… The workman's cottage was certainly next door to the very grand Queen Anne establishments belonging to the doctor or the lawyer.

The Plymouth plan spoke the Reilly/Morris language, deploring the conse-quences of an Industrial Revolution that had destroyed the coherence of society and created a 'labour pool for the large industrial works – soulless and meaningless'. The plan evoked the solidarity stimulated by the Blitz: 'Experience in the war has exemplified the fact that when the cause of the community is at stake, individualism must be subordinated.' Rebuilding Plymouth, in other words, would be as heroic and as concerted an effort as fighting the war had been. The pre-war city's haphazard, sprawling, 'discordant development' would give way to a harmony based on the 'human, personal scale'. A muted Morris note is struck in the plan's suggestions that it 'should be possible to incorporate art in the design and decoration of the home'.

Reilly had retired from teaching in 1934 because of a heart condition, but he was still very much on the scene and keenly interested not just in Jill's film but also in Jill herself. Liam MacQuitty, who would again act as Jill's on-site producer, reports in *A Life to Remember* that they went to see Reilly, who was 'full of enthusiasm and helpful ideas'. In Jill's copy of Reilly's book *Representative British Architects of the Present Day* (1931), the author wrote this inscription:

> The owner of this book is Jill Craigie, in my opinion not only a lovely creature but far cleverer than any of the architects described here. I have fallen for her in spite of being in my 70s – deeply!
>> Charles Reilly
>> Jan 1945

By the time Jill met Charles Reilly she had read her man – prompting another inscription in her copy of his autobiography, *Scaffolding in the Sky* (1938):

> I have just heard, dear Jill, bought this book before she knew me & apparently has kept it since. It makes me very happy to hear this.
>> Charles Reilly
>> Jan 1946

In *Scaffolding in the Sky*, Reilly claims to have been 'a very square toed person' in his youth. If so, he certainly matured into a well-rounded William Morris man (the Labour Party at its December 1944 conference passed a resolution approving his 'ideas for community planning'). He relished his socialist principles, attacking the 'individualism of scrambling competitive commerce' that ruined the coherence of English towns and despoiled the countryside. A man of 'baroque instincts' – so it was said at the conferral of his Liverpool University honorary degree – and a seductive performer, he had charm and guile.

Reilly described many adventures with his 'women friends', and so he has to be added to a long list of admirers that Jill juggled while still married to Jeffrey Dell. That romance was on the architect's mind is evident in his inscription in Jill's copy of *The Reilly Plan*:

I wish Jill Craigie was part of my plan. She would be in any real 'new way of life.'

Charles Reilly
Jan 1946

The plan's author, Patrick Abercrombie, proved easy to work with: 'It was a great triumph to get him to appear in the film,' Jill remembered, 'though he was glad enough to be in it because he liked being made up. It's extraordinary how all men seem to like being made up.'6 J. Paton-Watson, the city engineer and co-author of the plan, was 'extremely efficient… the whole town was very ordered. Everyone did what he said. He was a bit of a dictator.' Jill could also count on the natural link to America in the story of the Plymouth pilgrims, and the 'Astors were big names,' she emphasized. 'I thought this would appeal to the Rank organization.' It did. The outspoken and controversial Nancy Astor (1879–1964), an American from Virginia and the first woman to take a seat in Parliament, had recently retired as a Conservative for Plymouth. She was a gallant and witty campaigner, devoted to the people of Plymouth, and during the war she exhibited a Churchillian courage as she walked among the ruins, rallying citizens of a city that had been bombed as badly as London.

Nancy's husband, Waldorf Astor, then Lord Mayor of Plymouth, endorsed the city plan, declaring that Plymouth would be 'rebuilt as a unity'. Important local political figures such as the Conservative candidate for the Devonport seat, Leslie Hore-Belisha, objected to the plan, and he decided not to appear in the film, Jill said, when she told him he might look like the villain. The 'mood of the moment' was socialist. As an interviewer said to Jill, in her film Lord Astor talks like Karl Marx. Jill added: 'Later, Lord Astor advocates nationalization of land, and my goodness they did it at Plymouth. They owned the land, they owned the whole centre of the city. So it was Tories and Labour thinking alike at that moment.'

Another person to feature in her film, although only allowed a cameo role, would mark a turning point in Jill's life. It was here that she became involved with her third and final husband, Michael Foot.

The end of the war in Europe in the spring of 1945 and Churchill's call for an election made Jill's pilgrimage to Plymouth especially rousing and promising. When Michael arrived in Plymouth to campaign in the early summer, Jill asked him for his schedule and filmed him at one of his speaking engagements. She admitted many years later that she thought it was a shameless piece of propaganda, but she was already falling in love with him – or as he later said, 'She fell in love with the Labour Party and me at about the same time.' Michael was the first man she had found to be both attractive and capable of actually changing the way people live.

With Del Giudice's help, the Rank organization got behind the film. But only just – explains Geoffrey MacNab in *J. Arthur Rank and the British Film Industry* (1993). Although discussion of a 'better Britain' certainly engaged the public and books on the subject became bestsellers, there was little evidence that 'enthusiasm for town planning extended to the cinema'. And as with *Out of Chaos*, Jill's plan to use 'real people' and actors, to script the film but also to base its dialogue on what people actually said and did, remained risky. 'Nor did this early British attempt at neo-realism, at combining fact and fiction, real life with invented drama, seem to have much box-office allure,' MacNab concludes. For the moment, however, Rank held in check his 'patriarchal conservatism'.

Not so Nancy Astor. As Jill's film began to take shape in May and June of 1945, Lady Astor became alarmed as she saw Jill honing in on the collectivist aspects of the Plymouth plan. As John Grigg notes in *Nancy Astor: A Lady Unashamed* (1980), she was a 'social reformer who felt that society should be improved largely on private initiative, with the State helping but not taking over'. More partisan than her husband, Nancy Astor accused Jill of making, in effect, a Labour Party film. Perhaps Lady Astor had heard that the crew members on Jill's film were spending their time campaigning for a Labour Party victory in the 1945 elections.[7] At any rate, Lady Astor called the company accountant John Davis and asked him to get Arthur Rank to stop the film. Liam MacQuitty remembered being summoned back to London for a meeting with Rank and Davis. Liam showed them the wonderful press the film-makers were getting. 'Look at these, John,' Rank said. 'We're too late.' Del congratulated MacQuitty on his quick work, but Liam decided to see Lady Astor, figuring she had only begun to fight. He showed up at her house without an invitation and was rudely received. But the persistent MacQuitty said he had come to show Lady Astor the script containing the 'key scene' in which her husband appeared. He followed her to lunch, noticing that both Abercrombie and Paton-Watson were there. Evidently the film was under discussion. Lady Astor abruptly asked Liam, 'What is it?' He showed her the script. She glanced at it and said, 'What is that bitch up to?' She thought of Jill as a Russian, Liam said – and a revolutionary one at that, no doubt. Liam reiterated that Jill had made sure Lord Astor had 'full recognition for his part in the Plymouth plan'. Lady Astor told him to 'sit down and have some lunch'. He hadn't come for lunch, Liam said, 'but I will take a drumstick'. She laughed. Liam wisely withdrew.

Jill retained considerable respect and affection for the first woman to hold a Parliamentary seat. 'The first thing she said to me was "For God's sake, take my husband from me,"' Jill recalled.[8] Lady Astor's record spoke for itself. As Jill put it, 'She faced, alone at first, both the ridicule and the freezing hatred of the male House of Commons. She bombarded the ramparts of prejudice with just the right combination of insolence, scorn, repartee and courage.'

The accounts Jill gave to film historians such as Drazin, Macnab and Philip Kemp detail only a confrontation involving herself, Rank and Davis. Davis said the film was not going to make any money. Of course not, Jill countered. It was a 'prestige' item. Davis scoffed. Then Jill showed Rank the press cuttings that praised him for making a film about Plymouth's plan to rebuild. She explained how she had 'turned Plymouth upside down' – even getting the police to stop traffic for the production. She pointed to the admiring notices of her as a woman director given her opportunity by Rank. 'You're going to look awfully foolish if you stop it now,' she told them. Jill then saw Rank turn to Davis and say, 'You see, John, it can't be stopped.' She looked at Rank and could see he was 'delighted'. Patrick Abercrombie wrote Jill to congratulate her 'on the conquest of Lady A'.

As a good socialist, Jill wanted plenty of ordinary people in her film, but as a professional film-maker she made sure they got 'tested', with the result that the less self-conscious 'naturals' were chosen. They got into the 'spirit of it', she recalled, when they invented some of their own dialogue. Mrs Copperwheat, for example, was a war widow who enjoyed doing the film. 'It did her a lot of good,' Jill said. 'It was very therapeutic for her.'[9] Jill saw no reason why so-called ordinary people could not entertain a feature film audience – indeed, she found such individuals far more flexible and spontaneous than the upper class and military officers. Some of the cast appeared by accident – for example, when Jill spotted an American sailor who was both a good dancer and eager to appear in her film.

The campaign quality of the film is exemplified in its closing scenes in which the city's young people carry banners, demonstrating in favour of the Plymouth plan. Here Jill capitalized on public sentiment to organize and create a scene that became part of the public's participation in the plan. *The Way We Live* represents the moment when Jill's socialism and film-making fused into a kind of apotheosis.

The documentary opens with a rousing overture and this bid for attention: 'This film is made for the people of the blitz in the hope that their newly built cities will be worthy of their fortitude.' The first shot is an aerial view that rapidly closes in on Plymouth, as a voice-over narrator announces, 'This is a tale of a town and of the town's folk', followed by scenes identifying the Lord Mayor and the corporation, big business, little business, the fishermen, the mothers and the Copperwheats. Each group turns to look at the audience as they are identified, almost like actors bowing. The narrator continues: 'But the heroes or villains – according to your point of view – are two men with a plan: J. Paton-Watson, the city engineer, and Professor Abercrombie' (the latter looking very academic with his monocle). 'What they have to offer is something of a challenge to the way we live.' Up comes the music as the credits roll over the model buildings of the Plymouth plan.[10]

A voice-over narrator, a soldier-writer, is then shown returning home on a troop ship. In a series of scenes he casts about for a story to write about. He is discouraged by what he sees of a drab, post-war Britain. Then he sees a shop window displaying books about town planning, including *The Reilly Plan* and Paton-Watson's and Abercrombie's Plymouth plan. Meeting discouragement from cynical newspaper editors, he nevertheless makes his way to Plymouth. Expecting a sunny resort atmosphere, he is disconcerted by devastated streets and by antiquated attitudes. The most energetic-looking person is an American sailor, who barely registers the Englishman's observation that the pilgrims left from Plymouth. 'So I've heard,' the sailor says.

The next day the writer walks out to a magnificent view of the Hoe and the harbour. The rest of the city looks cramped and featureless, with 230 people to an acre, in conditions as primitive and unhealthy as the Middle Ages, he observes. Shots of crowded streets and small family kitchens, with children playing on floors and mothers making meals in the midst of chaos, are contrasted with Plymouth's triumphs as a port city, its role as the gateway to America and the world, its election of the Virginian Lady Astor, its natural advantages, its 'rolling farmlands, shimmering streams, lush valleys, old world villages, winding lanes, and a windswept moor. It might be the most beautiful setting in the world.' But that natural setting has been marred by unplanned housing, sprawling suburbs until… The sounds of bombers are heard and the scene shifts to an aerial view. Explosions and fires roar across the screen, followed by scenes of houses and other buildings ripped apart. The voice-over switches to the sneering voice of Lord Haw Haw (William Joyce), whose wartime broadcasts taunted the British people. 'Plymouth,' he announces, is 'beyond repair'.

The scene shifts to a long line of weary people, including the Copperwheat family, who are without homes. Mr Copperwheat, a dockyard worker, and his wife live with their three children and their grandmother. They are trucked to Mrs Hines' home where they have to make do in very cramped conditions –

the oldest daughter will sleep in the kitchen, Granny and the two younger girls will sleep with their mother in the bedroom, and Mr Copperwheat will occupy the only other space, a makeshift sitting room. The writer, interviewing Paton-Watson, wonders if his ambitious plans are not rather 'remote'. Paton-Watson tells the incredulous writer that he should visit a 'mothers' meeting' at a housing estate. The writer hears their complaints about houses situated too far from shopping, inadequate washing facilities, poor plumbing (they have to fill baths with buckets of water), inadequate space for larger families and children without play areas. The writer then presents the village green concept to the receptive women. Walking away from the meeting, he strides with a sense of purpose he did not have after leaving the troop ship. And he reflects: 'What was it Shaw said? "Man's house hasn't changed as much in a thousand years as a woman's bonnet in a score of weeks." And yet when he goes out to kill he carries a marvel of mechanism.'

On the Hoe, young Alice Copperwheat and her friend Dorothy meet a couple of sailors, one of whom takes Alice's hand and swings her into a dance. He is so good that Alice wishes she could go on dancing in the open air all night. 'And dancing and dancing and dancing on the Hoe, just as they did all through the ages,' the voice-over of the writer is heard, quoting Shakespeare's lines about this 'other Eden … this little world … this precious stone … this earth … this England'. Those grand words, however, are set against scenes of the unsightly ravages of war and its aftermath, which in turn give way to Lord Astor's, quoting 'to each according to his need. We want to build so that everyone will have a chance of leading a full life. That is the philosophy of our plan.' 'But is it really practical?' the writer wants to know.

Representing the plan is Patrick Abercrombie – shown lecturing an audience about why the city cannot be rebuilt as it once was. Abercrombie and Paton-Watson handle the sceptical questions, showing how unplanned sites will only worsen the entire area, especially with the destruction of the countryside, where villages have been torn in half and the agricultural economy harmed. Similarly, planning is needed in order to cope with the cars that now clog access to the city and cause accidents that take more lives than the bombing did. 'Why should we remain behind the times?' he asks. The audience assents, although one man is heard snoring. 'All we have tried to do is plan the ideal city the way we would plan an ideal home.' This vision of a city with 'spaciousness and beauty for all' is greeted with cheers. But as the meeting breaks up, Mr Copperwheat asks, 'it sounds all right, but who's going to pay for it?'

Citizens are shown debating the plan – women seated around a sewing circle, fishermen working on nets, small and big business representatives, and Lord Astor speaking to the House of Lords endorsing the plan. 'Such was the power of the Lords,' the writer comments, that 'nothing happened'. He then encounters Alice standing before a Plymouth plan model. She tells him that she does not think the plan will make any difference. Her sailor companion adds, 'They don't have the kind of go ahead that Americans do.' The writer tries to make them understand that 'they' is 'we'. They can have the plan if they want it. But the young couple simply do not seem to care. 'So much easier to kill an idea than look into it,' the writer grumbles.

Then the film presents the Plymouth council's consideration of the plan. 'Everything they said in that meeting, they had said at a previous council meeting – I didn't cheat at all,' Jill said, 'and I wanted to be absolutely fair to everyone, and let them all have their heads, and I did – and just left it at that.' It is a rousing, contentious discussion that eventually results in endorsement of the plan. And still nothing happened, the writer reports. The community's mounting frustration is exemplified by Mr Copperwheat's fretful speech about the crowded living conditions, but just then Alice interrupts to say she is going to the Hoe. When her father doubts her word, she invites him to come along, and to her dismay he does, accompanied by his wife. A silent choreography then ensues as Alice walks with her parents on the Hoe and surreptitiously signals the sailors to keep their distance. The Copperwheats sit, joined by Dorothy, on a bench and engage in desultory conversation, as Alice wistfully suggests it might be rather nice to live in America. 'Well, suppose you bring him over and let us meet him,' Mrs Copperwheat says to her daughter, who feigns surprise, with Dorothy helping her out by saying the sailors are her friends. But Mrs Copperwheat is not fooled and sends the girls off to bring the boys to meet her and Mr Copperwheat, who asks his wife how she knew 'something was going on'. 'I think I know my own daughter,' she replies. The wary father says that 'with her looks you can't be too careful'. 'Perhaps you can, George,' his wife replies.

It is difficult to believe any male film-maker would have put such a scene into a film about the rebuilding of Plymouth, linking this young girl's restlessness to the spirit of adventure that created the city. Her father is proud to think that his family might have fought alongside Drake, but he is quite complacent about his place in Plymouth and cannot begin to imagine newer worlds. Alice's younger sister has already expressed a wish to go out on her own, no matter where, just to escape the confinement of post war Plymouth. Jill projected her own biography into the yearnings of these young women. Even though they have no interest in the Plymouth plan, they represent the new spirit it has tried to express. Watching his daughter, Mr Copperwheat realizes how he has come to expect so little. He thinks of the 'dole, then there's the war, then there'll be exports... one day I suppose the workers will wake up'.

Mr Copperwheat's outburst provides a transition to the writer's voice-over explanation that 'out of the growing discontent new leaders arose to fire the citizens with hope'. This speech is followed by a shot of a poster: 'The Labour Candidate Michael Foot Speaking To-Night.' The next shot pans over an attentive and receptive audience, including the applauding Copperwheats. Then Michael is shown, dressed in a neat, double-breasted pinstripe suit and speaking expansively about the rebuilding of Plymouth: 'We say the burden must be shared', so that the people of Plymouth are not left to pay for reconstruction while other British cities that escaped bombing remit nothing. He is stiff, his hands hang somewhat awkwardly at his side. But then the camera angle changes to a tight close-up, reinforcing his determination and the forcefulness of his words: 'By this plan we can make ours one of the most beautiful cities in the whole wide world.'*

Even so, the voice-over narrator describes an 'apathetic' people weary of still living in their bombed-out city. The dejected writer strolls on the Hoe, gazes at a war memorial, and notices 'something odd'. Coming within camera range are young people carrying banners with message such as 'Less Monotony Please', 'Premises Not Promises', 'Bigger Houses', 'Roads Designed for Safety', 'Youth Wants a Theatre'. Groups with banners parade through the town, as a marching band is shot at eye level to create a sense of the action being carried to the audience; a high angle shot shows them crossing a pedestrian bridge with banners aloft to the sky; a low-angle shot displays the bright banners emerging out of shadows – a stark contrast to dark, interior city walls. Soldiers, sailors, scouts and other boys' and girls' clubs converge in a collective demonstration that fills the main street lined with crowds. The film ends with this scene (MacQuitty numbered the crowd at 3000), as the London Symphony Orchestra plays a triumphant finale, and the writer concludes: 'The cities of tomorrow. Who can tell what they will be. Their story is still being written by the citizens of today.'

In the end, the Plymouth plan was adopted, and to this day the film is shown regularly in the city as an integral part of explaining the community's recovery from the war. To Jill, however, the plan did not nearly go far enough in

---

* Jill thought, 'Thank God, there's a Labour chap who is actually interested in aesthetics.' In Michael Cockerell's 1997 documentary on Michael, Jill is shown addressing Michael: 'I later found out that you're not that mad on aesthetics. You like a good view...' Michael interrupted to say: 'You mean I was just an ignoramus.'

implementing a democratic 'village green' environment. And she would later attack architects for failing to deliver on their promise of better designed cities.

Jill Craigie's democratic/socialist aesthetic is especially striking when she is compared with another woman documentary film-maker: Leni Riefenstahl. Riefenstahl was a genius at handling crowds, at displaying the dynamism of youth and flag-waving patriotism, and superb at allowing the visuals to tell the story – at making movies move. But in Riefenstahl's films, crowds gather around a supreme leader, and the aesthetic is fascist: the sense of community is centred on adoration of an individual. In *Triumph of the Will* physical and mental strength are equated with power and there is no place for conflicting arguments. Indeed, Hitler's triumph is presented as the victory of uniformity over criticism. Jill Craigie's aesthetic, on the other hand, is all about debate and disagreement. Michael Foot may be the hero of the moment, but he is heard speaking only for a minute.

The final moments of the film grew out of Jill's discussion with a cynical group of young people who told her that the plan would never be implemented. Like all good agitators, Jill provoked them:

> 'What are YOU going to do about it?' I said democracy is rather like marriage. It only works if both sides work. And out of this discussion they said: 'Well we'd better have an exhibition – better have a protest march.' And it was their idea... The council stopped all the traffic for us.

The Way We Live premiered at the Plymouth Odeon (a Rank theatre) on 29 July 1946 to an enthusiastic audience. Liam MacQuitty points out in *A Life to Remember* that in September the film 'received outstanding praise' as the first documentary shown at the Cannes Film Festival. *The Way We Live* accomplished a 'very difficult thing,' one reviewer noted, weaving 'out of a large number of threads a pattern of democratic discussion ranging over the whole area of Plymouth and its surroundings'.[11] The *Times* critic concluded: 'The film on the whole is admirable in being at once generously ardent in spirit and nearly impartial in argument.'

Yet John Davis tried to kill the film by showing it in an East End theatre where he knew the audience would not have the patience to sit through a documentary. 'I was depressed because it got booed, got the boot,' Jill said. But then she was told, 'That's nothing. They threw tomatoes at the screen at *Henry V*!' But according to Geoffrey Macnab, *Observer* critic C.A. Lejeune 'rallied her colleagues to the cause', hailing the film as 'intelligent, thoughtful, comprehensive', and *The Way We Live* found a distributor.

*

Unfortunately, most documentary film historians – many of whom have probably not had access to Craigie's work – do not acknowledge her. Paul Rotha in *Documentary Film* provides her with this mixed tribute:

> To Jill Craigie went the credit for getting the film industry, in the form of the Rank Organisation through Two Cities, to back *The Way We Live*... A far more expensive and larger production than a M.O.I. [Ministry of Information] film, it enjoyed a considerable success despite initial opposition from the associated Rank cinemas. For continuity the film resorted to the well-worn device of the visitor, a journalist... the family who were the principal protagonists were adequately directed, but the film as a whole broke no new ground.

Jill herself disclaimed originality, but saw what made her different from Rotha: 'I wanted to translate my films into more human terms. I tried to do that, to have characters, real people in it. His [Rotha's] was an intellectual argument, wasn't it, *Land of Promise* [a documentary on housing in post-war Britain].'

Ambition and self-doubt tore at Jill Craigie's sensibility: 'I was nervous. I looked self-confident in front of these chaps, but I wasn't... Once I'd finished the film, of course, I could only see the mistakes and I was horrified. I wasn't good enough, in fact. I could have been good enough.'[12] She regretted that the studios provided no opportunities for women to learn the technicalities of film-making, to move up the ranks from tea boy to cameraman to director of B pictures, mastering their trade. The war had abruptly opened a window of opportunity that just as quickly closed when the fighting ended. Such sudden breaks for women had no 'roots'. When she offered to become part of the production team for Rank's *March of Time* newsreel/documentary series, 'in any capacity... I was absolutely black-balled out of the industry, I couldn't get work anywhere,' she told Charles Drazin. Jill believed that her outspoken socialism harmed her in an industry dominated by Conservatives – an obstacle she would continue to confront into the 1950s. Although she bluntly called her films 'bad and amateur', she mitigated that harsh judgement by observing, 'They weren't nearly so bad and amateur as some of the boys' first films.'[13]

Film historians Annette Kuhn and Susannah Radstone single out Jill Craigie's 'ability to bring out the best in "ordinary people"' and her 'political commitment', without noting how remarkably she blended her feminism and socialism in *The Way We Live*.[14] Critic Philip Kemp ably captures what makes Jill's work distinctive:

> *The Way We Live* was something quite new: it set out to show how planning, that panacea of the postwar Labour government, affected the lives of 'ordinary people' –

and how they, in their turn, could influence the planning process… But more, it was an exceptional – and in Britain, virtually unheard of – example of filmmaking as activism, the creative and political processes intertwining and advancing each other in a way that even the Soviet filmmakers of the 1920s had only rarely achieved.[15]

'You had the city in your pocket in May/June 1945, didn't you?' an interviewer asked. 'Yes,' Jill agreed. With the making of the film, with the Labour triumph in the election, with the arrival of Michael Foot, she felt the millennium had come.

'No Socialist who saw it will forget the blissful dawn of July 1945,' wrote Michael Foot in his classic biography of Aneurin Bevan:

> The great war in Europe had ended; the lesser war in Asia might be ending soon. This background to the scene in Britain naturally deepened the sense of release and breath-taking opportunity. And those who had served the British Labour movement for generations, renewing their faith after each disaster, in 1919, 1926 and 1931, had their own special cause for exultation.

Jill had come to the party late, so to speak, through Malcolm MacDonald and then Michael Foot, but she felt the full force of that recovery from catastrophe. In 1919, Malcolm's father had led the party to a crushing defeat. In 1924, as Prime Minister in a minority government, MacDonald pursued an extremely cautious programme that deeply disappointed members of his own party and ended ten months later with a decisive Conservative victory. Worst of all, MacDonald and his Cabinet had failed to capitalize on their 1929 majority, and by 1931 had drastically cut unemployment pay and united with Conservatives to form a national party. His brilliant early years as the first leader to make Labour the largest party in Parliament were eclipsed by his anti-Labour policies. During World War II Aneurin Bevan feared that the Labour ministers in Churchill's coalition government might make the MacDonald mistake yet again, which is why he aggressively advanced the view that the country would abandon Churchill's old-fashioned heroics as soon as the war was over. Bevan stood virtually alone, 'against all odds and orthodox prophecies' that presumed the popular Churchill would model himself after the Lloyd George of 1918 who united peoples and parties into one patriotic government. But Bevan was proved right: the attack on Britain had focused the people on the 'promise of a new society. Suddenly the vision of the socialist pioneers had been given substance and historic impetus by the radical political ferment of wartime.' Indeed, the 'discipline of war could be used to buttress the necessary planning for the future'. Labour would not err again by eviscerating reformist expectations. 'When the scale of the Labour Party's victory became known on the night of 26 July,' Michael reported, 'bonfires were lit, people danced in the streets, and young and old crowded into halls all over the country to acclaim their elected standard bearers.' Jill's dancing scenes on the Hoe, seen in the light of the 1945 victory, seemed prophetic.

Adventures and Amours
(1944–7)

Among the friends to whom I have read this play in manuscript are some of our own sex who are shocked at the 'unscrupulousness' meaning the utter disregard of masculine fastidiousness, with which the woman pursues her purpose. It does not occur to them that if women were as fastidious as men, morally or physically, there would be an end of the race. The pretense that women do not take the initiative is part of the farce. Why, the whole world is strewn with snares, traps, gins, and pitfalls for the capture of men by women… It is assumed that the woman must wait motionless, until she is wooed. Nay she often does wait motionless. That is how the spider waits for the fly.
      Bernard Shaw, preface to *Man and Superman*, underlined by Jill Craigie

When Jill met Michael Foot her personal life was far from simple. Indeed, it even verged on the scandalous. Although Jeffrey Dell's last wife, Barbara, did not think there was much left of the Dell/Craigie marriage when she arrived in 1941, Jill and Jeffrey remained in touch and, indeed, were collaborating closely on *The Flemish Farm* as late as 1943. They also continued to share many of the same friends. Charles Reilly's letters to Jill, for example, suggest that during the making of *The Way We Live*, she had no trouble in maintaining an orbit of men around her that still included Jeffrey. Reilly wrote to her on 15 April 1945 that Jeffrey had told him she was making 'fine progress' on her film. Reilly added, 'To make a town your hero, and such a town, is to break new ground in a splendid way. You must not feel any obligation to me or anyone else to fit us in if we don't really fit. This is a grand theme you have got hold of & you must not let anything spoil it.' Reilly had heard from Michael Foot on his way to San Francisco to report for the *Herald* on the establishment of the United Nations. He told Reilly that Jill had been 'good to him', and he had 'great hope' of her 'further help'. If Michael did not get back in time to campaign for Parliament, 'you had better fight it for him!' Reilly urged Jill. 'I haven't seen you, you know, since you disappeared in a back street one dark

night in Soho & MacQuitty would not let me steer you to safety through the
masses of ravening American soldiers. I never heard how you fared – except
that you got on very well with Abercrombie, but that you were bound to do.'
Writing to Jill on 9 July 1945 he reported:

> I spoke to Jeffrey on the phone last night after my dreadful journey and told him all
> I had seen & how you directed crowds. He was so pleased & happy & enthusiastic
> and said he would certainly come down... he wanted to see you in action. He
> thought you a wonder of the world as indeed you are. Something very nice came
> into his voice, a quiet happy tone, when he heard of your doings – I loved it.

Barbara Dell thought Jeffrey had buried himself in his work. He was a self-
possessed man who kept his feelings to himself, and Barbara believed he had
tolerated Jill's straying because of the extraordinary wartime conditions and
because the couple were no longer in love. But one of Reilly's letters to Jill
suggests that Jeffrey had not given up on the marriage: 'How wonderful of
Jeffrey to have taken such a house! What faith he must have not only in you
but in himself!' Reilly believed Jeffrey was justified: 'This film of yours about
a real live town will come home to everyone. I feel you have done something
really great in it I can admire you as well as love you & that's the best of all!...
This is your great work. Make it the best & sacrifice everything to it.'

Jeffrey wrote Jill a detailed, enticing letter about Chase Farm and the new
country house he had found in Haslemere, Tennyson country, where 'Green
Sussex fading into blue/With one grey glimpse of sea' aided the poet's composition of his Arthurian saga. The house included a large kitchen, a fireplace,
three bedrooms, some nice oak panelling, nicely painted walls, a tiled
bathroom, a separate lavatory and a room upstairs. There had been no time to
discuss the purchase with Jill, since forty-five other people had also enquired
about the property and Jeffrey felt he had to take it 'there & then'. He hoped
Jill would 'approve what I've done'. In a postscript he admitted that she would
be horrified to find that there were 'NO cupboards!! or practically none.' But
he was looking for some, as well as for kitchen items. And they could sell
anything she did not want later. 'Also as we've dined on our laps for nearly 2
years we can probably do so for another few months – until we find the right
table, which is your particular flair, and I shan't even look for that sort of
thing.' He was searching for a 'bit of coconut matting like old Reilly's, so that
our floor is not too bleak even to start with. Oh I do hope you can come &
see it soon!'

Julie's friend Gilly visited her at the Haslemere farm and was impressed
with the fantastic swing Jeffrey had built for her friend. The house was on a

hill, and you walked down a slope and you swung over a valley. 'He built me an igloo of bracken,' Julie recalls, and though she called him Jeffy ('When is it Jeffy's birthday?' she asked her mother in a letter from boarding school), and she was not allowed to call him 'Dad, or anything like that', he acted like a stepfather to her. 'He had been in my life as long as I could remember.' Jeffrey made the country seem a paradise. 'I always wanted to live in the country,' Julie emphasized.

Purchasing the house may have provoked Jill into declaring her intention to dissolve the marriage. Ten-year-old Julie, who spent part of her time with her mother during the shooting of *The Way We Live*, was already aware of her mother's complicated love life, having witnessed, for example, an episode of her mother crying on the phone, the only time she had seen Jill in tears. 'I knew she was talking to Laurie Friedman. Don't ask me how I knew, but I did.' Barbara Dell remembered trying to keep Julie out of the way, but Jill's affair with her cameraman Friedman was obvious to everyone on the set – and elsewhere, for Kay Mander, a documentary film-maker, had heard about it.

Julie cannot put a date on the traumatic scene. It probably occurred sometime in 1946, when she visited Jeffrey at the new house:

> There were two attic rooms that were going to be mine. I came leaping downstairs. I had worked out a way we could connect the two, and it would be great when Gilly came to stay. I could have my horse permanently here. It was my idea of paradise. Jeffrey took me for a walk. He was a tall man, and he knelt down and put his head on my shoulder and burst into tears and said: 'You're not coming to live here. Your mother is leaving me.'

Devastated and furious, Julie felt she had lost the only real father she ever had. Gilly remembers how Julie had announced her move to the country. 'Then suddenly you were back,' she reminisced with her friend. All that remained of Jeffrey were the bits and pieces of furniture Jill had acquired during their marriage. They remained a fixture, Julie remembered, in her mother's later homes.

In 1946, the affair with Friedman apparently over, Jill moved out of Malcolm MacDonald's house, Frognal Lodge, and into Liam MacQuitty's Hampstead residence, Holly Berry House. 'It seems very strange to me now,' Julie reflected, 'how we lived in these different men's houses when she belonged to another man.' Liam's explanation was that Jill refurbished and looked after his place while he went off on film and television projects. Michael Foot, on the other hand, had no doubt about Liam's intentions. 'He wanted to go off with Jill. I haven't the slightest doubt. I don't blame him.

There were quite a lot like that.' But Liam insisted he never had any intention of marrying Jill, and he adamantly rejected the idea of a romance with her.

According to Michael, Charles Reilly first introduced him to Jill in late 1944 at a party in London. Reilly's son Paul, one of Michael's Oxford classmates who had convinced him to forsake his family's Liberal Party affiliation and embrace Labour, had brought his father and his friend together in Brighton, where Charles Reilly lived in retirement. Michael had already established his reputation as a radical journalist writing for the leftwing publications like *Tribune* and the *Daily Herald*, and then as the brilliant editor of the *Evening Standard*.

At their first meeting Jill had told Michael about her plans for *The Way We Live,* adding that she wanted to film him campaigning. 'You arranged to meet at the Ivy, which was a very posh restaurant,' Jill said to Michael during Michael Cockrell's 1997 BBC documentary about his career. 'I remember thinking ... that's the kind of socialist for me. I was prejudiced in your favour right from the start.' Although Michael certainly found her alluring, there is no doubt that Jill pursued him. However, his mother, not Jill, first planted the idea of marriage. Watching Jill expertly manage the filming of the debate over the Plymouth plan, Mrs Foot excitedly phoned her son: 'She'll do. That's the girl for you.' Unfortunately, as Michael told his mother, 'The girl is already married.'

'Jill Craigie was a raging beauty let loose on susceptible wartime London,' Michael reminisced in 'A Love Under Wraps' (*Evening Standard*, 19 May 1993):

> I could not take my eyes off this original apparition. She had the colouring of an English rose but everything else was a romantic, mysterious addition. She was half Scottish and half Russian, not a tincture of English reserve in her make-up. She had Celtic and Russian fires and passions intermingled with what seemed an inborn gift for appreciating painting and music and, as it seemed to me, every other art.

Jill resembled the Duchess of Sanservina in Stendhal's *The Charterhouse of Parma*, one of Michael's favourite novels. Jill always had 'something new and entertaining' to show him. Like the Duchess, she coupled beauty with a 'spontaneous character' and a 'soul ever sincere, which never acts *with discretion*, which abandons itself wholly to the impression of the moment, which asks only to be swept away by some new object'. Hemmed in by all sorts of compunctions himself, Michel admired her drive and determination: 'What she wanted she wanted forever,' as Stendhal writes of the Duchess.

Michael never met Jeffrey Dell but he soon heard about men on Jill's list:

Paul Nash, Henry Moore and Charles Reilly. There were others like the painter Dennis Matthews who, like these three, had featured in her films. 'Dot Hyson and Jill played up a lot of men,' Michael acknowledged. 'They were two amazing, scandalous women, believe me.' They would unscrupulously invite men with certain pretensions out to the top restaurants in London, but the men would find themselves 'no further along after paying for the meal'. Michael had a good time imagining these men 'falling in front' of these women who 'put them aside'. To him, they had a 'mystique… a secret way they did it'. He never learned their 'trick'. 'She led men one hell of a dance,' Julie said of her mother. 'She was in full swing from chap to chap and full of dreams and ambitions when she met Michael and not looking to make a man her life's work.'

At boarding school Julie nonetheless recognized 'there was an oddity going on'. Dennis Matthews, also known as Hampstead's 'Housewives' Choice', a nickname derived from a BBC radio programme of that name, 'fell for my mother big time'. Julie described him as an 'extremely beautiful' and unattached man, and Michael called him 'a cheerful, good looking chap'.

Ralph Vaughan Williams (1872–1958), yet another admirer, wrote a page of music for her birthday. His letters to Jill, like Reilly's, are rather wistful and yearning. He lamented that he was so 'sorely old' and she 'so very young'. Jill remembered he was 'very decrepit but very happy… the best company'. They had worked together on *The Flemish Farm*. Tired of the war scenes, he asked her, 'Can I write some pretty nurse music today?' He loved to joke – even about the serious music he loved. The mention of Schoenberg prompted this remark to Jill: 'Oh yes, my next symphony is going to be of the wrong note school too.' At the same time Jill took Julie and Gilly to Henry Moore's studio, and it was apparent to Julie that her mother and the artist were drawn to each other.

To Jill, Michael was not like the other men she had known. 'I liked that myopic look in his eyes and I liked what he had to say. I felt he was honest, and integrity means a lot to me in a chap… He was a little shy, didn't make a pass at me or anything like that, but he was such a good listener asking questions… I didn't make it very obvious that I'd fallen for him. Women were not nearly so forward in those days as they are now.'[1] Michael had no sense that he was being pursued. 'I thought I was being consulted,' he said. 'It didn't happen all at once.' He had no music in his Park Street flat. Jill brought a phonograph and played Mozart. 'She made me understand what music was. She taught me all such things. She made that flat musical.'

Michael suffered from eczema so badly that he had days when he just wanted to stay at home. He also suffered from asthma. Both conditions had made him timid with young women and envious of chaps who confidently courted them. 'For quite a long time I didn't think that any woman would look at me,' he confessed. When Michael went to work at the *Evening Standard*, after being recommended by his political hero, Aneurin Bevan, Michael marvelled at the ease with which Max Beaverbrook (1879–1964), the newspaper's owner, acquired mistresses. Similarly, Frank Owen, Michael's predecessor as editor of the *Evening Standard*, had every woman falling for him, Michael recalled, and 'he was tremendously good in what he gave back to them'. Michael watched him as he had watched his Oxford friends, those 'stunningly good looking gay sparks' Tony Greenwood and Paul Reilly 'at work. I was absolutely in awe of them. And I thought, "How do you do that?"' Then he met and read H.G. Wells and learned about how he had overcome his inhibitions. 'Caught' by Wells's stories of sexual liberation, especially *Ann Veronica* (1909), he took notes, determined to overcome 'my disabilities'.

When Michael met Jill he was thirty-one and had comparatively little sexual experience – though Jill would later mention visiting his London flat and seeing women's perfume bottles in his bathroom, and other accounts claim he was quite a lady's man during the war. Certainly his position as editor of the London *Evening Standard* bolstered him, but he discounted his rate of success with women. 'I hadn't had any great sex life before Jill,' he declared.[2]

Michael did not have eczema or asthma the day Jill met him. And it might not have mattered so much if he did. 'She didn't seem to take any notice of it at all,' Michael said. Julie saw Michael as a 'white eczema-covered creature with a wheezy cough'. It astonished her to hear her mother call him her Adonis. 'I don't believe it,' responded Michael, who had found his physical disabilities such an impediment when courting women. 'I fell for him straight away,' Jill said. Liam remembered meeting Michael in Plymouth in Jill's company: 'He was talking Jill's language.' The Plymouth plan inspired great orations in Michael. 'Where there is no vision, the people perish,' Liam quoted, 'and here was a man with vision.' Jill attended all of Michael's political meetings, she told his biographers Simon Hoggart and David Leigh. At the eve of the Poll meeting in Devonport's town hall, she watched an enormous, excited crowd queuing up to hear Nye Bevan, Michael's hero and the prophet of a Labour victory, speaking on Michael's behalf. 'Nobody is going to stop the Labour Party,' Jill said. She had almost joined the Communist Party during the war, she told Michael, because it seemed to be getting on with it, agitating for the 'better Britain' imagined in the Beveridge Report (1942), which he described as a country that 'aimed to conquer the five giant evils – want, disease, ignorance, squalor, and idleness'.[3] Bevan had taunted not only Churchill but also the Labour ministers in his coalition government when they seemed to stall on setting up a programme of social insurance that would carry out the Report's recommendations. Now he had come into his own. Constance Cummings, the actress and a friend of Nye and later Jill and Michael, described him as, 'a great flowing furnace. You warmed yourself in his company and he lifted your spirits.'

In a sense, Jill became a believer in Michael Foot's destiny before he did. He came from a distinguished Plymouth family. Two of his brothers, John and Dingle, and his father Isaac – all Liberals – campaigned for Parliamentary seats in the 1945 election. All of them thought they had a better chance of winning than Michael. Even Bevan expected him to lose. When Michael won by a little over 2000 votes while the other three Foots lost, only Jill was not surprised. She watched Michael, hoarse with passion and pale with exhaustion, carried off to his victory party – aggrieved that she was not invited. So she arranged a private showing of *The Way We Live* and invited him to it. He did not appear. So she arranged a second showing and sent a car for him to make sure he attended. 'Being a beautiful young woman, she was used to getting what she wanted,' Julie observed. Jill told this story to her daughter many times, saying, 'If you set your heart on a man, make sure you get him. There are ways. Shall I tell you about Michael?'

Jill introduced Michael to Hampstead Heath, where they made 'good use of the excellent hedgerow shelters for loving couples'. It was a love, as he wrote, 'under wraps'. His mother, a 'strict non-conformist, like the vast majority of my potential constituents in Devonport ... would have disapproved most strongly of any departure from marital conventions'. (Michael's mother died on 17 May 1946 without ever having met Jill.) Marriage, in fact, would have to wait, since Jill was still married to Jeffrey Dell, and neither lover seemed especially keen to formalize their relationship. And they did not live together. Michael only had his small flat and Jill had no home of her own to offer. Liam MacQuitty remembered declining her suggestion that he move into Michael's quarters and that Michael move in with her at MacQuitty's house.

Jill and Michael realized that they were a study in contrasts, which made them all the more fascinating and necessary to each other. The shy Michael had loving parents, supportive siblings, an Oxford education and was rooted in a community and its traditions – all of which Jill craved. The bold Jill had a sexual assurance and an aesthetic flair that seemed magical to Michael – as if it had come out of nowhere. How could someone become Jill Craigie? It astounded him, and he would often repeat, 'she did it on her own'. Michael admired Jill's poise. Her eye for colour and composition intrigued a man who had a deep and abiding love for literature. He did not have Jill's ability to focus on form, to shape a life itself as a work of art. Yet Jill admitted that she was not as confident as she looked, and Michael provided her with a stronger link to a wider world. Del Giudice began to say to her, 'I think you should go into politics and represent the film industry, and have a voice there.' He invited her to dinner when he had 'politicians at his table,' Jill recalled, 'so that gave me a kind of insight … not many people had, because not everybody went down so well with the politicians'.[4]

For Michael, Jill represented the fulfilment of his quest for 'passionate mutual love', as Bertrand Russell called it in *Marriage and Morals* (1929), Michael's bible on the subject. 'Nature did not construct human beings to stand alone,' Russell wrote. 'The best thing that life has to give,' he continued, is 'happy mutual love', which produced 'a new being composed of two in one'. H.G. Wells called it the search for a soulmate, the very term Michael would use years later in describing his feelings for Jill. 'Ever since I had seen the happy smile on the face of Bertrand Russell, the champion of companionate marriage, I had been in favour of it.' And so was Jill, Michael thought. She was, he wrote in 'A Love Under Wraps', the 'girl of my theories, but the girl of my dreams too'.

Approaching the summer of 1946, Michael yearned for a holiday, a 'luxurious honeymoon' that would take the couple away from their fitful Hampstead trysts and to Nice, where he had enjoyed the opulence of Lord Beaverbrook's hospitality in 1939. Michael promised do his best to emulate his former employer's extravagance, and off he went with Jill to the Hôtel Negresco, still situated in its 'late-Victorian splendour' and 'eerily empty'. They thought it prudent to take a room each, and 'barricaded in separate suites', he evoked the Churchillian grandeur of their rendezvous: 'Never in the realm of marital experiment had such lavish facilities been made available for so few.'

The tentative twosome emerged into the corridors of the great hotel, explored the French coast to Juan-les-Pins and Gulfe-Juan, the site of Napoleon's landing from Elba and now the setting for Picasso's court. Craving real eggs – having only had the powdered variety during wartime – Jill ordered in her excellent French '*une omelette enorme*', spreading out her arms in an all-encompassing gesture. The waiter took her at her word – as she liked to recall with child-like delight – producing the 'largest omelette ever served on the French Riviera'.

They had ten days to themselves, bathing in the bluest water they had ever seen and sunning on beaches they could enjoy in Napoleonic solitude. Nary an English voice was heard, and after this delirium of delight they sneaked back to London – Michael to Park Street and Jill to Holly Berry House, where reporters greeted her: 'We have reports that you've been away in the South of France with Michael Foot. What do you say?' She rang Michael, who instructed her to issue the following statement:

> Michael Foot offers his fraternal greetings to his fellow journalists – and the reminder that, if anything appears in the newspapers about his visit to France, he will be happy to reveal his latest information about the love affairs of Lord Beaverbrook, Lord Rothermere and a select list of other newspaper proprietors.

As Jill told Michael, the reporters 'just melted away'.

Blue Scar
(1946–9)

I stood in the ruins of Dowlais,
And sighed for the lovers destroyed
And the landscape of Gwalia stained for all time
By the bloody hands of progress.

From Idris Davies, Gwalia Deserta (1938)

The period after the making of *The Way We Live* proved stressful for both Jill and Julie. Jill was still scrambling to sort out both her love life and her film career. As her mother became involved with Michael Foot, who began staying overnight at Holly Berry House, Julie got angrier and angrier. 'I wasn't supposed to know they were sleeping together. My mother would ruffle up the spare bed, but I could see that it had not been slept in properly.' Gilly remembered how Jill used to 'vaguely unmake' that bed. She also remembered a beautiful chaise longue situated in front of a window. 'I never saw my mother sit down,' Gilly said when thinking of her own homelife. 'She was always doing something.' As Gilly entered Julie's home, Jill would be lying down, 'looking *so beautiful*, so elegant'. Jill would say, 'That you, darling?'

For a brief time Jill stayed with Michael in his bachelor flat at 62 Park Street. It seemed to Julie that she had lost her mother's attention: 'She always asked me what I would like her to cook for dinner! After Michael moved in, she always asked Michael, not me.' Mother and daughter had grown closer as the Dell marriage slowly disintegrated, and then Michael Foot barged in – or so it seemed to Julie. To Michael, Jill seemed a wonderful mother. 'I admired all the time she gave to Julie – right from the beginning. I don't think Julie fully appreciated that.'

Jill's peripatetic life took a toll on Julie, who hated boarding school and had trouble learning to read. She was unpopular with Tory teachers because she had spoken up for equal pay for farmworkers and expressed pro-Labour sentiments. On Guy Fawkes Night a gang of Tory students tied Julie to a stake. 'They had Clement Attlee, Bevan, Guy Fawkes and me; the others were dummies, but I wasn't.' They started a bonfire in the distance and danced around her and a schoolmate whom she had 'corrupted'. She did not tell her mother.

Julie yearned for those periods when she could be home and have her mother to herself.

> I would come home, and I would never say how much I hated it, because as a child if you hate something very much and it's all bad news and bad memories, you're very intelligent – you don't do what adults do. You come home in the holidays and you know you have four or eight weeks of unadulterated pleasure, and are you going to spoil it by explaining or whining about it. Children really live for the day.

Rudyard Kipling, Anthony West and generations of children unhappy away from home have voiced similar sentiments, and it always comes as a blow to their parents when their children later write or talk about their miserable childhoods. 'I'm whining about it now,' Julie said. 'It came as a terrible shock to my mother when I told her [much later].' The story of their misunderstanding would thread its way through much of Jill's later biography.

Julie left her second school, The Causeway in Horsham, with poor marks and 'a giant-size feeling of inferiority', Jill wrote to Mervyn Jones (26 May 1994):

> Nothing I could say convinced her that what she could do was just as important as what she could not do. I never had any doubt of her abilities. She had an extraordinary facility with complicated mechanical contraptions … She was good at art with a good eye for composition and a sense of style. She was also extremely creative in her play.

Jill struggled on – getting no support from Julie's father and only disapproval from his family, who did not like the company Jill was keeping. Except for her mother, Julie had only Gilly, who greatly admired Jill. Gilly remembered walking up Holly Hill in Hampstead and seeing Jill walking down the opposite side. 'She didn't see me. And she was *so beautiful* that I couldn't bring myself to talk to her. She had a beaver coat on and a beret and looked so gorgeous I was overcome with embarrassment.' Gilly recalled this complicated period when Jill and Julie were living in Liam's house and he was wooing Jill while Jill was wooing Michael. 'I remember us being trapped in our bedroom and not allowed to go down when she had Bill MacQuitty there and somebody had called. Manoeuvring all these men was like a Whitehall farce.'

Michael and Julie believed that Malcolm MacDonald wanted to marry Jill
when he returned from Canada. 'I'm not sure how high up the list Malcolm
was,' Michael speculated. 'Well, he must have been quite high up, considering
that we lived in his house and he bought me a horse,' Julie countered. Michael
recalled that Malcolm gave Jill many lavish gifts, including works of art. Jill
wrote in *Odd Reflections*: 'The more you take, the more you are loved – so
foolish are men.' She told Julie that she could not marry Malcolm because of
his protruding teeth. He also lived in the shadow of his father, and though he
served in many distinguished diplomatic posts, he referred to himself in his
autobiography *Constant Surprise* as 'one of those smaller men', and composed
this epitaph for himself: 'He was superficially good at many things, and
profoundly good at nothing.'

'Who would you most like me to marry,' Jill asked her daughter. 'Michael
or Liam?' Julie said Liam. 'He was fun, good looking and paid lots of attention
to me. Michael was ugly and he didn't say boo to me.' But Jill demurred
because money meant too much to him; besides, he did not share her socialist
politics. He found schemes like Aneurin Bevan's National Health Service
idealistic and unworkable. Later, when Jill told Liam she was marrying
Michael, according to Julie, Liam replied: 'I have this terrible buzzing in my
ear, and it's all your fault.' Michael recalls that 'Liam was always very nice
about it, I must say.' Liam did not remember that buzz but rather recalled Jill
telling him that she had been to a gypsy who had forecast that she was 'going
to walk in high places'. Jill, a bit of a gypsy herself, Liam suggested, believed
her marriage to Michael had been foretold. 'She knocked Mike right off his
perch. At the beginning he considered her half a witch and half a bitch. Spitch
was the combination of the two.' Michael believed the term derives from 'spiv',
slang for (strictly speaking) a petty criminal, though Michael seemed to have
in mind Jill's spirited and unorthodox nature. In August 1947 Michael wrote
in a copy of *William Morris: Selected Writings*: 'To my beautiful spitch, with
love from Michael.' Jill favoured Michael but Liam remained on the scene,
keeping that twinkle in his eye, and 'Jill never stopped flirting with every man
who walked through the door,' Gilly said. 'There was never a period I
remember when there weren't men on the scene.'

At the same time, Jill's career faltered as the Rank Organization suffered
several setbacks, including 'spectacularly huge expenditure' on prestige
products such as *Caesar and Cleopatra* and *London Town* – one a boring Shaw
adaptation and the other a 'dud musical' – costing well over £2 million with
'no obvious return'.[1] John Davis targeted the extravagant Del Giudice, whose
over-budget productions now made him vulnerable. By 1947 Del had sold his

shares in 'Two Cities' – Jill's main funding source – and Rank had effectively ended a three-year 'mission', in Geoffrey Macnab's words, to 'broaden the base of the industry'. Rank now abandoned his aspiration to make Britain a world power in cinema, taking on a wide range of subjects and styles. The fragile infrastructure Jill counted on had been demolished.[2]

Confronting a film industry in a post-war slump, Liam MacQuitty established his own company, Outlook Films. Building on the confidence he had in Jill, he self-financed an ambitious film about the Welsh people and the nationalizing of the coal mines, a controversial Labour government action taken in 1946. Liam got half their funding (£22,500) from the Coal Board. In July, Jill attended the annual miners' gala in Durham, a spectacular event involving virtually the whole city, with miners from all parts of the world marching and speakers addressing the assembly at the miners' special invitation. 'When the invitation comes,' Michael remarked, 'You're very pleased, and I did get the invitation right then.' Jill came up with Noel Newsome, then the Coal Board's public relations officer. 'He was quite interested in Jill and quite a nice chap,' Michael remembered. Indeed, in an inscription to *Voices from Britain, Broadcast History 1939–1945*, with a foreword by Newsome, he had written: 'For Jill. Best love from Noel and here's hoping!' Whatever his hopes, 'We managed to do him down in the hotel,' Michael reported. 'She went to the miners' gala with Noel and she came home with me.' Jill met all the important figures such as Arthur Horner and Will Painter, Communist miners' union leaders, and she began to think of doing a documentary about the gala itself, saying to Michael: 'It's the greatest working-class festival. It ought to be properly recorded.' According to Denis Forman, then at the Ministry of Information, such a film would have fallen 'on the margins' of what might be accepted for funding. Denis remembered hearing about Jill's project but did not recall that Jill approached him directly, although Michael believed she received a 'disheartening reply'.

Liam had to match the Coal Board funding with his own money and what he could obtain from his father and brother. As with *The Way We Live*, the film would be shot on location, obviating the scramble for expensive studio space. Liam bought a van to transport equipment and coaxed his technicians to work on a profit-sharing basis rather than on full salaries. A publicity item about the film reported that Emrys Jones, the film's star, agreed to work for a 'reduced salary' because he liked Jill's script for *Blue Scar* so much. In his autobiography, MacQuitty does not understate the enormous risk of making the film without a distribution guarantee. But he could not wait for what he probably could not get; besides, he had 'absolute faith in the film we were

producing'.[3] Asked why she did the film, Jill replied: 'I wanted to do something important, and what is more important than coal today? When you
think of coal, your thoughts go immediately to Wales – the singing, the
valleys.' Movies had already created a mythic, romantic Wales – the country
of director John Ford's *How Green Was My Valley* (1941) and Emlyn Williams'
The Corn is Green (1945). Ford shot his film in a Hollywood studio, dismissing
critics who griped that he had not even visited Wales: 'It's a Celtic country,
isn't it?' What more did he need to know? 'They're all micks, aren't they?' Jill
was quite aware that she had a tendency to romanticize the miners, but she
wanted to ground herself in documentary fashion in the Welsh countryside,
in home life and in the mines. All the while she would be exploring, as
Williams did, a 'theme popular in modern Welsh literature': the 'preoccupation with education as a means of career advancement and as an escape
route from communities impoverished, parochial or repressive'.[4]

Michael Foot recalled that Jill scouted several locations before settling on
Abergwynfi, a compact South Wales village with 3500 people – 'almost
unbelievably photogenic', Jill said. She checked into the Western Hotel, where
Julie and Gilly came to visit, getting in the way of the crew and playing
hopscotch on the hotel roof. The girls were on their own – their nominal
guardian, Barbara Dell, had her film duties to perform. Right after the war,
hotels did not have much to offer: 'There was always the smell of cabbage,'
Gilly noted. 'Then we discovered pit heaps.' Knowing only Hampstead Heath,
they did not realize what they were walking on and would come back to the
hotel all black.

Jill commenced by observing the miners and their families, determined to
absorb a sense of their daily routines and concerns. At a public meeting she
faced a sceptical audience none too pleased with Hollywood's rendition of the
Welsh. 'How do you see the Welsh miner?' asked one challenger. The outsider
replied that she saw 'a man with humour in his make up, with music in his
soul, with some heroism and plenty of grievances'.[5] The audience responded
'hear hear'. She offered a cash prize for the best short article on 'What I think
about while working in the mines.' She learned how bitter the Welsh could be
about condescending outsiders. She found it extraordinary that miner's homes
were so neat and clean when their work involved so much dirt. The pianos
that graced so many miners' cottages confirmed her belief in their aesthetic
sense.

Blue Scar also demonstrates that Jill did not neglect the business of mining
and the consequences of nationalization. New machinery had just been
introduced into the mines, and she asked a miner if his work had been made

easier and safer. 'Well, you see Miss Craigie,' he answered, 'with these pneumatic drills we can no longer hear the earth speak' – a line she used in her film. He explained that when miners used the pick, they could hear the cracks in the roof. She also sat in on many meetings between managers, other officials and the miners. She interviewed all of them to get the details right; she did not downplay the complexities of nationalization. She pressed the miners to get an insight into the 'problems underground', recalls local historian Terry Witts, who began in the 1990s to interview the few surviving members of the communities Jill visited. She asked permission to attend a meeting about declining coal production. 'That's okay,' the manager said, 'but remember the language will be blue.' When the men came up from underground to the meeting, the manager said: 'What the hell has happened to production?' They replied: 'It's those bloody sprockets. They've sent the wrong bloody sprockets down again!'

The village queued up to see the film, astonished to see the actual row shown virtually word-for-word. 'You should have seen the manager's face,' they told Witts, who then went to see the manager's wife. 'Terry,' she said, 'he went every night of the week to see the film.' Comparing her stay in Abergwynfi and Llanharan to reports in the national press and to reading history books at school, Jill said: 'It came as a shock to discover how one-sidedly the miners and mining communities had been portrayed.'[6] To Terry Witts, she wrote: 'You're much too complimentary about my visit to Abergwynfi ... Do write whatever you like about me and my film. I think I could have made a better one if I'd been doing it today.' It was a characteristic response – and an honest one.[7]

The first shot in *Blue Scar* is of a Welsh valley superimposed with a title: 'A story that might have happened anywhere in South Wales.' Jill commissioned a woman, Grace Williams, to score the film. Williams' music conveys a sort of muted triumphalism, a mood that both celebrates the Welsh spirit and evokes the land's sombre realities. Jill used nine miners in the film as well as The Port Talbot Municipal Choir and the Afan Glee Society.

It is October 1946. In crisply filmed opening scenes the miners are shown ascending to the surface of a mine shaft and entering the manager's office to argue about coal production. The exchanges are so rapid that the dialogue is barely understandable. The manager demands increased output. As the miners sing in the showers, Tom Thomas (Emrys Jones), remarks that he will not apply for a promotion until 'there is a change in the system'. But much of the banter is about Abergwynfi and the girls there.

Tom is off to see his girl, Olwen Williams, whose family is shown in their

living room discussing her aspirations to become an opera star, a dream that
the men think is preposterous, although an Englishman is courting her, and
Olwen's mother clearly thinks her daughter has a future beyond Wales.

The first two scenes admirably convey the social, sexual and political
tensions of a Welsh mining community, and they represent the best moments
in a film that rises far above any previous work on the subject – as film
historian David Berry recognizes. But the second scene also introduces the
love story of Tom and Olwen, which, Liam MacQuitty noted, he and Jill felt
forced to include in order to secure the work's distribution as a feature film.
Gradually this factitious element will infect a film that promised so much
more than conventional fare.

But in these early scenes, Jill's command of her material is superb, as
Olwen's father (Ted) and his son (Thomas) argue over the merits of
nationalization – Thomas cynically doubting that change of ownership will
make any practical difference in the miner's life. Ted, obviously suffering lung
damage from years underground, rejects Thomas's dire warning that if he
does not quit and go on reduced salary, he will be a dead man. But the family
needs the money badly, Ted insists, and the situation is made worse, we later
learn, because Thomas tends to be a slacker who does not show up for enough
shifts. Although the film is 'avowedly socialist', Andy Medhurst acknowledges,
it does not make the *Tribune*-reading Thomas into a paragon of virtue.

A knock at the door interrupts the family's celebration of Olwen's
scholarship. It is Alfred Collins (Anthony Pendrell), the English industrial
psychologist who has fallen in love with Olwen. Once in the crowded living
room, the smartly dressed Englishman becomes self-conscious: 'I say, I hope
I'm not gate-crashing a party.' Olwen's mother makes him welcome, and her
father asks Olwen to introduce Alfred to everyone. Each identical greeting
from friends and neighbours all named Williams or Thomas ('Pleased to meet
you') is correct and polite, with only Thomas putting a bit of an edge in his
voice. The uncomfortable Alfred attempts to make a joke: 'You know I think
you all have the same name on purpose. Just to embarrass the English.' Tom,
whose expression has changed from a look of doubt to hostility, replies, 'The
English embarrassed? That hasn't happened since Lady Godiva.' Tom and
Thomas will have none of Alfred's attempts at self-deprecating humour. As
Olwen sings and the group joins in, the disconcerted Alfred spots the torn
wallpaper. Still, he overcomes his uneasiness and for a moment, at least, joins
the ensemble in song, so that even Tom is able to say a pleasant goodnight to
his rival.

The remainder of the film focuses on Tom and Olwen as their different aspirations and attitudes toward their native land erupt. Olwen does not want to 'pass' Tom, and she urges him to give up mining and 'better himself'. He can only better himself, he replies, by making his and the miners' lot better. Jill would have noted this conflict not only during her filming in Wales, but also in her discussions with Aneurin Bevan, who was becoming as much a hero for Jill as for Michael. For Bevan, the only way for the Welsh to succeed as individuals was to succeed collectively as a people concerned with another's welfare. Although an anti-English attitude pervades *Blue Scar*, a deeper vein of resentment over class distinctions runs through the film. Tom believes that Olwen is asking him to reject his class. He cannot satisfy his ambition unless he is ambitious for his fellow workers.* But she believes all his studying at night will avail him nothing because he will remain 'right at the bottom of the social ladder'. Yet Olwen's desire to escape is powerfully supported, critic Andy Medhurst points out, by the film's photography: 'The streets of Abergwynfi are drab and harsh, with broken pavements and a complete absence of any cinematic beautifying.'

Tom extols the 'spirit of the valleys' that binds the people together. Olwen won't find that in the big cities, he asserts. Indeed, the film endorses his romanticism with magnificent shots of the valley and the mountain atop which a football match is to be played. At a worker's institute, Tom enters the convivial atmosphere of card games, darts, dominoes, drinking and singing. He takes his beer upstairs to the library. He opens a book and turns to a page titled 'A Socialist's Creed', but his reading is disturbed by superimposed images of Alfred and Olwen dancing together. Medhurst notes that the 'whirling waltz' reveals Tom's 'intense jealousy. This brief overlapping of politics and fantasy has an intensity and complexity that marks it out from the rest of the film.' Going downstairs, Tom picks a quarrel with a table of men who disgust him with their talk of 'money, money, money'. Told to pipe down so the singing can be heard, Tom exclaims: 'Singing, football, night classes. That's how we keep ourselves alive!'

Tom returns to the mines while Olwen heads off to college and then on to London, where she marries Alfred and pursues a singing career. The documentary strengths of the film are evident when Tom descends to his job in a shot Liam MacQuitty singles out in *A Life to Remember* with justifiable pride: he 'strapped' his Newman Sinclair camera 'pointing upwards, on top of the lift cage. As the cage went down in the shaft, the camera recorded the

---

* In *Aneurin Bevin: A Biography, Volume 1: 1897–1945*, Michael writes of his hero. 'His ambitions were communal and collectivist. He wanted to rise with his class, and not out of it.' When one of Bevan's friends, David Minton, decides to emigrate to Australia, he responds: 'I'm going to stay here and fight it out… [I]f all the young men were to leave, who is to continue the fight?'

circle of light at the top growing smaller and smaller until it finally disappeared.' Better than any dialogue, the shot puts us in the miner's cell.

This desolate absence of light and the figures of crouching miners drilling and picking at the coal while overmen (supervisors) taunt them is interrupted by a scene in a posh restaurant where Alfred and Olwen are celebrating her birthday. The camera tilts upward from their table to show walls decorated with rather primitive human figures reminiscent of cave paintings – a choice at odds with atmospherics such as crown moulding and placid background music. The disparity intensifies as the camera tilts downward and the music becomes strident and brassy in a brief shot of a coal-blackened hand outlining a naked female form on the coalface. Such visual touches once again accomplish much more than the dialogue, although Tom's comment that the pneumatic drills dull the senses is a fitting accompaniment to that lone hand drawing on a cave wall. Tom is shown taking charge of production, having earned his step up.

In *Blue Scar*'s denouement, Olwen invites Tom to London to hear her singing debut on the radio. The city is pictured with crowded, noisy streets, filled with bewildering street signs and confusingly numbered buses – a frenetic, fragmented realm of such human density that the camera can glimpse only body parts. Tom makes his way to Olwen's cramped flat, where there is to be a party in her honour. The kitchen is hardly bigger than a small closet, and in addition to a tiny bathroom there is only the living room where Olwen and her husband eat and sleep. 'You know, Tom, the slag heap has nothing on the London suite,' she says. He responds, 'They talk of miners bathing in the kitchen. I didn't know that Londoners eat in the bedroom.' Olwen has hardly been a success – 'I haven't even started,' she mutters disconsolately, then cries as Tom realizes how little she has gained. When the party begins, Olwen instructs Tom as to how to greet everyone. Tom then meets various London types: a sardonic agent, a drunken clubman, a pretentious artist. Olwyn points out that they will not say 'pleased to meet you' but 'how do you do?' Tom wonders why: 'Are they pleased to meet each other?' Olwen considers: 'Not really.' London – the very city that made Jill's career possible – is treated as the home of the artificial and the insincere. At the end Tom rejects Olwen's hint that they could have an affair, and he is seen returning home to his magnificent Welsh valley.

Like every other film Jill and Liam worked on together, *Blue Scar* had trouble finding a distributor. 'You don't even speak our language,' said Sir Arthur Jarrett, head of the ABC theatre chain. Nothing came of discussions with the

Rank Organisation. Then Jill met with Harold Wilson, Minister for the Board of Trade, and Wilson's favoured film-maker, Alexander Korda. In *A Life to Remember*, MacQuitty describes their meeting in Korda's 'plush private viewing theatre in Park Lane'. Wilson only wanted to know what his driver thought of the film. Wilson said he always relied on his driver's film criticism. The driver liked it, yet Wilson offered no help. MacQuitty watched Korda and his cigar, half of it grey ash he flicked off onto the sumptuous carpet. 'A bad omen,' MacQuitty thought. All Korda wanted to know was how much the film cost. When MacQuitty said he had kept costs down to £45,000 by paying 'cash for everything', Korda replied, 'Never pay cash.' Korda did, however, speak to Arthur Jarrett, and Jill and Liam eventually got a trial distribution in seven theatres. The film did well but went out to an expanded circuit as a co-feature that limited MacQuitty's returns to £18,000 – just enough to pay back his family. Jill deftly organized a press campaign. 'Jill the Giant Killer', which appeared in *Reynolds News* on 12 June 1949, is typical of articles that extolled her beauty, her unconventionality and her resilience, helping her score a 'triumph over the knowalls of the film industry'. Another piece (unidentified in Jill's papers) related how director and producer had struggled to get their funding, with Jill investing her savings and 'selling her jewellery to help'.

Blue Scar's reviews were mixed to negative. *The Times* (9 April 1949), for example, praised its documentary elements while noting that the 'blend of romantic story and objective demonstration of the ways of the Welsh mining villages is not always harmonious'. Jill's politics and her view of nationalization were deemed 'muddled', but she was a master at depicting village life.

Like *The Way We Live*, *Blue Scar* continues to enjoy a vivid life in the communities where it was filmed. Over the years Jill received numerous letters from fans of these films, many of them recalling that her work had made a deep impression on them in youth. Scholars and local historians also contacted her, testifying to the value of her films. This correspondence confirmed her view that film could shape public opinion in ways that government did not understand or exploit.

In *A Life to Remember*, MacQuitty is tactfully silent about his opinion of *Blue Scar* and about the end of his years with Jill, saying only that Jill married Michael and, 'I continued the battle alone'. Jill and Liam remained on excellent terms, phoning one other and seeing each other from time to time. Liam also retained a cordial relationship with Michael after Jill's death. In conversation, Liam said that Jill 'realized after *Blue Scar* that she was not a director of films in the sense that Ronnie Neame or David Lean were'. Julie remembered how devastated her mother felt after putting everything she had into the film: 'It flopped and she was fairly shocked.'

In *Documentary Film*, Paul Rotha dismisses the film with a phrase, saying it failed to 'master its subject'. Film historian Philip Kemp calls the film 'uneven, often awkward', although he cites Andy Medhurst's remark that 'what is so startling about *Blue Scar* … is that it is a British feature film that is consciously political, avowedly socialist'. David Berry's critique – the most comprehensive so far – acknowledges the film's failings but praises its 'raw authenticity'. And he perceptively notes that Jill's 'film projects almost had to be *too* ambitious for her to make any kind of impression and counter the pervasive sexism in the industry'. On 19 October 1988 *Variety* published an 'Archive Review' of *Blue Scar*, which concluded that Jill's work was 'uneven but shows promise, apparently never realized with another fiction feature'. This judgement echoes Berry's: 'a genuine screen talent prematurely extinguished'.

In retrospect, the scenes portraying the lives of miners underground and the deft evocation of domestic interiors, in which the tensions between men and women and their families emerge, seem the most authentic. Much of the rest, as William MacQuitty acknowledged, was rather forced – an inept effort to graft a love story onto a documentary. This kind of failure, however, in an experimental film that did not capture the mainstream imagination hardly proved Jill was unfit to direct. And she still believed, with some justification, that her talents as a director had yet to be fully developed.

My Dear Child

(1947–9)

Ah, love, let us be true
To one another! for the world, which seems
To lie before us like a land of dreams...

Matthew Arnold, Dover Beach

A letter (26 September 1947) that Michael sent to Jill from Jamaica while visiting his brother Mac (Hugh),* reveals how passionate he had become about her and how they had already fallen into the rhythm of their lives together:

> I love you, my sweetheart. I have told you ten million times already, but you must know that it is true ... I think of you my darling, & wonder how you are getting on with all your struggles. Just after I had left you I opened the Times... I saw a letter signed 'JILL CRAIGIE.' As my mind happened to be on that subject at the moment, I almost fell off my seat in the bus. So all the way to the airport I was able to bask in the thought, not only of your beauty but also of your genius. It was a fine letter & the last sentence should endear you even more to John Davis.[1]

The letter is addressed to 'My dear child', the term of endearment Michael would employ for the rest of their lives together. Depending on the occasion and the observer, the term could seem affectionate, curt, playful or condescending. To a casual friend like the author Margaret Drabble, Michael was like many men of his generation who used such terms without intending any offence. 'My grandfather [Isaac Foot] was the same,' said Alison, Michael's niece. Jill's first reaction to this phrase cannot be recovered; later, her response

---

* Hugh Foot, Lord Caradon (1907–90), had a distinguished diplomatic career in posts that included Palestine, Cyprus, Jamaica and Nigeria. He was the government's permanent representative to the United Nations from 1964 to 1970, and was made a life peer when he joined the government in 1964.

would vary with her moods, the tone of her husband's voice and the company. Publisher Mike Bessie, who first met Michael during the war and would later edit Michael's books for American publication, recalled:

> I spent so much time with Michael and Jill. I have this picture of them – we'd be sitting in discussion and she'd say something that either he disagreed with or he thought was naive – 'My dear child' is the way he would begin. I don't think I ever saw him – although I knew what he was feeling – ever lose his temper with her. 'My dear child' – well, for me it would be a little like 'one, two, three… ten' before I opened my mouth.

How did Jill respond? 'What that evokes is the whole question of their relationship,' Mike answered. 'Sometimes quite heatedly. Jill didn't give ground, even when it was a matter when Michael had good reason to believe he knew better.'

Michael's letters from Jamaica in September and October 1947 aimed to dispel her 'bleak' outlook: 'We must never have holidays apart from one another again,' he vowed. Just then she was having some trouble with UNESCO, which had commissioned her to direct a short documentary, *Children of the Ruins*, about the impact of the war on youth across Europe. He wrote that she should tell them to 'go to hell', adding that 'just about the first intelligent thing' they had done was to 'get a first-class director for once' in an organization 'cluttered up with a lot of third-rate saboteurs'.

Jill's ten-minute short, a production of the Crown Film Unit, presents children playing in rubble, crouching in rags, emaciated and forlorn, stretching out their hands for food. A voice, clearly Jill's, asks whether the war effort tended to rate industrial might more highly than concern for human values. Shots shift to children in crowded, dingy, poorly lit schoolrooms – 'as if they could really learn this way', remarks a male voice. The situation in the US is better, the narrator continues, but scenes of picketing teachers and headlines about strikes emphasize their low salaries and the teacher shortage. Children are shown going to school barefoot. The plight of girls in other parts of the world (India, for example) is such that they receive 'hardly any education at all'. A whole generation was brought up,' says the male voice – 'or shall we say dragged up,' Jill's voice interrupts – with the 'consequences of war'. Children are dehumanized and transformed by the war machinery, the narrator notes, as brief shots of Hitler and his slavishly saluting youth corps dominate the screen. Amid scenes of book burning, the narrator quotes Isaac Newton's view that to destroy books is to destroy reason itself. Since the war advances have been made, but three-quarters of the world's children are brought up uneducated. Not the destruction of the cities but the break-up of homes and families is the greatest tragedy of war, the narrator insists.

'The whole world was on the move.' Jill's film portrays the history of the twentieth century as the saga of displaced peoples. Shots of children digging up the bricks between streetcar tracks, hauling water in decimated landscapes and bearing huge bundles on their backs are accompanied with the narrator's observation: 'To be young and to live meant to be old beyond one's years.' Children learn survival skills, but 'what is going on in their minds?' The film's shots of children clamouring for bowls and cups and of camps with no parents suggest that the work of relief organizations seems noble but horrendously inadequate.

This world problem becomes the focus of a UNESCO conference – 'What, another committee?' – Jill's voice breaks in. 'And what's it all going to cost?' The male voice replies: 'Well, what would you do?' The propagandistic intent of the film now emerges: UNESCO thinks of the world as 'one place' and aims to provide the 'tools of learning' (pencils and books) and teachers. 'If we have a scrap of humanity,' the narrator emphasizes, the crisis of the world's children cannot be ignored. 'Difficult to feel for people when they are so far away, but our neighbours matter.' Shots of a devastated Hiroshima follow scenes of teachers and aid workers dealing with children of all ages, races and colours. Shots of children with radiation poisoning convey Jill's realization that it was not merely the bombs but the ramifications of nuclear energy programmes that had to be fully investigated and controlled if there was to be a sane world and a comity of nations.

This little-known film is an idealistic view, to be sure, but one that exposes the high cost of doing nothing, of taking refuge in scepticism or cynicism, or in concentrating only on one's immediate surroundings. Through its focus on children, the film makes the world seem like a neighbourhood, a community – almost a village in which the suffering of others becomes everyone's concern.

Besides her beauty, talent and charm, Jill's passionate involvement with such urgent social issues endeared her to Michael. At his first lunch with Jill in the White Tower restaurant, Michael in typical fashion recommended Winwood Reade's prophetic *The Martyrdom of Man* (1872), a 'great heretic's poem', which declares: 'Theology is an excellent nurse, but a bad mistress for grown-up minds' and 'Doubt is the offspring of knowledge.' The book spoke both to their brooding over the new anxieties of a nuclear age and their irrepressible hope in a vibrant new future. A curious cross between the biblical and rationalist idioms, *The Martyrdom of Man* contains sentences that 'linger in the memory like verses learnt in childhood', Michael observes in *Loyalists and Loners*. Thus Reade exhorts: 'The time is coming when the crowned idea will be cast aside and the despotic shadow disappear.' Reade's 'combination of an excitement or foreboding about the future with a reverence for the past', as Michael puts it, spoke to his own and Jill's feeling that they were on the verge of a thrilling but dangerous epoch. Their country after 1945 seemed to have arrived at a perilous but also promising turning point, and the sceptical yet ever-questing mode of Reade's history of civilizations, which so disturbed conventional Victorians, now appeared to have found its proper time and audience. Futurists like H.G. Wells paid tribute to Reade, and Michael would later write: 'He seeks to discover how new civilisations made their great leaps forward and how living societies were turned to stone.' Either outcome now appeared possible for post-war Britain.

During this period Jill became pregnant. She was still married to Jeffrey Dell (they did not divorce until the spring of 1948). What did Michael want to do? He did not propose marriage. The couple did not regard the institution with any deference. They had been living as 'openly as anyone did at a time when such liaisons were not mentioned in the newspapers', Mervyn Jones notes in *Michael Foot*. But an MP with a 'small majority and a Methodist tradition in the constituency' fathering an illegitimate child risked ruin. Michael said he loved Jill and would abide by her decision. She wanted his love on terms that left them both free, and she wanted to get on with her film career. She had the abortion – a very big decision, as such operations were illegal and dangerous. Later, when it became clear that she could have no more children with Michael, she looked back at her choice with regret and remorse.*

Less than two years later the couple married. Jill was now free of Jeffrey Dell, and marriage made it safer for Michael to live with her. Perhaps just as important, they knew the marriage would please Michael's father. Isaac had already accepted Jill wholeheartedly, but marriage in his eyes would seal the affair. In a BBC documentary about Michael, 'Labour's Old Romantic' (1997), Jill said that she told Michael, 'If you ever have any extra needs, I don't want to know, and even more important I don't want anyone else to know. That's

---

* Jill seems to have had at least one abortion during her marriage to Jeffrey Dell. In her papers an undated letter (*c*. late 1930s, early 1940s) signed by Donald, a film director, begins: 'My dear Jill – my dear Jill! That was a dreadful thing to go and do. Apart from everything else it must have frightened Jeffrey out of about ten years growth. Even his description of the callous Harley street surgeons [who would have been repairing the damage caused by the illegal operation] discussing whether to operate or just leave you to rot made my toes curl up, so what must it have been like at the time doesn't bear thinking of.' Test results showed Michael capable of having children. Years later he found his 'certificate of virility'. Jill believed that her abortions contributed to her inability to have another child.

the price you have to pay [she laughed]. And I think that's quite a decent attitude, isn't it? And that's how he is, he's pretty secretive.' In that same programme Michael agreed, 'That was a perfectly sensible thing to do.' It was the 'same principle on which Nye [Aneurin] Bevan and his wife Jennie worked, I think'.

Jill and Michael married at the Hampstead Register Office on Trafalgar Day, 21 October 1949. Michael remembered rising at Liam's house on the morning of the great day but pretending 'I was coming from somewhere else'. Michael listed his age as thirty-six and Jill put hers as thirty-five (she was actually thirty-eight) on the marriage certificate. In the box for rank or profession of the bride's father, there is only a diagonal slash next to the name of Arthur Craigie. Isaac Foot (identified as 'Privy Councillor' on the marriage certificate) along with Paul Reilly witnessed the marriage. The couple listed 62 Park Street and 9 Holly Place as their separate residences. Michael did not remember Jill's mother's presence. 'I don't think so. Jill wouldn't have had her. She was the last person Jill would have wanted at her wedding.' Julie was away at school. Michael (without Isaac, the teetotaller) went to the Savoy Hotel for drinks with Paul Reilly and Frank Owen, his former colleague at the *Evening Standard*.

Isaac was utterly charmed with Jill, and she loved him. 'My father must have been just about the happiest man who ever lived,' Michael wrote in *Debts of Honour* (1980). Like his son, Isaac had a 'zest for living and reading'. Both father and son were 'happy warriors' – the Wordsworthian term Michael applies to Isaac. He shared Jill's enthusiasm for Oscar Wilde. Indeed, Isaac had been in London during Wilde's trials. That Isaac, a staunch Liberal Party man, lost more elections than he won did not dim his spirit or his principles. He remained, as A.L. Rowse reported in *A Man of the Thirties*, convinced that someday the Liberals would return to power. He had a voice, Michael wrote, 'as rich and memorable as Devonshire cream'. And he was certainly the kind of supportive father Jill never had.

When Jill told stories about the Foot family, Isaac often had the starring role. She adored his sense of humour, which, like hers, could be self-deprecating and down to earth. 'He always went about with his hands in his pockets,' Jill said, and he was 'very slovenly in his clothes, though a very eminent gentleman. Somebody came up to him in his native town in Cornwall and said, "Mr Foot, I have great respect for you, but I don't think a gentleman of your eminence should walk about with your hands in your pockets." To which he replied: "Well now, most lawyers have their hands in other peoples' pockets."'[2] Michael could not imagine how his father, the most unworldly of lawyers, earned his living looking after other people's business.

Both Jill and Julie (despite her original antipathy towards Michael) welcomed their entrance into the Foot family. 'It was so exciting – all these people,' Julie recalled – and many of them were her age. It had always been just Jill and Julie and one other (usually Gilly). Both mother and daughter had had lonely childhoods and now they had a family at last – and one that (like Michael) took them as they were. 'We used to have these family gatherings at Pencrebar,' Michael's nephew Chris Highet remembered, cousins and uncles and aunts with 'powdery faces'. It was a large house with land that accommodated all of the visiting Foots, as well as many dogs and horses. Jill had her pick of extraordinary personalities. Chris called Mac the most exuberant. Julie thought him the most handsome Foot. He would retire for the evening by 7.30 or 8.00 p.m., saying, 'Let's get started on tomorrow', for tomorrow was sure to be 'an exciting day'. On her first visit to Pencrebar, Julie was given the 'bible room', stocked with Isaac's precious collection of bibles. She awoke at 5.00 in the morning. 'Ringing out through the whole house was Bach played on the large radiogram downstairs. There was no chance of sleeping anymore.' Michael thought John the 'best talker',* though no one could surpass Isaac (a staunch Methodist) 'in the pulpit or on the political platform – he didn't make much distinction between the two – attacking the bloody Tories'. Chris, Jill's favourite, visited her and Michael in London and thought of her as his 'London mum'.

The feminist in Jill, however, perceived a less pleasing side of the Foots. Although Michael affirmed his mother Eva's support for women's causes and her great admiration for Lady Astor, Julie remembered that 'my mother was very critical of the way the Foot family were brought up'. The girls (sisters) were 'second class citizens. The boys were everything and the girls were there to serve the boys', which meant, for example, making the boys' beds and 'fetch this for your brother, fetch that for your brother'. They did not get the same education – an especially sensitive point with Jill. Her friend Moni Forman remembered Jill would say, '"My God, you know everything is done by the women. The men sit back and don't do a thing." She did not approve. The sisters did everything for the brothers.'

Jill found an ally in John's American wife, Anne. Both Anne and Jill admired Eva, who had been a woman active in many public causes, but they learnt how disappointed she would be at the birth of a girl, since the boys were more likely to do 'interesting things'. Eva reserved certain items – like asparagus – for the men. During rationing Michael got the butter because 'Michael loves butter.' Anne wondered, 'Who doesn't?'

---

* John Foot (1909–99) became the senior partner in the family's law firm in Plymouth. He ran unsuccessfully as a Liberal candidate in four elections. He was awarded a life peerage in 1967.

Yet Jill 'pandered to my father', Michael rejoined, 'serving him the sweets he liked. He was looked after in our home the same way as he was looked after in his.' Julie suggested that her mother was a 'man's woman'. She tended to give them favoured treatment at dinner parties. She could spend a whole evening enthralled with a husband and ignoring his wife. Jill flirted. 'It was a bit of fun. She liked it, especially with attractive, well mannered men. But you had to pay attention to her. She had no time for boors,' said Moni Forman.

Michael believed that Jill took his family in her stride. 'I don't think Jill was awed by our family. She was moving around in film industry and theatre circles, after all. She got on with them all.' Michael's brothers thought her 'much the most beautiful addition to the family for generations', he claimed. 'They were greatly mystified as to how I had got this raging beauty. I'm saying that seriously.'

33 Rosslyn Hill
(1949–52)

I was taking Michael away from the peace and privacy of his tiny flat in Park Street, which he loved, to live with two females in the wilds of Hampstead.

Jill Craigie to Mervyn Jones, 26 May 1994

Soon after their marriage, Jill and Michael set up a home (with a lease from the Ecclesiastical Commissioners) at 33 Rosslyn Hill, on a main thoroughfare in Hampstead, which still exuded both a village ethos and the cosmopolitan flair Jill had come to cherish during the war. This part of London always had a pastoral air. As Al Alvarez explains, 'For the unreconstructed Londoner, Hampstead is the best possible substitute for the country.' He evokes the 'heavy scent of Hawthorn' on the Heath, the natural ponds for swimming in summer, and the autumn bushes 'thick with berries'. At one point the Heath even had a winter ski jump. Yet Hampstead had always been bohemian – a 'gentle nest of artists', as Herbert Read called it. The war brought refugees who made the streets look and sound different; they established shops and restaurants, making Hampstead seem more 'foreign' than the rest of London.[1] But in 1949 it remained a community, as Jill later commented, with shops 'handed down from father to son since the early 19th century'.[2]

Jill came into the marriage virtually wiping her slate clean. Michael does not remember her saying much about her previous marriages. He heard nothing at all about her father. In fact, Jill hardly ever referred to her past to anyone, except for anecdotes about artists, theatre people and film-makers. Michael showed little curiosity about her history. Jill regrouped, so to speak, in the Rosslyn Hill years, forming new friendships and meeting many Labour Party luminaries – some of whom welcomed her, some of whom treated her with scepticism or incomprehension. When Jill mentioned to one prominent socialist that she worked in films, he replied, 'Oh, I never go to the pictures.' It seemed a 'point of pride' with him.[3] Tony Greenwood's wife, Jill, looked at the Henry Moore drawing of the underground shelterers, which took pride of place in Rosslyn Hill, and said: 'What an ugly picture to have in a sitting room.'*

Although Mike Bessie, now pursuing a career in U.S. publishing, took an instant liking to Jill, his wife Connie did not. Connie had met Michael during the war, and he had fallen in love with her. She was the daughter of Morris Ernst, a prominent attorney famous for his work defending authors such as James Joyce in censorship cases. Michael had met and admired Ernst and now formed a close friendship with Connie. 'I don't think she liked Jill because Michael and Jill were married,' Mike said. 'She felt that Jill chose Michael not for love, but for status and a future and ambition.' Mike did not agree. But Connie's perceptions gradually changed because the affection between Michael and Connie was very strong, and Connie gradually came to appreciate – if never really to love – Jill. Barbara Castle, a close friend of Michael's, looked at Jill askance. Jill's primary attribute, in Barbara's view, was her beauty, and Barbara realized, as she put it in her autobiography, that she was not beautiful enough for Michael. As Jill told Elizabeth West many years later after her and Salman Rushdie had befriended Jill and Michael, Barbara made her feel that she was 'unworthy' of Michael. To Barbara, Jill simply did not count and could be safely ignored when she and Michael had a political discussion. That Jill did, in fact, have an intense interest in politics meant nothing to Barbara. After all, what had Jill done? Jill, in and of herself, simply did not measure up as a political asset, and for many years Barbara held the same opinion.

Richard Crossman, on the other hand, included Jill in his list of 'wonderful political wives', along with Celia Strachey and Dora Gaitskell: 'All of them are possessive women who fight for their husbands like tigers and all of them … are politicians themselves and not merely interested in politics,' he wrote in *The Diaries of a Cabinet Minister* (1975). Indeed, Crossman liked to argue with Jill. When she announced at one of their early meetings that she was a 'William Morris socialist', he scornfully replied, 'That's all over and done with.' In turn, Jill disdained the idea that Morris could ever be out of date. Both enjoyed their rousing arguments.

It gratified Michael to see that Lord Beaverbrook, who had done so much for Michael's career in journalism, take to Jill. Michael knew that the old man

---

* Anthony Greenwood (1911–82), Michael's Oxford classmate, entered Parliament in 1946 and held a number of governmental posts, including Minister of Housing (1964–6).

usually did not like his journalists' wives: 'He wanted exclusive rights.' But Jill 'knew how to deal with him from the very first meeting, how to awaken and sustain his curiosity, how to keep his eyes on today and tomorrow and not the past, how to appreciate all those human sides of him which the outside world believed not to exist'. Some observers on the left thought of Beaverbrook not merely as press lord and a Churchill crony, but also a malevolent influence in British political life – a 'kind of Dracula, Svengali, Iago and Mephistopheles rolled into one', wrote Michael in *Debts of Honour*. Yet not only did he and Jill conduct a lively, shrewd correspondence about politics, he also sponsored Jill as he had Michael, opening up an *Evening Standard* column for her in the mid- to late 1950s. 'He had infinite charm,' Jill recalled. So did the whole family, she added. As revealed in *Debts of Honour*, neither Jill nor Michael cared the slightest that their friendship with Beaverbrook might arouse disapproval, since they did not feel corrupted by his support. When A.J.P. Taylor asked Michael if he could reveal in his Beaverbrook biography that his subject had contributed £3000 in support of *Tribune*, one of the lightning rods of Labour activism, Jill joined Michael in saying 'put it in'.

It pleased Jill that Michael's principal hero, Nye Bevan, and his wife, Jennie Lee, became two of her intimate friends. Jennie Lee (1904–88) was a feisty coalminer's daughter who created a sensation in her first Parliamentary term (1929–31), and then again as the wife of the controversial but beloved leader of the Labour left. Jennie had become Jill's indispensable companion and, in a way, Jill's model. Like Jill, she exhibited an extraordinary complex of attributes that made her a living contradiction: she was a powerful woman who had relegated herself to a supporting role. As Jill wrote, 'The price Jennie paid in quiet desperation in subordinating her considerable ego to his and in becoming, of all things, a wife, struck me as the most moving and fascinating aspect of this story; a story rich in drama, conflict, high endeavour and love, sacred and profane.'[4]

Like Jill in her later years, the young Jennie was drawn to Rebecca West, jotting down while still in college West's memorable statement of 1911: 'A strong hatred is the best lamp to bear in our hands as we go over the dark places of life, cutting away the dead things men tell us to revere.' Like Jill, Jennie befriended suffragettes and 'longed to have broken windows and to have suffered in prison with them'.[5] Jennie had contended with the Labour hostility to women and had taken her place in Parliament when 'feminism was a dirty word', writes Patricia Hollis. Jennie served in Parliament at a time when women like the MP Ellen Wilkinson, a women's suffrage proponent before

World War I, now downplayed women's issues.* Jennie erupted as such a force among these women that she made Lady Astor look like a 'fluttering girl,' said Ellen Wilkinson.

Like Jill, Jennie's looks commanded attention: 'When she walked into a room, no other woman existed. Men had eyes only for her and that sultry, smokey beauty.' But Jennie had no time for flirting, and most men, including Nye, suffered her rebuffs. She had supreme self-confidence, which 'countless men found quite irresistible', her biographer reports. She shared with Jill a 'frank, physical and uninhibited' manner. A member of the Independent Labour Party (ILP), she was to the left of most Labour Party MPs in the 1930s, and she could not abide the cautiousness and conservatism of Labour Party leaders. Indeed, she didn't believe the party was capable of changing society in any fundamental sense. And she only accepted Labour Party affiliation with the advent of the war. Nye Bevan, of course, had much to do with Jennie's turn towards Labour, since he represented the alternative to the Party's cautious leadership that believed only in gradual reform. He had boldly struck out against Churchill and the Tories even during the war when they seemed invincible, predicting a Labour Party triumph that hardly anyone, save Jill, it seemed, believed likely.

Nye and Jennie were the reverse image of Michael and Jill. Like Jill, who transformed Michael into a much more culturally well-rounded person, Nye introduced Jennie to his 'range of friends inside and outside of politics, and [to] his interest in the arts, music, painting – worlds which were unfamiliar to her'. Both couples sought out a remarkable spectrum of friends that transcended political boundaries and, indeed, politics itself.

Jill and Jennie did part company on one issue. Jennie was part of a generation of women who were socialists first. When Barbara Castle argued on behalf of equal pay for equal work, Jennie responded, 'We cannot ask for equal pay when miners's wages are so low.' Castle replied, 'We will wait for ever.' In *Odd Reflections*, Jill recorded Jennie's sayings about men, such as: 'Jane's young enough to think one man is better than another.' And yet, 'women's issues bored her', Jennie Lee's biographer concludes.

By the time Jill met Jennie, the 'young priestess of the ILP, guarding the flame of pure socialism' had become second to Nye, and Jill could see why: 'He was wonderful company, witty with a brooding, soaring imagination and, as often as not, he had something fresh to say. The mere thought of him conjures up vivid scenes like a montage in a film,' Jill wrote.[6] Nye would jump

---

* The female narrator in Jill's next documentary about equal pay, *To Be a Woman*, pointedly asks whether women MPs have forgotten their sex.

to his feet as the radiogram played Handel's *Love in Bath*. He might dance; he might conduct his own orchestra, improvising with the best of them, like Peter Ustinov. More visceral than Ustinov, Nye had the 'capacity to lose himself in the music and with so much delight amazed us'.

Patricia Hollis suggests that by 1945, when Jennie re-entered Parliament, she had 'lost her nerve'. She could not 're-master' a House of Commons after a fourteen-year absence. That gap was not unlike the one that opened up for Jill after the war (1946–60), when it became impossible to direct and she had to take the subordinate role of writer. Hollis's words for Jennie seem apt for Jill: 'She chose to give up a career that it was unlikely she would command; she renounced what she might well not be offered.' Indeed, Jennie said of Nye: 'He was doing what I wanted done, infinitely better than I could have done it.' What Nye needed, what Michael needed, was a secure home base: 'It is the woman's part to give way, to make life smooth, to walk by your side,' Jennie wrote in a note to Nye she never sent. 'It is the man's part to accept the social easements on the domestic front but even in accepting to be satisfied and satiated. Dreams are reserved for the women who take, not for those who give. Giving is dowdy.'

Patricia Hollis observes that Jennie and Jill made the same decision to marry powerful men. Other women, like Barbara Castle, married men who served them essentially as wives. In Barbara's case, the marriage left her free to pursue sexual liaisons without the encumbrance of children.

Nye had a 'faculty rare in politicians', Michael notes in his biography, a 'strong visual sense' that endeared him to Jill. A man with Nye's politics who could also *see* proved irresistible to her. 'He was almost as much at home with painters as with poets,' Michael reports. As Minister of Housing as well as of Health, he 'never allowed anyone working in his department to relapse into the delusion that building houses was solely a question of economics or business. People had to live in them.' A disciple of Lewis Mumford, Nye believed housing should be part of the 'living tapestry of a mixed community', mirroring the ideas Jill had encapsulated in *The Way We Live*. Jill enjoyed the man her husband described this way: 'He never moved anywhere without looking – at the use or misuse of the countryside, at the way towns and cities had been built, at the pictures on the walls of every house he entered.'

Nye was viciously attacked in the press for incompetence (it was said his ministry did not produce enough houses) and for tyrannizing the medical profession (it was alleged he wanted to turn doctors into government employees). Doctors feared that the NHS would deprive them of their professional independence and destroy the direct relationship between doctor and patient. Yet he prevailed in the most spectacular and bitterly fought-over achievement of the Attlee government.

Nye endured as the happy warrior Michael celebrated in his father and emulated himself. Nye liked good food and theatre people – tastes right up Jill's alley. He argued the merits of *King Lear* and 'fatuities and misapprehensions of Shakespearean critics' with Dot Hyson and her husband Anthony Quayle.[7] The captivated couple became a part of Nye's company – Bevanites converted on the spot. And he did just as well with the civil servants who helped him to create the National Health Service. Nye's outspoken politics had created the impression of a strident man, yet he earned Jill's adoration because of his ability to inspire not only loyalty, but also love. Like Michael, Jill adored the sheer gaiety of the man. He 'seduced men and women alike', reports Patricia Hollis. Nye could be crude with women, but Jennie insisted he was 'an incredibly sweet tempered husband'. Jill certainly saw him as a gentle giant.

Called a 'medical Führer' by the Tories and their press, Nye remained unmoved. 'If we wait for everything to be ready,' he said, 'it will never be ready.' To Jill, whatever its shortcomings, the National Health Service – which signed up 90 per cent of the country's doctors and 95 per cent of their patients in its first year – was a phenomenal success. The aftermath of Nye's triumph, however, demonstrated to Jill why politics was a 'blood sport' – the word she chose to describe what happened to him in the partisan arena of public affairs. He got into trouble for a speech in which he tried to correct Prime Minister Attlee's praise for 'other parties' for their help in creating the 'new social services'. Nye recalled the reactionary governments of the 1930s: 'That is why no amount of cajolery can eradicate from my heart a deep burning hatred for the Tory Party. As far as I am concerned they are lower than vermin. They condemned millions of first class people to semi-starvation.' In the weeks that followed, his attack on a political party was made to seem an abuse of the eight million people who had voted Tory. His words 'undermined democracy itself', one paper announced. Attlee rebuked Bevan. The Conservatives formed Vermin Clubs and distributed Vermin Badges. Nye's house became the site of an extraordinary series of attacks. He came home to find the cream-coloured facade of 23 Cliveden Place defaced with huge black-painted words 'VERMIN VILLA'. The hate mail was the least of it. He found his letterbox full of 'dead mice, dead rats, animal droppings, even human excreta'. A newspaper tried to contrive an assignation with a prostitute, but he knocked the camera away before a picture could be taken.

In an atmosphere that now seemed surrealistic to Jill, she watched Nye day after day, turning up 'jubilant', saying, 'Tomorrow tens of thousands of people will hear who cannot hear today.' Nye saved his hatred for the press, rejecting Jill's advice that he put on a charm offensive. 'What do you take me for? A political gigolo?' he asked her. Then Churchill attacked, charging Nye with having called 'at least half the British people ... lower than vermin'. He suggested that a 'morbid hatred' had unbalanced the Minister of Health who had become a Minister of Disease. Bevan's allies now saw Churchill move in for the kill. Out for the evening to watch a film, a man pushed Nye and said, 'You haven't a clue', but Nye did not take the bait. Jill watched this powerful man powerless to change the terms of the debate. What did it matter that he had many Tory friends, that the Health Service benefited everyone and that Nye had attacked an institution, not a people?

Bevan recovered from this public assault – duelling effectively with Churchill in Parliament and rallying his own supporters – and, as Jill saw, Nye's battle strengthened his relationship with Jennie: 'Jennie felt a great compassion for Nye, admired his courage and resilience, especially his firm adherence to principle ... I think too she fell in love with Nye at that period, perhaps for the first time.' Jill felt a similar compassion after Michael's terrible election defeat in 1983, when she had to armour herself against the way the press ridiculed and demonized her husband.

To the Rosslyn Hill house came an impressive array of dinner guests. In the journalist Milton Shulman's memoirs, *Marilyn, Hitler and Me* (1998), he remembers animated evenings with Aneurin Bevan and Jennie Lee, Barbara and Ted Castle, Harold Wilson, Richard Crossman, Randolph Churchill,* actor Roger Livesey, director Frank Launder and journalists Paul Johnson and Paul Foot (Michael's nephew), whom Michael predicted would have an 'explosive effect on Fleet Street'. Paul Foot was one of Jill's favourites. Still a public school boy, he felt daunted by the distinguished political and intellectual company surrounding Jill and Michael, but she encouraged him to voice his opinions. 'She was always sticking up for me, sticking up for anyone with a point of view – even if she disagreed.' She would say, 'Shut up, and let

---

* The conservative Churchill might seem an odd friend for Jill and Michael to have cultivated, especially since he had run against Michael and lost in the 1950 election. Jill made speeches questioning Randolph's statements about coal production: 'I do know something about coal, having spent a year just recently in the mining areas,' she told voters. But the men had been colleagues on Beaverbrook's *Evening Standard*, and during their election contest Jill had noticed that Randolph seemed 'at a loose end' after a day's campaigning (according to Mervyn Jones). A word from her to Michael resulted in the two candidates and their wives having a convivial dinner in an out-of-the-way pub in Dartmoor.

the boy speak.' Paul did not want to speak.* But Jill believed that you could not get anywhere without an argument.

Paul Foot remembered visiting Rosslyn Hill, 'sitting there feeling fantastically embarrassed' as Nye Bevan fondled Jill. He was a 'groper'. In retrospect, Paul felt that Jill 'had worked it out. You don't defeat sexism by just getting on your high horse.' She used humour to deflect Nye's advances. Occasionally, she would take a teasing tack. As Nye made a pass in a taxi, she asked: 'What would you do if I called the police?' Nye answered 'I'd say: "Officer, can you blame me?"' In *Odd Reflections*, Jill wrote: 'Better to be treated as a sex object than a sexless object.'

Julie took greater offence as she watched politicians flirt with Jill. She hectored Michael about it. He would reply that of course men accosted Jill. She was an attractive woman. Malcolm Muggeridge could keep up an easy flow of conversation with Jill while making passes at her, Michael remembered. 'He was doing it all the time.'† Never a jealous man, Michael called Julie 'Iago'. He emulated the Bertrand Russell of *Marriage and Morals*: 'The purely instinctive man, if he could have his way, would have all women love him and him only; any love which they may give to other men inspires in him emotions which may easily pass into moral condemnation,' an emotion that only leads to 'melodramatic orgies of jealousy'. Michael endorsed Russell's argument that attraction to one person did not preclude 'serious affection for another'. Michael made passes at other women. He would wait for an opportunity, Drusilla Shulman said, when he had Drusilla (a remarkably beautiful woman) all to himself in a lift.‡ Russell advised: 'Each party should be able to put up with such temporary fancies as are always liable to occur, provided the underlying affection remains intact.' Michael seconded Russell's dictum that the 'serious love between man and woman' constituted the 'most fructifying of all human experiences'. Jealousy jeopardized this love by keeping husband and wife in a 'mutual prison' with no toleration for 'lapses'. Jealousy, indeed, was a 'form of persecution' placing a 'veto upon the actions of others in the name of virtue'. Jealousy came out of the religious world of taboos making 'most men and women ... incapable of being as whole-hearted and as generous in the love that they bring to marriage'. Michael was determined to overcome the restrictiveness of a conventional upbringing that prevented most couples from feeling decently about sex and marriage. In *Odd*

---

* Listening to Paul reminisce about Jill, Michael said: 'It all rings true, except that he didn't want to speak!'

† Michael has suggested that this biography should include an appendix of all the men who made passes at Jill, but such a project is beyond my capacity as a researcher.

‡ Michael's response to Drusilla Shulman: 'It depends on what you mean by a pass.'

Reflections, Jill wrote: 'Nothing will convince me that life has anything better to offer than a marriage in which both parties rate each other's welfare and happiness of supreme importance – give or take a few adulterous moments.'

Did Jill suspect that Michael had a 'few adulterous moments' at Labour Party conferences? She certainly had her suspicions, noted in *Odd Reflections*:

> Never trust secretaries.
> The most sinister of all relationships is that between a husband and his secretary.
> A secretary has more power over a man than his wife.
> The subservience of secretaries is disgusting.

It is possible, of course, that these statements have to do with power, not sex, although it is not easy to separate the two in such cases. Keenly sensitive to the rhythms of her mother's life, in her childhood Julie was unaware that Michael had been unfaithful or that it upset her mother. She only saw a wife 'besotted' with her husband. But later, when Julie was an adult, Jill would confide her suspicions to her.

To Gilly, 33 Rosslyn Hill presented a view of another world. 'It was the first house I had been in that had sheer, full-length curtains that used to billow.' Jill created ideal conditions for Michael to write, including 'plenty of wall-space for books'. As Isaac had said to her, 'Let the boy be known for his library.' She ordered a magnificent set of bookshelves made of Chilean laurel, which she had installed in the L-shaped sitting room with impressive parquet floor.

Julie relished her days with Gilly, the only real friend she felt she had. She resented being 'sent away'. At fifteen she departed for La Châtelainie, a finishing school in Saint-Blaise, Neuchâtel, Switzerland. 'I did not see it as a privilege,' she said, although she admitted liking the school and wrote enthusiastic letters to her mother, which Jill kept. Jill thought it would 'boost her morale' for Julie to learn a language, she wrote to Mervyn Jones (26 May 1994):

> I scoured the particulars of every school in Switzerland known to cater for foreigners and chose for Judy the one which offered the widest choice of subjects to study and which also organised the most exciting excursions and ski-ing expeditions. Unfortunately, it cost as much as sending a boy to Eton. For the first and only time I appealed to the father's side of the family for help, without success, though they were far better off than I was. They had never contributed so much as one garment towards Judy's maintenance.

Julie felt that her poor performance at school disappointed her mother. Jill admired high achievers and lived in and respected that world. Julie did not come up to expectations. At home with Jill and Michael in Rosslyn Hill, Julie found herself in dinner parties among writers like Milton Shulman and Arthur Koestler. 'If I ever opened my mouth, I was talked right over. Nobody was interested in anything I had to say. I don't blame them because I suppose I didn't have anything interesting to say. But it made me silent.' Jill 'put a lid on it' when she told Julie: 'Darling, don't talk about yourself. It's boring.' Julie felt stupid.

While Julie felt unappreciated, Gilly saw a different Jill. 'Jill was always encouraging me, which my parents never really did. I never sat down with my parents and said, "Should I go to a high school. Should I do this? Should I do that?"' Jill wrote in Gilly's autograph book:

> I'm sorry to harp on this dreary question, but I do think as you are a very bright girl you should make a real effort to get to the university. As for your headmistress who does not think you have the ability, I say 'to hell with school mistresses who decide in advance what girls should do.' Her job is to inspire you to make the supreme effort to rise to the top of the tree where you belong.

Jill had given Gilly a pound for the autograph book and Gilly had purchased it for ten shillings and deposited the rest in her bank account. 'Julie would have gone out and spent two pounds,' Gilly observes, 'and work out how to get the other pound out of someone else.' Jill wanted Gilly to go into the film world. Jill even offered to get her a job as a continuity girl. They would watch films together, and Jill would point out what people were wearing, how their hair was done, where they propped a bicycle, and say, 'That's in the wrong place. In the last shot it was in that way.' But the idea of a career in film appalled Gilly's parents. 'It was like going into hell.' Gilly experienced two worlds that did not mix: 'I think that if I had suggested that we have Jill and Michael to tea, my father would have thought it was a bit like inviting the devil.'

Jill praised Gilly on a regular basis. 'That's interesting,' Julie observed, in an interview with both women. 'I know what you see it [the praise] as,' Gilly said. 'Controlling,' Julie added. 'Oh no,' Gilly replied. 'Controlling was never a word in my vocabulary. I never thought of anyone as trying to control me.' 'If my mother said I couldn't do it, I believed her,' Julie confessed. 'You'll never make a writer,' Jill said to Julie after looking at one of her daughter's compositions. Without a father, the 'shy and mouse-like' Julie depended on her mother for 'everything'. Gilly agreed – 'You were terribly shy' – and usually Julie got the worst of it when Jill compared the girls: 'Gilly, you were very bright. Julie couldn't read until she was twelve.' As Gilly put it, 'There was always this sting in the tail of the praise.' Julie never resented Gilly; she resented her mother. 'Your mother had an amazing knack for hurting you. She knew just where to strike. She always went straight for the throat,' Gilly told Julie. 'I suppose she did. I never understood why she would want to,' Julie wondered. 'Julie, this had gone on from the year dot, except that as you got older, it became more hurtful,' argued Gilly.

Jill praised Julie for accomplishments Julie did not think were very clever: '"You're a great swimmer!" I wasn't a great swimmer at all. I could swim better than her. "You're a great horsewoman." I never got a first prize ever. She thought she was encouraging me and praising me for what I loved doing and was good at.' In later years Jill's friends like Glenys Kinnock remember her as taking immense pride in her daughter's achievements. After Julie had published three books, Jill said, 'You've accomplished more than me.'

Jill's keen interest in Gilly would find its parallel in Jill's involvement with other young women Julie would befriend in the 1950s. Jill was like no mother they had ever encountered. 'You should start wearing a bra, Gilly,' Jill advised an embarrassed thirteen-year-old. A shocked Gilly said, 'Oh, I don't think my Mummy thinks I'm ready.' Jill replied, 'Well, have a look. I think you are. I will get you one.' So home Gilly went with this 'thing', and her mother said: 'Oh, if Jill says so.' And that was it. Look around Gilly's home today, and you can see Jill's influence everywhere. Jill never saw the house. 'It would have given her great joy,' Julie said, for Jill would have recognized how much her taste had shaped Gilly's. 'There's nothing of my mother here,' Gilly pointed out. From Jill, Gilly learned 'acquisitiveness' – not a mere grasping after material objects, but an exquisite affinity for beautiful things that make life a work of art.

Jill had the same impact on Julie, whose talent for homemaking earned her mother's admiration, but the criticism – Gilly insisted – 'kept pouring out'. It had become an entrenched feature of the mother-daughter duel. In later years – whenever Gilly visited Jill – 'we all plunged back fifty years'. Jill heaped her dreams on Julie, wanting her daughter to be more feminist, more independent and more successful than she herself was. 'If only she could have stood back and seen what she really had, she wouldn't have been so critical,' Gilly concluded. But Jill had the attitudes of the self-made woman and of the ambitious parent: having no support from her mother, writing off her father, on her own in London at such an early age, struggling through two unsuccessful marriages, raising Julie by herself and then finally meeting a man of

Jill Craigie, 1943. This publicity shot was taken after the filming of Jill's first documentary, *Out of Chaos*. The picture was a favourite of her third husband, Michael Foot.

Jill's first marriage to Claude Begbie-Clench, an assistant studio manager for Alfred Hitchcock, 1933. Claude had an aesthetic sensibility, and Jill said he was a lot of fun, but the marriage quickly fell apart.

Jill on her wedding day with Claude's 'Unckie' Sidney, Aunt Maude's husband. Jill looks deflated, as if marrying into Claude's wealthy and conservative family overwhelmed her.

Jill's only daughter, Julie, with her father. Jill and Claude separated when Julie was a baby.

Jill's second husband, the screenwriter and playwright Jeffrey Dell, whom she married in 1938. Jeffrey helped Jill get her break in films, and they collaborated on several projects before the marriage ended.

A promotional picture taken for a feature in *The Sketch* magazine. The original caption reads, 'Reflections and Impressions ... Clever young film director, Jill Craigie, pays as much attention to her looks as she does to production details. Something a successful career woman should never forget.' Jill wanted to be taken seriously as a director and would be quite scornful in later years about the sepia glamour shots, but she also realized that the publicity brought her to the attention of the public she wanted to reach with her films.

Jill on the staircase of Frognal Lodge, Hampstead – home of the government minister Malcolm MacDonald – which she and Jeffrey Dell moved into after their house was destroyed in the Blitz. Jill apparently met Malcolm in the company of the actress Dorothy Hyson. A portrait of Malcolm's father, Ramsay MacDonald, adorns the staircase.

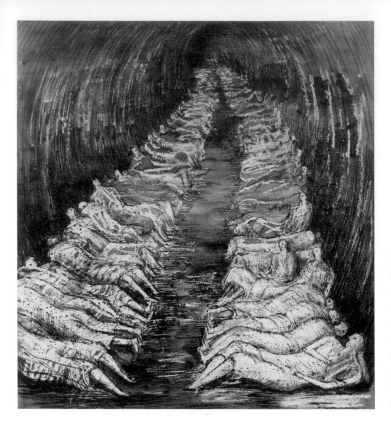

Henry Moore's wax drawing *Tube Shelter Perspective* (1941). Both artist and drawing featured in *Out of Chaos*, and Jill and Moore wandered the 'tomb'like shelters together. To Jill, the dimly lit figures looked like 'rows of Egyptian mummies'.

Jill standing in a dump for wrecked German war planes, the scene of Paul Nash's painting *Dead Sea*, which turned the wreckage into a symbolic, almost allegorical landscape.

Jill on set for *Out of Chaos*, talking to her producer Liam MacQuitty while the artist Stanley Spencer scribbles in his notebook.

Jill with (l–r) Henry Moore, Roland Penrose, the photographer Lee Miller and Moore's wife, Irina. Jill kept this photo in her *Out of Chaos* scrapbook.

Jill on set. Jill's producer, Filippo Del Giudice, sent Jill into the studio for publicity shots and played up her role as a woman director in charge of a forty-man crew. Jill noted in her scrapbook that the only other woman on the production was the continuity girl.

Aerial view of Frankfort Street, Plymouth, 1941. Plymouth had suffered grievously from German air raids that damaged not only the port installations but also large areas of civilian housing and public commerce. Jill chose to set *The Way We Live* (1946), her film about post-war reconstruction, in Plymouth because, despite the devastation, it was so picturesque 'half-surrounded by water, with stunning cliffs and two harbours'.

Jill with Liam MacQuitty (left) chatting to Sir Patrick Abercrombie during *The Way We Live*. Jill considered it a 'great triumph' to get Abercrombie, one of the architects of Plymouth's post-war reconstruction, into the film.

Jill has written on the back of the photograph: 'For Judy [Julie]. People say I look rather like you in this one.'

Jill filming with MacQuitty. They worked together on four films from 1943 to 1951 and would remain good friends. MacQuitty admired the 'very determined' Jill.

Michael Foot campaigning for the Devonport seat, Plymouth, filmed for *The Way We Live*. Jill met and fell in love with Michael during the making of this film, attracted to his capacity to change people's lives.

Jill relaxing on set. She later admitted: 'I was nervous. I looked self-confident in front of these chaps, but I wasn't … Once I'd finished the film, of course, I could only see the mistakes …'

promise who took her on her own terms. These all contributed to her feeling that now she was in some sense established. As the next generation, Julie should have gone on from there. I've taken it this far, the industrious parent says, and now the child has a running start. When the child does not appreciate this advantage, the parent is aggrieved and apprehensive. To Michael, Jill seemed so concerned about Julie, so caring and so involved with her daughter's life, that he found Julie's grievances against her mother excessive. For him, the method and the style of Jill's regard for Julie never became an issue. Focused on Jill, he defended her to the last, even while gradually forming a closer tie with Julie. 'Don't be taken in by Julie's view of her mother,' he warned. 'You knew one Jill. I knew another,' Julie responded.

Gilly watched Julie manipulating her mother, and she could imagine her friend working it out: 'There will be a problem. My mother's going out, and we're not going to be included.' Julie would immediately 'hatch up a plan', Gilly remembered, and the mother/daughter dialogue would play out this way:

'Gilly and I are going to do this…'

'You can't do that because I've got to go to the studios.'

'Well, in that case we will have to go to the studios with you.'

'Oh, that would be very awkward.'

'Well, we can come to the studios. You can take us to lunch and the car can take us back.'

'It was amazing,' Gilly said, 'and it never changed.'

Coming from a rock-solid household, Gilly represented a durable alternative to Julie's fitful upbringing. Not even politics stood in the way, even though Gilly's father voted Conservative. Gilly would return home from a visit to Julie's home and mention a guest who had discussed politics. 'Oh that would be *Labour* politics,' her father would say. Gilly did not like to start arguments; they frightened her. 'There was a rule when Aneurin Bevan and Jennie Lee were around,' Gilly recalled. 'Politics were not to be talked about because they upset me.' Abashed, Gilly did not know how to cope with all the political fervour in Julie's home, especially since nearly everything said contradicted her father's opinions. 'Everyone thought the Labour Party was wonderful, and there was a lot of banging and thrashing about that never happened in my household.' During one vehement argument, Jill saw Gilly whinging and interrupted: 'You mustn't talk politics in front of visitors. It's embarrassing.' Julie spoke up, 'Gilly's not a visitor. She's a regular customer.' Politics could not be discussed until the girlies went to bed. Aneurin Bevin used to sit there and say, 'Isn't it time for the girlies to go to bed?' Gilly liked

Bevan. He was jolly, different – full of loud Welsh talk. He seemed the same in the kitchen as in his public appearances. Gilly's relations would ask her, 'Are you still friendly with that Michael Foot's daughter? He is dreadful. He says terrible things. He will drive this country into ruin.' Gilly never became a political person, although much later she did once call Jill and Michael to report that she had voted for a local Labour candidate (but it was the man, not the party, that had appealed to her).

After boarding school, seventeen-year-old Julie decided to become an actress. She studied at the Preliminary Academy to the Royal Academy of Dramatic Arts (PRADA). She disliked her last name, which people were always getting wrong, and changed it to Hamilton. She brought her friends home. Michael remembered actresses who flirted with Aneurin Bevan. At PRADA Julie met sixteen-year-old Lizzie Parker. When Julie saw her classmate's 'piggy sort of accommodations', she said, 'Why don't you come and live with us. We have a nice big house with room. Come and meet my mum.' When Jill opened the door, Lizzie thought 'she's so tiny'. Yet Jill exuded power and beauty – especially in the depth of her eyes. She made Lizzie feel completely at ease. 'When you met her, you felt you were the only person in the world. She concentrated completely on you.' Lizzie looked around this gorgeous Rosslyn Hill home and thought, 'Why not?' Jill said, 'Right, yes, you can come. How much are you going to pay?' Lizzie hesitated and began to explain she was on a grant. 'Thirty shillings enough?' Lizzie, then paying £5 a week, said 'YES!'

33 Rosslyn Hill was 'an easy house to relax in'. It had a handsome square-shaped garden and three floors done in cool colours. They spent a lot of time in the spacious basement kitchen. A huge living room on the first floor and the bedrooms on the second provided ample room to entertain and for Isaac Foot to stay over when he visited London. Julie and Lizzie had their boy-friends in all the time and gave fantastic parties when Jill and Michael were away. 'We had total freedom in this majestic house,' Lizzie recalls. Mrs Sadler, the cleaner, was one of a succession of women Jill would employ, all of them completely loyal and on intimate terms with Jill. Lizzie thought that Mrs Sadler served as a kind of mother figure to Julie. Indeed, Julie remembered meals at Mrs Sadler's house, especially after Jill and Michael moved out of Rosslyn Hill and were looking for a new home. 'Her flat was a refuge for me and I spent many hours there regularly.' Julie would later become godmother to Mrs Sadler's daughter's son.

Lizzie watched Jill and Julie row – 'in the kitchen across a huge table, a classic shouting, screaming match about Julie not having enough attention because of Michael'. Lizzie remembered feeling embarrassed, thinking that 'Julie was in the wrong.' But then Julie did not talk about her grievances. 'Nobody's taught to be a mother. We don't have lessons in motherhood,' said Lizzie. 'Jill was the best mother she could be to Julie – in the circumstances and at the time of life I met her.' But Michael and Jill were public figures and involved in their own careers. Michael was the new man in Jill's life, and Jill was giving Michael some of the affection that Julie craved. Julie did not feel she had a family. She needed someone like Lizzie. 'She called me her cousin,' Lizzie remembered. 'Perhaps Jill ignored Julie to an extent, but on the other hand, they were really close and they could talk about things I could never talk about with my mother.' Lizzie said to Julie, 'I'm so envious. You can talk to your mother about sex and about your relationships. You have to think about that. She's not a sort of sitting at home, knitting mother.' Jill took Julie's actress friends 'under her wing'. With Michael, Lizzie had the sort of jokey relationship he had with many of Julie's friends. 'What are you two chicks up to now?' he would ask. 'What fellow will be calling at the door this week?' He always seemed to be 'in his head', yet at parties he could suddenly focus on 'dizzy Lizzie'. She was drawn to his magnetic humour and affectionate teasing. Even better, he liked to be teased. Like Julie, Lizzie had been initially repulsed by Michael's asthma and eczema and could not understand what attracted Jill to him. Yet when she came to know him, Lizzie had no trouble understanding Jill's devotion.

'In those early years,' Julie recalled, 'my mother was extremely untidy. She was not methodical. She would open letters and stuff them into the pocket of whatever she was wearing or leave it on the mantelpiece. She would look at something like her divorce papers and say, "Oh, this is horrid," and screw it up in a dressing gown, which would subsequently get thrown away.'

Paul Foot remembered visiting Rosslyn Hill on 2 June 1953, Queen Elizabeth's coronation day. He was thrilled to get the tickets to the ceremony that neither Michael nor Jill wanted. He attended the event with Julie, Paul said: 'We were absolutely bored stiff.' They returned to Rosslyn Hill. Jill opened the door and she was still in her dressing gown at 5.30 p.m. 'They were both smoking hugely then, and I remember thinking, "God, this is dissolute and degenerate." And here these people are just lying around enjoying their day. I was deeply shocked.'

To Be a Woman

(1948–51)

The fact is, the Labour Party has never regarded creative artists and craftsmen as being in the least important… It is this indifference that has lost the two most powerful media of the age, films and television, not only to Socialists but to independent-minded people whoever they may be.

Jill Craigie, 'I Call This a National Calamity', *Tribune*, 28 October 1955

In the early post-war years, cinema peaked in popularity, with over one third of the British population (20 million) attending at least one film a week presented by nearly 5000 cinemas. As President of the Board of Trade from 1947 to 1951, Harold Wilson sought ways of promoting this booming but chronically vulnerable industry, which needed government support in order to fend off an aggressive American presence. Without a quota system specifying that a certain percentage of British films had to be shown in England, Hollywood could easily have swamped Rank or Korda or any other British film company by offering cheap movies that British distributors could not resist booking. Indeed, since Rank had his own distribution chain, he could (at the urging of John Davis) obtain the cut-rate American product while trying to fabricate his own blockbuster films that he hoped would do well in both the British and American markets. British documentaries, always considered 'poor relations'[1] to feature films, were especially vulnerable. Given a choice, John Davis would much rather show a cheap (regardless of the quality) American film than a home-made documentary, no matter how good it might be. And since there were only two film distribution chains (controlled by studio executives like John Davis), there was not much chance that independent film-makers could find a niche in the domestic market.

At the Board of Trade, Harold Wilson wanted to help an industry he found glamorous and to accommodate the studio bosses who courted him. Philip Ziegler, Wilson's authorised biographer, suggests that Wilson spent more time on the film industry than it deserved in the total scheme of economic planning: 'The making of films, though not insignificant, was hardly central to Britain's economy.' On the other hand, the cinema's cultural importance, as Paul Foot argued, merited special consideration. Charles Drazin has shown that, as never before, British studios of the 1940s produced films of outstanding quality and social importance. Film had a great part to play in the rebuilding of Britain, no matter what criteria might be applied to its products.[2]

Wilson arrived on the scene at precisely the moment when Jill's own fortunes as a film-maker fell. She had placed her hopes on the development of an independent distribution circuit modelled on the lines of the BBC, which would provide opportunities for film-makers like Filippo Del Giudice and Michael Balcon – producers who were 'passionate about the film medium' and not just about the business, she told film historian Charles Drazin.[3] Surely a socialist government should not simply follow the line of the Wardour Street capitalists who bankrolled Rank and Korda, she contended. She took heart from the support of the Boulting Brothers, John and Roy, twins born in 1913, who, like her, were writers, directors and producers with a 'predilection for the socially angled theme' and for 'dashing into public controversy and tilting at the establishment'.[4] As she remarked in 'I Call This a National Calamity', their film *Pastor Hall* (1939) 'showed their Socialist faith to anyone who would listen'.

Although Jill knew Harold Wilson and he occasionally came to 33 Rosslyn Hill, she did not warm to him. Ben Pimlott, Wilson's biographer, observes that 'fellow MPs, especially middle class ones ... were variously puzzled, hurt, or contemptuous at the Wilsons' failure to join in the dinner party rituals which oiled the wheels of political intercourse amongst Labour intellectuals'. Although the Wilsons lived in Hampstead Garden Suburb, the 'Hampstead set' found him 'heavy going' on subjects such as the statistics of 'nylon stocking importation', notes Philip Knightley. This 'suburban family man' could not have been more out of sync with Jill's thinking. It made her 'blood boil', she told Drazin when she remembered how Korda 'made a bee-line for Mary Wilson, and wooed her, and flattered her'. Invited to a dinner – 'I didn't know what this dinner was, so, you know, I didn't even put on a wonderful dress or anything' – Jill found herself seated between Laurence Olivier and director Carol Reed, and among the most prominent members of the film community. Then, in front of Harold and Mary Wilson, Korda stood up and said, 'You see, I've got the British film industry – here it is.' Korda got $2 million from Wilson, and Del, Balcon and the Boultings got nothing. Then

Korda lost the $2 million, 'as we all could have told him', Jill concluded. 'It was all Harold's fault, and Harold never understood about the monopoly, he never went around with the right people anyway … he never met any socialists in the industry.'

'There are a lot of rats in the film industry,' Jill charged. Even fine film-makers like Carol Reed and David Lean were only 'concerned in their own projects and getting a break. They were hardly aware of what was happening, actually… the political significance of all this and the Korda/Harold Wilson set-up.' But she saved her ammunition for the President of the Board of Trade. In *Fighting All the Way*, Barbara Castle, a Wilson confidant, remembered how Jill 'used to corner' him 'at our parties … and attack him for not doing enough for the British film industry'. According to Castle, Jill got no support from Michael, who 'used to be as brutal with her as he often was with me: "Don't do that. No. Come off it."'

Jill was very hard on Wilson. She was equally critical of Wilson's prede-cessor, Stafford Cripps (1889–1952), who had begun this Labour relationship with the industry reactionaries. To Charles Drazin, Jill confided: 'Lady Cripps shocked me, because she used her position, and he was supposed to be the most upright fellow ever, but Lady Cripps was always saying "And can you fit dear Henry in for some job," and she rather used her position to get jobs for her relatives.' That sort of nepotism seemed to Jill no different from that exhibited by Korda, who hired family members and did little to promote British talent. Jill seems to have felt a special bitterness for Korda, judging by her attack on him during an interview with film historian Philip Kemp. Denis Forman remembers that for a brief period she tried unsuccessfully to become a part of Korda's circle.

According to Knightley, Wilson was not quite so taken in by Korda as Jill supposed. When Korda told him about *Bonnie Prince Charlie* and another film set in the sewers of Vienna (*The Third Man*?), Wilson 'groaned' and said both projects would lose money. Most commentators agree that the National Film Finance Corporation (NFFC) that Wilson set up in 1948 did some good in sustaining the British film industry – certainly more than a Conservative government would have been willing to do. But Paul Foot's assessment is sound: Wilson missed a great opportunity to create a government-sponsored alternative to the monopoly that basically shut out the independent pro-ducers who had been responsible for many of Britain's greatest achievements in film. Jill's argument that Wilson never bothered to understand the dynamics of the industry gains strength with Knightley's comment that 'Wilson loved details', and did not always see the 'wood in spite of the trees'.* Knightley also seconds Foot's point that Wilson and Wardour Street spoke the same language, 'unabashedly capitalistic and chauvinistic'. The consequences for independent film producers were disastrous. As Ernest Betts concludes: 'The language of the shareholder falls naturally into place and that of the independent film producer or director is more or less irrelevant or limited to the submission of projects.' Jill lived in Wilson's own neighbourhood, so to speak, and the man simply would not listen! Wilson did not build on what Paul Foot calls the 'new idealism … born out of contempt for the political and cultural sterility of the inter-war years and the hope of a new socialist era'. In his *Memoirs* (1986), Wilson reveals his complete misunderstanding of British film when he calls Sir Stafford Cripps, his predecessor at the Board of Trade, a 'soft touch' for an 'immigrant film producer named Del Giudice'. Cripps, 'counting every penny for the welfare state', was nevertheless 'ready to raid the tills for Del'.

One man who did listen to Jill, Mervyn Jones points out, was Michael Foot. In a Commons speech he proposed that Wilson's creation, the NFFC, provide loans for scriptwriters as well as producers. The ideas came from writers, he well knew. It was 'absolutely fantastic to say there is a shortage of ideas or talent', he declared. He deplored a state of affairs that subordinated the work of artists and technicians to dictatorial distributors and studio regimes.

Jill watched in dismay as the socialist, democratic ethos of the war years evaporated: 'The debutantes came back. It all came back overnight. It was something to do with the *Daily Express* and *Daily Mail*. They helped sort of change the mood. It was alarming… It was a return to the class system in a big way.' Jill believed that although the war had seemed to liberate women, in fact it consolidated anti-feminism. How wonderful that women became fire-fighters, welders and tractor drivers, she agreed, but these were thought of as men's jobs temporarily held by women. The changes during the war had no 'deep roots', and afterwards women were driven 'back to the home'. Jill's feminism isolated her: she imagined people saying, 'there's something rather wrong with her, you know'.[5]

Films reflected the shift in political attitudes. Interest in documentaries waned, Ernest Betts notes, and the 1950s – Drazin's 'decade of Family Entertainment' – dispatched films into the doldrums, so that even the greatest documentary film-makers had almost no scope for their work. If Humphrey

---

* Paul Foot gives Wilson more credit than Jill did – at least for understanding the issues – arguing that those in favour of a third, independent circuit had his backing. In the event, however, the NFFC did nothing whatsoever to break the monopoly. Wilson opted instead for what Foot calls a 'shoddy mixture of statist interference and patronage'. See Charles Drazin's treatment of Korda's manipulation of Wilson in *The Finest Years*.

Jennings, who died in 1950, had lived longer, he would 'have to have done a feature, and he wouldn't have lasted a week', John Krish, a director of British features in the 1950s, told Drazin.

At the start of the 1950s Jill was without work, managing to pull off just two projects: *The Women's Rebellion: A Dramatised Impression of the Suffragette Movement*, broadcast on BBC radio on 13 March 1951, and a documentary arguing for equal pay, *To Be a Woman* (1951), with money raised by women's organizations and under the auspices of William MacQuitty's company, Outlook Films. With the suffragettes and feminism now a forgotten cause, she sought to raise public consciousness.

Jill's radio play aimed to shatter the 'picture of a hysterical spinster of amazonian proportions making herself ridiculous by chaining herself to railings. This is so far from the truth that it is a little shocking that none of our historians has yet treated the subject conscientiously,' she wrote in the *Radio Times* (9 March 1951). The play demonstrated why the suffragettes believed they had to abandon fifty years of peaceful effort to get the vote. Aside from the narration, virtually the entire dialogue of *The Women's Rebellion* is taken from the historical record and from the testimonies Jill had solicited during the early 1940s. The play offers a swift, incisive vignette of the Votes for Women movement, easing listeners into the sounds and sights of Edwardian England: 'Life moved at a dignified pace to the gentle accompaniment of horses hooves.' But this world of etiquette books and women in bustles attached to chaperones was already threatened by the 'absurd looking monster of the motor car', the politics of Labour leader Keir Hardie (Emmeline Pankhurst's friend, and a supporter of votes for women), the agitation of trade unions and a swelling atmosphere of rebellion. The voices of a Lancashire mill girl, a middle-class woman and other women of different ages and classes quickly follow, evoking the drudgery of women's lives, their confinement in limited domestic roles and their vulnerability in marriages their husbands could respect or repudiate as they liked. A working-class woman cries out: 'If I don't work, how can I feed them [her children] and pay the rent? And if I *am* working, how can I care for them during the day?' The play then introduces Emmeline Pankhurst, whose work as a Registrar of Births and Deaths on the Manchester City Council brought her a palpable understanding of poverty and the lack of legal protections that put 'political shackles' on women, preventing them from vanquishing their plight.

'Liberals all over England,' the narrator notes, shared Mrs Pankhurst's belief that the 'vote was the only means of ensuring justice for women'. Pankhurst became the focal point of women, who believed her position gave her the visibility to raise the issue in the public's mind. The play reveals how early on Jill staked out her position along Mrs Pankhurst's lines – emphasizing that neither the labour union movement nor socialism *per se* were enough in so far as making a just world for women was concerned. When a woman explains that the Manchester Technical College provides no training for women and will not admit them even to bakery and confectionery classes, and that the trade unions object to educating women, Mrs Pankhurst observes: 'And I once used to think that the Trade Unions would be our greatest champion.'

The play accelerates to four years later when Christabel Pankhurst asks her mother how long she has worked to get the vote. The answer is 'a lifetime', to which Christabel makes her famous reply: 'For my part, I mean to *get* it.' She then embarks on a career of militancy, interrupting the great Liberal politician Sir Edward Grey and demanding to know when women's suffrage is to be made a government measure. Scenes of Christabel, Annie Kenney and numerous women pressing Winston Churchill and other Liberals to answer this question shift to brief speeches by Keir Hardie standing out as a lone male voice in Parliament arguing the suffragette case. With the formation of the Women's Social and Political Union (WSPU), headed by Mrs Pankhurst and marshalled into action by Christabel, groups of women confront the Prime Minister (Campbell Bannerman), pointing out that a majority in the House of Commons is already prepared to give women the vote. But with his Cabinet 'not yet fully agreed to the issue', he preaches the 'virtue of patience'.

Events escalates throughout 1907 and 1908, as the newspapers dub Christabel 'Queen of the Mob' and the public splits over how to respond to the spectacle of women in full, open public protest: 'But the more the Suffragettes aroused sympathy, the more they aroused opposition.' Male voices are heard discounting women's rights because they do not fight in wars and they cannot win their place by arms as men do; women would impose impossible moral standards and enter Parliament in such numbers as to dominate the making of laws. When Christabel assembles masses of women to 'rush' the House of Commons, she is hauled into court on a charge of 'incitement to riot'. The finest scenes of the play unfold with Christabel confronting first Lloyd George and then Herbert Asquith, turning their political statements against them and towards support of her own actions. Trained as a lawyer, she notes that *Chambers Dictionary* defines 'rush' as an 'eager demand' and an 'urgent pressure of business'. She forces Lloyd George to admit that MPs speak of 'rushing' bills through Parliament. In her crowning moment she asks him about the author of these words spoken in Trafalgar

Square: 'I am sorry to say that if no instructions had ever been addressed in political crises to the people of this country, except to remember to leave violence and love order and exercise patience, the liberties of this country would never have been attained.' When Lloyd George cannot identify the author, Christabel informs him: 'Those were the words of William Ewart Gladstone.' Thus in a courtroom full of Liberal statesman and establishment figures, she throws at them a great Liberal leader's own incitement. Christabel goes on to show that Lloyd George himself and Joseph Chamberlain and other Liberals have taken extra parliamentary action when they wanted to pressure or 'rush' Parliament. She quotes Herbert Gladstone's own words to him in court: 'There comes a time when political dynamics are far more important than political arguments,' a time when the 'necessity for demonstrating the "*force majeure*" which arms and actuates a Government for effective work'.

In spite of Christabel's brilliant performance, she and other women lost the case and went to prison. Yet by 1909, the narrator notes, the WSPU had a 'credit balance of a million pounds'. While their paper, *Votes for Women*, sold 16,000 copies a week, government opposition hardened and the police became brutal – 'arms twisted, skirts pulled over heads, bodies knocked and dragged about the streets'. Mrs Pankhurst replied to such assaults: 'Let it be the windows of the Government, not the bodies of the women that shall be broken.' Carefully calculated public acts of violence – assaults on property and disruptions of Liberal political meetings, including the spectacular scene of Charlotte Marsh and Mary Leigh on the roof of the building where Prime Minister Asquith was to speak hurling slates at the police, who hose them down – express the determination and exhilaration of women fighting for their rights. 'The water is very refreshing. Do you know I am really enjoying it,' says Marsh, who with Mary begins to sing.

This exuberance is suddenly cut off by a very brief scene of forcible feeding, immediately followed by a doctor's protest that the use of a rubber tube with a hard end inserted into the mouth and down the throat into the stomach or forced up a nostril produces nausea and laceration of the throat and is liable to cause other grave injuries resulting in septic pneumonia. Heart attack and even death may follow. Two hundred doctors and prominent public figures such as George Bernard Shaw and John Galsworthy decried the government's actions. Labour leader George Lansbury is heard telling Asquith: 'You will go down in history as the man who tortured women.' Suffragettes did have their health permanently damaged and some did die, prompting Mrs Pankhurst to say: 'I am no longer a human being. I am an instrument of faith, and as such I shall be given my niche in history.'

Sylvia Pankhurst has a very minor role to play in this drama, but she does come in towards the end and is credited with assembling a 'huge deputation of women from the East End of London who at last wrung from the Prime Minister, Mr Asquith, the first words of promise'. He at last seems to acknowledge the inevitable: 'If the change has to come, we must face it boldly and make it thorough going and democratic in its basis.' The play then comes rapidly to a close, as Mrs Pankhurst and Christabel suspend their agitation to throw themselves into the war effort. 'We women must put our country first,' Mrs Pankhurst declares, calling for the 'industrial conscription of women'. The narrator observes that, 'It was said that help was promised in return for the vote at some future date.' Jill leaves open, in other words, whether or not such a precise quid pro quo was arranged – largely because, as she would later write, she did not believe that Mrs Pankhurst was anything other than a patriot first.

The play ends with the narrator's quick summary of the suffrage bills of 1918 and 1928 granting women their rights as voters, the statue erected to Mrs Pankhurst, and Charlotte Marsh's words – the very words spoken to Jill at Mrs Pankhurst's statue: 'I lived for the Movement. We gave up everything for it. Our personal lives, our freedom. I was forcibly fed 136 times. I would do it all over again. Women have no idea how much they have gained.' The speech goes on to enumerate the fifty acts of Parliament that made lives better for women and children. 'Today, women have rights,' Charlotte concludes.

After the broadcast, letters poured in – praise from suffragettes and from others with memories of them. Some sent snatches of campaign songs: 'I beg you all to note/That we mean to get the vote/Or we'll all become most obstinate resisters.' One correspondent remembered how her usually meek mother could not abide her domineering husband's attack on Mrs Pankhurst and jumped to her feet telling him to 'shut up', saying, 'I wish I was at Mrs Pankhurst's side – carrying a banner – I'd show some of the men.' Another wrote to tell Jill how at seventeen she would spend her Saturday afternoons dressed in prison clothes driving on lorries round Holloway Prison 'cheering the women in there'.*

This spirit of activism also fuels the outrage expressed in *To Be a Woman*. The film opens with shots contrasting a young woman dressed in the fashion of 1950 on the way to work with a woman walking in the formal, confining dress of the late Victorian age. How do these women compare, the female

---

* The only sour note came from Jessie Kenney, who felt her sister Annie had not been given enough credit for rousing the suffragettes into action. She accused Jill of shortchanging Annie because Annie had not co-operated with Jill's plans to make a film about the movement.

narrator (the actress Wendy Hiller) asks? How does the modern woman match up to the woman whom John Stuart Mill found in a state of subjection (a subtitle reads 'Women, Criminals and Lunatics May Not Vote'). 'Can she develop her individual talents? Can she create the kind of society she wants?' the narrator asks during shots of a young woman typing. 'What does it mean in twentieth-century Britain to be a woman?'

During shots of women employed in various industries and businesses, the narrator observes: 'If anyone dares to resurrect that cliché that woman's place is in the home, let them contemplate the sight of millions of women outside of the home earning their own living.' Almost a third of these women are married. Two men look askance at a woman delivery driver, prompting the female narrator to say, 'Women work while men weep. Not that they've ever wept much over this [shots of a woman on her knees washing stone steps] or for that matter this [a scene of women dancing the can-can].'

A male voice intrudes: 'But it seems that young women with their lives before them can do what they like.' Women can rise to Cabinet rank and have career and marriage at the same time, he asserts. 'What more do women want?' Shots of very young, rather wistful-looking girls introduce a series of statements by leaders of women's groups, noting women do not have equal opportunity for training in all professions and technical specialities; they are not yet represented in large numbers in Parliament or in local government; they do not have their incomes assessed and taxed separately.

Then a cut to a woman knitting prompts the male narrator to say, 'Isn't she more representative of the average woman?' The knitter says she does not believe in 'all this equality nonsense', and would rather stay at home and raise a family. Besides, women don't like to work under women, she says. And, she asks, who would employ the average woman? Her remarks are overridden by the introduction of prominent women in the arts, medicine, engineering, publishing and trade unions, shots that in turn segue to the female narrator, who intones: 'Prejudice dies hard. Sometimes it even finds quite lucid expression.' Then an older man, seated in a plush chair, his paunch protruding, plays 'devil's advocate'. It is Professor Joad, a national figure at the time who often appeared on the *Brains Trust* radio programme with Michael Foot and other public figures. Joad argues that 'on the whole' the entrance of women into the workforce has been a 'mistake'. The 'general level of happiness', he contends, is 'lower since women left their homes'. Are women making great discoveries or creating great works of art or ruling countries? 'Of course they're not. They are acting as drudges for the men.' The female narrator counters: 'But what are the facts, Professor Joad?' A shop window displays books by women, and the narrator mentions that painters like Berthe Morisot and Frances Hodgkins have international reputations. A shot shows Jill pointing at a painting in a window and arguing with her male companion. Then a shot of composer Elisabeth Lutyens follows (she composed the music for the film).

The film attacks the argument that men need higher wages than women to support their families. Shouldn't a man with a family get more than a spinster? a male voice breaks in. Well then, the married man should get more than the bachelor, the female narrator responds. Less than half of the male workforce supports families. Most women are doing two jobs: taking care of home and family and teaching school or doing some other job outside the home. The scene shifts to a married man at his breakfast table while the woman is cooking and cleaning up not only for him, but also for an elderly gentleman, presumably her father or his. The man is getting 'value and service'. The wife is hardly a 'dead weight'.

Ian Mikardo, Michael's colleague in Parliament, is introduced as an industrial consultant.* Mikardo explains what work costs in a factory. The way to keeps costs and prices steady is 'not to pay the person doing the job but pay the job. The State looks after the extra needs which come out of the extra responsibilities of wife and children to a certain extent through family allowances, income tax rebates and provisions for education and the like. The same job done with the same level of skill and effort must always be paid for in the same way,' he concludes.

Then the film begins its peroration, the narrator pointing out that women now staff many industries that men once dominated. 'Women are cheap labour' becomes the refrain, as scenes follow of women making glass, operating cranes and entering new industries such as plastics and radio, where 'employers hardly consider taking on men at all'. The woman who sells shoes gets less than the man who sells shoes (shot of a man ogling a woman clerk in a shoe store). Where there is male unemployment, it has often been caused by employing women as 'cheap labour. When unemployment was at its peak in Britain, the number of women employed was steadily rising.' This process of undercutting male labour leads to unemployment, even when government invests in industry. 'But where women are paid the rate for the job – in the BBC and in Parliament – the men are none the worse.' Is a man's job safe as long as women are able to undercut the men?' The male voice intrudes again,

---

* Ian Mikardo (1908–83) was elected in the 1945 landslide and became a confidant of Michael's and a Bevanite. He remained a backbench leftist his entire career – respected and feared by not only the opposition but also his own party leaders because of his formidable debating style and firm grasp of business principles.

'But all political parties agree with the principle of equal pay. But now isn't the time.' The female narrator rejoins, 'Now is never the time,' as footage of suffragettes parading and protesting is shown. 'Women were fighting for the rate for the job even before they went to prison to get the vote.'

The narrator now raises her voice, asking if some of the women in parliament have forgotten the 'cause of women'. The male interrupts, 'But the Chancellor of the Exchequer has told them that it will lead to inflation', to which the narrator responds: 'We who represent millions of women and all political parties – civil servants, teachers, bank clerks, businesswomen and industrial workers ask: "Would anyone of integrity mention difficulties paying him [a man with a shovel digging out a rail track] less for the job because he is a Catholic? Or him [a man stirring cement] because he is a refugee? Or him [a glassmaker] because of the colour of his skin? Or him [a man washing windows] because he has ginger hair?" But we insult women in this way.' The narrator points out that Britain has signed the universal declaration of human rights, which specifies equal pay for equal work. 'Was this signed in good faith or in hypocrisy?' the narrator asks. The film concludes by returning to the modern woman now leaving her employment. The narrator asks: 'Isn't it time we in Britain make it a proud thing to be a woman?'

In spite of its provocative tone, Jill's film roused little interest and was not widely reviewed. It did not have a theatrical release. She kept only one brief unidentified news item about the documentary in her papers. Later, for the television program *Fifties Features*, she dismissed her film as 'very cheap', saying it was 'not very good and I wasn't very satisfied, but I did my best at the time'. Like many of her dismissive comments about her work, this one has to be viewed with caution, since she judged herself by the highest standards, and like most artists felt disappointed when her work did not live up to her ideal conception of it. On the same programme Jill characteristically expressed pride in having employed composer Elisabeth Lutyens at the suggestion of Sir Arthur Bliss, who told her Lutyens 'makes amazing sounds, you must have her'. Lutyens gave her exactly the kind of 'really good modern' score Jill wanted, an intermittent, percussive aural commentary that is virtually all drumbeats, clashing cymbals, gongs, xylophone riffs and ringing bells.

In this film Jill is at the end of her tether. It is a passionate, uncompromising work. It is full of good argument but it does not have the playful, cunning tone that might have disarmed an audience and an industry that had little patience for the film's subject matter. When Mervyn Jones told Jill how much he liked the film, she called it 'rotten', adding 'I'm not proud of it.' *To Be a*

Woman marked, in Jill's own mind, her final bitter effort to survive as a documentary film-maker.

To Be a Woman is not a bad film. Indeed, it is a striking document made at a time when the political tide was against making women's issues a pivotal concern. Jill's ability to see beyond the immediate demands of rebuilding post-war Britain makes her film more relevant than ever to a vision of society based on the equal treatment of the sexes.

13

Rape
(1952)

On 4 May 1952 the writer Arthur Koestler (1905–83), an acquaintance of Michael's, phoned Rosslyn Hill and Jill answered.[1] He announced his decision to settle in England, and he said he wanted to celebrate by going on a pub crawl. Jill said Michael was away for the weekend, but that made no difference to Koestler. Jill felt she could not refuse him after he had been so hospitable to her and Michael during their visit to Verte Rive, France, the previous summer. They had stayed at his private suite in Fontainebleau, and he had taken them up to Montmartre. Michael took a special delight in Koestler: 'He could make you laugh, you know. Throughout the war, I think I knew him as well as anybody.' In *Loyalists and Loners* (1986), Michael wrote:

> Who will ever forget the moment he read *Darkness at Noon*? For Socialists especially, the experience was indelible. I can recall reading it right through one night, horror-struck, over-powered, enthralled. If this was the true revelation of what had happened at the great Stalin show trials, and it was hard to see how a single theoretical dent could be made in it, a terrifying shaft of darkness was cast over the future no less than the past.

Koestler proved no less formidable in person than in print. Michael had met him in London in 1940, when Koestler 'brought ashore with him a distinctive knowledge of how the continent had been subdued, and how we too might be engulfed by the new barbarisms'. Michael did not agree with all of Koestler's opinions, but Koestler seemed indispensable, the 'most powerful arguer I ever met', combining 'logic, passion and historical insight' in a relentless onslaught on anyone who engaged him.[2]

Koestler's mesmerizing power was 'quite a feat', Michael adds, for a 'shy, fragile, rootless, self-conscious, guilt-ridden Hungarian Jew who arrived near-penniless on our shores'. Michael 'fell an immediate swooning victim to his wit, charm and inordinate capacity for alcohol'. By 1941, as acting editor of the *Evening Standard*, he had hired Koestler to write a column – to the delight of Beaverbrook, who recognized how much Koestler had to tell the English about what had happened on the Continent. But the column ran afoul of censors and Michael realized that his new friend could be troublesome – indeed, frightening: 'Koestler got you in a corner, with all escapes blocked and machine-gunned', with 'mounting, insensate, satanic virulence'. Drink made Koestler especially aggressive and a 'different kind of man altogether', Michael said.

Koestler arrived at 33 Rosslyn Hill early in the day, and Jill immediately set off with him to point out the homes of the prominent and the pubs of the celebrated. Koestler had a drink at every stop but he showed no signs of getting drunk. Jill, never a big drinker, had ginger beer. He behaved quite properly and Jill had merely been sociable. 'There was no sign of him flirting with me,' she recalled. Suddenly Koestler demanded that Jill fix him lunch. She demurred, saying she had been working on a film and did not have much in the house. Why not a typical English roast beef lunch in a pub? No, he insisted on a home-cooked meal and she relented, taking him home for an omelette. Afterwards he helped her wash up. She hoped this would put him off. Taking him round had been a chore: 'I felt that I had been lumbered with him. If I'd been interested in the fellow, I'd have sat down and offered him some brandy.' As she put down her dish cloth, he grabbed her hair, pulling her down so brutally that he banged her head on the floor. Jill, nearly knocked out, struggled to recover her senses, finally fighting back and managing to break free.

Jill sat outside on the house steps in her torn clothes, just a short way from the police station across the street. She could have been there in a minute. But she had admitted Koestler to her home. 'It did not look good,' she thought. She imagined the headlines and concluded, 'No woman could have stood that. I couldn't have done that to Michael.' She thought of the publicity, of the prying questions she would be asked, of how she could possibly explain what she had been doing with Koestler. Instead, she waited to see if he would emerge from the house. When he did not, she went in, supposing he would have calmed down and realized he had made a fool of himself. 'I took a chance ... which was rather stupid of me,' she told Koestler's biographer, David Cesarani decades later, after the rape had become public knowledge. Koestler attacked again, this time grabbing Jill's throat. 'I was worried about my life, not my honour,' she told Libby Brooks. Terrified and exhausted, she gave up the struggle: 'There's a limit to how much strength one has and he was a very strong man. And that was it.' Jill had always imagined, she told Michael years later, that she would be able to resist a rape attempt, but Koestler had caught her by surprise. Koestler got up with these parting words: 'I thought you always had a bit of a yen for me.'

Jill knew nothing about Koestler's relationships with women. 'I just thought he had gone mad. I never knew he could do such a thing.' But his ruthless and experienced assault made her suspect that he had raped other women.* The assault was not about sex but about the desire to exert his power, and this man had the confidence to believe he could get away with it.

What should Jill tell Michael? She did not mention bruising in any of her accounts, but how could such a violent episode not leave marks? Cesarini reports that she 'merely said' to Michael that 'she had been in a terrible fight with Koestler'. But Michael did not remember Jill mentioning a fight with Koestler or saying anything that would have aroused his suspicion.

Jill confided in director Ronnie Neame the day after the rape, when they met, as scheduled, for a script conference.† Contacted in Beverly Hills nearly fifty years after the rape, he did not know that Jill had discussed it publicly and was reluctant to say anything about it. But after assurances that he was not betraying a confidence, he confirmed that Jill had entrusted her secret to him. After so many years, it is not surprising that his recollection differs from hers in some details, though the essential facts remain the same. In Ronnie's version Koestler had left the house after a visit and then returned, forcing his way in with a foot in the door, telling Jill, 'This is going to happen whether you like it or not.' How much Jill might have struggled, Ronnie could not say – perhaps Jill did not say. But when he heard that Jill said she did not tell Michael, Ronnie was astonished: '*Really?* That I find very hard to believe. I was always under the impression that she had told Michael and that he had understood "up to a point", and that the matter was then dropped. It's a big surprise to me that Michael didn't know.' Perfectly willing to admit he might have got Jill wrong, Ronnie nevertheless emphasized his impression that she had told Michael by the time she talked to him. Jill would later confide to Libby Brooks that she had told 'her producer' about the attack and that he said, 'Don't tell Michael, for God's sake.'‡ She had been married to Michael for less than three years, and she 'only had eyes for him. I didn't regard Koestler as a celebrity, just as a friend of my husband's. Michael would have felt that he ought to sock him.'

---

* The circumstances in which Jill revealed the rape and in which it became public knowledge have been misreported many times. See Chapter 29.

† Jill's relationship with Neame is discussed in the next chapter.

‡ Was Jill referring to Ronnie Neame or to his partner John Bryan, who produced Neame's films? Neame does not think Jill told Bryan (now deceased).

'I was anxious to bury it, to suppress it,' Jill said. But 'it kept recurring in my sleep. I had nightmares.' Over the years she confided her burden to a few friends. Julie first heard the story sometime in the late 1970s when she had taken a 'terrible risk' with a man. Michael never met Koestler again. They had parted over 'differences about the bomb'. They no longer shared political sympathies. Asked what he would have done if Jill had told him, Michael said: 'I don't know. I think I would have written him a letter – something like that … "our friendship is at an end".'

For Jill, any course of action entailed appalling consequences, and inaction only served to increase her pain and isolation. Her rape brought home the truth that women remain singularly vulnerable. 'Her rape is pretty central to the story of her life,' David Leigh, one of Michael's biographers, observed:

> The world that made it impossible for her to do anything about the rape is the same world that made it impossible for her to do a lot of other things, I thought when I heard about the rape. How could you suppress that? How could you be suppressed about that? Because you learn to accommodate yourself to being suppressed about so much. When you do not deal with such a violation, it does enormous damage.

As Jill sat on the steps of 33 Rosslyn Hill, she thought of calling Jennie Lee and Nye Bevan, whom she regarded now as her closest friends. But they were away in Nye's constituency. She apparently never did tell them. Instead, the rape became a story refracted only through Jill's sensibility. The rape, in effect, became a parable of everything Jill could not say, of everything she felt she could not change about the condition of woman.

Decades later, during a conversation with intimate friends in her home, Jill blurted out the story of the rape, a story that Michael would then allude to in a newspaper book review, causing a public controversy that would shadow the last years of Jill's life. Michael Scammell, Koestler's authorised biographer, would attack Jill's credibility, and only then would the full implications and consequences of the rape be revealed.*

* See Chapter 29.

Screenwriter
(1952–8)

The terrible thing is to have ambitions … I met Harold French, and he was a lovely man, very, very modest, and he said that what he wanted to do was to make his film, and then go home and play bridge. He didn't mind what he made, just made whatever he was told to make, and that was fine, and he had a happy life as one of the most sought-after directors, and that was the recipe for contentment.

> Jill Craigie in conversation with Charles Drazin, 14 November 1994

Personal happiness and the success of her marriage began to outweigh any hopes Jill had of remaining a film director. Writing kept her at home and at Michael's side. Jill had 'very good ideas,' says director Ronald Neame (1911–) and 'an inventive mind' – as he discovered when he consulted her about the screenplay for *The Card* (1952), starring Alec Guinness. Other directors came to her with problems. She had worked (uncredited) with director Henry Cornelius (1913–58) on a wartime documentary, *Painted Boats*. Cornelius wanted her advice on the making of *Genevieve* (1953), a comedy that every important producer turned down as 'too slight' but which Jill thought a masterpiece. Although everyone except Jill seemed to think the film would be a box-office disaster, it became a very profitable and critically successful film, with an Academy Award nomination for best story and screenplay.

Jill encouraged Cornelius to employ Larry Adler, blacklisted in the US, to do the musical score (which was also nominated for an Academy Award), and she helped him find financing from a wealthy communist troubled over how much money he had. His psychiatrist thought he would lose his 'guilt complex' if he lost money on a picture.[1]

Jill told an interviewer: 'I did quite a lot with Henry Cornelius, although I don't have a credit, but I did work a lot with him in *Genevieve*, actually. He was very funny.' It is difficult not to see Jill's influence everywhere in this film. The plot concerns a husband, Alan McKim (John Gregson), who is far more attuned to the workings of his prize vintage car, Genevieve (whom he calls 'the old girl'), than he is to his beautiful wife Wendy (Dinah Sheridan). Alan bullies his bored wife into driving from London to Brighton in Genevieve every year to attend his vintage automobile club's annual event. The car breaks down repeatedly – as does the relationship between Alan and Wendy. Alan's oafish friend, Ambrose, does not do much better with women. He rides to Brighton in his vintage car with his girlfriend Rosalind (Kay Kendal). To both women the men seem silly, engaging in bets and male tests of prowess. Cars become a perfect metaphor for the driven male ego, 'pompous and stuffy', as Wendy remarks when she sees that Alan is jealous of Ambrose, whom he suspects might have had an affair with Wendy. That her husband could so misread his best friend's character at first amuses then disgusts Wendy. When Alan and Ambrose engage in an adolescent fight, Rosalind asks, 'Isn't this becoming a bit frantic?' Rosalind reflects the temper of the times when she surprises everyone in a club by playing a jazzy trumpet far better than the professionals. Although Ambrose is elated, her performance (imagine, a woman can blow her own horn!) does nothing to check his boorish treatment of her.

Jill thought sex the perfect comic vehicle for exploring the differences between men and women. She delighted in exposing men's sexual posturing and how women got caught up in their own contradictions and absurdities in sexual matters. Wendy, for example, drops her objections to Alan's vintage car excursion when she rediscovers the Edwardian hat and dress she wore on their first motoring trip. Now the trip becomes romantic and she can relive her courting days. The trip also becomes a chance to display her handsome ensemble – and then Wendy's own vanity is affronted when the car backfires and she spills coffee all over her grand costume.

The male, competitive world – there is a good deal of shoving women about in *Genevieve* – is made to appear absurd, not reprehensible. This slant reflects Jill's own feeling at the time that humour, rather than the earnestness of *To Be a Woman*, might be her best weapon. In any event, she turned next to working with men on comic scripts (William Rose wrote the script for *Genevieve*). She liked and trusted Ronnie Neame, with his big, blustery and kind ways. 'Come in and talk to Ronnie,' Jill would say to Julie and Lizzie, who found him always genial, humorous and genuinely comfortable and interested in their company. 'He was around a lot,' Lizzie recalled, 'a noticeable presence' at Rosslyn Hill.

Ronnie first met Jill in the late 1940s and remembered that her socialism more than her feminism set her apart, although she got along with Tories much better than Michael, Neame believed. She was also more free to criticize the left, he suggested: 'She used to have quite a go at Nye Bevan.' She was outspoken and frank about Michael's political allies, 'but not in a bitchy way'. Neame got his start in the film industry as an assistant cameraman on Alfred Hitchcock's *Blackmail* (1929) and established himself as one of the finest cinematographers in British film history. After a successful partnership with director David Lean, he was just embarking on his career as a director when he befriended Jill after her election to the British Film Academy. Neame welcomed her into an organization that had few places for women and that needed her energy and experience as a young and enthusiastic documentary film-maker modest about her accomplishments and eager to learn. Attractive ('very pretty,' Neame emphasizes) and personable as well, Jill was irresistible.

The Film Academy board met once a month, and Jill often stayed on to join a 'warm, friendly' group of three or four at a pub. She soon introduced Ronnie to Michael, whom he had always heard called a communist and 'not a very nice man'. People used to come up to Jill and say, 'What a shame you're married to that awful man.' Jill took it in her stride, Ronnie said. 'It never really upset her.' Ronnie found Michael 'an absolute sweetheart, a charming man'. Like Liam McQuitty, however, Ronnie thought Michael was 'up in the clouds, completely unrealistic. He would like a world that is just not practical or possible.' The public saw only the strident 'soapbox' Michael Foot, Neame realized. They did not know that after his combative television performances he would dine amicably with his political opponents. Neame would have friendly arguments with Michael about his socialism: 'Michael, if you made everyone equal, within a few years there would be rich ones and poor ones, and successful ones and unsuccessful ones.' Ronnie came to Jill with the idea for *The Million Pound Note* (1953). His partner, John Bryan, had read Mark Twain's story and thought it would make a fine film. The concept was simple, Ronnie Neame explained, 'You don't have to have money to succeed; you have to appear to have money.' Two wealthy old gentleman living in Belgrave Square agree to draw on the Bank of England one of only two £1 million notes ever issued. They decide to give the note in a sealed envelope to a poor man, who must promise to return the contents of the envelope in a month's time in order to receive a large reward. The film concerns the dilemma of a poor man forced to cope with a fortune he cannot spend even as it wins him respect. 'I think this is wonderful,' Jill said, 'and I think I might be able to fill it out.' Ronnie replied, 'All right, give it a go.' Jill wrote a script that was 'so good', Neame recalled, 'that we had the audacity to send it to Gregory Peck, and to our utter astonishment he accepted it and said he'd love to do it.' In fact, according to Tony Thomas in *Gregory Peck* (1977), Peck was the first major Hollywood star with 'current box office clout' to make a deal in Britain. Ronnie worked late into the night with Jill and saw little of Michael, who seemed utterly absorbed in his Commons career.

Neame remembered script conferences between 'Greg and Jill', in which he wanted a few changes in dialogue. Jill found Greg Peck entrancing. 'She really fancied him,' Lizzie said. 'She would tell us about him.' Before Peck appeared on the scene, Jill would spend the morning in a dressing gown smoking a cigarette and cook breakfast for Julie and Michael in her usual disarray. But during the filming of *The Million Pound Note*, 'She would come down as though going out to a dinner party,' Julie recalled. 'Look at my mother today!' Julie said to Michael. Jill was so open about her 'crush' that Julie did not suppose for a moment that Jill was having an affair. Nearly fifty years later, Gregory Peck wrote: 'I regret that my only recollection of Jill Craigie is of a good looking young woman who occasionally visited the set. Not much else, except that she had an engaging smile. Was she cheering us on as the writer of the piece, or was it a bit flirtatious? I never found out.'[2]

Jill's creation of the two smiling eccentric English brothers, Oliver and Roderick Montpelier, intent only on amusing themselves with their wealth, is a fine touch, copied virtually intact in the American remake, *Trading Places* (1983). Such is the power of money that all Henry Adams (Peck) has to do is show his £1 million note and everyone (from restaurateurs to tailors to hoteliers and tradesman, high society and charities) fawns over him. Newspapers celebrate his arrival in England. Jill adds a vivid vignette: a sudden breeze whisks the pound note out of Henry's hands and he sets off in chase after it, getting his coat caught on a fence spike, and charging after his prize through various encounters before he is able to pounce on it. These moments show off Jill's gift for visualizing scenes Twain did not create, scenes that are only possible in a film, which can keep that note hanging in the wind with no words at all and provide the actor with a set piece of physical business.

Another nice touch is Henry's employment of the 'mute weightlifter *cum* valet created entirely by Jill', Ronnie notes in *Ronald Neame: An Autobiography* (2003). 'Jill's forte ... was inventing characters and devising situations.' Such moments are sly comments on the English class system, the pretentiousness of its institutions and the *folie de grandeur* of a country in decline. Americans aren't spared either: Henry finds himself suddenly welcome at the American consulate, although when he first arrived penniless, he was turned away. A nobleman who is kicked out of his suite to accommodate Henry is outraged and tells the hotel manager: 'Are you trying to tell me that American money means more than an Englishman's name ... This country is going to the dogs.'

Henry's fate vacillates depending on his ability to produce his £1 million note (at one point it is stolen by his chambermaid). *The Million Pound Note* is, in short, a capitalistic farce that Jill exploits for comic purposes well beyond the whimsy of Twain's story. When the note is returned to Henry by the English nobleman who had instructed the chambermaid to hide it, the nobleman remarks that he does not like Yankees and what they do with their money, but 'the things we do for it is a dashed sight worse!'

Ronnie Neame called the film a 'wonderful opportunity for Jill' that garnered her good reviews. While not an 'exceptional film', it proved very successful and received mixed to good reviews. Subsequently, critics have treated it with lukewarm enthusiasm, calling it it 'earnest and well-crafted'. If the film did not make a greater impression, it is perhaps because, as the *New York Times* reviewer Bosley Crowther noted, the satire is so mild (28 June 1954). In part the problem is pacing – more of a weakness in the direction than in the writing.

What might have been Jill's greatest screen credit, *Trouble in Store* (1953), became, in her view, such a fiasco that she refused a writer's credit. The film features the debut of comedian Norman Wisdom, who remains grateful for Jill's contribution. In his memoirs, *My Turn* (2002), he mentions that Earl St John, the producer of *Genevieve*, hired Jill to write a script 'specially tailored' for Wisdom. She did so in six weeks, delivering 'the goods'. Wisdom bluntly says: 'I loved it.' But the Rank Organisation reacted with alarm because of her sharp satire on a 'big store in a Chaplinesque vein, with plenty of scope for slapstick'. Wisdom recalls an 'uproariously funny' screenplay that stimulated him to 'stretch the ideas to the limit'. His version jibes perfectly with Michael's recollection of Jill's profound appreciation of Chaplin's work. Undoubtedly she was aiming in this script for something like Chaplin's *Modern Times* (1936). But the Rank Organisation rejected her fusion of social criticism and comedy, transforming satire into slapstick. Vestiges of Jill's conception can be found in the tramp character Norman, a lowly, maladroit stockboy, who takes a few mocking jabs at the pomposity of his superiors. Jill's ability to make the visual medium tell the story is evident in Wisdom's comment, 'Without a word being spoken, everyone knows exactly who we are.'

Although Jill's decision to take her name off *Trouble in Store* did her no good in the film industry, she continued to work on scripts at Pinewood Studios throughout the 1950s, including *Windom's Way* (1957) and *The Horse's Mouth*

(1959),* thanks to her relationship with Ronnie Neame and John Bryan. *Windom's Way* is her adaptation of James Ramsey Ullman's novel, set in an unnamed country in the Far East. Dr Windom (Peter Finch) operates Selim General Hospital, a thatched hut in a village where he is revered by the natives. He thinks, with dread, about the arrival of his estranged wife, as he listens to a report about his patients delivered by Anna Vidal, the beautiful, dark-featured head nurse who is in love with him. Jill uses dialogue sparely: Windom is seen against the backdrop of his world – all in accord with Jill's notion that in film the visual should trump the verbal.

Windom is estranged from his wife Lee (a silvery blonde Mary Ure) and at odds with Patterson (Michael Hordern), the plantation owner whose brutal treatment of rubber workers outrages the doctor. Windom's protests are dismissed, and Patterson attributes local unrest to the 'Reds', an explanation Windom rejects as just an excuse for punishing the workers and their families. The trouble is really about the workers' desire to grow their own rice, which is part of their traditional way of life. Patterson is charging them high prices for what they should be producing themselves. It is the old story of the company store, an enforced infantilization of a people in the interests of an imperialistic market economy.

When the workers strike, Patterson calls the police; Windom counsels negotiation. Patterson says white men should work together. Windom refuses. A village revolt ends in a machine-gun massacre. The villagers burn Patterson's plantation. The next day Windom surveys the wreckage at the plantation and convinces the men to rebuild it, saying he will support their demands if they return to work for Patterson. But Patterson has gone to a government commissioner alleging that Windom is implicated in the violence and that he may be a subversive. Selim is soon to be targeted by a rebel army, a military official predicts, and Patterson is promised immediate action if there is any sign of sabotage.

The commissioner arrives with troops and takes command of the hospital. Under interrogation, Windom is made to seem not merely a rebel sympathizer, but an instigator of rebellion. Lee intervenes, inviting the commissioner for a meal, exercising the tact and charm her husband lacks. Over dinner, in a more relaxed mood, Windom asks: 'Aren't we becoming so

---

* Alec Guinness is credited with the screenplay adaptation of Joyce Cary's novel. In Jill's study there is a folder titled 'Script for *The Horse's Mouth*.' But in fact the folder contains other matter. Julie photographed Alec Guinness on the set and recalled her mother working on the film, while Lizzie remembered Jill got her a job as an extra. Jill would have been a valuable adviser given her friendship with Stanley Spencer and her knowledge of Augustus John's work – two artists who are said to have been Joyce Cary's models for his painter, Gulley Jimson.

obsessed with what we're against that we've forgotten what we're for?' He
works out a deal predicated on his promise to bring back the workers who
have fled the village. Lee points out how deeply her husband has become
implicated in politics – in spite of his wish to serve only as a doctor. His
political naivety results in disaster, with workers having been co-opted by the
rebels. 'I've botched the whole thing,' Windom admits, regretting his
involvement.

Jill effectively shows how the male ego's drive damages even an altruistic
character like Windom. As Jill argued in a book review, 'The personal is really
political.'[3] The reviewer from *The Times* called her script a 'brave piece of work'
and praised the film's 'courage to think for itself'. But the critic also identified
a major weakness: 'Where exactly are we, geographically and politically,
supposed to be?' To be more specific, though, would have committed the film-
makers to a much deeper engagement with politics than the Rank
Organisation, which funded and produced the film, is likely to have tolerated.
To be more specific would also have muted the film's allegorical quality – its
stark political/moral drama and its probing of male/female dynamics.

Jill called *Windom's Way* a 'terrible flop', even while she acknowledged its
'rather good reviews'. Part of her disappointment had to do with her lack of
control over the final product. 'The director is king,' she told an interviewer,
and the writer only a 'junior partner'.[4] She also expressed frustration that even
Ronnie Neame and John Bryan – professionals she respected – looked askance
at some of her feminist suggestions. Although she had convinced Neame of
the cinematic possibilities of her suffragette project, he never did follow up
her lead. Reflecting on his years of collaboration with Jill, Ronnie Neame
observed: 'To be absolutely honest, her ideas were better than her ability to
put them down on paper.' He termed her dialogue 'moderate'. But her ideas
were 'original' and she had 'so many splendid ones', Neame emphasized. 'One
sensed that right from the beginning … and she did learn a great deal about
the technique of making films from us and was grateful.' Neame singles out
the contribution of his partner John Bryan, 'one of the best set designers in the
world'. In 1963 Neame left to pursue his career in Hollywood and did not
resume his friendship with Jill and Michael until the mid-1980s.

Jill watched in dismay as the film industry of the 1950s became more and
more inane and abject. At one point she attempted to collaborate with writer
Philip Oakes on a series of television programmes adapting the work of D.H.
Lawrence. Jill had first met Oakes at a press showing of *Windom's Way*, which
he did not like and which led to a 'dust-up' with Jill. But Jill did not hold it
against Oakes, a wonderful raconteur, who also developed a romantic interest

in Julie. But the project went nowhere in a television climate that had yet to portray the working-class world he and Jill wanted to dramatize. Oakes also thought that Michael's politics did Jill no favours in a conservative industry. He called her a 'very competent film-maker – certainly equal to most of her contemporaries – perhaps even better than that'. Still, 'Why when you're as nervous and neurotic as a producer should you take a chance on Jill Craigie?' Oakes asked.

Jill explored the 1950s political climate in her *Evening Standard* column,[5] shrewdly predicting what would happen to *A King in New York* (1957), a film Chaplin was making at Shepperton Studios. Now a blacklisted director (McCarthyism had survived McCarthy's political demise, she noted), Chaplin had warned his American actors that they might be jeopardizing their careers by working with him. Pressure would be put on distribution companies not to show the film. Liberals would defend Chaplin's right to show the film but deplore its impact on Anglo-American relations. Communists would embarrass liberals by championing the film. Right-wing and left-wing papers would find fault and merit in the film, while 'Labour Party leaders will hesitate to be seen at its premiere'. Only a comic masterpiece could buffer Chaplin from this onslaught. To Jill it seemed extraordinary that this 'writer, composer, actor, director, producer casting director, and financier all rolled into one … an artist of absolute integrity … a genius' should not be valued as a 'miraculous … phenomenon'. She would forgive any man who so 'consistently combined the belly laugh with an appeal to the heart and intellect'.

Chaplin's case was not unique. Other actors and scriptwriters Jill knew became unemployable if they were not 'politically in the clear'. Many Americans had taken refuge in England so that they could work. 'I cannot believe,' Jill concluded, 'that we'd lose the friendship of the Americans by standing up to them on this issue.' She then used Michael's 'favourite American quotation': 'If there's anything that cannot bear free thought, let it crack.'*

In 'Now, why didn't Sir Laurence employ Miss Monroe' (*Evening Standard*, 18 February 1956), Jill attacked Conservative and Labour governments alike for taxation policies that made it virtually impossible for stars like Laurence Olivier to form their own production companies. Consequently, the profits would go to the Americans, and British actors and crews would work on salary for stars like Marilyn Monroe, whose company had bought the film rights to Terrence Rattigan's play *The Sleeping Prince*. Since Alexander Korda's

---

* The quotation is from Wendell Phillips, the American abolitionist orator.

death (1956), the Ealing Studios had closed, movie attendance was down and British producers were looking to America for funding. Michael Balcon had been able to continue producing pictures in Britain only because of his pre-war savings, she pointed out. 'No wonder some people get a little weary of the never-ending attack of socialist MPs on film stars' salaries. Socialists believe in a juster society. So they devise a system of taxation that strengthens vast combines at the expense of the artist.' She had made a similar attack on Labour in *Tribune* (28 October 1955).

In the hope of reviving her career as a director, Jill turned to Sir Michael Balcon. He seemed the perfect choice – a 'remarkable combination of judiciousness and idealism,' as Charles Drazin puts it in *The Finest Years*. Balcon was no buccaneer. He tended to form long-lasting relationships and to live by the code of the gentleman. Balcon's biographer, Philip Kemp, provides an anecdote about Balcon's agreement with Alexander Korda, whereby Mick (as he was known to his friends) could employ a certain actor before Korda. When Balcon discovered that Korda had gone ahead and hired the actor despite their 'gentleman's agreement', Korda said, 'Mick, for there to be a gentleman's agreement, there have to be two gentlemen.'

Balcon believed in realism and social relevance, and rejected Hollywood escapism. He had produced Robert Flaherty's classic documentary *Man of Aran*, even when industry insiders mocked the budget overruns and spoke of 'Balcon's folly'. Balcon's Ealing studios gave its name to many of the classic British comedies of the 1950s.

In one sense, Balcon was for Jill the next best thing to Filippo Del Giudice (who could no longer get financing for films). In another he was worse than any opposition Jill had confronted in the Rank Organisation. Balcon, who sat on Rank's Board of Directors, vetoed the suggestion that Muriel Box, wife of producer Sydney Box, should direct, even though she and her husband had just won an Academy Award for *The Seventh Veil* (1945). Balcon 'wasn't sure a woman had the qualities necessary to control a large feature film unit', Drazin reports. He had rejected Kay Mander's request to direct in 1950, telling her bluntly, 'Women can't direct.'

How much Jill knew about Balcon's anti-feminist side is not evident. Although he shared her commitment to socialism, he had a conservative temper and advised her on 21 January 1953 not to write about the censorship of British cinema, fearing that she might antagonize the Colonial Office and the Bank of England, both of which had provided facilities for film-makers.[6] Perhaps she relied on his well-known reputation for fairness and openness. Perhaps the fact that she and Michael socialized with the Balcons gave her hope. For a period – perhaps five or six years – the Balcons were 'one of our closest friends', Michael said.

On 12 January 1958 Jill wrote to Sir Michael:

At the risk of boring you – and I'd hate to do that – I've decided to put the case for my directing a film for you. I know you have your own team, that even if you hadn't there are plenty of talented directors around and that, if it comes to trying out someone new, a more exciting choice would seem to be one of the bright so-called Angry Young Men.

All the same, at this particular moment in the history of British film making I think I have something to supply that most of our films lack. You will judge whether my reasons are sound. And if you don't think they are, I know you will be kind enough to forgive me for bothering you.

But first I'd like to answer any doubts you may feel about my technical knowledge. If my documentaries taught me anything it was how little I knew about the craft. Admittedly I came to this painful conclusion rather slowly, but once I did, I made up my mind to do something about it. That's why I persuaded Ronnie and John to try me out as a script-writer. With all their experience, I knew they had loads to teach me. And they did.

You see with them I wasn't just a script-writer. I was brought in on everything right through to the dubbing. We worked as a team. On the *Million Pound Note* I was on the floor all the time – mostly without pay just to learn.

Of course one must have flair too. But no one has ever suggested I lack ideas, on the contrary. And I think I've always had a bit of an eye for composition as anyone must who is interested in painting. As you well know, this is one of Sandy's [Mackendrick]* strong points – and a weakness in some of our directors, Corny [Henry Cornelius] for instance.

Anyway, I know Ronnie and John believe that I could shoot a film with style and polish. Indeed they often talk about producing one for me: but I guess they'll always be too engrossed in their own productions.

They'd tell you all this, also that they have confidence in my ability to handle actors and actresses. Many of our stars often ask me why I don't direct. As for the technicians, don't think there's any resistance to women what with Murial [Box], Wendy, and Betty [Box]. I never had any difficulties on that score. I think all that technicians ask is that directors know what they're doing. And they like to be on a good picture.

But now for the core of my case. Can you honestly say that any of our directors, even Sandy, ever shoot pictures that really get under the skin of their women characters? Has your wife or your daughter ever said to you about British films – I mean during the last six or seven years – that is me, that is precisely how I would

---

* Jill and Michael socialized with Mackendrick (1912–93), director of *The Man in the White Suit* (1951) and *The Ladykillers* (1955).

have felt under these circumstances? Curiously, American directors seem to succeed in this, but rarely the British.

And consider what is happening in the other great mass media, to use a horrible expression. Take Fleet Street. Every Fleet Street editor, even the editors of the most high-brow papers, rely on women to cater for women. This trend is growing so much that a one-time serious paper like the *Evening Standard* has almost become a woman's magazine.

Eighteen months ago I wrote a couple of humorous articles based on observations of my daughter and her friends. I was asked for more – a whole series. I delivered the goods. The circulation and advertising managers were so delighted with the results that I was offered the editorship of the woman's pages in place of Eileen Ascroft. I turned it down because, as you know, I prefer films.

Consider the fantastic circulation of women's magazines, horrible though they are. And the increasing time given on television to women and teenagers' programmes.

Today, the people with the most money to spend on themselves are the young girls at work before they're married. They buy the records, they go out for their entertainment. But anyone wanting to cash in on this market in films automatically thinks of Rock N Roll, Tommy Steele and the Doctor series. Not that I'm against this thinking – it brings the girls in – but it's possible to do better.

Ever since my daughter was sixteen my house has been filled with her friends from the polytechnic, R.A.D.A., Fleet Street. She brings home shop girls, typists, out-of-work actresses, photographic negative retouchers, junior copyrighters, girls from every walk of life.

And they all have certain things in common. Their goal is, very naturally, marriage. They either live at home or in bed-sitting rooms as in *Look Back in Anger*. It was bed-sitting room life, incidentally, that I described in my [newspaper] series and accounted for its success. And the main conflict in the mind of these young girls is whether to hold out for their dream-man, who is rather like a movie star, or settle for reality, which is nothing like what they were aiming at. But many hold out until they are twenty-three or even twenty-seven because they can afford to. And in the meanwhile, they learn quite a lot about men and giggle a lot about the type of passes men make. They worry because so many married men behave like bachelors. A lot of them like classical music at least as much as jazz and they go abroad for their holidays.

It sounds as though I am suggesting a story for you, which I'm not though I could. But our films are made as though we're completely unaware of this new generation. We ignore modern trends to such an extent in dealing with youth that I sometimes wonder whether our better directors know what is happening.

What I'm saying is that I am at least on the wave-length of youth, particularly young girls. And what the girls are up to affects their mothers, their land-ladies, the shops, the courts, everyone in society.

Surely in pictures we should wake up to these new trends?

I would very much like you to see a French Film called *Mitsov*, directed by a woman. It is very French and bears no relation to the society we live in, but even so it is far nearer the mark in looking at life through the eyes of a young girl. It is also the kind of film I would like to aim at. It has humour which I think is essential.

I hesitate to write any more, though I would love to chat about it. But if I have completely failed to interest you, it would be a great kindness to tell me so.

And again please forgive me if I have wasted your time.

Jill

Balcon replied two days later, saying he found her letter 'more than interesting' but was beset with many production problems, which he proceeded to enumerate. Certainly he wished to hear more about her ideas, but he wanted to 'make it quite clear, to prevent any misunderstanding, that there seems to be no immediate possibility of our working together on a picture'. He did not disagree with her, but he had 'certain commitments'.

The subjects Jill might have made into films stud her *Evening Standard* columns of the mid-1950s: absurd laws that allowed women to sue for breach of promise, perpetuating the notion that women had more of a stake in a marriage promise than men did; the foolish obsession with stars like Marilyn Monroe (men would not stand it if their wives actually devoted all their time to being glamorous); the bias against Cockney actresses and anyone who did not speak standard English; the tyranny of the fashion industry; the appalling atrophy of the imagination brought about by television, a medium for midgets. 'We are subhuman, in every way smaller than life with petty virtues and tepid emotions. The fifties will be notable for the adulation that was lavished on the midgets,' she wrote in her column of 29 December 1955. 'Jill had a great deal of integrity,' Ronnie Neame noted: she would not have accepted work on projects that she did not believe in. 'She was no hack.'

If Jill had enlisted Balcon's support, she could have shown him the *Evening Standard* series on working girls, derived from her experience with Julie's friends. In 'London's Bachelor Girls,' (20–24 February 1956), Jill explored the personal and working lives of women in their twenties – some living at home, some on their own, employed in the retail industry, in television, in theatre, in business as secretaries and assistants. Jill interviewed them about their attitudes towards career and marriage. They wanted their own homes and families, but they did not see giving up work as necessarily the outcome of finding the right man. They had no trouble finding employment but they confronted considerable difficulties getting promotions, since their employers presumed they would marry, relinquish their jobs and therefore were not worth investing in. These young women were sophisticated – listening to classical music, reading books, playing golf and travelling. Jill admired them greatly but regretted their 'total lack of interest' in 'politics and social problems':

> the girl in her twenties enjoys her status and rights without the least curiosity as to how they were won. She behaves like a feminist but has turned feminism into a dirty word. She is passionately eager to live both more fully and in more beautiful surroundings then her parents without understanding that her ambitions are related to politics.

Indeed, these women parroted their parents' politics and showed no 'glimmering of the rebel'.

Jill informed her readers about the basics of such a young woman's life – how much she made for a living. Gilly, one of the girls working in retail, earned a little more than £6 a week, contributing to her family's income while paying for her fares and lunches. But she would have to wait a decade or more to be promoted as a buyer. Women working as garage attendants, research workers, receptionists and others in clerical jobs might earn as much as £12 a week – more than their fathers took home as bus drivers or railway workers. In their families they still had to put up with the 'lingering feeling a woman's place is in the home'. These women ought to read about Mary Wollstonecraft, Madame Curie, Dr Garrett Anderson and the Pankhursts, women who succeeded without 'sacrificing one jot of men's admiration'.

Housing in London, Jill reported, was a horror for a young woman. It was very difficult to find decent accommodation that did not eat up half or more of her salary. Jill recommended Lizzie's solution – find a friend to share the rent of a larger flat. Otherwise the digs could be quite squalid – indeed Dickensian – with rude landladies, dirty bathrooms shared by several roomers, poor heating and broken furniture. In such circumstances a young woman preferred to spend her money on making a good appearance, which meant a 'semi-starvation diet'. Even so, Jill found few young women willing to marry men for a meal ticket; on the contrary, they would not think of marrying unless it was for love.

In an article addressed to the parents of these young women, Jill advocated encouraging daughters to stay at home – provided they were given a room of their own and their privacy was respected. This meant relaxing rules about being prompt for meals and also staying out of their daughters' love lives: 'It is far better to enthuse over your daughter's less desirable companions and keep quiet about the rest.' Daughters had to do their part, too: helping out in the house, exercising tact and keeping the noise down.

The *Evening Standard* series proved to be quite popular and Jill filmed Gilly, Lizzie and other young women for ITV in 1958 or 1959, her first foray into commercial television. (Very little of this work survives.) Gilly remembers that Jill provided her with clothes for her camera appearances and filmed her walking to work along Oxford Street. But this television venture was to Jill a pale shadow of what she had hoped to show on a motion picture screen. It is doubtful that she told her husband about her letter and Balcon's reply. Michael had no recollection of the letter, and when it was read to him along with Balcon's reply, he felt keenly about Jill's dashed hopes. When Philip Kemp, researching a life of Balcon, found this letter at the British Film Institute, he contacted Jill, who professed to have no memory of it.[7] When he interviewed her about it, she seemed embarrassed and regretful, calling it a 'rather begging letter'. It is not too much to say that Jill always looked at the world through the eyes of a young girl and that she relived her own start in life through the young girls she met and wanted to film. It is hard to believe that Balcon's response did not break her heart.

The pain and self-doubt of these years comes through in a later interview:

> I would have made a good, competent director who could have held her own with anyone, without being tops, that's my own assessment. But it was very difficult for a woman, really ... It's a marriage. It was easier for Betty and Muriel Box, because Sydney was a producer and he could sponsor them, and bring them along. But I hadn't got anyone like that to look after me ... The real artist will sacrifice relationships. And personal relationships mean a lot to me. I couldn't do that for my career. I don't think my career is so important that society's the worse for not having it ... I sort of drifted out of films.

32A Abbey Road

(1954–9)

… it is so difficult to recapture the spirit of 1945.
Jill Craigie, 'I Call This a National Calamity', *Tribune*, 28 October 1955

The years at Rosslyn Hill ended with the short-term lease sometime in 1953. 'We so loved the house,' Jill later wrote to Mervyn Jones, 'that Michael tried to persuade the Church Commissioners … to sell us the freehold.' But they were adamantly opposed. Jill found the house hunt discouraging: 'Estate agents have lowered their standards of honesty,' she wrote to Beaverbrook.[1] She visited flats and houses that had inadequate heating and the 'wrong' colour schemes .

Jill was working at Pinewood Studios and the couple lodged in a pub/hotel, The Crooked Billet, in Denham. For a while they lived in a rooming house in 4 Hampstead Hill Gardens. Then they stayed with generous friends – for six months with J.P.W. 'Curly' Mallalieu (1908–80), Labour MP for Huddersfield for thirty-four years. Michael and Curly were Bevanites who assembled 'every Tuesday lunch-time while Parliament was sitting at Dick Crossman's house at 9 Vincent Square', Michael reports in his Bevan biography. In an introduction to Mallalieu's autobiography, *On Larkhill* (1983), Michael mentions his 'careless, uncalculating quality, an overflowing, never-failing sense of humour, a gift for comradeship, a faith in our common humanity'. But Jill had a row with Curly's wife Rita, and she and Michael moved out.

During this homeless period, Jill and Michael travelled to America in the height of the McCarthy period (they wanted to understand firsthand why their American friend the musician Larry Adler had been blacklisted). Like everyone else in New York, they sat in front of television sets, watching congressional hearings and admiring domestic labour-saving devices Jill decided to install in her own home. They met Dorothy Parker, one of their favourite writers. 'New York ruled the world,' Michael recalled.

Beaverbrook became their benefactor when he offered Jill and Michael a cottage at Cherkeley, his estate, as a temporary residence while they were house hunting (later the cottage became a weekend home). Isaac Foot, no stranger to friendships with Conservatives, gave his blessing when Jill consulted him. Jill also conferred with Aneurin Bevan, who said 'go ahead', although he had rejected a similar proposition from Beaverbrook – so hated by the left that Michael called him Beelzebub, a flattering, grandiose allusion, since the name put Beaverbrook in the same burning lake as Milton's Satan. They accepted the cottage rent-free, but Jill spent a considerable sum restoring the derelict dwelling and improving its market value.

Weekends at Paddock Cottage appear to have been idyllic, judging by Michael Ward's splendid photographs of Michael and Jill on a sofa (his hand delicately touches her hair), of Michael in the kitchen helping Jill to wash up, of Michael in a hammock and of Julie sunbathing, and of Jill darting forward, her feet off the ground – the very picture of health and happiness. The cottage stood in a field, and Jill made a garden and put a fence around it, exercising her gift for making a home into a paradise.

Michael called the cottage a writer's 'hide-out'. Jill kept Beaverbrook informed about the improvements she had introduced, including gas heating and electrical wiring. She painted the cottage white and planted hundreds of bulbs. 'It's a fine place for work,' she wrote to him on 27 December 1956. 'I think too Mike is much healthier than in town.' Somehow, the cottage caught fire and burned down. Jill, a reader of P.G. Wodehouse, saw the humour of it. So she went to Beaverbrook and announced: 'You're a cottage short, old boy.' Beaverbrook did not seem to find Wodehouse terribly funny.

On 10 or 11 December 1954 the couple moved into a permanent home at 32A Abbey Road in St John's Wood.[2] At £6000 this modern house – so out of tune with Jill's aesthetic and removed from Hampstead – was what they could afford. 'They had looked at many many houses for sale,' Julie remembered, and 'they had a very modest budget'. Michael did not like the idea of builders in the house, and the newly built Abbey Road residence needed no improvements. Nevertheless, on moving day Jill became upset because her furniture did not look right in her new house and there was not enough room. Michael appreciated the ground-floor garage and the two floors of living space – 'quite a nice little house,' he said, although, 'it wasn't quite good enough for the books'.

It is unlikely that Jill regarded Abbey Road as anything other than a temporary abode, although they would stay there for nearly a decade. Julie admired the way her mother made it a 'lovely home'. Jill created a garden, although gardening was not yet the passion it would become at Pilgrim's Lane two decades later. She had a char lady, Abby Clifford, who saw to the cleaning (Julie cannot ever remember her mother doing housework). 'Jill never had any kind of quarrel' with Abby about how to run the house 'and the rest of it. They were friends,' Michael recalled. 'My mother always formed close relationships with the people who worked for her,' Julie agreed. 'She became a part of their lives.' Jill sorted out their problems. Abby had 'serious man troubles', Julie remembered. When Abby's man 'buggered off', Jill helped her with the serious legal problems that ensued. Jill wrote letters on her behalf and advised her how to deal with lawyers (Jill's columns in the *Evening Standard* demonstrate a considerable understanding of the courts – in part, derived from her marriage to Jeffrey Dell, who began his writing career creating successful court dramas).

Arriving at Abbey Road, you went up the stairs to the living room. There would be boxes of a hundred Gold Flakes cigarettes lying around. Jill and Michael would go through a box in the course of a day. Paul Foot would bring his Oxford friends around to meet his hero, Uncle Michael. Michael would often be out at the House of Commons, and Jill would say, 'Oh, just sit there, he'll be back.' On one occasion Paul told Jill he had been studying T.S. Eliot's 'wonderful poetry'. Jill said, 'It's all absolute rubbish. Eliot? Absolutely awful.' Paul objected, 'That's not true,' and he recited a bit of Eliot. 'It sounds all right when you say it,' Jill admitted, 'but he was deeply reactionary.' Michael would come in and go straight up to the bedroom, and you could hear them chattering away about the day. Then Michael would come down and 'make clear he wanted us to go away,' Paul remembered.

Jill and Michael had friends in the neighbourhood: their doctor, Jerry Slattery, the novelist Olivia Manning, and her husband Reggie Smith, the hero of Manning's Balkan trilogy. Jerry and his wife would go off on holidays with Olivia and Reggie, and Michael and Jill accompanied them on a visit to Venice and Rome. Jerry, who was 'so full of life', his friend Mary Noble recalled, made house calls, saying, 'I'll be round. Get the gin.'

Beginning in the late 1950s, Jill and Michael took holidays every year, many of them in Venice, which for Michael was the city of romance and the renewal of his love for Jill, the city where he wooed her by reading from Ruskin and Hazlitt and Stendhal and Byron and virtually every writer who had celebrated the virtues of Venice. 'We go every year,' Jill told a television audience in the late 1980s:

We just wander round. I wish all the British architects would spend five years in Venice. Not to build little pinnacles and campaniles – which are marvellous – but there are no cars, no loneliness. There are these beautiful squares where kids play and the mothers and the grandmothers and fathers of all ages mixed up in the cafés and you can sit there all day. It's all out of danger and everything is within reach. It's the most fabulous place for a holiday.

Jill and Michael would spend a fortnight in the city, at Easter or in the summer or in September, and amassed a large library about Venice. 'We knew every inch of Venice,' Michael claimed. To him the city was pure theatre. Even the look of a doorway invited a sense of drama. 'The churches are like theatres, the theatres like churches,' he would say. They fell in love with it in the same way a man falls in love with a woman, by 'crystallization' – Stendhal's term for the mental process by which the lover 'draws from everything that happens new proofs of the perfection of the loved one'.*

But the Abbey Road period wasn't always idyllic. While Jill and Michael's relationship continued to blossom, relationships outside the couple were less harmonious. During her time at Abbey Road Jill went through two painful trials – a deep conflict with her daughter and, during a particularly fractious time in the Labour party, Michael's fall out with his best friends Nye Bevan and Jennie Lee over the subject of unilateral disarmament, which was becoming increasingly important to Jill. At the same time, Jill was struggling to come to terms with her own professional frustrations and to give Michael the unwavering support she felt he deserved.

Julie was now in her early twenties, living at home and pursuing a career as a Fleet Street photographer. She had given up thoughts of an acting career. Jill bought her a new Leica camera after *Picture Post* photographer Bert Hardy assured Jill that Julie needed one.† Believing that Julie was her responsibility and embarrassed to ask Michael for money, Jill maintained her proud and independent stance by selling her works of art, including a Renoir (apparently given to her by Malcolm MacDonald), which fetched what seems like a

---

* In *De l'Amour*, Stendhal retrieves his metaphor from this phenomenon: 'At the salt mines of Salzburg, they throw a leafless wintry bough into one of the abandoned workings. Two or three months later they pull it out covered with a shining deposit of crystals. The smallest twig, no bigger than a tom-tit's claw, is studded with a galaxy of scintillating diamonds. The original branch is no longer recognizable.'

† According to Alan Rusbridger in a *Guardian* obituary (22 June 1990) of Sir Tom Hopkinson, editor of *Picture Post* (1938–1950), Jill was among the young reporters 'who first made their mark' with Hopkinson's encouragement. I have not found any articles in *Picture Post* signed by Jill, but she may well have contributed anonymous items or worked on pieces attributed to celebrity authors.

pittance now: £2000. Michael did not seem to understand Jill's predicament and later said, 'I don't know why she felt she had to sell the Renoir.'

Julie had her share of suitors. 'I had boyfriends ringing me,' Julie recalled, and Michael would answer, 'Hello, darling', and Jill would answer, 'Hello, darling.' Or Jill would answer and the boy would say:

'Oh, is that you Julie? This is John.'

'Which John?'

'WHAT?!!'

When Michael heard one of Julie's admirers coming up the stairs, he would sing in a deep bass voice 'Ma, he's making eyes at me.' To Julie's great embarrassment, 'he'd sing the whole bloody thing'. Among the distinguished suitors to receive this royal welcome was the Earl of Kimberley. 'My mother never stopped Michael. She never defended me,' Julie said laughingly.

Julie dated actors, although her mother disapproved. 'You can't marry an actor,' Jill said. 'Jill was very suspicious of actors, it's true,' Michael remembered. They are a vain lot, she told Michael, who admired Claude Rains until he met the man, who could only think of himself, at which point Michael realized the wisdom of Jill's sentiments. In April 1956 Sean Connery – just beginning his career – appeared in a play along with Ronnie Fraser, Lizzie's boyfriend, and Sean joined Ronnie and Lizzie and Julie for a drink. 'He just stood there staring at me,' Julie recalled. He wore old jeans. He smiled. She saw his gold teeth. They shook hands. He had tattoos on his right forearm, proclaiming 'Scotland Forever' and 'Mum and Dad'. He said hello in the Scottish accent he had carried with him from an Edinburgh tenement block. 'God, what a yob,' Julie thought. He was gorgeous, but he was also just another aspiring actor.

Sean started phoning her, but at the time Julie was involved with another man. Then several months later at the Buxton Club, a film actor's hangout, Peter O'Toole, one of their group of friends, approached Julie and said, 'For God's sake, go out with him. He's been in love with you for ages. Go out with him!' Julie could not resist. At Lizzie's wedding, Ronnie wore a kilt and so did Sean – the 'whole Scots gear, and he looked absolutely devastating – the most beautiful sight, I remember thinking, I'd ever seen in my life', Julie emphasizes. Sean escorted Julie (a bridesmaid) home to Hampstead and caused a 'minor sensation'.

Julie spent part of the week with Sean and part at Abbey Road. Julie did her best to further Sean's career, taking many photographs of him and talking him up. 'We went everywhere together,' Julie said. 'When I gave Sean the chance, he was a sweet, gentle guy.' Together they picked out a dog for Jill and

Michael, which Michael promptly named Vanessa (after the object of Jonathan Swift's affection). Then Julie came home to Abbey Road one morning:

> I went to my mother's room and said, 'What would you think if I said I was thinking of marrying Sean?' She leapt out of bed and screamed 'You can't marry a navvy with gold teeth and a tattoo.' Michael, who had been in my room sleeping, came into the room and said to Jill, 'My child, my child, you can't talk like that.'

Julie began to cry. A few hours later Sean showed up at Abbey Road. 'My mother, who had been perfectly nice to him, froze him out. I tell you her frosting is as nasty as her charm is welcoming.' She hardly opened the door and Sean could see Julie in tears. He wanted to know why. 'It went on like that for months.' Michael stayed out of it. 'It's only your happiness I'm interested in,' Jill said. That did not make sense to Julie, and the relationship between daughter and mother turned hostile. Nonetheless, deeply influenced by her mother's view of actors, she turned down Sean's marriage proposal.

Julie and Sean found a small house in Waverley Mews, off Abbey Road. He managed to get a mortgage on the strength of his developing career, and the couple fixed up a home, but they split up after they had been together about two years, 'Biographies of Sean give it a year,' Julie pointed out.

Jill later acknowledged her role in breaking up Julie and Sean. Jill said Sean was 'uncouth' and did not know how to treat a woman.[3] She told a later housekeeper, Kathy Seery, about her dismay at watching Julie, suitcase in hand, lumber across the lawn to Paddock Cottage accompanied by Sean (oblivious to Julie's burden and Jill's disapproval). Michael liked him, 'But we had no idea of the success he was going to be, the film actor of the age,' he said. Jill made Sean out to be rather unreliable, but Julie called him an 'honourable man'. Jill objected to the idea that she was a snob. 'My collier friends in Tredegar could have given Connery a lesson in polished social behaviour,' she wrote later to Mervyn Jones. Resenting Mervyn's treatment of the episode in his biography of Michael, she added: 'The idea that I did actually love my daughter and feared that she might be hurt never enters your head.'

By all accounts the Michael Foot of these years was consumed with politics and journalism. In addition to his position as an MP, he was editor of *Tribune* in 1948–52 and 1956–9,* and heavily involved in debates over how far to the left and to socialism the Labour Party should swing. Never a strong supporter

---

* Even when not officially editor, Michael often seemed to take charge of *Tribune* when its outstanding journalists moved on to more lucrative positions – often in the Beaverbrook press.

of Attlee, whom Michael deemed a far too cautious leader, Michael hoped that his hero Nye Bevan would one day become leader and fulfil the party's radical mission to transform society. After the rousing election victory in 1945, the Labour government had continued in power with a severely reduced majority in 1950. Bevan had resigned from the Cabinet when his rival and Cabinet colleague, Hugh Gaitskell, successfully headed the drive to require patients to pay for items such as medications. To Bevan these charges represented just the beginning of an effort to dismantle the concept of universal and free health care that had been the cornerstone of his programme. Tensions increased between Bevan and Gaitskell, when Gaitskell became leader in 1955 and attempted to move Labour away from its roots in trade unionism in order to appeal more strongly to the successful middle-class professionals who voted for Harold Macmillan and the Conservatives in 1955 and 1959.* By the mid-1950s Gaitskell's opposition to unilateral nuclear disarmament – advocated strenuously by Michael in *Tribune* – became another rallying cry of the far left Bevanites, a hard core of perhaps two dozen, with nearly twice as many joining the group on certain issues.

Jill entered into Michael's world entirely – as her letters to Beaverbrook demonstrate. Julie called it a 'very stressful time for Jill'. Jill was in full sympathy with Michael and the other Bevanities like Richard Crossman, Tom Driberg, Barbara Castle, Ian Mikardo and Harold Wilson, who had been attacked by the Labour Party leadership as a 'party within a party'. As Michael put it in the second volume of his Bevan biography, 'Those conspiratorial weekly meetings were truly more memorable for the zest and gaiety and the genuine argument than for any detailed plotting done.' But the outspoken leftism and articulation of Bevanism in *Tribune* angered their opponents on the Labour right. In short, a Bevanite wanted Labour to hew to a line independent of America's Cold War belligerency, to continue aggressively Labour's programme of nationalization and to make the party itself more democratic and the leaders more responsive to the rank and file in the unions and the constituency parties. To the Labour right, the Bevanites seemed to threaten party unity and were out of touch with an electorate moving toward Conservatism.

Meanwhile, Jill became increasingly upset about the burdens placed on

* Specifically, Gaitskell wanted to abandon Clause 4, the part of Labour's constitution that committed the party to the 'public ownership of the means of production'. This brand of socialism he deemed old-fashioned and partly responsible for Labour's electoral defeats. Clause 4 also became the symbol for Gaitskell and other revisionists of undue trade union power within the party. At the 1959 conference Gaitskell attempted, in effect, to enhance the power of the MPs, but he was not able to persuade the party's membership to do so. A special conference in 1995 finally abolished Clause 4 and with it the radical programme of the Bevanites.

Michael. Personnel at *Tribune* changed frequently. The best journalists, like the talented Bob Edwards, departed to work for Beaverbrook, for example, in order to secure higher salaries and a larger audience of readers. Consequently, Michael's work at *Tribune* increased significantly. Some time in 1955, Jill 'hit out' at Jennie Lee about the journal's exploitation of Michael, and Jennie hit back in a long letter that she apparently never sent.[4] Nye was one of the founders of the journal and Jennie had been on its board of directors since 1945. She reminded Jill that '*Tribune* has been a source of intolerable punishment for both of us.' Both their husbands had used them as a 'weeping wall'. Jennie referred to Jill's worry occasioned by a libel suit against Michael for the headline 'Lower Than Kemsley', a swipe at the press lord's lack of ethical standards. Although the case was ultimately decided in Michael's favour, he emphasized that the uncertainty of the outcome made Jill increasingly anxious, since a Kemsley victory would have wiped out Michael's modest savings and resulted in the loss of their home. Jill decried the endless weeks of work on the paper that absorbed Michael's 'creative energies', the rancour over efforts to raise money for the publication and the loss of the staff Michael had trained to better-paying papers. 'Short of beating me up physically, nothing was left undone to drive home your attitude,' Jennie wrote before breaking off the letter.

Approaching the election of 1955, Jill wrote two *Evening Standard* columns that defined her concept of the political wife. In 'Does a wife pull in votes?' (30 April 1955) she doubted that she could make an impact even if she possessed the shape of Marilyn Monroe and the fervour of Mrs Pankhurst. True, a male candidate could not appear on a platform without his wife during an election campaign, and she had to visit hospitals, factories, women's groups, etc., but as for Jill: 'I, personally, have never succeeded in changing anyone's mind about politics. I believe our views are the result of temperament rather than reason and are modified only by events.' In her view, better to buck up her husband's spirits than to suppose she could do anything else that might actually sway the outcome of an election.

Jill noticed that Michael's Conservative opponent, Joan Vickers, who had come from a career in the Red Cross, seemed 'quite the model', praised for her slim figure and 'beautiful suits and dashing hats'. In fact, Vickers waged an aggressive campaign, getting out into the streets talking to people in shops and cinema queues. 'She's here, there and everywhere. Why don't you come down more often and provide some feminine opposition?' one of Michael's constituents asked Jill. Her reply demarcates the space Jill tried to reserve for herself: 'Because I work for my living and because I don't wear hats.' A fashion contest would not help Michael, Jill implied, and it would transform her into the relentless campaigning political wife. Not that she could not catch 'election fever', she admitted: 'I've acquired some cunning little numbers on the A-line.'

Part of Jill's scepticism about her own role – and her effort to maintain a balance between her career and Michael's – had to do with her discouragement over the feeble role women played in British political life. 'How curious it is that when women fought for the vote more than 2,000,000 joined the suffragette movement,' she wrote in the *Evening Standard* (16 May 1955). 'Apparently when women could not vote they were interested in politics.' Having observed several brilliant hardworking MPs, Jill deplored the cynicism and apathy that led women not to vote. Overcoming her initial resistance to campaigning for Michael, she now professed to enjoy her involvement in his electioneering, moving about in a loudspeaker van trying to tell women in 'vivid language' what they were missing. Children followed her van, and when she had attracted fifty or so, she would send them home with messages for their mothers. She had thus overcome her 'election allergy'.

In 1955, with a depressed Labour turnout, Michael lost by 100 votes. Isaac, used to losing his share of elections, sent Michael a consoling note and the first edition of a book by Jonathan Swift, one of Michael's heroes. Michael himself took the defeat in his stride. As Jill told an interviewer: 'He never looks back, ever, and he – the minute he has a setback – he sees what he can do about it, and he says: "Well, now I can write that book I've been dying to write" … He never envies anybody … has no malice in him. He just gets on with what he's got to do, and it's a great way to live.' As for Jill: 'I thought it was dreadful. I made a fool of myself … I wept in public.'[5]

Michael went to work on *The Pen and the Sword* (1957), his riveting account of the duel in 1710–11 between Jonathan Swift, 'the prince of journalists', and the Duke of Marlborough, the 'greatest of English soldiers', over whether England should continue the War of the Spanish Succession (1701–13). 'Public opinion with the press as its main engine, in the country at large and particularly in the London coffee-houses, was now a considerable force. It could help sway votes in Parliament, sink the public credit or raise a mob on the streets.' Another of Michael's great heroes, William Hazlitt, would say as much about the power of public opinion, fuelled by the press, to foment the French Revolution. In other words, Michael Foot out of power was still Michael Foot in power. Jill wrote a column on town planning for the *News Chronicle*, as well as a wide range of pieces for the *Evening Standard* in 1955 and 1956.

Journalist Geoffrey Goodman, who first met Jill and Michael in 1949 at a Labour Party conference in Blackpool, frequently visited Abbey Road with his wife Margit. The couples would rendezvous at the Gay Hussar restaurant, which had a private top room where Bevanites and the likes of Tom Driberg (1905–76), a flamboyant journalist-politician, held forth. 'He had an unhappy life, in many respects,' said Michael. 'He was taking terrible risks with his homosexuality. He couldn't have sex with men of his own class… He didn't talk to me about these matters, but he talked to Jill.' In a postscript to Driberg's *Ruling Passions* (1979), Michael adds: 'She comprehended long before I did how his ruling homosexual passion had condemned him to a life-time of deep loneliness.'

Geoffrey remembered 'tremendous moments at Abbey Road'. He referred not merely to the galvanizing political talk, but to the ambience Jill created. 'Not only was she a wonderful cook, it was the way she *deployed* the whole table. She was a masterly organizer. Whether she organized Michael or not, I do not know. It's for him to say.' Michael, sitting next to Geoffrey at the Gay Hussar, did not say. Geoffrey and Margit met as a sixsome with Michael and Jill and Frank Cousins[6] and his wife Nance. Cousins (1904–86) became general secretary of the Transport and General Workers' Union (TGWU) in 1955 and a national political figure, employing the TGWU block vote to back the Labour left and the Campaign for Nuclear Disarmament (CND), founded in 1958. Until then, the Bevanites had had the support of the constituency parties but the Labour leadership had employed the Labour union bloc vote to stymie the left.

They dined at each others' houses. 'I was awestruck the first time I went to St John's Wood,' Margit said. 'But it was very easy. They made us very comfortable straightaway.' Next to going out with Nye and Jennie, Frank and Nance provided Michael with the 'best kind of political discussion. If Frank had come into the management of the TGWU earlier, the whole shift of the party might have been better,' Michael supposed. Nance Cousins, a 'formid-able character', struck up terrific dialogues with Jill. Nance would round on Frank: 'Frank, you're talking rubbish!' Then Jill would take up that line, and it would be Jill and Nance versus Michael and Frank. The target was often Harold Wilson, whom Nance disliked as much as Jill did. Michael and Frank had a different opinion, and one of them would begin to say, 'Well, that's not quite true …', but between Jill and Nance, 'they pretty well tore Mr Wilson from bow to bow', Geoffrey reports. 'They thought he was putting one line to us, another to others,' as Michael put it, 'and he did.'

In the early 1950s, Wilson began to be mentioned as a successor to

Clement Attlee as party leader. Wilson sided with Bevan in his rivalry with Hugh Gaitskell, and Wilson followed Bevan's lead in resigning from the Labour Cabinet in 1951. Thus Wilson solidified his credentials as a left-winger, although his canny efforts to remain on good terms with all factions in the party aroused Bevanite suspicion. Against Bevan's wishes, Wilson (backed by Dick Crossman) replaced him after he resigned from the Shadow Cabinet in 1954, thus reinforcing Bevanite speculation about Wilson's intentions and convictions.

Sometimes the dinner parties included Dick Crossman, journalist Ian Aitken and their wives. Jill loved to argue. 'Well, that's all very well but ...' she would begin, or, 'Surely you don't believe ...' Geoffrey would hear her say. She created an 'ethos', a special atmosphere that allowed each individual to speak out. 'She was always the one to stimulate the difficult discussions,' Geoffrey and Margit agree. 'It was that sort of demanding question,' Geoffrey remembers 'that gave an original slant to the evening.'

Jill and Michael were members of CND from the beginning. Although she never took a prominent role in the organization, she did join CND marches and occasionally spoke at events.

In Brighton, Jill joined a group of forceful speakers that included A.J.P. Taylor, Benn Levy* and Mervyn Jones. She made a very moving speech. She said, 'Any woman who has given birth and knows what it is like to have a child – and how dear it is to you – is horrified by the thought of this child suffering and dying.' She put it so simply and brilliantly, Mervyn recalled. Jill realized that the horrifying consequences of radioactive fallout made the idea of storing, let alone using, nuclear weapons anathema to civilization. 'She was even more of a unilateralist than Michael,' asserted Mervyn. In 1958, approximately 4000 people marched from London to Aldermaston (the weapons research facility) to demand an end to nuclear testing. Jill and Michael joined them. For the previous four years prominent scientists – including Nobel Prize winners Hermann Muller and Linus Pauling – had questioned governmental attempts in the US and the UK to minimize the perils of fallout. Closer to home, Alice Stewart, a scientist working at the Royal Free Hospital in Hampstead, had published in 1956 a preliminary study of x-rays showing that even very small doses of radiation doubled the risk of cancer in children. 'That was what we found and that finding has determined the course of my life ever since,' noted Stewart, who went on in the 1970s to expose the workplace risks for American nuclear industry employees.[7] Jill

---

* Benn Levy (1900–73), playwright, Labour MP (1945–50), a Bevanite, married to the actress Constance Cummings, a good friend of Nye, Jill and Michael.

may not have known about Stewart's work, but she was certainly aware of such concerns and studies, and to her dying day she would remain committed to a regime of strict controls – if not outright banning – of nuclear devices.

Spike Milligan befriended Jill and Michael during the first CND marches. He was briefly engaged to Julie. Jill and Michael regarded Spike as a comic genius on a level with the Marx brothers and Oscar Wilde, but Spike had a savagery in his humour, a rage about the human condition that drew him to the marchers, who were not only protesting weaponry, but also the perversity of human blindness to its own suicidal tendencies. *The Goon Show*, Michael later wrote, was the 'proper antidote' to the times – the Conservative era Jill had so decried in her columns, a period epitomized by the Macmillan ethos that soothed the populace into thinking 'you never had it so good'. Without Spike there would have been no Monty Python or a generation of comic minds that tore apart the pretensions of British institutions. Jill and Michael shared his sense of grievance that his creation of the show had been over-shadowed by the success of his collaborators Peter Sellers and Harry Secombe. With a tendency towards depression, Spike often relied on calls to Jill to cheer him up. The two would commiserate over their indignation at the way people treated their children.[8]

All these friendships thrived in the solidarity of the CND marches. In the second volume of his Bevan biography, Michael notes the significance of this new movement: 'National pride and disgruntlement, scarcely less than intelligent alarm about the bomb, found notable expression in the limpid beauty of Bertrand Russell's English, in the humanity of J.B. Priestley, in the invective of John Osborne, in the release which many of the young describe as a "new kind of politics".'

Peter and Mary Noble hosted a big party for the exhilarated marchers, 'just around the corner from Jill and Michael'. A journalist (a *Tribune* contributor) and film pundit, Peter had many show-business friends in common with Jill and Michael. Mary, an actress, appeared as Vivian Darkbloom (an anagram of Vladimir Nabokov) in Stanley Kubrick's *Lolita* and introduced the couple to the director.* She had also worked with Jeffrey Dell. Mary, a big fan of Michael's, used to enjoy riding the bus past 32a Abbey Road, where she would see Michael working and feel all was well. Michael's and Jill's other friends, like journalist James (Jimmy) Cameron (1911–85) and cartoonist Vicky (Victor Weisz 1913–66), shared Spike's 'hilarity and despair', Michael wrote in *Debts of Honour*, and no one captured that complicated mood more than

---

* Michael believes that Kenneth Tynan introduced Jill to Kubrick at an even earlier date.

Cameron, the 'prince of modern journalists'. Jimmy and Vicky were appalled at the horrors of the nuclear age.

As late as the autumn of 1957, Jill and Michael thought Nye would support the unilateralists. In *Tribune*, Nye had declared: 'The existence of nuclear weapons can no longer be regarded as a deterrent to war, but as making war a certainty... We must apply our minds to the destruction of nuclear weapons before they have a chance to destroy us.'[9] But Michael and Jill did not press him for an outright call for British nuclear disarmament, believing that he would have to arrive at that position sooner or later. Barbara Castle knew, however, that Nye was ambivalent about what to say in October 1957 at the Labour Party Conference in Brighton – especially since he seemed the likely choice for Foreign Secretary in a new Labour government under the leadership of his rival, Hugh Gaitskell, who opposed the unilateralists.

In volume two of *Aneurin Bevan*, Michael emphasizes Nye's desire to maintain party unity after years of acrimony between the Bevanities and Gaitskellites. In 1956 Bevan and Gaitskell had worked well together in opposing Anthony Eden's appalling Suez adventure, and though Bevan remained critical of Gaitskell, he saw that a refusal to support Gaitskell would damage the Labour Party. For the first time Bevan found himself marginalized by a leftist mass movement that Michael (out of Parliament from 1955 to 1960) acclaimed.

By the time Michael did confer with Nye about the bomb, his hero's mind was set, and the only concession Michael could wrest from him was Nye's remark in his Labour Party conference speech that unilateralism might be a future alternative to current policy. Emotions ran high. Frank Cousins said, 'I have a six-year-old daughter and I will not compromise with anybody about the future of that child.' He demanded that his party condemn the 'maintenance and manufacture, by ourselves or by anyone else, of this idiot's weapon'. Nye had to speak next, and his words chilled his admirers: 'You will send a Foreign Secretary, whoever he may be, naked into the conference chamber.' In other words, unilateralism destroyed diplomacy; it was no way to end the Cold War. Mervyn Jones, sitting next to Michael, saw him 'wince as though he had been stung by a wasp'. Some thought Nye's reference to 'naked' meant 'without the bomb', though he intended the expression to mean 'without allies', since the US would not support unilateralism. Nye then made matters worse by calling unilateralism an 'emotional spasm' that would contract Britain out of its 'commitments and obligations entered into with other countries and members of the Commonwealth – without consultation at all'.

Nye was, however, speaking to the majority of his party, which voted down the unilateralism resolution. At dinner Michael, Vicky, James Cameron, Geoffrey Goodman and Ian Aitken – all Bevanites – held their wake for Bevanism. 'I'm finished with him,' Vicky said. Michael took a more moderate tone, but his twenty-year comradeship with Nye was in jeopardy. They had never before disagreed on a fundamental issue. Jennie Lee, who had been a unilateralist, supported her husband, accepting his view that Labour would never win a general election with a unilateralist policy. She joined Nye in demanding that *Tribune*, the very organ of Bevanism, make no comment at all and just report the conference and print readers' letters. Michael wanted a full airing of their disagreement and a clarification of Nye's views. How could he, as editor of the journal, not take a stand? On 11 October 1957 he wrote to conciliate Nye, acknowledging his old friend's loathing of nuclear weapons, but also challenging him:

> Nothing I have heard persuades me that the possession of a few bombs which can never be used except as an act of national suicide and which as long as we produce them will impose enormous burdens on our economy will assist in making Britain's voice more powerful in the world. Indeed, I still believe – as I am convinced a growing number of people throughout the country will believe – that Britain's readiness to renounce the weapon which we all regard as an invention of the devil could capture the imagination of millions of people in many lands.

A host of the country's intellectuals and artists joined Michael's side, and *Tribune* became a staunch CND supporter. Nye and Jennie protested, and Jennie even went so far as to urge Howard Samuel to drop his subsidy of the paper, effectively killing it. But Nye would have no part of a vendetta against Michael. Still, Jill put her attitude succinctly in a letter to Beaverbrook on 16 December: 'Nye said goodbye to the left, and, as it seemed to me, though Michael denies it – to Michael in particular.'

Jill watched in dismay as Michael's influence inside the party seem to wane in the mid-1950s. In a letter to Beaverbrook (*c.*1956), she worried about her husband's 'suicidal tendencies', by which she meant his devotion of his 'energies to *Tribune* and turning down safe Parliamentary seats in favour of contesting the Plymouth seat once again'. 'Michael seems to me to be becoming more and more isolated,' she wrote to Beaverbrook on 29 December 1957.

Whatever qualms Jill had about the direction of her husband's career, her letters reveal that she enjoyed the world of celebrity and high living Beaverbrook's largesse afforded: 'I think it was quite something getting Mike into a dinner jacket, don't you? Furthermore, it was voluntary. I had merely packed it,' she wrote to Beaverbrook. At the Danieli hotel in Venice she had watched the 'diverting spectacle of Michael setting off for his morning bathe in the hotel motor launch in the company of Sir Oswald Mosley,* Profumo,† a Conservative minister whose name I've forgotten, I think it was Maud,‡ George Strauss,** and various Italian starlets. What a picture for photopage!' In his *Autobiography* (1960), a hostile Herbert Morrison†† dismissed Michael as a dilettante who could not be taken seriously as a politician. He called Michael 'a kitchen revolutionary... who has drifted into the socialist movement from the serene backwaters of a fairly comfortable middle-class environment'. But a good deal of the passion in politics was extra-parliamentary and fuelled into movements like the CND. There were periods when Parliament seemed soporific, observed Michael in a *Daily Express* book review (20 June 1959), which referred to the 'snores we hear today'.

While Michael held his ground, Nye advanced. 'Apparently, he could not believe that it was beyond his power, for the first time in their long association, to bring Michael round to his way of thinking,' wrote Mervyn Jones. Nye stormed out of an encounter at *Tribune*, slamming the outer door with its frosted glass panel so hard that the clanging could be heard throughout the building. Jennie Lee found Michael's moralizing insufferable, saying he was 'like a priest!'[10] She called CND an 'hysterical middle class lobby' now dominating the Left.[11]

The next summer (1958), drinks at Abbey Road that were meant to lubricate a reconciliation only raised blood pressure, and in an unusual outburst Nye shouted at Michael: 'You cunt! You cunt!' Clutching one of Jill's prized Sheraton chairs he banged it on the floor, breaking its elegant legs. Jennie Lee thought the men had almost come to blows.[12] Somehow Jill smoothed over the incident, calling up Nye the next day. He came to Abbey Road and 'made his peace' – although he persisted in his efforts to convert Jill to his views, as he had done with Jennie.‡‡

* Oswald Mosley (1896–1980), leader of the British Union of Fascists, had once been a promising Labour Party member, whose ideas Michael Foot found, for a brief time, attractive.

† John Profumo (1915–) is best known for the sex scandal that forced his resignation as Secretary of State for War in 1963.

‡ John Maud (1906–82) held various posts dealing with fuel, power and food in Conservative governments.

** George Strauss, a founder of *Tribune*. Jill and Michael were often guests at his home.

†† Herbert Morrison (1888–1965), one of the primary architects of the Labour governments of 1945–51. A brilliant administrator, deputy leader under Attlee and leader of the House of Commons, this supreme organizer could not win Attlee's assent to succeed him or the hearts of his party. In the second volume of his Aneurin Bevan biography, Michael ridiculed Morrison's efforts to control government policy through a series of committees and subcommittees that slowed down the aggressive socialism that Michael and Nye believed the country was prepared to undertake.

‡‡ Mervyn Jones quotes Nye's words during the fight with Michael, who in volume two of his Bevan biography only states that Nye used 'four lettered responses' and accused Michael of 'sterility'.

Then Prime Minister Harold Macmillan called for an election on 8 October 1959. Michael thought he had only a slim chance of regaining his Parliamentary seat, but he and Jill returned to Plymouth on 20 September and he opened his campaign with an uncompromising call for unilateralism: 'A nuclear war could well destroy us all. We are alarmed by the thought of it and so are the Russians.' Nye promised to campaign for Michael, but he could not fulfil his pledge because of a prolonged illness, soon to be diagnosed as cancer. Michael lost again – this time to a Conservative majority of 6454 votes. With a tearful Jill at his side (she had become completely absorbed in her role as supportive wife), he took the defeat with his usual grace, offering no complaints or excuses – and no regrets about entering the contest. He had fought on principle and vowed to continue his campaign against the H-bomb.

The election solidified the Conservative majority and put an end to the ailing Bevan's efforts to reach an accommodation with Gaitskell. It also put an end to the hard feelings between Michael and Nye. In hospital for an emergency operation just after Christmas 1959, Nye may have realized he was dying. 'Quite humorous and very much his old self', Nye gently chided Michael for quixotically attempting to regain his old Parliamentary seat. Nye then said: 'Now you'd better look properly for another seat. Perhaps you needn't look further than Ebbw Vale.'*

* Ebbw Vale was Nye's safe seat and one that, with Jennie's support, Michael could easily win. In 1983 Ebbw Vale was renamed Blaenau Gwent.

10 Morgan Street
(1959–63)

Of course, many people are now saying that if the worst happens to Nye, Michael must step into Nye's shoes.

Jill Craigie to Max Beaverbrook, New Year's Eve 1959

The drama of Nye's final days seemed to consume Jill's energy. 'Of course, if Nye did die, the effect on the Labour Party would be disastrous. Gaitskell and Co. would go out for a big kill of the left,' Jill wrote to Beaverbrook. But then what should Michael do?

> I think Michael's heart is in writing and newspapers and something of a tug of war goes on in him as to which he should do most wholeheartedly. He is not really cut out for political intrigue. The only time Michael has really enjoyed his work fully was when he was on the *Standard* and I am not saying that to please you. I think we both know that is true. All the same, it wouldn't surprise me if he doesn't go flat out on the political front, even though he has started a new book.
>
> Because if he doesn't, he must sit back and watch the complete disintegration of the Labour Party. And the trouble really is Gaitskell ... At a party the other day, where numerous political journalists from every paper were present, Gaitskell was talking quite openly about Annie Fleming [his Conservative mistress]... This sort of behaviour in public does not inspire the fanatical devotion that leaders require. Only the job hunters rally round Gaitskell and people see through them. Even ambitious characters like Dick Crossman and Barbara Castle become disgusted with him. Not that they mind what he does in private; but his indiscretions and opportunism disgust them. Harold Wilson is playing a kind of early Stalin game and he might well oust the leadership from Gaitskell, but Harold is so pompous and conceited and such an uninspiring character, that he won't do the party much good either.

On 6 July 1960 Aneurin Bevan died. A bitter Jennie Lee wrote: 'Spiritually he recovered from the wounds inflicted by the unilateral disarmers in 1957 and 1958, but they had done their deadly work. Until their attacks began, he never had so much as a stomach ache ... He did not die, he was murdered.'* A devastated Jill and Michael made a vow never to antagonize Jennie again and to remain, for the rest of her life, devoted friends. Michael rushed to Jennie's side, and out of their reconciliation came their agreement that he should write Nye's biography.[1]

Of all the Bevanites, Mervyn Jones suggests, Michael seemed a likely successor to the fallen hero. Others were not left enough or did not have the temperament for leadership. Yet Jill knew Michael had little appetite for a star turn. When his friend Alan Brien pressed him, Michael replied, 'No, no, it's not my role. I'm not a leader.' Lady Beaverbrook would later write to Jill: 'I wish Michael were more ambitious – he will never put any pressure to bear for himself, it is always for an ideal – this is the way of all martyrs – the only one to suffer is themselves!'[2] Indeed, Michael prized the calling of the backbencher and admired independent leftists such as Leo Abse, elected an MP in 1958, and Ian Mikardo, who remained a fiercely singular leftist back-bencher throughout his entire career. The right choice for Michael, then, was to take up Nye's own hint that he should succeed him at Ebbw Vale. Jill assented enthusiastically, given the affinity for the Welsh she felt while filming *Blue Scar*. As Leo Abse put it, Jill put no brake on Michael's romanticism. 'She was, after all, a woman of the film world.'

After a setback – when Michael did not make the constituency party's first shortlist† – he launched a rousing campaign that took up where Nye left off, attacking Gaitskell for failing to unite the party but also pro-moting the unilateralist cause and public ownership. The *Evening Standard* provided a portrait of Jill in action. In a small village hall jammed with a hundred people, 'Jill Craigie, in a red shortie coat with a black Hussar hat set rakishly on the side of her head, was gazing at her husband ... occasionally she interpolated the speech, so that when he declared the Soviet Union spent more on education than Britain, she quickly added "per

---

* Bevan suffered from high blood pressure and frequent chest colds. As Patricia Hollis in *Jennie Lee: A Life* (1997) notes, he had his 'share of ill health'. According to volume two of Michael's Bevan biography, he suffered from a 'touch of pneumoconiosis' from his days as a miner. It is a dubious idea that emotional stress causes cancer, although that theory remains popular with many people searching for a reason behind the illness. See Susan Sontag's *Illness as Metaphor* as a corrective.

† As Nye's heir apparent, Michael had the backing of the Bevan family, and it was assumed that the local party would want another MP like Nye, with an international reputation, but sentiment evidently tended towards a local candidate and it took some doing on Jennie Lee's part to break up the group of lesser contenders who had combined to keep Michael off the list.

capita".'

Jill thought the Welsh were at least as witty as the fabled Irish. 'She was absolutely out to make a success of it,' Michael recalled. She revelled in gossiping with Welsh housewives – indulging in frank talk about their 'delinquent' husbands and their sex lives. Their confidence in one another impressed her. They were ardent, but humorous about politics, and she liked that: 'The Welsh often laugh that they may not weep. I think now I understand how the people of the valleys have emerged from the years of Depression so effervescent and yet so serious a people.' She liked to talk to women voters about the suffragettes and the importance of the vote. Sometimes she got carried away. Addressing a crowd of men and women, she heard herself say, 'And there is one big difference between men and women' – and then stopped, as the gathering convulsed in laughter.[3]

Michael's majority was 16,729, several thousand votes shy of Nye's high watermark, but far more than the 12,000 votes it was said he needed to prove himself. On 17 November 1960 Michael called his father with the good news. Isaac said, 'When they fight the Foots, the Tories bite granite.' When a reporter remarked, 'God help Gaitskell', Michael replied, 'You said it.' Vicky produced a cartoon showing Gaitskell's gazing at Michael's glowing face in the newspaper. A gloomy Gaitskell said, 'Oh dear, we've won.' Three days later Michael took his parliamentary seat wearing, according to Hoggart and Leigh, a wrinkled suit. The Conservatives cheered Michael and waved for Gaitskell to join them. 'The Labour leader managed a smile as crumpled as his newest member's clothing,' Foot's biographers report.

Gaitskell could never forgive Michael's Bevanite attacks. On a 1962 trip to Portofino, Jill sent Beaverbrook a report of an encounter with their nemesis: 'We turned round and there was Gaitskell and party… Did Gaitskell give us a nod? Did he smile? Did he invite us over? Not at all. He cut us dead. Only Maurice Bowra [a friend of Michael's since his Oxford days] left Gaitskell's table to speak to Michael and was afterwards, so he told us, reproved for his disloyalty. So how's that for magnanimity on Gaitskell's part? I was quite sorry that one of your reporters was not lurking about.'

On 13 December 1960 Isaac Foot died. He had celebrated his eightieth birthday during the summer, and though the family could see he was failing, his death from a heart attack surprised them. Jill felt his loss keenly. Just before he had died, Isaac had given Jill one of his treasured volumes, Oscar Wilde's *Ballad of Reading Gaol*. He had left behind a massive collection of books and debts. 'All his wealth is tied up in his library,' she confided to Beaverbrook, and 'Michael, as might be expected, would rather hang on to the books than get any money.'* He had experienced the worst attack of asthma ever, Jill wrote to Beaverbrook, asking him about the effectiveness of the cortisone he took for his own asthma attacks.

Jill and Michael had stayed with Isaac at Pencrebar during Michael's days as an MP from Plymouth, but in Ebbw Vale they wanted their own home in the community. They bought a dilapidated miner's cottage at 10 Morgan Street, right on one of Tredegar's main streets. Michael only had to step outside his home to see the handsome iron clock, the town's focal point and a symbol of its industrial history. Michael remembered that the terraced cottage cost £300 and was in such bad condition (the roof was falling in) that he and Jill were advised not to purchase it. But it had solid thick walls and Jill saw its promise, beginning on a renovation aided by a £2000 government grant.

While establishing this second home, Jill made her own friends as a 'talented women who flourished on her own', agreed Alan and Megan Fox.† 'But she never had a major role,' Alan emphasized. She would attend an annual dinner of this or that organization, appear at an opening of an event and canvass where it seemed appropriate. 'But the role of the woman was to be a supporter,' Megan confirmed. Employment for women was a problem. Given the area's industrial development, there were few jobs deemed fit for women. Women were maids, kitchen help, typists, secretaries, 'but there were no serious career opportunities as late as the 1960s and 1970s', not even in the local Labour Party, Alan said. A woman doctor was a rarity.

'Michael would come down regularly on a fortnight and all his time was taken up with constituency matters,' Megan recalled. 'And was she to tag along?' Alan added, 'Lots of his dealings would have been with male-orientated industries – coal, steel and light industries. She was not deliberately excluded; there was just a cultural change, a chasm', between the constituency and the smart world of London. Jill would rely on couples like Alan and Megan, saying to them, 'Come and tell me now what you think of this situation. What's the view in Tredegar?' Like Michael, she loved to listen. 'Sometimes she would throw a spanner in the works just to see what would happen,' Megan said, laughing.

---

* The Isaac Foot library of 52,000 books was sold to the University of California for £50,000.
† Alas, most of Jill's closest friends in the constituency died before this biography was begun.

Alan and Megan describe how the cultural gap* opened up when Jill decided to employ two respected local builders, Ivor and Howard, to help her refurbish 10 Morgan Street. 'The thought of this bloody woman telling them that she wanted a large roped handrail instead of a wooden handrail – where were they to get this?' Well, Jill got the item and they put it on. Then they went on about the fireplace. She wanted an open grate. 'There are so many modern grates about, you know,' they told her. 'Everyone is getting rid of these old things.' But Jill knew she had a Victorian mantelpiece, and she kept it, admiring its shape and quality. The floors creaked but she insisted on keeping the original wood and had it rubbed down and stained. 'Well, they weren't happy with that.' At every stage, they complained. 'Don't you want a nice handle on that?' they asked Jill. 'No, I want the old latch left,' she replied. 'Yet when it was finished,' Megan said, 'they had to admit that Jill was right. She had an eye.' She was always looking for Victoriana and would buy an ornament and pop it on a shelf – for example, a black and gold cow (a cream jug), which she gave to the Foxes when she and Michael sold 10 Morgan Street in the mid-1990s. The item is worth well over £400 now. It was just like Jill to pick up, say, a pair of candlesticks for a few pounds that would later fetch £40.

Jill put in beautiful William Morris wallpaper and installed a large Welsh dresser with lots of willow-patterned china. Much of the lighting came from old paraffin lamps rewired for electricity. The cottage was a time capsule. In the cupboard Jill kept election posters from Michael's first Ebbw Vale election. An oil painting on the wall featured a Welsh valley scene, and the rocking chair had a rush seat.[4]

Michael appreciated Jill's gift for homemaking but did not inquire about the items she selected. He appreciated the cottage layout: the kitchen/parlour below street level (which Jill had opened up, putting in a door as a rear exit), a spacious street-level room with a little spiral staircase in one corner (she resisted the builders' advice to tear it out), and then at the top a bedroom and a bath. Michael liked the thick walls: 'It was all very snug.' Michael wrote the first volume of his Bevan biography (published 1962) in the kitchen, where he would also meet with some of Nye's own friends. He often phoned his constituents and would invite them for a session in the living room.

If Jill's role in Ebbw Vale remained limited, there seemed to be no strain in

---

* The idea of a cultural gap should not be overstated. Martin Westlake in *Kinnock: The Biography* (2001) notes that 'Mrs Lily Tagg, a Morgan Street shopkeeper… was renowned locally for having visited every major opera house in Europe.' Indeed, Michael remembers her fondly as a good next-door neighbour and friend who often looked after 10 Morgan Street when he and Jill were away. Michael also admired her husband, who shortly before his death fulfilled his promise to take his wife to La Scala.

the marriage. 'She used her talents in the best way she could without compromising Michael's career, which she regarded as the more important one. If it would have been reversed, they would have been just as sincere,' Alan believed. 'They were dotty-eyed about each other. Michael is a hopeless romantic, isn't he?'

On a weekend in 1963 two college students, Neil and Glenys Kinnock, were introduced to Michael by Labour Party councillor Bill Harry, who suggested the young couple might like to accompany Michael on one of his Sunday morning walks and 'discuss the plight of the masses'.[5] Neil had campaigned actively for Michael in 1960, and according to Mervyn Jones, 'Michael spotted his political talents and decided to keep an eye on him.' Glenys and Neil had only recently become a twosome. Like Neil, Glenys had been active in Labour Party politics from an early age, becoming a CND campaigner at fifteen. She remembered being 'overawed' at the prospect of meeting Michael and thrilled when she and Neil were invited to 10 Morgan Street:

> I remember going down that little winding staircase and having one of Jill's lovely dinners. For me, even though it was this little house, it was all hellishly sophisticated. I was eighteen, and Michael Foot was my father's hero. But that didn't last because they were so hospitable and friendly. Women always say Jill was not good with women, and I noticed that she often wasn't, yet she was always extremely generous in every sense to me. We had lots of chats – and excellent gossip was shared with me.

Glenys and Neil, as 'two working class kids' who had lived in the kind of council houses Aneurin Bevan had built after the war, intrigued Jill and Michael. Jill always wanted to know 'where you were coming from, what your background was, what made you what you were. She engaged with me seriously. She was never one of those women who put me down at the bottom of the table. I always sat next to her.'

Glenys found it amusing and fascinating to watch Michael and Jill:

> He would say, 'Oh my dear child! Don't talk such bloody rubbish!' The bout would go on, and Jill would just flutter her eyelashes, look at me, roll her eyes, and then start another conversation to detract attention from this outburst from Michael. Some might say they were not well matched, but this was not the case. They were so comfortable with each other, and so deeply in love. Neil and I are a volatile pair, and so we could identify with all the shouting.

The 'rubbish' would usually be political gossip that Jill had elaborated into a

riveting allegory. Leo Abse thought that Jill, like his Welsh wife Marjorie, had
an artist's sensibility. Jill and Marjorie saw each other often because their
husband's constituencies were close together. Both women were 'fantasists',
Leo argued:

> Marjorie had a tendency to conflate fact and fiction as only the Welsh can. Jill could
> tell a tale, which had a kernel of truth, but it did not necessarily happen. To some,
> this may have been disconcerting, but I lived with this for years. Drama is a
> necessary ingredient of life in Wales; nothing is prosaic. Then it follows that you are
> tolerant towards people who heighten the mundane and make it exciting and
> delightful. All this was Jill. Marjorie would sometimes come home when she had
> been with Jill and start telling me something, and I'd say, 'Of course that isn't right.
> How do you know?' Marjorie would say, 'Jill told me.' 'Take it easy,' I said. The
> stories about politicians or politician's wives may or may not have been true, but
> they would certainly indicate the yearnings, if not the realities of those people.

Glenys found Jill a rather fascinating study in ambiguity, doubt and
misunderstanding:

> She was uncertain about a lot of things. She was uncertain about what her role was
> and where she fit into the Party. Her heart was in the right place, and her radicalism
> was never in question. We had once, however, had a serious row about the pill. One
> of the emancipating things for women was that they could plan their families. Jill
> was totally against it. She said, 'This is a danger to women's health, and they should
> be very careful about this form of birth control.'

To Glenys, Jill could seem rather old fashioned in an odd way.

> Jill did not have Michael's gift for being at ease with people regardless of their class
> background. During canvassing on a doorstep, she might inadvertently say
> something inappropriate. She didn't always know the nuances, the vocabulary or
> even that feminism was taken with mother's milk in South Wales. A woman comes
> to the door, you look over her shoulder, and you see it's a single mum with lots of
> kids running round, and you'd say 'ah', and know these people and they moan about
> everything – whereas Jill would say, 'Oh, this is terrible.' And you'd say, 'Jill, you just
> have to think what these people's lives are, what these women are doing.' But she
> would never have thought or understood because she'd never experienced that. It's
> not knowing what poor people expect you to say and not to say.

Glenys pointed out that 'Michael never wanted to think badly of anyone,' and
Jill had to be his 'eyes and ears':

She would confront the stark reality and this was important. She often said he was being naive about his political opponents who would denigrate him behind his back. She was very protective and very aware that betrayal was on the cards. She had a special way of wheedling out information, opinions and ideas. There would always be lots of questions. You came in, she greeted you, you had a glass of wine or very strong gin and tonic, and then there would be the questions, lots of questions, fluttering eyelashes and tossing of the head.

Glenys never thought Michael dominated Jill. 'She made her own personal contribution. Feminism is about generosity and caring, and Jill certainly promoted the cause of women's rights.' Glenys never regretted the years she devoted to raising her children (Glenys worked as well), and Jill 'understood that. That was another identification we had.' Making a family, a home and a successful marriage was an achievement both women rated highly.

Neil Kinnock remembered meeting first Jill, then Michael.[6] Asked whether he was aware of her fabled flirtatiousness, he responded that 'it was very subtle. She was very gentle.' She would put her head to one side, smile slightly, toss her hair and look absolutely enchanted with you, conveying a sense of complete devotion. In a mood to argue, she would put her head to the other side and exhibit a truculent stiffness. Arguments at Morgan Street might begin with the seemingly trivial issue of haircuts, and that would lead to some extreme political statement. Neil took issue with Jill about the length of men's hair, and she promptly became the champion of every beatnik style you can imagine, and then Neil would counter-attack, deploring any man who did not have a crease in his trousers.

Neil loved Jill's beautifully pitched voice, a voice of the 1930s. At the suggestion that Jill had a 'plummy' tone, Neil agreed, but quickly added, 'it was the only thing plummy about Jill'. He considered it a voice 'frozen in time, a bit of frozen history'. Yet Jill was always in the now. He did not remember her ever mentioning her mother or father. If she quoted anyone from her past, it would be an artist: 'Augustus John used to say …'.

The young Neil Kinnock met a couple completely devoted to each other, and he marvelled at the curious dynamic between them. 'If I ever said, "my dear child" to my wife, I'd get acid straight back.' Jill would handle Michael, breaking down his first name into two syllables. Jill was the one to say 'be careful Mich-ael' and 'do you really think' to her sweet and trusting husband. If Jill said, 'You know best', Neil knew you should take that the way all wives meant it (as bullshit). 'Jill had a bloody good memory, for both the bad and the good things.' She also had a 'feel for the nooks and crannies of history'.

She would begin by saying, 'Of course, you know, don't you?' And you'd have to listen, because of course you didn't know. Jill was an expert at getting people to listen to her. Jill had 'great expectations' and felt that ultimately good would triumph over evil. In that sense, she had a core of 'innocence', Kinnock concluded. 'It just felt good to go in and inhale a bit of that atmosphere', even if he would come away with the sceptical thought, 'Oh, if only that was true.'

Jill obviously enjoyed Neil and Glenys's give-and-take. Glenys would mimic Neil's pompous talk, and though nettled, he could not help laughing. 'It's a sign of Neil's strength. A less secure man would not like to defer to his wife as much as he does,' Jill observed to biographer Robert Harris in *The Making of Neil Kinnock* (1984). If the early Neil Kinnock had a fault, it was his tendency to be a 'little glib', she told Harris. Responding to the biographer's question about Michael's and Neil's 'father–son' relationship, Michael's one word answer was 'balls'. Glenys and Alan Fox (a close friend of the Kinnocks) felt Neil did become a kind of son, but understandably neither Neil nor Michael wanted a relationship that was anything other than that of equals.

The Kinnocks were only the most important of a younger generation that always found a welcome in the Jill Craigie/Michael Foot household. It must be put that way because Jill's home – wherever it might be – became the citadel, the arsenal, the playground and the court of Michael Foot's life. Leo Abse put it well in his memoir, *Private Member*: 'Jill Craigie, winsome and creative, has her own province in the Foot home.' She had her own name and identity – yet as Abse's own sentence concludes, it was berthed in the 'Foot home'. 'Politicians seldom like women,' Abse remarked, and often forget that women constitute half of the electorate. He admired Jill and his wife Marjorie – both spirited women – and appreciated their aesthetic view of the world (expressed in their joint antique-hunting forays). Most MPs have 'submissive, almost apologetic wives', Abse said, and the ones that did not were made into better men, like Tony Crosland, who might have become effete without his wife Susan, or Sir Elwyn Jones, whose 'original and disconcerting wife', Pearl Binder, kept her husband from becoming just an 'urbane smoothie'. 'Winsome' was the word Abse used about Jill again during an interview. To be young is just an age, Frank Lloyd Wright once said, but youth is a quality, and if you have it, you never lose it. Jill had that sweet and innocent quality associated with youth, but she also governed – she had her province. While Michael had a tendency to circle round and round a subject, she grounded him and brought him and his arguments home.

17

Facing It
(1963–4)

Keep her facing it. They may say what they like, but the heaviest seas run with the wind. Facing it – always facing it – that's the way to get through.

Captain MacWhirr's advice in Joseph Conrad's *Typhoon*,
often quoted by Michael Foot

More than anything else, Jill conveyed to Julie the importance of making a home and a family – a complete world – although Julie wanted more of it than Jill had had with Sonia, and Julie had had with Jill. She wanted home, family, and several children – they would mean much more than a career ever would. In 1960 Julie married Victor Lehel, a handsome and talented Hungarian architect (a seemingly perfect choice for Jill Craigie's daughter). The next year she gave birth to a son, Jason, and Jill became a fifty-year-old grandmother.

On 21 October 1963, their wedding anniversary, Jill and Michael were driving from 10 Morgan Street to London with two-year-old Jason and their dog Vanessa, while Julie, who had just had an operation on her back, was convalescing after more than a month in hospital. Taking a scenic route through Herefordshire, Jill, never a good driver, entered a junction, cutting off the right of way of a lorry that crashed into the car's passenger side, throwing both Michael and Jill out of the car. Like most cars in those days, theirs did not have seatbelts.

Jill landed on the road, and the lorry, before it could stop, ran over her left hand. The driver phoned for an ambulance while Vanessa jumped out of the car, only to be recovered some hours later. Jason, in the back seat, remained safe in the wreckage. That he escaped without injury was what Isaac Foot would have called a 'crowning mercy', Michael later wrote to Jill.

At the end of an 11-mile ambulance ride to Hereford General Hospital, Michael managed to say, 'Mind you don't put me in a private ward.' Always a stout defender of Nye's National Health Service, Michael wanted to avoid even the appearance of special treatment, refusing to be transferred to a London hospital, although he couldn't prevent the specialists that flocked to help him on Julie's request. Characteristically, he later wrote an article demonstrating that the pioneering methods of the NHS and its effort to spread quality care throughout the country had saved his life.

Jill urged the doctors to treat Michael first; he urged them to care for her first. Michael had every rib broken, perforated lungs and a crushed left leg; the doctors thought he might die. Jill's injuries were also quite serious. She had a broken pelvis and a shattered hand. Both husband and wife underwent operations and suffered immense pain. With a caved-in chest, even breathing became a torture for Michael. Jerry Slattery, their doctor, acknowledged Jill's agony (28 October 1963): 'A fracture of the pelvis is one of the most painful of all afflictions. Every movement sends waves of pain throughout the whole body.' It would take the better part of year for them to recover.

The next morning Julie arrived (having been driven by a friend all the way from East Sussex, where she had been convalescing). She was told Michael might not last the night. Michael's brother, John, a lawyer, arrived and told Julie that if Michael died, Jill might be charged with manslaughter. It would be ten days before Michael would be considered out of danger. He had been advised not to speak because of his damaged lungs, so he wrote a note to Julie, then staying in a hotel near the hospital, 'How is Jason? Do you need money?' (Jason had spent the night of the accident at a policeman's house until his father Victor arrived to take him home.)

Julie had contacted Jill and Michael's GP Jerry Slattery, a 'remarkable man', and 'he rushed to Hereford to make sure all possible was being done. He made sure the best anaesthetist was on the job of looking after Michael; the anaesthetists saved Michael's life,' Julie emphasized. She also contacted Dr Lipman Kessel, a top orthopaedic surgeon, who had just operated on her back, to make sure her parents got the best treatment. Julie would stay in Hereford until Jill and Michael were released from hospital a month later. Julie's husband had taken charge of Jason.

Jill and Michael were buoyed by Julie's attentiveness and aggressiveness on their behalf. 'Marvellous having Judy around – makes all the difference,' Michael wrote to Jill. 'Her action, I think, may have saved your life,' Jill later wrote to Michael from her hospital bed. 'She's a very good girl. No words of praise too high – not only for what she has done, but the charm with which she had done it,' he concurred. They were also deeply worried about the strain she was under, since she herself had been out of hospital for only a few days.

Michael did not dwell on his own injuries. His extraordinary courage and cheerfulness astounded the hospital staff. His concern quickly turned to Jill. A doctor told him that they would have to amputate Jill's hand. Michael solicited other opinions and the hand was saved, although it would need many operations, continuing care and would never be right. Later Jill went to a specialist in Rugby to have her hand rebuilt, but for the rest of her life she would try to conceal it with a bandage.

Jill was put into a private room. Julie did not tell her mother how grave Michael's condition was: 'She had no idea until much later.' Jill and Michael began exchanging notes almost immediately. 'For my part,' Jill wrote to Michael:

> although I do my best not to relive the accident, it keeps coming back to me like a vivid nightmare & the thought of risking your life, your oh so very precious and special life, my darling, is far more unendurable than any amount of physical pain. The latter I am getting used to.
>
> The hold-up to your book [the second volume of the Bevan biography] also distresses me, but I am trying to figure out ways in which I could help to produce the necessary conditions in which to complete it.

Michael replied:

> My dear child,
>
> Thanks for your note. Please don't worry about how the accident happened. The only thing that matters is that we should both get well together & that I think is what is going to happen. And then we shall need each other even more than we did before.
>
> So sleep, don't be impatient & do what you are told. When we're better we'll go on a good holiday together.
>
> Love,
> Michael

'Poor girl, she suffered much anguish,' Michael wrote to Beaverbrook, and Beaverbrook wrote to Jill:

> You are meeting your dreadful calamity with courage. You have much to do in nursing Michael back to health when he escapes from the hospital. Do not, my dear Jill, dwell on the past. The circumstances of your accident should not – must not distress either of you. There is no use in saying it might have been different if only & c. Remember the song 'Che sera sera.'

The hospital staff tried to conceal any bad news from Jill (they did not allow her any newspapers). She wrote to Michael:

I am one mess of aches, pains, frustrations, furies, sadness, irritation &
impatience all of which, according to our competent Dr Slee, means that I am
making real strides towards recovery. My hand seems to be macabre, to put it
mildly, but at least it is saved & I gather getting it to function depends on my own
will power.

Darling, I have just been cleaned up for the evening. And although I remain, with
my strings & pulleys, like one of Heath Robinson's less successful contraptions,* I
feel sufficiently human to drop you a note. Have patience, you say & I expect you
have. But how to have patience when the aches & pains are too irksome to make
even reading possible, I don't know.

Later she wrote:

the contraption on my leg has been changed & in place of the old 'Study in
Wire & String' by Francis Bacon,† I now have a primitive plaster after the style
of Barbara Hepworth. But, leaving aesthetics aside, the result is LIBERATION.
My leg has worried me every second of the day; but now, suddenly, the torture is
over.

Like Jill's left hand, Michael's left leg never returned to normal. He continued
his vigorous walks but with a stick for support.

It was typical of Michael to credit his long hospital stay (until 19
November) with affording him the opportunity to read Joseph Conrad's
novels and to develop an intense absorption with Montaigne. His asthma
vanished after the accident. During the early days of his hospital stay, the
doctors told Michael that an attack of asthma might kill him. (The asthma
returned only in Michael's dreams.)‡ Michael also quit smoking, which no
doubt helped to alleviate his respiratory problems.

By 5 November 1963, Lady Beaverbrook was praising Jill's 'warrior spirit'
and sending her two boxes of pink champagne, which Jill and Julie drank
during the hospital stay. After five weeks in hospital, Jill and Michael returned
to Abbey Road, and then in January 1964, they decided to spend their holiday
at Capponcina, in the South of France, at the invitation of the Beaverbrooks.
'I thought I was done for,' Michael recalled, meaning that perhaps the accident

---

  * Heath Robinson (1872–1944) satirized the machine age with his elaborate and exquisite drawings of
gadgets that would raise one's hat, shuffle and deal cards or recover a collar-stud.
  † Francis Bacon (1909–92), as critic John Russell notes in *The Oxford Dictionary of Art* (1988), 'is known
for his handling of paint, by means of which he smudges and twists faces and bodies into ill-defined
jumbled protuberances suggestive of formless, slug-like, creatures of nightmare fantasy'.
  ‡ His eczema had gradually abated in the 1950s after treatments of Vitamin C administered through a
sun lamp personally delivered by Nye Bevan, who had recommended the procedure.

and the operation had 'interrupted my sexual possibilities'. But the holiday proved otherwise. Jill would later tell Julie that the first years of marriage were her most sexually fulfilling. But holidays were a time of romantic revival. 'We never wanted to miss them. Whenever we had differences, we had wonderful reconciliations on holidays,' Michael emphasized. In the in-between times the marriage's sexual life would 'fade', he acknowledged, though he discounted Rebecca West's theory that most men lose sexual interest in their wives after the first five years of marriage. Michael, in a mood for sex, said Jill 'could do what she wanted' – tease and be playful? ('oh yes!'), become aggressive? ('NO!'). 'She thought sex was a matter for ridicule and comedy. She would laugh about it.' Sex might have its sacred aspects, but 'it ought to be treated with mockery as well'. When Michael began to read Byron in earnest, he enjoyed reading to Jill those parts of *Don Juan* that expressed her own contrary view of sex.

The couple went on to Morocco in February for the winter sun. While staying at the La Mamounia Hotel in Marrakesh, Jill and Michael enjoyed a reunion with Randolph Churchill, who remained a convivial companion even though he was ailing, still unable to quit his habit of smoking eighty cigarettes a day. Jill charmed the irascible Randolph and 'looked after him', Michael recalled: 'Lots of people found it difficult to be nice to Randolph, but not Jill. We had lots of fun, and it assisted our recovery, although it may have finished off Randolph. He would say, "All these other people – these weaklings – have gone to bed and here we are sitting up drinking all night."' Although Michael had been deeply critical of Randolph's father, Michael shared Randolph's abiding passion: his lifelong campaign against the appeasers – Chamberlain and the whole pre-1938 lot that Michael had attacked in *Guilty Men*, the famous pamphlet to which he contributed. Randolph's two losing campaigns against Michael in Plymouth had only endeared him to Michael and Jill. 'He was so unpopular amongst the Tories – you can't imagine his rudeness to them – and by the end of a campaign they would not come to see him off at the station. So Jill and I would see him off.' Jill and Michael even stayed with Randolph at his home in Suffolk while he was working on the first volume of his father's biography. Jill and Michael admired Randolph's indomitable spirit. Later Jill visited him in London after a lung cancer operation. He sat there drinking, smoking and telling off his distinguished physician: 'Stop treating me like an invalid.' He died in 1968.

During their holiday in Morocco, Jill's hand 'became very painful' and had to be treated with expensive antibiotics. She went home to Abbey Road and prepared herself for a series of operations on her hand. Michael returned to stay with the Beaverbrooks at Capponcina for another period of recuperation.

But a message from Jill disturbed his repose: 'I am mystified & horrified by our conversation this morning. You may not believe it but I cannot bear to think that you are made unhappy on my account,' he wrote to her. He would come home as soon as he could make the travel arrangements. 'The only thing that sets my mind at rest is that I am quite confident that we can settle anything & everything by a talk together ... I wrote to you when I was in hospital to say that what I wanted was THIRTY GOOD YEARS of life TOGETHER. That's what I want & that's what I am sure we can have.' Michael wrote again the next day: 'I was relieved to get your telegram, although I am still shaken by our conversation.' He planned to return home in three days.

What had so disturbed Jill? Pamela Berry had sent Michael a book with a note attached. 'Jill thought it showed a closer relationship than was the case,' Michael said. Pamela Berry, the daughter of the Earl of Birkenhead and wife of Michael Berry (Lord Hartwell), chairman and editor-in-chief of the *Daily Telegraph* and the *Sunday Telegraph*, had become President of the Incorporated Society of Fashion Designers in 1954. Dick Crossman extolled her 'slap-up political-social occasions', which had 'all the brilliance of intimate gossip'. There one could meet Roy Jenkins, *Washington Post* owner Katharine Graham, newspaper editor Hugh Cudlipp, historian Arthur Schlesinger Jr, Tom Driberg, American journalist Joseph Alsop and writer Virginia Cowles – to name just a smattering of the British and American figures who revelled in the give-and-take of political intrigue. According to Crossman, one became known as a 'Pam Berry person' by entering her 'hard-boiled, political, journalistic atmosphere'. She was 'male-oriented,' Crossman emphasized.[1] Jill had been confiding in Julie her deep resentment over Michael's attendance at Berry's salon. He had dined with Berry and had never protested that Jill had not been included in the invitations. Jill felt 'Michael was disloyal to her', Julie said. Jill, a saloniste who would shortly make herself the cynosure of her own new home, saw in Berry a competitor. Michael, always attracted to bright and beautiful women, had what Stendhal called a 'French gaiety', so much more pleasing than the English spirit of reserve and dignity. Or as Stendhal put it in *De l'Amour*, one of Michael's cherished texts, 'Which of our successive Governments did commit the frightful atrocity of *anglicizing* us?' Michael was, in other words, an enthusiast with a taste for exotics who needed careful watching. 'He notices beautiful woman,' Jill's friend Jenny Stringer remarked. 'He's flirtatious.'

Michael found Berry's lair enticing because 'she made friendships all over the bloody place' – in other words, irrespective of Party. But he was able to convince Jill that he was not having an affair with Berry. Jill's suspicions were evidently allayed, but she would remain wary of the bonds Michael formed with women. He loved to stay up late drinking with Beaverbrook's granddaughter, Jeanne Campbell, a journalist full of riotous stories. She could match any man drink for drink. Jeanne was just a teenager when Michael first met her in the late 1930s. 'She was a very attractive woman, there's no doubt at all,' Michael asserted. 'We got on like a house on fire. Jill was a bit suspicious about my friendship with Jeanne.'

After his respite at Capponcina, Michael returned to the offices of the *Daily Herald*, where he had been writing a column since 1944. 'When I got there, they said I was sacked.' Under a new name, *The Sun*, and a change of ownership (Rupert Murdoch) the paper took a political line that no longer jibed with Michael's. But the new management had blundered, believing they were getting rid of a freelancer. A paid-up union member, Michael was entitled to compensation and settled for £5000. He and Jill then sold the Abbey Road home for £12,000 to purchase a decrepit but eminently restorable Victorian home in Hampstead for the same amount. They had just about broken even, since it would cost about £5000 to rehabilitate the structure. Actually, Michael felt he was ahead, because he accepted Beaverbrook's invitation to become the chief book reviewer for the *Evening Standard* – in some ways the 'best job of my life', he believed, since he had the first claim on biographies, histories and criticism that also went free of charge into his ever-growing library.

By the middle of March, Jill was in a London hospital, writing to Beaverbrook on 10 March: 'despite ghastly picture in the *Express*, I am fit as can be, feel and look, so I am told, years younger'. But she was facing an ordeal with skin grafts, 'in and out of hospital for a week or two every two months until the end of the year'. Michael wrote to her:

> I hope you have settled in & things are not too terrible. If they are, just grit your teeth & bear it. You have been very brave & patient about the whole wretched business & I hope you won't have many more trials to endure over it... I am looking forward to our new home enormously, more than I can say.

Even a week away from Jill was too much, Michael wrote: 'I feel I would like someone to hit me on the head so that I could stay unconscious until we meet. Still, we'll make up for it.'

Jill was just as excited as Michael about the prospect of a new home. There was only one problem: she didn't like the name of the street, Worsley Road. It would be so much better if it became in name what it was in fact: an extension of Pilgrim's Lane. In a few years Jill would successfully arrange the name change, just as she had arranged her own.

18

Pilgrim's Lane
(1964–70)

She delights in detailing the transformations she has effected on their various homes. 'They were all derelict when we started but there's so much you can do without spending a lot of money.' Their present one in Hampstead reflects an uncluttered taste – white walls, burnished sanded floors, plenty of books and pictures.
Susan Raven and Carolyn Faulder, 'Mrs Wilson says goodbye to her diary ... which wife is next?', *Evening Standard*, 21 March 1976

On 17 January 1964 Hugh Gaitskell died. He was only fifty-six and at the 'height of his power and prestige'. He had 'come to be seen as the next Prime Minister ... blooded by battles and triumphs ... acquiring an appropriate gravitas'.[1] After a contest with George Brown and Jim Callaghan, Harold Wilson succeeded Gaitskell as Party leader on 14 February. On 12 March, Beaverbrook passed on this judgment to a receptive Jill: 'Wilson has not improved what is now popularly called his image. Probably it is good enough without any improvement, but he is not a growing asset. Tell that to Michael.' But Michael overcame his concerns about Wilson and wrote his campaign biography, sensing that Wilson's superb tactical and diplomatic manoeuvres would unite the Party and bring it back to power. On election day, 15 October 1964, Labour won, but with only a five-seat majority, making it difficult to reduce the 'weight of the old society' that had burdened previous Labour governments.[2]

With a 20,271 majority in Ebbw Vale, Michael threw himself into politics with a renewed vigour. 'Michael, I assure you, has never been fitter,' Jill told Beaverbrook, 'nor has he ever looked so well. Bronze, brown with his face filled out, or rather, not nearly so drawn, since he eats rather more having given up smoking.' Leo Abse observed a far more confident man stride into the House of Commons.[3]

Barbara Castle, now in Wilson's cabinet, acknowledged Michael's brilliant backbench oratory, but she was put off by his stridency. He showed no interest in joining the front bench, and he became one of the government's ardent critics – holding it strictly accountable, as Nye had done, to its socialist principles. Jill, who had always distrusted Wilson, found Michael's independence, indeed his argumentativeness, invigorating and inspiring. In her writing about women and about town planning for *Tribune* and *The Times* among other publications, Jill would hold the new government and its supporters accountable to its putative socialist democratic principles.*

It was an exciting time for Jill. 'We had always wanted to get back to Hampstead,' Michael said. She liked nothing better than renovating a house that now suited her furniture. Lady Beaverbrook sent Jill a Regency desk: 'I know only too well how much you appreciate old things with a flavour of the romantic' (5 December 1967). One of Jill's better purchases (30 July 1969) was an antique pine 7-foot breakfront bookcase (*c*.1830), which cost £350. The property had considerable water damage and required other repairs and improvements, including knocking down walls for an enlarged kitchen and dining room downstairs and a spacious sitting/living room on the ground floor. Yet, 'in a relatively short time, we were living in a very comfortable house', Michael recalled. Jill sold one of her Henry Moores to fund her decorations and furnishings.

Michael now lived just a few minutes from Hampstead Heath, where he liked to take Vanessa for long walks – two or three miles in just under an hour. On weekends the walks were longer. Jill, a good walker, sometimes accompanied him, but just as often she was 'very pleased to see me off', he said. The untrained Vanessa made walking on the heath 'somewhat hair raising', according to Julie. 'You'd call the dog, and if it did not feel like coming ... well, if the dog wanted to swim, it would swim. Or it would run across the road.' Julie evoked the spectacle of Jill or Michael standing on Hampstead Heath and shouting: 'Vanessa, come here!', while the dog swanned about as if to say, 'I'll come when I'm ready.'

Why didn't they do obedience training? Julie laughed: 'That's almost a ridiculous question! Can you see Michael taking a dog to a dog school?' What about reading a book? 'Their minds were on higher planes. If I said, "Come on, train your dog," the response would be "My dog's perfect!" There was no chance. They loved the dogs to pieces.' Julie watched Michael return home from an outing, only to greet Vanessa with, 'Oh my beauty, my lover, oh how are you?' and then turn and say, 'Hello, Jill.'

---

* See Chapter 19 for a description of this work, which included Jill's return to film-making.

Then there was the time when Vanessa went missing after a sumptuous dinner at Dennis Mathews' house. Jill gave a full account to Julie. The party searched everywhere in the pouring rain with no luck. Dennis persuaded Michael and Jill to stay the night and called the police. Jill lay awake listening for Vanessa's bark. Michael 'went straight to sleep, as he always does'. At 4 a.m. Jill heard Vanessa and woke Michael. She had lost her voice and could not call the dog. Michael 'staggered out of bed', dressed and set out after Vanessa. Even with a torch the search proved frustrating, the dog sometimes sounding nearer, sometimes further away. Michael stumbled into some barbed wire, then heard his dog whimpering. Eventually he brought the drenched Vanessa back to the bedroom. They dried her off. Michael got back into bed and dropped soundly off to sleep while Vanessa, 'mad with delight started pushing the chair all round the room making the most awful clatter'. Michael slept on. But not Jill.

One of the first friends Jill made on Pilgrim's Lane was Jenny Stringer, a friend of Victoria Reilly, who was Paul Reilly's daughter, Charles Reilly's granddaughter and Michael's goddaughter. Jill was just past fifty when Jenny met her, and Jenny regarded her as a stunning beauty. 'Jill was my mentor,' Jenny said. 'She was a great cook', who really knew how to run a house and who did not disparage such talents.* Jenny had married young and had had four children. By the time she met Jill, she was 'frustrated in lots of ways'. But 'Jill made me see the value of what I was doing.' Jill said the mother's role did not get the respect it deserved. But she also supported Jenny's desire to study and to do more with her life.

Glenys Kinnock had similar memories of Jill: 'I think she assumed that I would have a direct political role, but she never said to me, as Barbara Castle would, "What the hell are you doing not standing for Parliament?" Jill understood that it was my own choice. I wasn't resentful and never have been, and at the age of fifty I got elected to the European Parliament. So I've had the best of both worlds. She was hugely supportive and hugely loyal.'

Jenny noticed that Jill had certain 'attitudes'. Jill would invite Jenny for a dinner party at '7.30 for 8 p.m.' Jenny would arrive at 7.55 and Jill would say, 'You're late!' Jenny would say, 'No, I'm not' and 'give it right back to her'. Jill did not like buffets. 'You had to sit down and it all had to be carefully arranged.' Jenny liked that aspect of Jill, who made an art of such occasions. Michael was the focus of these parties. 'They come to see Michael,' Jill would

---

* Jill had learned cooking from scratch, knowing virtually nothing when she married Michael. 'She was naturally creative,' says Julie, who herself became a fine cook and author of a culinary column in the *Ham & High*.

say to Jenny, and then laugh. Jenny did not see any sign of bitterness in Jill, although Jill told Julie that she wondered how many friends she would have left if Michael died before she did.

At a Pilgrim's Lane dinner party, you could find A.J.P. Taylor, Mike and Connie Bessie, Malcolm Muggeridge or Stanley Kubrick. Jill considered Kubrick to be one of the few contemporary film-makers worthy of the medium. In a piece for the *Observer Magazine* (11 January 1980) she called *Dr Strangelove* 'a work of art', devoid of 'visual clichés', with a painter's sense of faultless composition. Kubrick reveals the grim realities of a nuclear world, yet 'he has us rocking with laughter'. These continual contrasts were complemented by the music – for example, 'jolly little renderings of "Johnny Comes Marching Home" accompany some of the most sinister sequences, wittily symbolising man's joyous sense of fulfilment in his own work, but regardless of the consequences'. She admired Kubrick's feeling for the obscene aspects of a male-dominated world: 'Never shall I forget the tone in Sellers' [Dr Strangelove] voice and the salacious gleam in his eye' when he envisions a post-nuclear holocaust world in which there will be for breeding purposes twelve women to every man. 'Since each man would be required to do prodigious services along these lines,' he argues, 'women will have to be selected for their sexual characteristics, which will have to be of a highly stimulating nature.' When Jill and Stanley met, Michael noticed that they formed an instant bond.

Sonia Orwell was another frequent guest at Pilgrim's Lane. Michael had first met her at Nye Bevan's home. Sonia said it all when she wrote to Jill and Michael on 29 April 1967: 'The whole atmosphere of your house is glorious: all those books & fires & flowers & nice people & marvellous food & drink & jokes – in fact my childhood dream of the Good Life!' Such evenings were so well done that guests like Sonia wondered at all the 'trouble' Jill went to on such occasions. 'I wondered if you eat like that every evening and if that explained why Michael seems so cheerful and well!'[4] 'When you went to dinner and Jill was not feeling well, she would not allow you to get up and clear your plate,' Moni Forman remembered. 'She'd say, "Sit down, it's all right."' The talk ranged from politics to the arts and it often lingered on after the party was over. 'You shook me last night when you pointed out that my arguments amounted to a denial that art was influential and my reply doesn't satisfy me this morning!' Benn Levy wrote to Jill.[5]

Moni Forman met Jill in 1969, shortly after Moni's marriage to James Cameron, and the women became very close friends. Jill told Moni that she could not do justice to her marriage and pursue a full-time career. 'That's not to say that she gave up her career for Michael. There's a big difference. She made a choice that this was important to her. It [marriage] hadn't worked before.' Moni found Jill a giving friend. Any little present you gave her, she made a fuss over it: "Oh, isn't that lovely," and she made you feel appreciated. She would fasten on some accomplishment of yours and say, "You really have done this beautifully." She had the quality of bringing out the best in you – if she liked you. I mean, how much time do we really have to spend on everyone?' When James Cameron was hospitalized, Jill came round nearly every day with goodies like smoked salmon, which she knew he liked. Her generosity astonished Moni because James had many friends but none who would do that kind of thing for him. He never forgot Jill's kindness.

Jill's mother, Sonia, lived at Pilgrim's Lane for the last few years of her life. Julie remembered that her grandmother gave Jill £2,000 to renovate the upstairs flat, which Sonia then occupied. Why Sonia came to stay with Jill is not clear. A friend's letter to Michael and Jill suggests that Sonia was ailing and had become one of Jill's worries.[6] Yet Jill hardly ever went up to see her mother or ask her down to dinner.

In December 1970 Sonia set the flat on fire by mistake and the same night had a cerebral haemorrhage. Jill told Julie about sitting with Sonia during her last hours. The nurses seemed rough with her mother, and Jill protested. They said, 'Ah! She doesn't know what's going on. She can't feel anything. She can't see anything.' But Jill felt otherwise. She would hold Sonia's hand and could feel a slight squeeze. Sonia died a few days later, on 22 December 1970. Her death certificate gives the cause of death as 'myocardial infarct due to coronary thrombosis'. Julie's husband Victor was very critical of Jill at the time, but 'my mother wouldn't talk about it. All she said,' Julie recalled, 'was that she felt so guilty.'[7]

Why did Jill feel guilty? It is hard to say, since Jill left so little commentary about her mother. Introducing Sonia to Jenny Stringer suggests at least some effort to include her mother in Jill's life. Yet most of the time, Jill set her mother aside, for she was unable to get over the hard feelings of childhood, when she felt her mother had neglected her. Sonia's death, however, changed the equation, so to speak. Jill had only her feelings to confront. Now, perhaps, it seemed to Jill that she had neglected her mother.

Who Are the Vandals?
(1964–72)

If we cannot learn to challenge some of the basic assumption of city architects, if the layman is unable to intervene in the domain of the expert, the signs are that – despite all the figures of housing records – we are busy devising on a mammoth scale, a new brand of twentieth-century slum.

Jill Craigie, 'People Versus Planners', *The Times*, 14 September 1968

The radicalism of the 1960s and the election of Harold Wilson seemed to galvanize Jill and to provoke her into expressing in film and newspaper articles her alarm that the socialist promises of 1945 remained unfulfilled. In *Tribune* (7 August 1964) she argued:

It is sinister enough when only a few men own between them most of the newspapers in the country. It is no less appalling when a tiny group of men own most of the cinemas, film production companies … theatres, film, theatrical and writing agencies and many more subsidiary companies as well.

But when these two tiny groups of men are also given the control of television channels and when, instead of competing with each other, they gang up to grab for themselves an even larger slice of the mass media, then their power over what we may hear, read, and see begins to reach Hitlerian proportions.

Her criticisms were not just reserved for the media. In 1967 she took on the Camden Council, irritating local Labour Party leaders because of her uncompromising attack on the failures of public housing. Jill was still avidly interested in town planning and this period of renewed energy was channelled in this direction. She responded to what Terence Bendixson calls the 1960s' 'ferment in thinking about cities. Futurism was fashionable.'[1] In 1961 Lewis Mumford published *The City in History*, a reworking and expansion of *The Culture of the Cites*. Suddenly Jill saw a second chance to remould the city with the same zeal that had inspired the Plymouth plan. This time it was not the war but the planners themselves who had destroyed the cities by putting up monstrous tower blocks. Michael remembered that Peggy Duff, a Camden councillor, attacked Jill: 'You're stopping us from building flats for people.' While Jill's efforts did not stop Duff, Jill did not relent: in effect, the consequences of poor planning had been criminal – giving rise to the title Michael suggested for her documentary *Who Are the Vandals?*, commissioned by the BBC. As she pointed out to an interviewer, the vandals were not the young boys marauding through the housing estates, but the architects who had condemned whole communities to substandard housing and degrading facilities:

> They think they can do it all on paper without proper consultation. They have quite a lot of mock consultation, don't they? I've been to quite a few meetings with Camden Council, where I've heard people boo the plan, actually … After the war, architects betrayed their ethics. They had all these slogans which I fell for, because I'm a great one for falling for slogans. They used to say, 'A town should be for a citizen what a country estate is for a rich man: a pleasant place to walk in.' Well you can't say these tower blocks they've built with these beastly little places … all draughty at the bottom, make pleasant places to walk in, can you?

The film opens with shots of the tower blocks in the Regent's Park Estate in the north of London (not far from Pilgrim's Lane), with the voice-over of a woman calling them 'rabbit hutches'. That the first voice is a woman's is important: 'I saw architecture from the feminine point of view,' Jill said. 'Today, I happen to think that one of the things that went most wrong with the Labour Party is its ignorance on this subject.'

A male voice overlaps with the woman's, pointing out how the units have grown and grown, as a group of boys run wild on roofs, climbing up railings, jumping off roofs. Another male voice speaks of the damage these gangs cause and of the chaos that ensues from the unplanned consequences of building. Children parade with signs protesting the dangerous conditions in which they have no room to play. Architect John Chisholm is shown approaching a group of women and children, introducing himself to say that he wants to talk with them about the housing scheme. He is personable, direct and comfortable on camera. He behaves like a man who actually practises architecture by talking to the people the buildings are meant to house. A handheld camera jerks in and out of a congestion of cars, children, bare patches of ground and high gates as Chisholm walks to his meeting with Peggy Duff, chairman of the planning committee in Camden Town. Chisholm is blunt. He asks her 'why on earth' so many roads intersect with the playground. She explains that the recreation area was put in after the rest of the development. Chisholm is relentless, refusing to take at face value Duff's comment that tower blocks were simply the style that seemed appropriate after the war.

MP Lena Jeger interviews an articulate housewife who provides a devastating analysis of how the Regent's Park estate has failed. She doubts her views would sway an architect who has his own ideas. Real change would come, she argues, only if public opinion carried more weight. Chisholm then zeroes in on Brian Smith, the award-winning architect for the southern part of Regent's Park. In scene after scene, Chisholm strips away Smith's defence of the tower blocks, exposing their bland uniformity, lack of shopping, the intrusion of roads into residential areas, obstructive railings and limited ground space. Chisholm sees sameness and standardization; Smith sees 'use difference' and 'visual contrast'. Jeger is then heard comparing the flats in Regent's Park to the cells in a honeycomb.

As alternatives to the tower blocks, Chisholm interviews architects and shows schemes in the planning stage and completed projects that provide cost-efficient, low-rise, high-density housing with large concentrations of shopping, a landscaped public concourse, pedestrian malls and special provisions for private living spaces (including gardens and balconies). The film takes the viewer step by step through architectural models – in this case while the architects themselves discuss the principles of planning. Architect Edward Hollamby describes his low-rise, intimate terraced housing in Lambeth, which accommodates as many people as tower blocks would on the same site while fitting in with the scheme of existing housing. He solicits public comment – Jill includes a scene with children questioning the architect about his provision of a play area.

Jill breaks the pattern of the film with a brief visit to William Morris's house. Hollamby says he is guided by Morris's belief in the symbiosis of the beautiful and the useful. Later in the film, loving shots of a shoemaker's tools emphasize how much is lost when whole neighbourhoods are demolished. Children come into a copper and brass worker's shop with metal pieces that the shop owner plates free of charge. A whole culture, in other words, is violated by the redevelopment scheme in Kentish Town (a part of the Borough of Camden). 'Learn to love the narrow spot that surrounds our daily life for what of beauty and sympathy there is in it,' wrote William Morris, the presiding spirit of *Who Are the Vandals?*

The film's denouement comes in Chisholm's showdown with Kentish Town planners and councillors. The architect chides them for destroying the street life that supports small shopkeepers and tradesman (second-hand bookshops, shoe makers, copper and brass craftsman) and for evicting people from homes they cherish and only wish to improve. The argument – the back and forth between Chisholm and the three borough representatives – goes on for a tenacious ten minutes, an extraordinary feat that few documentaries in the age of sound bites would dare to attempt. Jill's film remains a fresh document today, a superb example of an activist film-maker constructing an argument and fomenting a sense of outrage that twenty-first-century documentary film students have compared to the work of Michael Moore.* Television critic R.W. Cooper called *Who Are the Vandals?* 'remarkably fresh and enlightening, largely because she lets people talk for themselves' (*The Times* 3 February 1967). Architects were not so happy about the film. Michael Foot remembered some threatened to sue Jill for jeopardizing their livelihood. It disgusted her to think that architects would seek this kind of immunity. All the arts benefited from criticism – as Oscar Wilde had taught her a generation earlier.

Jill buttressed the impact of *Who Are the Vandals?* in the press, writing two articles for *The Times,* 'People Versus Planners' (14 September 1968) and 'Judging Britain's New Towns' (2 November 1968). The tower blocks, she pointed out, were not an isolated phenomenon. On the contrary, they were part of the spreading megalopolis that Lewis Mumford had deplored and which Jill termed 'grandiose monotony'. She provided a historical context by invoking Charles Reilly's vision of the village green, of communities on a human scale, and touting Tony Greenwood's White Paper, 'Old Houses Into New Homes', which called for a blend of past and present that would preserve but also enliven the 'rich texture of metropolitan life'. Reilly had excoriated his own profession for refusing to criticize itself, and Jill castigated architects for talking only to other architects. No wonder hideous designs won prizes and competitions when architects were merely creating plans that they knew would please each other. 'Have we reached a stage in the history of British architecture when members of the public must teach the professionals their job?' she asked in 'Threat to Parliament Square' (*London Illustrated News*, November 1972).†

* Moore's films, especially *Roger and Me* and *Bowling for Columbine*, share Jill's populist democratic mentality and her sheer joy in argumentation. My students at the City University of New York, who come primarily from the five boroughs of the city, were amazed at how contemporary Jill's concerns were and how she had pinpointed the nature of their own metropolitan life.

† The article pleads for the second prize scheme by Tom Hancock to be adopted for the New Parliament Building. His design continued the scale and rhythm of the adjacent House of Commons in the form of a tight group of related buildings. The setback between gave the impression of oriels and the skyline was fretted by the roof structures – as against the ruthless and sheer 'glass box' of the winning scheme.

Jill also attacked the way planners' belief in the efficiency of motorways destroyed communities and actually increased the congestion in central London. See 'London's Motorway Box-up', *New Statesman*, 7 February 1969.

Tom Hancock, a brilliant young architect, commenting on Jill's article for this biography, said, 'Jill was an inspiration to me.' The article could have been, he insisted, a 'turning point in urban design practice. But, alas, the message which Jill was attempting, some decade or so before urban design theory caught up with her, was that context should be directly respected in modern architecture. She really used my scheme to begin that discussion. It was a feminine intuitive understanding with which we are just catching up.'[2]

Hancock had been appointed master planner for the new town of Peterborough in 1964 at the age of thirty-three.[3] Thus he became part of a select cadre of planner/architects working on a cluster of new 'counter magnet' cities, purposely created at a distance from their parent cities, notably London and Manchester. Under the Labour government elected in 1964, the New Towns Act created three new cities: at Peterborough, Milton Keynes and the Lancashire New Town at Preston. In 'Judging Britain's New Towns', Jill wrote that Tom Hancock, the 'youngest town planner in Britain … has exploded into the architectural firmament like a brilliant, disturbing phenomenon from outer space'. Hancock favoured preserving as much of the old town and village life as possible, checking the sprawl and preserving green belts and rural surroundings while introducing more efficient public transportation, building the type of terraced houses that had accommodated rich and poor alike for generations, modernizing existing housing and segregating traffic from residential areas. The Hancock approach, Jill believed, would modify the sameness of the new towns and the rather rigid planning schemes of architects. In other words, in Tom Hancock she saw Charles Reilly reborn. Here was a man to awaken the country out of its 'visual apathy'. He was Jill's young Alexander.

When Hancock got the go-ahead to submit a plan for Peterborough, he put all design work on hold until he had looked at it. 'Amazing cheek,' he recalled. The language in Hancock's plan echoed the futuristic rhetoric of the Plymouth plan: 'People will lead a new kind of city life: easy and delightful journeys within their city region to the new and old centres of education, culture and recreations; homes in great variety clustered among the woodlands and rivers; great parklands within the fabric of the city.'

In the spring of 1968 Jill had sought out Hancock after seeing his BBC *Panorama* film *The New Cities*. They soon became friends. He remembered how on 15 February 1969 Jill arranged for a babysitter so that Tom and his wife Jan could have dinner at Pilgrim's Lane with Paul Foot, Tony Greenwood (Minister of Housing and Local Government 1966–70), and several others. Later, after Tom and his wife divorced, he continued to see Jill and Michael in the company of his partner, Yvette. When Michael called Jill 'My dear child', Jill would nudge Yvette, and say, 'You musn't get married.'

Jill and Tom did not agree on all things architectural. Tom thought she overrated Hollamby, who like most architects, Hancock observed, tended to be self-serving and insufficiently attuned to the political and practical nature of planning. For example, Hollamby wanted Hancock to design flat roofs in Lambeth, even though such roofs leaked. Only after a very carefully arranged argument did Hancock get Hollamby's grudging assent to pitched roofs. 'Jill used to say, "He's a good man, Hollamby", almost pleading with me. He lived in the Red House [the William Morris residence featured in *Who Are the Vandals?*], so he had touched the hem of greatness.' Hancock's comment suggests how completely Jill adopted aesthetic arguments and could be swayed by ideas alone.

Tom thought Jill's lifestyle:

very beautiful – that she could be a craftsman with film-making, organizing her home, her parties, her flowers, her relationships as an art. I could see her working with Michael on that relationship. It was a modern marriage – the sort we dream about but very rarely realize: that people can be open and have a degree of freedom and respect and not be chained together.

Tom found Jill 'more than attractive. She was affectionate and very much with you and very well versed in all aspects of life.'

In retrospect, Tom describes his younger self as 'very raw'. He became Jill's

disciple … I relied on her to guide me … what is the general direction? How does an architect or planner do more than just decent buildings? So I can blame her for getting me involved in the social dimensions of planning, which is a maverick thing to do, and in the establishment served me very badly. They thought this man was a radical and not reliable, working for Shelter, which was the national campaign for the homeless.

Peter Cuming, an architect who later befriended Jill and Michael, and who had worked for Tom Hancock, saw Jill as stuck in an earlier era of the garden city and the village green. Her Mumford/Reilly aesthetic could only take her so far. 'I think that's quite acute,' Tom agreed although he believed that her concern with the human scale of architecture remains valid and transcends its historical roots. After Mumford, there is no project, Hancock observed; by the 1970s and 1980s there is only pragmatism.

*

Although Jill never lost her interest in architecture, Cuming's analysis helps to explain why she increasingly turned her concern toward her continuing fascination with the suffragettes. Around this time she embarked on a project that would consume her energies for the rest of her life. First as a film, then a screenplay, finally in a book, Jill began to explore the history of the suffragettes.

In a provocative twenty-eight-page essay, 'The Suffragettes', dated 24 May 1967, Jill declared:

> No woman has been more maligned and misunderstood by male historians than Dame Christabel Pankhurst. In writing about the suffragettes and their leaders, the academic brotherhood seem to be so carried away by their preconceived ideas that they disgrace their own standards of scholarship. Just a few who wrote on the subject – for example, Dr David Morgan in his 'Suffragists and Liberals', or J.B. Priestley in 'The Edwardians' – have shown more perception, but even they have been partly led astray by previous, highly-biased interpretations. Right up to the present day eminent historians have taken little trouble to check their facts, or they have tended to twist them to make them conform to an unconscious anti-feminism. That is a strange and serious accusation; it can, I believe, be justified to the hilt.

Writers such as Roger Fulford in *Votes for Women* (1957) had ridiculed Christabel and Emmeline while suppressing the absurd behaviour of Prime Minister Asquith, whose performance had been likened to 'that of a trap-door acrobat in a pantomime'. Fulford had taken the lazy way out, simply cribbing from Sylvia Pankhurst's attacks on her mother in *The Suffragette Movement* and curiously deciding, 'it would be unfair to consult the great survivors of the movement because they had been parties in a dispute'. So distorted were Fulford's and other male writers' versions of the suffragette movement, Jill observed, that an appalled Sylvia made common cause with Christabel – from whom she had been estranged for many years – to mount a campaign that forced Fulford to amend at least some of his more outrageous misstatements of fact and ill-founded interpretations.[4]

Jill then attacks the historical fraternity of George Dangerfield, Brian Harrison, Peter Rowland, Kenneth Morgan and Andrew Rosen for their distorted accounts of the suffragette movement. If she mentions no women scholars, it is because there were none that took Jill's position and certainly none who wrote with her verve. Her polemical jabs anticipate the kind of feminist audit of male inadequacies that would make Kate Millett a star two years later with *Sexual Politics* (1970). Soon a new generation of women scholars would be quite literally knocking on Jill's door, seeking entrance to the mountain of evidence Jill had fashioned out of thirty, then forty, then fifty, and finally sixty years of engagement with her project.*

This stirring essay reads like a book proposal – which perhaps it is. In Jill's papers there is a letter dated 1 July 1969 from the managing director of Hutchinson Publishing to Jill: 'I am delighted to learn that the book is going ahead and that you have agreed [to] the proposals Harold Harris put to you.' But more than a year later she does not seem to have made progress. On 21 October 1970 Michael wrote:

> My dear child,
> Here is a present to celebrate our 23 or 24th anniversary, whichever it may be – a preparation for the celebration of many more.†
>
> The idea is that you can use 300 of it to put your mind at ease about your book. You can, if you want, refund the publishers but – better still – you can write the book – & be another 300 quid to the good.

All thought about this book apparently stopped when Jill and Michael confronted the greatest crisis of their marriage. As with every other interruption of her suffragette project, when Jill resumed work she would recast her ideas in yet another new form that reflected the ever-broadening scope of her mission.

---

* See Chapter 24.
† Jill and Michael often argued over dates and did not try to look them up. They had, in fact, been married for twenty-one years.

Obsession
(1970–72)

[H]ow had the spirit of William Hazlitt (died 1830) entered and enslaved mine? Even if I had known I could not have stopped myself.

Melvyn Bragg, *A Time to Dance* (1990)

Is every man a victim of his penis?

Jill Craigie, *Odd Reflections*

When Michael Foot read Melvyn Bragg's novel *A Time to Dance*, the story of a retired fifty-four-year-old bank manager who falls victim to the 'violent sensations of uncontrollable erotic love' for an eighteen-year-old working-class girl, he recognized the story as his own and wrote in his first edition: 'Read (with great enjoyment) in one gulp at Grasmere & on the way back to London, Aug 10–11 1990. Takes its place properly on the Hazlitt shelf.' The novel is a modern version of *Liber Amoris* (1823), William Hazlitt's account of his own romantic obsession, which Michael read for the first time in 1938. Hazlitt fell for the daughter of his boarding house owner and became so infatuated, despite any evidence of a mutual attachment, that he divorced his wife, only to be spurned by the object of his obsession.

For Michael, obsession was more complicated. 'It is possible to love two women at the same time. I don't think it's a rarity, but not so many are willing to admit to it or describe it, and the ones who have done so have done me great liberations,' he declared, only gradually and never fully disclosing what the eruption in his marriage meant to him and how Jill reacted to his passion for another. Jill would eventually seize control of the story by writing it down in letters to Julie and discussing it with her housekeeper Kathy Seery, Paul Foot and other female friends like Jenny Stringer. The closest Michael comes to revealing his *amour-passion*[1] is through his prismatic essays on two of his heroes, William Hazlitt and Jonathan Swift, in *Debts of Honour*.

The Hazlitt of two minds, the romantic and the realist, is complemented (in Michael Foot's book) by Swift, the lover of two women – particularly in a passage that concludes with words Jill would echo in her correspondence about her husband's obsession:

> So with all idea of perversion, mild or monstrous, set aside, let us return to the Vanessa–Stella mystery. No solution is offered here – except the simplest: that is, that he loved them both and that his heart was torn between the two. It is hard to read of his long years with Stella, the poems he wrote to her, and the *Journal* without believing he loved her; and if it wasn't love, it was something of his own invention very like it. As for Vanessa, it is impossible to read the poem to her without believing it was love, and that he must in some way have avowed it.

'I don't say that Jill approved of my idea, but she understood what I was saying about Swift. She knew all about that,' Michael insisted. He read Montaigne to Jill, just as Swift read Montaigne to Vanessa. Michael Foot never fell out of love with Jill Craigie, but he did have a love affair which was important enough to report here, since it had such an impact on his wife. She would never quite fathom Michael's mania. 'Jill called me secretive, I used the word about Swift, too.' Michael produced no *Liber Amoris* of his own, but he provided the biographer with guidebooks: *A Time to Dance*, *Liber Amoris* itself with its startling subtitle *The New Pygmalion*, and *De l'Amour*, Stendahl's French equivalent of Hazlitt's book, which Stendahl, in fact, gave Hazlitt to read and which, Michael conjectured, helped Hazlitt to put his own passion into perspective.

The identity of Michael's *amour* is best disguised under the name of Lamia, that figure of Keats' romantic poem, who resembles Hazlitt's Sarah, a demon/damsel who, in Michael Foot's words, 'almost destroyed him with her wiles, her titillations, her prevarications and her treacheries'.* 'She was a beautiful black woman, as black as you can be,' Michael said of his own lover. Michael and Lamia began their affair, carried on mainly at her London flat, sometime in 1970. 'It did not last long, but I must say I was absolutely taken by it,' Michael confessed. Why he felt this obsession, he did not know, so he re-read Hazlitt, realizing how closely his case resembled his hero's. In Hazlitt's story, Sarah takes him to the breaking point. Michael's story would have another ending: 'I had a separation with her. I said we can't do anything about

---

* Realizing he has made out Sarah to be the villainess, Michael adds: 'Let it not be forgotten, by the way, that no one has ever told Sarah's side of the story; what a find that would be!' In this account, Lamia's story, based on her notes to Jill and Michael, will provide some balance, although I have not, for this biography, sought out the woman here called Lamia.

this because it would be too damaging to Jill and to everybody else. And she didn't mind all that much.' Perhaps not, though Michael's sentiments seem to reflect a memory that has annealed events that were far more scorching to Jill and Lamia.

'I think it was when I had broken it off, pretty much, that I told Jill,' Michael suggested. Jill was 'obviously hurt, and didn't like it, but I don't think she was altogether surprised'. Michael put it mildly: 'She felt sore about it and went off to Venice by herself on a kind of protest, I think, wondering what she was going to do.' Did Michael think Jill might actually leave him? 'Well, I was very shaken. I didn't know what... I couldn't bear the thought of her being there without me.' She stayed away a fortnight.[2]

But why did Michael have to tell Jill about Lamia? 'Well, it came up,' he answered. 'How did it come up?' He mused but did not reply. Julie supplied an explanation:

> One morning I went to see my mother and she was drifting around the kitchen in a very peculiar state. I said, 'What's the matter? There's something wrong.' She said, 'Oh, I'm not going to talk to you. I'm not going to talk to you.' I said, 'Yes you are. There's something wrong.' My mother noticed that Michael was taking perfumed baths daily and taking a little more care about the way he dressed – a sure sign. And there were an *awful lot* of all-night sittings in the House. You *know* when your husband is being seriously unfaithful.* She was very troubled.

Then Jill found in Michael's clothes a letter from Lamia of a 'sexual nature' that 'absolutely laid it out'. Jill rested on the large sofa in Michael's library in a distressed state. 'What's the matter, my child?' Michael asked. She tried to get him to admit to the affair without actually saying she had found the letter. When he did not, she produced the evidence.

It is Julie's recollection that her mother was not sure that she wanted Michael back, and that Michael 'could not make up his mind. He wanted to string them both.' Julie's second husband, Mike Randall, then managing editor of the *Sunday Times,* came over to Pilgrim's Lane and told Michael: 'You have to shit or get off the pot.'† Both Jill and Michael respected and liked Mike, and during the crisis Mike and Julie became Jill's confidants.

In mid-April, a distraught Jill wrote to Julie and Mike from Venice: 'I still feel pretty demented. I have a horrible feeling that Michael does not love me

---

* From reading *De l'Amour*, Michael would have known that, 'Women are very clever at feeling the imperceptible changes in the human heart, and at distinguishing nuances of affection... They have a sense-organ for this, that men have not.'

† 'He used that exact expression. I was there,' Julie said.

enough to give up the girl.' Michael did not seem to have the heart to 'come back to me in the true sense'. Hence her 'feeling of impending doom'. She said he woke up every morning with a 'load of weight ... because of what he has done to me ... but he gives me the feeling that he regards it as impossible ever to make love to me again'. She imagined him picking up the phone to 'inquire how the girl is and then, of course, the whole thing will start again'.

Caught between despair and anger, she noted: 'He blames his puritanical upbringing. But that isn't my fault. Why should I have to suffer for his upbringing? But I do, like hell I do.' Michael had grown up in a household where Cromwell was king, where his father had several busts of the great Puritan prominently displayed. Jill's letter then acknowledges that Michael had not made love to her for quite some time. She had made no secret of the fact – telling her housekeeper Kathy Seery that Michael had not made love to her 'in years'.[3] Jill had also discussed her sex life with Julie. Jill was now furious because she had been so patient and forgiving. 'What other woman, I ask myself, particularly a younger woman, would show him the loyalty and devotion as I have? He would have only a few years happiness and then, probably, he would go through hell.' That Jill had not given way to frustration, to neurosis or to sleeping around as an act of revenge showed that, 'I have felt too deeply for Michael and I felt too that I was sharing a problem with him... But it took some doing, I can tell you.'* Jill doubted that most women would have been so self-denying. This was no conceit on her part, she added: it had to do with the kind of man Michael was, with his 'capacity to inspire great devotion'. But what woman would not 'feel furiously insulted if the man she loves cannot make love to her'?

It was characteristic of Jill to involve those closest to her in this moment of crisis. She asked Mike to talk to Michael, to 'disabuse' him of the idea that 'it is almost normal for a man not to make love to his wife. He once suggested to me that this is true of fifty per cent of husbands. That, as you know, is nonsense.' Jill was prepared to 'accept failure after failure', if only Michael would resume love-making.

Jill was now sixty years old. 'We are approaching old age. This is the time, surely, to enrich our marriage by finding each other again, slowly and painfully, I've no doubt, but any other course will render our relationship more and more empty and he will either turn into what is known as a dirty

---

* Was Jill ever unfaithful to Michael? I pursued this question with due diligence. Jill seems to have made the same decision as Jennie Lee. After finding the right man for her, she saw no point in having love affairs. Jill would have agreed with Jennie Lee, another highly sexed woman, that 'affairs aren't worth it', even though Nye Bevan, in Patricia Hollis's words, 'had a more casual attitude to such matters'.

old man or he will destroy both the girl and myself.' She then brought her letter to an excruciating climax, contemplating her years of observing the man she still loved:

> I sometimes wonder if Michael isn't just a little too greedy for life. He has fulfilment in his work – that alone is a privilege – the adulation of the public, a devoted wife and now a mistress. But none of us can have our cake and eat it. It can't be done. At any rate, not without paying a very big price. Even without letters and bits of paper, as Judy says, a woman knows if she is being deceived. Indeed, she only searches for evidence to confirm her fears. She scents danger and it becomes imperative to find the proof by whatever means. It is almost like an animal compulsion. I know very well when Michael's heart is elsewhere. I allowed him to deceive me in the past because I had faith he would cause me no injury and, in any case, he did give me the feeling that I came first. But now the girl comes first, that is the feeling he gives me whatever attentions he pays me.

How could Jill be so sure that Michael no longer put her first? Because he had failed her on the most important point: he no longer cared to argue with her.

> The attention he does pay me, the one that matters most, is the one of giving true considerations to what I say or write. He appears to dismiss all I say. He won't even argue with me or point out where I am wrong. Or why any suggestion I may make is absurd or impossible.

He did not want to discuss 'intimate matters'. Jill felt that his 'inhibitions on that point are somehow bound up with his other inhibitions'. Even that, though, Jill could accept if only he gave her the feeling that his 'love and emotions' were not 'lavished elsewhere'. She had no desire to become just an 'anchor or mother figure'. The trip to Venice was an ultimatum:

> If I can't live without Michael, I certainly can't live with him while his affair continues. I am quite adamant on that point. I have made such a terrific compromise for him. I have built up his self-confidence, I have done nothing to wound his self-esteem, whatever other mistakes I may have made, while he has done the very opposite for me. So I think the time has come when he should show the same integrity in his private life as he does in his public life. If he chooses the girl, I shall accept defeat. He would then have no need to wake up feeling a great weight on his back. He will have made the choice in a straightforward manner. Equally, if he gives up the girl, he will be lifted of that weight, but he really will have to give her up for good and try starting afresh with me. I would give him such a welcome it would be as though I had never been hurt. My God, how I love him! Too much, far too much.

In a way, the most extraordinary fact of this letter is that Jill made her marriage a family matter. She was also still arguing. Couldn't Michael see how unmanly and undignified his behaviour was? 'Or don't you agree, Mike?' Jill was not just venting her own troubles: 'I leave all my hopes in the loving hands of you two. Whatever would I do without you?'

Jill worried that her 'incoherent' letter only reflected her 'demented state'. Yet it is a powerful document: Jill and Michael were speaking in virtually two different languages about love. He was a man besotted with the Hazlitt hero who realizes that the world may call him a fool, and worse, but who finds that his 'dreadful passion' has given him a 'kind of rank in the kingdom of love'. Jill returned home, and the 'future looked promising even from physical point of view', she wrote on 6 July in a fourteen-page, typed, double-spaced letter to Julie and Mike. Then Michael had a relapse: 'Chance remark from woman at Hampstead hairdresser confirmed my suspicions.' Remaining calm, she told Michael he had been seen with Lamia in the Casa Pepe restaurant. Was he still 'hooked on the girl', she wanted to know. An angry Michael attacked Jill for 'having spies, listening to tittle-tattle'. But all this was bluster to Jill, as she wrote to Julie and Mike: 'The expressions on people's faces are so much more revealing than the words they use.' She said to him, 'I just don't believe you and so you'd better tell the truth.' Michael then admitted that after a message from Lamia relayed by his nephew Paul, he had seen Lamia to talk about her troubles. 'So when you see her... you then want to make love to her.' He replied: 'Well, I left the options open.'

Jill called Paul [4] and asked him: 'Just what am I fighting?' To set him at ease, she indicated that she knew all about the affair. Paul called her a 'sexy, trendy girl expensively dressed in the latest suedes'. She had been ringing *Private Eye*, where Paul worked, every day for a week before he met her. He thought he would be seeing a desperate 'little waif' instead of the 'flamboyant creature' who was on a mission, in other words, to liberate Michael from his books, his 'Hampstead set', and his corrupt politics. The last point truly astounded Paul, who revered his uncle's integrity. At the same time Lamia threatened suicide and broke down, crying in the office canteen in front of everyone and softening Paul up enough to arouse his 'chivalry'. He told her: 'You can't expect me to be neutral in this affair. I certainly won't intercede on your behalf, but I will deliver the message.' Paul did, and Michael said almost nothing and then went off to Ebbw Vale. Over dinner with Jill, Paul said he did not want to annoy Michael, and he was supportive of Jill.

Jill brooded about the dinner and worked herself into a 'furious temper'. When Michael called to tell her what train to meet him on, she replied: 'I've seen Paul and everything's finished between us, finished.' She hung up before he could reply. She was not home to welcome him but returned late and on the attack, calling him 'criminally selfish from the sexual point of view'. He put up no obstacles to a divorce in her favour, but he said he did not want a break and that he wanted to try again and that he would give up the girl.* A weary Jill replied, 'I've heard it all before.' But she went on to tell Michael everything Paul had told her. Michael listened, then said: 'She has no great passion for me.' He thought Lamia's comments on politics were a joke, since she knew quite well that Paul was an international socialist and to the left of Michael. Lamia probably thought Paul would be pleased. Michael confirmed what Paul had said: he had given Lamia money and, in fact, was shocked at her avariciousness. Michael actually said, according to Jill, 'Such a good theme for a novel.' Jill wondered where Michael was getting the money – £350 to Lamia at the start of the affair. Jill wanted him to leave but he pleaded to stay, and an incredulous Jill heard him say, 'The hotel would be expensive!' Michael got into bed with her, and 'I couldn't bring myself to make him leave that either,' Jill confessed.

The next morning Michael said he would meet Lamia at the Waldorf Hotel and break it off. That night he reported to Jill: Lamia laughed when Michael said it was over. 'She too had heard all that before.' What was so terrible about an affair? she asked. 'Everyone did it.' Besides, she relied on Michael for advice. He said she was not to call him or see him, but she could write to him. He gave her £40 for her rent and left. The part about writing made Jill uneasy, but she held her tongue, believing that Michael was finally telling the truth.

The next day a letter from Lamia arrived at Pilgrim's Lane. Michael offered to show it to Jill but said it would be 'hurtful' to her. Jill told him to give her the 'gist'. Lamia wrote that she was 'desperately in love' with Michael. She felt abandoned, ill and had no friends to rely on. What should she do about the flat? Jill thought Lamia was resorting to blackmail, although Mike had advised her that the press would not abet Lamia because journalists adored Michael. Michael then showed Jill a letter he had written to Lamia, which Jill thought quite clever. It was firm, but not provocative: 'I've tried to help you, and I think I have done so. You have all your life before you and a great capacity for enjoyment once you get me out of your system.'

Suddenly Lamia's motivations, Jill told Michael, seemed transparent:

* According to Jill, Michael also asked if she was determined to go through with a divorce, would she allow him to continue to live in the house in July and August so he could finish a book he was writing. 'There was no way he was going to move out of that house,' Julie observed. 'There was no way he could move all those books.' And move in to a small flat with Lamia? 'No way,' Julie concluded. The house was in Jill's name, a provision that protected Michael should he be sued for libel and lose (always a possibility for a man as outspoken as Michael; he had had a narrow escape in a libel suit brought against him by James Kemsley (1883–1968), Chairman of Kemsley Newspapers).

This is a girl, I told him, who boasts of her sexual prowess. She's very proud of the power she has over you through your body. She's said it to me and she's said it, in effect, to Paul. Has she by any chance a power bug? Does she see herself as a kind of Kitty O'Shea?* Does she want to play on an open stage the role of the other woman in the life of an important man? Could that be it, I added. Suddenly Michael sprang to life. 'My God, that fits,' he said... 'she tried to involve me in a public scandal. And she's tried to make scenes in public. I've had a terrible time with her. And she has a furious temper, a vicious streak. Yes, that fits. Everything is clear now.'

Jill had completely broken through the spell, and a grateful Michael kept saying, 'You're a good girl. You've saved me from catastrophe.' The only way Lamia could win now, Jill thought, was to get herself pregnant.

Lamia wrote again. Michael again offered to show the letter to Jill. Jill again preferred a précis of what turned out to be the same complaints and pleas. 'Is this a great bore?' Jill asked Julie and Mike. If Michael would not see her, Lamia wrote, she would have to 'Go and see other people and tell them.' Jill was struck with Lamia's political timing:

Well, it so happens, and this is a deadly secret Mike so please be careful not to mention it, that Michael has agreed to stand for the deputy leadership. Or rather contest it. The left in the House are cock-a-hoop for the first time in years convinced that they are on to a winner. All they are scared of now is that something might happen that would muck up their chance of victory. They believe they can bring about a general election next year by holding up legislation in the House of Commons on the common market and with the assistance of a few more government losses at by-elections. And Michael is their leader. Some, as you know, even want him to contest the leadership.†

* Charles Stewart Parnell (1846–91), the great Irish politician who converted Gladstone and the Liberal Party to the idea of Home Rule, had his magnificent career ruined when he appeared as a co-respondent in a divorce case brought by Captain William Henry O'Shea against his wife, Kitty. Parnell lost the support of the Irish Catholics, and his refusal to give up his mistress led to a split among the Irish nationalists. He died five months after marrying Mrs O'Shea. R. Barry O'Brien's two-volume *The Life of Charles Stewart Parnell* (1898) served as a model for Michael's two-volume biography of Aneurin Bevan.

† After Harold Wilson's surprise defeat in 1970, Michael had been elected to the Labour Shadow Cabinet – the only member who had not held office in the 1964–70 Labour government. Even though he had been critical of Wilson, Wilson liked him and shrewdly perceived that for all his oppositional tendencies, Michael was at heart a party man, a loyalist and a believer in Party unity so long as dissent within the Party was not subject to Gaitskellite efforts to silence criticism. For his part, Michael, nearing sixty, knew it was now or never if he wanted to actually exercise power and not merely to appraise it. Bevan, his hero, had not blinked when Attlee called him to the Cabinet. In October 1971, Wilson appointed Michael Shadow Leader of the House, and as biographer Mervyn Jones notes, 'his star was rising'. He led the forces against Edward Heath's Common Market legislation, which Michael called 'Britain's entry into the rich nations' club'. He was not opposed to the concept of a common market but rather to this 'narrowly conceived, Little-European Common Market'. As usual, Jill remained suspicious of Harold Wilson. In an undated letter to Julie, she claimed Wilson was trying to 'muzzle Michael now. A lot of those old lags in the Shadow cabinet, as he calls them, are really jealous of Michael's popularity and his power of oratory.'

Responding to Jill's political nose for blackmail, Michael decided not to write to Lamia again. Instead he would see her once again and give her more money because, he told Jill, Lamia was 'penniless'.

This drama went on, Jill pointed out, while Michael continued his busy round of work in Parliament and in the media, where he appeared frequently on television and radio. Lamia had become a liability and an irritant for a public man who found himself called away to an extra division in the House of Commons just ten minutes into what was supposed to be his farewell meeting with Lamia. She was sick, and he left her with the £70 that he meant to be his final payment to her. Now he was sure she would ask for another meeting. 'The trouble is, Michael is totally incapable of being ruthless, which is really what the girl needs for her sake as much as his,' Jill concluded.

So far, according to Jill's total, Michael had given Lamia £460. Jill suspected he had spent much more – perhaps as much as £2000 ('all our savings'). Jill had been reluctant to ask Michael 'for the sofa for my birthday, which, by the way, he now uses all the time! I doubt if I shall be so soft with him about financial matters in the future. And Mike, I did pay my doctor's bill and for the new curtains and carpet, etc., out of my mother's money. Am I an utter fool I'm beginning to wonder.'

But Jill's mood had brightened. It was now just a matter of figuring out how to dispose of Lamia. 'She sounds to me the type whom men fuck and then drop. I don't think she'll ever keep a job. Paul agrees she is very dangerous.' Michael might have 'lingering longings' for Lamia, but he now realized 'for the first time that his salvation lies in solving our problem'. But would that be the end of it? 'Sometimes now, I even find myself wondering whether we shall stay together. I think I've had about as much as I can take.' She asked Mike: 'Can you think of any way of dropping that wretched girl in the Thames? How many of us can say we have never felt murderous in the course of our lives?'

On 13 August 1971, Lamia wrote a letter to Michael, which he showed to Jill and which Jill kept. Lamia had written on her birthday, announcing that she would be contacting Jill. The previous year Lamia had declined Jill's invitation to come to Pilgrim's Lane or to Julie's house, and Lamia had countered that they should meet for drinks or tea 'outside of homes'. Now a beleaguered Lamia accused Michael of disloyalty and treachery. She had abandoned her friends and work so as to be on call for him, and now he had cut off all communication with her. She had lost weight, was coughing blood and did not have the money to pay her rent. She no longer could afford a phone. She wanted to settle up and take a holiday.

Jill replied to Lamia, sending a copy of her letter to Julie, with a note: 'But will this do the trick, I wonder. I doubt it. Michael read my letter and approved.' Jill began her letter to Lamia: 'Since you have said you would come and see me, Michael has showed me your letter.' Jill was not 'unsympathetic, quite the contrary. I think you are having a hard time. I have asked Michael to help you out financially, but I have written the cheque in my name as that may be less embarrassing to you.' But Lamia had to understand that 'this is the very last time when you can expect financial help. It really is.' Michael simply could not afford to support her, and it was best that Lamia learn to stand on her own feet. No other route to happiness seemed likely to Jill.

Jill knew what it meant to take an 'emotional battering', to suffer 'absolute defeat and despair'. Even so, if Lamia searched her heart, she would have to see that 'we cannot shift responsibility for our own actions entirely on to others'. Lamia had made a 'false judgement – no shame in that. We all do. Better to confess that mistake, though, than to continue making that same mistake. Men can be very selfish,' Jill acknowledged, but accusations, even just ones, only frustrated the accuser.

As to Lamia's health, if she was spitting blood, either she had tuberculosis and should go immediately to hospital where the NHS would care for her, or she had some sort of gum problem that could be treated easily. As to Lamia's loss of weight, Jill had lost even more during this period. Lamia had complained of her sprained wrist. 'How lucky you are … My hand was crushed in a car accident. I have to hide it whenever I can, I can hardly use my fingers and it's very uncomfortable all the time. And it will be for the rest of my life. No one can give you sympathy, especially in this household, for such silly things as sprained wrists or ankles, but your courage might be admired if you made light of such trifles.'

Jill thought Lamia risked wrecking her life on 'false hopes' and was seeking refuge or escape in illness. 'London is full of opportunities for young beautiful girls provided they have the guts and the determination to stand on their own feet and not to use others as crutches.' Jill had given the same advice to her daughter. Get a job, work with her own generation – that was the ticket. Jill saw no point in their meeting. 'There is absolutely nothing you could say to me that would make any difference whatsoever and nothing I could say to you that would be any help. It would only turn into a painful scene. That would be pointless. I'm sure you can see that for yourself.' There was to be no more communication. It all came down to a sentence that had a sort of omnipotence to it: 'Decisions have been made and they will be stuck to and no decision was forced on anyone, I assure you.' Jill concluded her *coup de grâce*: 'So I do sincerely wish you luck and once you face the realities of the situation, I'm sure you will get it.'

But Lamia would not let up. She showed up at Pilgrim's Lane. Jill and Michael were out and she left a note, asking them to contact her because she had to see them 'very soon'. When neither Jill nor Michael responded, Lamia returned – this time to be met at the door by Kathy Seery. Lamia asked to see Jill. 'I knew it was her,' Kathy said, 'by her description.' Kathy told Jill, 'there's a young girl out there wants to see you'. Michael was upstairs in his library. Jill approached Lamia and shouted: 'Fuck off! Fuck off! Fuck off!', slamming the door.

Lamia wrote Michael one more note. She reminded Michael of their meetings in the Casa Pepe. She remembered the way he put his arm around her back and his 'falling about' in happiness. Now his 'stupid wife' had acted the part of the 'wronged one'. But then Jill and Michael were part of 'another generation, and you two conspired again to come and deliver another blow'. This was her farewell: 'How can you both deprive the two of you and myself of so much happiness? You are both so soaked in so much hypocrisy… I just want to [sic] like a wounded animal to go away quietly and die, some where.'

Jill herself provided a coda a year later. She had found in her mother's papers a typewritten excerpt from a work of literature (unidentified) that speaks of the inevitability of loneliness and the struggle to come to terms with it. 'Perhaps we are not really worth much until we love our loneliness and consort with her for ever. Perhaps loneliness is not the terrible thing we believe it to be. Perhaps achievement begins at the point when we have changed it from a negative to a positive state, from a barren to a pregnant.' Jill wrote on her mother's typewritten page:

> Re-read November 21, 1972. It made me feel very guilty, especially as I feel very lonely myself. The thought of that terrible woman who was not even beautiful whom Michael loved well enough while the infatuation lasted to consider leaving me made me wonder what he might have done if he had fallen for somebody who was really charming & beautiful. Mrs Seery thought no man would have looked twice at her.* Deep down I have never believed Michael would leave me & he thinks the same really. But he can be heartless.

In *Odd Reflections*, Jill wrote: 'Michael paid me the compliment of calling me his "soul-mate." It is not true. An academic, someone for whom Swift & Hazlitt or Byron are living people, would fit into that role. But we are complementary.' Jill had once asked Michael why Hazlitt had not put the

---

* Perhaps Kathy Seery wished to spare Jill's feelings. In an interview Kathy said, echoing Michael, that Lamia was indeed very dark and very beautiful.

woman's case in *Liber Amoris*. The question would reverberate in Michael's Hazlitt essay:

> Considering how original were Hazlitt's ideas on almost every theme which captivated him, considering how he could race ahead to anticipate the thought, in the field of psychology, say, no less than politics, of the whole ensuing century, it is the more surprising that he never seemed to turn his mind to the great question of the rights of women. He was certainly no feminist, not that the word had yet been invented nor even that the thing itself was common. He was a frequent visitor at the house of William Godwin, and one of his gleaming sentences casts a kindly ray of light across the countenance of Mary Wollstonecraft. Yet the extraordinary fact is that he did not write much more about her; seemingly, he had never read her *Vindication of the Rights of Woman* or it left no mark whatever.

It is safe to say that but for Jill Craigie, it is unlikely Michael Foot would ever have written this paragraph. And surely for Jill Craigie, Michael Foot revealed the same limitation as his hero: an inability to comprehend fully the woman's story.

Recovery
(1972)

My daughter says that I am the most subservient feminist in existence.

Jill Craigie, Odd Reflections

Julie remembered that her mother, who had begun to get plump in middle age, lost a good deal of weight – 'she went as thin as a rake' – in the aftermath of Lamia. Jill looked wonderful. For quite some time she watched Michael carefully and went with him everywhere. 'She did not leave his side,' Julie said, even accompanying her husband to the House of Commons. In an undated letter (c. March 1972) to Julie and Mike, Jill reported:

> On my birthday, I heard him whispering to himself with nauseating sentimentality, 'My child! My child!' Well, it wasn't to me he was whispering ... that was evident. So it does appear he's having a hard battle with himself. So I feel sorry for him too and it's all painfully complicated. Little did I think our relationship would ever come to this.

It was a sorrow to Jill that their sexual life did not prosper, although Michael 'kept trying', Jill told Julie. Gradually she came to believe once again that he put her first. In late May 1972 she wrote to Julie that 'he is making such an effort to please me in every way that he can'. Julie felt her mother gradually became 'more in love with Michael than ever, which is what can happen if you feel your husband might be straying. It heightens the obsessive aspect of love. It turns you off other people and makes your husband more attractive.' The same might be said of Michael. 'I begin to feel that for the first time since we got married, he thinks it not impossible I could leave him and is rather alarmed,' Jill wrote to Julie.

Jill pursued a full social, cultural and professional life with renewed vigour. She consulted Tom Hancock about her articles on architecture and liked the way he debunked his profession (the same way Jerry Slattery did with doctors). Closer to home there was Jenny Stringer. Jill liked talking to her. Jenny, a full-time student with a job, a single mother coping with four children on a very modest budget, got Jill's staunch support. Jenny said Jill did not want her to 'feel in the least sorry for myself'.

Jenny's circumstances, and to some extent Jill's own, informed a *New Statesman* article, 'Old Fashioned Ideals' (2 August 1974), which also derived from Jill's research on Votes for Women:

> Basically, the struggle for women's rights has always been a struggle for status. If there is one thing every women of every class resents, it is being thought of as a mere servant or dependant. With this in mind, politicians might do well to take a fresh look not at the status of the woman who goes out to work but at the position of the woman who actually chooses to remain where men for so long insisted she ought to be. No one today is made to feel so inferior as the woman who prefers to bring up her children herself and practise the manifold skills required to look after a family. Whatever her contribution, which may be immense, however much her husband, children and sometimes a grandparent may depend upon her, she is still regarded and officially classed as a 'dependant'.
>
> Mrs Pankhurst wanted a law to induce husbands to pay their wives the rate for the job, or at least to share the money fairly. For almost three quarters of a century, from Gladstone to Asquith, political leaders fought a fierce battle to keep woman in the home. Now, by an ironical twist in history, they give her little or no incentive to stay there.

Jill had experienced these attitudes toward her own stay-at-home life:

> We went to an amazing party at Norman St John Steven's place. Heated marquee in the garden with drink and Champagne flowing, a galaxy of high powered tories, left wingers, millionaires, and Princess Alexandra. But everyone seemed to want to meet Michael. The Tory women called him their favourite Labour M.P. Jacky Astor, who was Tory M.P. for Plymouth when Michael stood for Devonport, hailed Michael with the words for everyone within hearing distance to hear, 'There is the one man I would die for. I'd die for him, I'd die for him. He's the straightest man who ever lived.' 'I'd die for him too,' Leo Abse chipped in. Michael chatted up Princess Alexandra without knowing who she was as if she were a fully paid up member of the Labour Party, which greatly amused me … A dreadful catholic bishop greeted me with the incredible question, 'And do you <u>do</u> anything, or are you only a wife?' I gulped and the question needed a witty reply, in fact, it needed Michael's wit, but I could only blurt out, 'I know what it is to have a career and to be only a wife, as you call it. Of the two occupations, I find being only a wife takes more out of me and, what is more, requires a subordination of the ego you Christians who preach

humility might find difficult to put into practice.' That shut him up. Then someone asked me whose wife I was. When I told them, everyone's attitude towards me changed, as if to be Michael's wife made me worth knowing. Is so much adulation good for him, good for anyone?

Jill had recovered her youth. At an amusing evening in Ebbw Vale a man had called her – 'don't explode with laughter' – Jill wrote to Julie, 'the sex symbol of the Labour Party!' In another undated letter from this period to Julie and Mike she mentioned seeing Dennis Matthews, a former flame and still a good friend. Both Dennis and Tom Hancock 'seem to have something more than a warm regard for me, but it's no use, I'm hooked on my man'. That Dennis still found Jill desirable was especially gratifying, since Jill knew he was 'still pursuing' her younger friend, Jenny. Jill was by turns proud and embarrassed, writing to Julie, 'Enough of this egotism.'

Part of Jill's excitement had to do with Michael's rising fortunes. He was in extraordinary demand as a speaker and was getting well paid for it. But even better, he seemed to be approaching the zenith of his political career.

> Did you see the bit in the Cross Bencher about Michael in *Sunday Express*, Mike? I have this feeling he may well get to Downing Street in the end, and I found a letter from Beaverbrook saying the same thing.[1] Michael says that's all rubbish, but I'm not at all sure now that he's as unambitious as he makes out. He's working very hard at turning enemies into friends, he's split the Jenkinsites and the press are absolutely cock-eyed in their assessment of the Parliamentary Labour Party. I hear all Michael's speeches in the House these days and there's no doubt whatever that he and, I'm sorry to say, Enoch Powell, absolutely dominate the place. The Chamber fills up when either of them is speaking and Powell's speeches are most moving, brilliant, and persuasive… You're right about Powell, he is indeed a mad genius.

In *Loyalists and Loners*, Michael pays Powell the supreme compliment: 'In the House of Commons, he can compel attention, even from those who detest what he appears to say or stand for, as no one else has done since Aneurin Bevan, almost alone, faced the all-powerful Winston Churchill with the wartime Parliament at his back.' For a time the House of Commons seemed to have become the Michael Foot/Enoch Powell show. Foot and Powell had first teamed up in 1969 to destroy Labour minister Richard Crossman's bill to reform the House of Lords. Michael had done star turns on radio and television – debating with every top Conservative – but to hold Parliament in his palm was quite another kind of achievement. This involved much more than oratory and the power to persuade. As Mervyn Jones observes, Powell and Foot shared a mastery of parliamentary procedure and a keen relish in the exploitation of its opportunities. Like a relay team, they produced and supported each other's amendments, mocking Crossman's bill and holding the House in thrall. In the first four months of 1969, for example, Michael made twenty-six speeches, which made the House of Lords seem so ludicrous that the only solution was to abolish it. Powell wanted no reform because he felt the monarchy would become the next target. Michael was aided tremendously by a reticent Conservative Party that supported the bill but did not want to speak out in support of a Labour measure. At one point Michael turned towards the Tory bench and said: 'Look at them, these unlikely novices for a new Trappist order, these bashful tiptoeing ghosts, these pale effigies of what were once sentient, palpable human specimens, these unlarynxed wraiths, these ectoplasmic apparitions, these sphinx-like sentinels at our debates – why are they here?'

Although Jill abhorred Powell's reactionary politics, she had no more trouble hosting Powell and his wife Pamela at Pilgrim's Lane than she had entertaining Beaverbrook. The Pilgrim's Lane dinners were kept a secret in an obvious effort to avoid political gossip. 'We never had anyone else at those dos,' Michael said. He had condemned Powell's infamous 'Rivers of Blood' speech (20 April 1968) suggesting that blacks were victimizing whites and that immigrant communities in Britain were organizing to attack British citizens, but he was aghast at the way MPs had made Powell a pariah. However abhorrent Powell's speech, Michael treated him with respect, slapping him on the back in the Commons library in front of a crowd of MPs and asking him how he was 'getting on'. The speech never got discussed at Pilgrim's Lane or at the Powells' Eaton Square residence in the ten years or so of dinners the couples enjoyed. Michael sensed that Pamela wanted to bring it up but both men changed the subject. In *Loyalists and Loners*, Michael explains why he found it hard to believe that a man of such learning and rectitude could possibly be a racist; rather, his words had been chosen unwisely and without any apparent consciousness of how they would instil 'fears and hatreds and antagonisms'.

Powell's reckless language had isolated him the way Bevan's attack on Tory vermin had, for a time, isolated Michael's great hero. Indeed, the friendship with Powell coincided with Michael's drive to complete the second volume of his Bevan biography, interrupted by the automobile accident in 1963 and an unusual period when Michael found it hard to concentrate on the book – a problem he attributed, in part, to cravings for cigarettes that persisted for a few years after he quit smoking. By the late summer of 1972 he was 'hard at work on the book', Jill reported to Mike Randall. The couple discussed the biography incessantly. 'He puts in quite a few of my ideas and I can refresh his memory on the more personal aspects, all of which is most gratifying to me.' Jill keenly observed the dynamics of how a biography got built and enjoyed her part in the construction, much of which did not show in the finished product:

We spent an evening with Jenny* Lee over the book and she was very emotional. She had discovered some old papers and bits of diary. She had written a letter to Nye which she told us that she thanked God she had never sent. She showed us the letter and her bits of diary but we weren't allowed to take them away. Anyway, in her letter she had written to Nye in despair because she felt her confidence had been completely destroyed. Her spirit was broken and she felt he could do more to bring out the best in her. Yet it was also a diffident, apologetic letter in which she said she hated to take liberties with him and often resented the way other people did and that she would be a fool if she failed to recognise how much greater his contribution was and so forth. What had happened was that all the burdens of domesticity had fallen upon her, everyone was ill – secretary, Ma,† cleaner and so forth, she had no time for shopping, her bras were falling to pieces and she had been asked to stand for the executive‡ and couldn't give her mind to playing, as she put it, political dodgems which she was very good at. Nye appeared to be blind to her moods, had never, never hurt her and thankfully, a letter arrived from him before she sent hers in which he showed his concern for her, saw she was very depressed and told her, 'We have our secret happiness.' Jenny said that she had a most aggressive ego and it cost her a lot to sacrifice that for Nye, how much no one would know, but she always knew it was worth it. On the other hand, she had much consolation in her private life as their devotion to each other never wavered. I think the latter to be true although I doubt if Jenny realises that Nye often made passes at other women, me especially, almost every time we met, but I doubt if he had much success with anyone and he did it most crudely. Comparing notes with Sonia Orwell, who had the same experience, we both agreed he never really robbed Jenny of anything. He never once said anything derogatory about her or flattered any women at her expense, his passes were really frivolous. Indeed, after I had laughed at him for about the tenth time for saying to me, 'When are we two going to fuck?' He replied, 'well it wouldn't make much difference to me if it was you or Judy!' How much more interesting are those things which cannot be published! I always used to tell Michael about Nye's overtures and he made no comment. I used to wonder why he wasn't a little shocked considering Nye was his best friend.

* This is Jill's spelling for Jennie Lee.
† Ma is Jennie's mother, who cooked for Nye and Jennie, as they had no kitchen skills whatsoever.
‡ Labour's National Executive Committee.

At the time Jill wrote this letter, she was engaged in revising her play, *Emmeline and Christabel*. Some time in 1971 Jill had gone to Mike Randall for comments, and he had provided shrewd criticism on how to cut scenes, sharpen dialogue and quicken the pace of the drama in general. The play pivoted between suffragette demonstrations in the streets and the celebrated court case in which Christabel took on Lloyd George, Herbert Gladstone and the whole Liberal cohort that had stymied the Votes for Women drive. This work built on Jill's radio docudrama of 1950, but it was more ambitious in its effort to show not only the women's struggle, but also the black comedy of male politicians attempting to thwart the inevitable. Indeed, the play is remarkable precisely because it uses humour to savage effect and employs music and songs as satirical motifs. Jill was obviously influenced by her admiration of Stanley Kubrick's use of similar methods in *Dr Strangelove*.

Out of the play had come a book proposal, *Emmeline Pankhurst and her World*, scheduled to be part of a series of coffee-table picture books published by Thames and Hudson. The picture book (with 20,000–40,000 words of text) had derived from a timely word from Elizabeth Thomas (who had worked as Michael's secretary) to Stanley Baronne at the publishing house. Jill told Mike that Baronne had phoned her, saying, 'he could kick himself for not having thought of the idea himself and that I was ideally placed to write it. He's coming here on Thursday to look at my collection.' Jill was indeed a publisher's dream because she had both the expertise and an archive of illustrations worthy of a small museum all packed into her one-room study. In the mid-1940s, Jill had begun collecting material on women's efforts to win the vote, her interest in the suffragettes driving her back into the nineteenth century in order to understand how it was women turned to militant protest.

All this activity, Jill observed to Mike Randall, occurred between 'shopping, getting meals and walking on the Heath' twice a day with Michael discussing *his* book. Julie and Mike were always coaxing Jill to stay with them in the country so that she could get on with her own work. 'Mike is longing to read your script again, how is it going now? When can we expect it?' Julie had written on 2 February 1972. By 25 August, Jill wrote to Mike, 'I cut <u>everything</u> you have suggested', and she had added songs and verses to replace newspaper quotes. But there would always be some reason why Jill could not leave Michael to get on with her work, even though she would complain about his constant interruptions. No matter how convenient Julie and Mike made their offers, Jill demurred. An exasperated Julie wrote:

Mike has always said to you that you are <u>very</u> <u>very</u> welcome to stay with us for <u>as</u> <u>long</u> as you like, (There was a time when the offer could have helped you in your problems, I'm very happy for you that you no longer need our help in that way) and we would have put off any one and every one else coming here so you could have had the comfort and privacy of our spare room and double bed; you would have been made very comfortable and we would have loved having you any way.

Jill's play, like her book, like her original idea to do a film about the suffragettes, kept evolving.* Her major project – to tell the story of how women got the vote and why getting the vote remained so important – could not be held apart from the shopping and the cooking and the architecture of homemaking and the entertaining and her envelopment in Michael's life. The project had to be done right in the midst of this multi-faceted career or the project was not worth doing – precisely because it would cut her off from the life she had invented for herself. Not that she didn't long, at times, for precisely that division between life and work, but the facts demonstrate that no strand in the tapestry of her enterprises could be torn out without damaging the whole composition.

In spite of Jill's considerable efforts to interest actress/friends like Peggy Ashcroft in her play, a production never materialized. The coffee-table book just grew and grew and eventually became subsumed in Jill's idea for a much more broadly gauged book that would tell, in epic fashion, the history of the votes for women movement.

Did Michael do enough to help Jill? Julie thought not. What had Michael ever really given up for Jill? Jill took the point, yet she did not press Michael for more. He took an avid interest in her writing and they would discuss her projects for hours on end. Indeed, he would remain the best source on how Jill conceived of her work on women's rights, and on how she was planning to write the later parts of her book. Great artists, she would always say, did their work no matter what. She did not consider herself great and did not see how anything short of greatness could justify demanding more from Michael. Jennie Lee's assessment of her relationship with Nye resonated with Jill: 'She

---

* *The Times* of 30 November 1972 announced that Jill had delivered the play to her agents, calling it a 'musical drama'. At various times Jill would interest her friends, the actresses Peggy Ashcroft and Constance Cummings, in producing the drama, but it never did find a venue. With the help of her grandson, Jason Lehel, Jill would later transform the play into a shooting script, *Incitement to a Riot*, which has not been filmed. The play also went through several revisions. Jill hoped that Carmen Callil at Virago Press would publish it, but Callil wrote on 5 September 1977 to say she was tempted to do so but plays were a hard sell and Virago had no playscript list into which Jill's work could fit. Several producers also had a look at the play. On 19 April 1977 Sir Bernard Miles at the Mermaid Theatre sent Jill a typical response: 'I like your play very, very much, but really can't think we could get around to doing it. There have been two very good suffragette series on T.V. within the last few years… this has a fatal effect on the Box Office.'

hated to take liberties with him and often resented the way other people did and that she would be a fool if she failed to recognize how much greater his contribution was.' Like Jennie, Jill never had it out with her husband, never did level with him about what it had cost her to support him. Like Jennie, Jill had to convince herself that she had made the right choice.

22

The Idea of India
(1973–98)

[T]he history of independent India appears as the third moment in the great democratic experiment launched at the end of the eighteenth century by the American and French revolutions.

Sunil Khilnani, The Idea of India (1997)*

Indira is India, India is Indira.

Deu Kanta Barooah, Congress Party President

In September 1973 Jill and Michael took their first trip to India. Krishna Rasgotra, the Deputy High Commissioner, invited them to join a delegation that included Jennie Lee and Michael English, a Labour MP, on a three-week tour, which stretched from Kashmir in the north to Madras in the south. Rasgotra's wife Choti – 'a tremendous raging beauty,' Michael observed – would become Jill's good friend and faithful correspondent, strengthening Jill's links to the country.

Jennie and Nye had supported independence for India before the war and had become friends with Jawaharlal Nehru (1889–1964), the country's first Prime Minister. When Nye died, Nehru established a visiting fellowship in his memory. Jennie's tie to Indira Gandhi, who had become Prime Minister in 1966, just two years after her father's death, strengthened in the 1970s, when Gandhi's opponents charged her with creating a cult of personality that menaced parliamentary democracy. Michael had joined the India League while still a student at Oxford, and he had befriended Krishna Menon (1896–1974), the League's founder and secretary and the foremost spokesman in England for

---

* Michael recommended this book as the best expression of the vision Jill had of the country. Both Jill and Michael met Khilnani in India, and Michael reviewed his book. It is worth noting that in defining the significance of India, Khilnani sweeps aside the Russian and Chinese Revolutions, which have had such an influence on so many leftist intellectuals, but which did not have the hold on Jill and Michael that India exerted.

Indian nationalism. 'He taught me a lot of my politics,' Michael says, referring to his anti-Empire, anti-imperialistic convictions.

In characteristic fashion, Jill and Michael also exploited the journey as a way of renewing their commitment to each other. 'A wonderful experience which Michael and I could share and about which we felt alike each adding to the other's observations; one of those events to look back upon which cannot be repeated,' she wrote in an unpublished journal, *Impressions of India written November 5th, a week or so following our return.* Jill and Michael were yearning for a cause they could celebrate. And the Indians delivered, welcoming Jill and Michael with a warmth and intimacy that made the couple India enthusiasts for life. 'Jill was mad about the place – right from the beginning,' Michael remembered. 'Some people hate the sight of India, the poverty, but Jill loved it.' Jill saw the poverty, too, of course, but the idea of India proved positively thrilling. Jill's India was the India of villages, a kind of William Morris India. In *An Indian Summer* (1974), James Cameron observes: 'More than any country in the world India *is* the village.' Eighty per cent of the population lived in 600,000 villages. For his beautifully written and candid report of his own obsession with India, Cameron had the advantage not only of having made many visits to India since the 1930s, but also of being married to an Indian, Moni, one of Jill's closest friends.

While Michael spoke with the eminent who wanted to meet him, Jill went off on her own expeditions with groups of women. She met prominent women, including female journalists. 'She saw the places where women were taking control and had greater impact, deciding for themselves if they would have children,' Michael reported. She was quite aware of the 'obscurantist parts', too. It was a country of 'tremendous contrasts'. She walked the streets without an official escort and returned to Michael with the intelligence she had gathered. 'She was teaching me all about it,' Michael said. 'India played a very big part in our lives.'

Neither Jill nor Michael wanted a junket. They had come to learn. If Jill had any preconceptions about India, she did not write them down. She had read about India, of course, and had brought with her a biography of Mrs Gandhi. Her companions provided the only sour note: both were 'singularly insensitive, heavy-going and although Michael English was no friend of ours and odious, unlike Jennie, she in a way was more of a strain'. Jennie fought with English – 'a terrible fellow,' Michael said – and she kept demanding to be taken care of. Even worse, 'She brought all her prejudices to India and saw nothing,' Jill wrote. She watched Michael – such a contrast to Jennie – 'eager to ask questions in his own tentative way'. Jennie pulled rank and talked incessantly about her friendship with Nehru. 'I never realised before what a name-dropper she is. She also likes to be the centre of attraction and very much the Queen Madam, as I have heard her called but hitherto could never understand why.' She did not walk the streets and meet the people, and consequently she 'got everything about India wrong', Jill confided to her journal.*

Although India was undergoing an industrial revolution that Jill likened to England's in the nineteenth century, she admired the government policy, the 'green revolution and all that entails is designed to keep the people in the villages and improve their lot'. She knew the rates of success varied greatly from state to state, but her aesthetic sense flourished with the 'vitality of the Indians, the colour, the pageantry, the beauty of the women in their saris, the grace of their movements, the animals, the political zest and the way many Indians seem to resemble the Welsh'.† Then there was the wonderful Indian dancing – perhaps a little too long – that Jill enjoyed at a school founded by Annie Besant (1837–1933), the British theosophist, socialist and birth control proponent, who created a sensation in India and was elected president of the Indian National Congress from 1917 to 1923. When Jill tried to question an Indian woman who knew Besant, Jennie broke in, 'We know all about Annie Besant.' Jill persisted, wanting to know what the woman thought of the biographies of Besant. The woman confirmed Jill's suspicion that they contained many errors. '"Write them, write them," Jennie advised the woman in a regal tone and swept off denouncing her later as a "phoney".' Out of Jennie's hearing, Jill gave the woman her phone number and asked her to call if she came to London. Jill had a special interest in Besant and collected books about her. Women like Annie Besant were more highly regarded there than they could ever be in Britain. The Indian story appealed to Jill because it was a key to open a door still half-closed in Britain.

Jill thought 'Nye's description of the Taj Mahal cannot be bettered – "like a piece of music caught in stone." It didn't appeal to Jenny.' Later, when Jill saw the monolithic carvings, especially the Elephanta, at the Mahabiliputm Temples, she wondered if Henry Moore had seen them. She 'felt sure he would have been bowled over'. When Jill admired the cottage industries that kept handicrafts alive, Jennie 'condemned' her for being 'arty crafty'. At one of the villages Michael bought himself a Rosewood walking stick, a token wedding anniversary gift that Jill insisted on paying for.

* Patricia Hollis, Jennie's biographer, suggests that Jennie was doing no more than was expected of her – behaving, that is, like a 'sister of Indira'.
† Jill romanticized the Welsh and the Indians alike, seeing in both a vivid contrast to the inhibited English.

Both Jill and Michael revelled in a country where 'nationalisation is not a dirty word'. She enjoyed the posh hotels (all nationalized) but deplored the bloated service staff. She believed the country had begun to cope with its population explosion, although improvement in health care meant more lives to support. She was gratified to see how many Indian academics had read Michael's work and respected it. They hoped he would become Prime Minister. 'I think he would make a most acceptable and excellent foreign secretary. But what a hope with Callaghan [the Labour shadow foreign secretary] hanging on!'

In the universities half the students were women, and she was impressed with the equal pay in the civil service and the important posts women held in government and industry. Of course, she realized this did not mean much to the majority of women in the villages: 'In India the women seem to be either more emancipated than in England or very much less so.'* She met a charming woman MP who thought the country fortunate to have a female Prime Minister, since women were so much more 'practical' than men. This MP, 'no beauty and rather fat', made large claims for her family planning campaign. She told Jill that she and her husband had decided not to have children; she used a dutch cap or he used a condom. 'She goes round telling women how to use it and claims, at the same time, to have a very good sex life with her husband, which made me rather envious. When I meet such women, I find myself thinking, if her why not me?'

Jill also saw the 'worst of India': the 'shanty towns, Bombay, the beggars, especially the children begging and the poverty which, nevertheless, is not so bad as we were led to believe serious though it undoubtedly is'. According to James Cameron, who had visited Bombay a few years before Jill and Michael, 90,000 people slept on the streets while 'expensive new apartment blocks were sprouting everywhere with names such as Monolith, Acropolis, and Flowerdene'. Cameron reported, Jill rationalized:

> Not everyone sleeps on the pavements because they have nowhere to live. Sometimes they prefer to sleep near their work, or they may have just arrived from a village. There are many reasons for sleeping on the pavement and in a hot country this is not a particularly distressing thing to do. At first, the sight horrified us and no doubt there are heaven knows how many hard cases; but we saw no one dying on the pavements or looking as if they were starving.

---

* In *An Indian Summer*, James Cameron points out that successful public women in India come from the upper and middle classes. 'There is not and never has been a working-class woman with a function in Indian politics, and it is hard to say when there ever will be.' His wife Moni told him, 'Give it another fifty or eighty years. Do not be impatient.' At the time only 10 per cent of women were literate.

Jill focused on Ashoke Bangalore, where Nehru had given Corbusier 'a free hand ... to build a modern city regardless of expense'. The result 'proved that Indians have nothing to learn from European architects and would do better if they never left their own country nor saw any western architectural magazines.* Bombay with its congested sky-scrapers is a disaster.'

Britain looked bleak after Jill's immersion in this country full of animals: 'Long live the sacred cow. And the bullocks, the goats, the pigs, the buffaloes, the elephants and the camels. The people live close to their animals which they seem to treat well, the villagers live a Thoreauite existence and the problem of the future will be how to retain the best of Indian values while raising the standard of living.' Jill was also attracted to Hindu men, 'taught to look after their women, to please them sexually, to buy them beautiful clothes and jewels ... The women wear much jewellery, even peasants, often consisting of gold or silver bracelets and ankle bracelets.'

Keen to know how arranged marriages worked, Jill had many conversations with Indian women who said their marriages worked because they had to work. Divorce was rare. The women would not stop their daughters from marrying whom they chose, 'providing they were moderately suitable', but they 'saw no chance of happiness in the so-called "permissive society"' of the West. Jill attributed their attitudes to a culture in which 'both girls and boys are taught that they must please their husbands and wives ... Great emphasis is made on the need to be unselfish.'

Jill and Michael travelled down long, narrow roads covering hundreds of miles. 'I was never bored. Michael dozed off just occasionally,' Jill wrote. Apparently she was not defeated by what James Cameron called the 'endlessness on the Indian road that you do not get even on the interminable plains of the American Middle West'. In villages and factories Jill enjoyed speaking with women workers but never got the chance she yearned for: to 'enter one of the huts in the Indian villages'. Jill wanted to know, for example, where women kept their saris and men their clothes. A 'daft woman' in Bombay said they used poles, but a Calcutta tea planter told Jill they had tin boxes for storage.

Jill liked Calcutta, 'a green city with plenty of open space swarming Indian style with animals and a beautiful river frontage'. Unlike James Cameron, she did not remark on the 'urban awfulness', a 'wretchedness that has gone not only past redemption but beyond description ... Nowhere but in Calcutta is there a beggary of such ubiquitous, various, ever-present and inescapable

---

* In a chapter on Indian cities, Khilnani provides a devastating analysis of Corbusier's failure to create buildings that suited the environment and the culture.

kind ... the lepers and tertiary syphilitics and pinheads and epileptics and normally starving men and women.' Jill, in contrast, delighted in the shop signs and advertisements – the baker who called himself the 'greatest loafer in the world' and bras touted as the 'passport to womanhood!' How could Jill not like a country where cinema was the 'favourite entertainment'. Films were shown even in remote villages, where the audience sometimes became so involved in the action that they tore a screen to ribbons shooting arrows at a tiger, or so Jill had been told. More than once Jill encountered a view of film as a piece of reality that intrigued her. Mr Rome, a Calcutta tea planter, told her about one of his workers who had seen the same film eleven times. 'Why?' Mr Rome asked. 'There's that train which just arrives in time to save the man. But one of these days it will be late,' the worker replied.

Jill contrasted the bumptious Jennie and her 'rich friend in Bombay', both complaining about their income taxes and the 'low castes', with the 'subtle' Michael who drew out his Indian hosts with wit. He had a teasing charm and an intense interest in how others thought; these qualities coupled with an ability to listen made him an irresistible confidant. A man of conviction and good humour, he incited his hosts to laugh and share their jokes with him. When Jill and Michael visited Nangal, where Nehru often stayed, near the Bhakra Dam, India's largest power station, there was a power cut. 'How strange that there should be a blackout here of all places,' Michael said. The Indian PR man did not skip a beat: 'The nearer the church, the further from God,' he replied, provoking a roar of laughter from Michael. Jill found touring the dam a bore but loved her guesthouse garden, where she watched 'fireflies in the moonlight and the palms and lake and the hot tropical atmosphere', all of which put her in a romantic mood.

Indeed, Jill had been caught by the romance of India. James Cameron had his wife Moni against whom he could test his perceptions of India. Jill had Moni as well, but Jill's idealism, Moni felt, could not be tempered. Moni ('a good old-fashioned left-wing socialist,' Michael affirmed) would say: 'You're too kind to India. You see a glowing, good India, which is not the case.' As Moni later reflected: 'She wanted to believe in the Fabian India that was the case when we were growing up.'

For Jill and Michael, Indira Gandhi was the incarnation of that promise of empowered socialism that had first joined them together in 1945. They met her on 11 October in New Delhi,* having come from Kashmir. Michael's brother Dingle had been the attorney for Sheikh Abdullah (1905–82), a.k.a.

---

* Jill kept the invitation in her papers.

The Lion of Kashmir, when the Indian central government prosecuted him for treason. Michael had been an admirer of Sheikh Abdullah ever since the days before World War II when Abdullah and Nehru had worked closely together for Indian independence. Sheikh Abdullah served as Chief Minister of Kashmir from 1975 until his death. 'He owed a debt of gratitude to Dingle, which he certainly showed when Jill and I stayed with him in Kashmir,' Michael said. They were his guests at the Governor's Palace in Srinagar, from which they set off on breathtaking rides into villages surrounded by snow-capped mountains. 'Whatever grievances the Sheikh had had with Nehru and the central government', he thought Kashmir as much a part of India as Nehru himself did. Nehru had been born in Kashmir, which added to Nehru's feeling about it, Michael pointed out. Jill and Michael's vision of the country grew out of Nehru's vision, expressed in his book *The Unity of India* (1941), which argued that the land could not survive in bits and pieces and that Kashmir is an integral part of India. Like her father, Indira always thought of herself as Kashmiri.*

Surprisingly Jill includes only one sentence on Indira in her journal: 'She wears no jewellery and only a simple cotton sari, but I thought her very feminine and not unattractive.' The words do not do justice to what Indira came to mean for Jill and Michael. They met both of Indira's sons, Rajiv and Sanjay, as well as Rajiv's new wife, Sonia. 'They were all friendly, right from the beginning,' Michael noted.† At that point Rajiv was resistant to any involvement in politics. 'A most attractive man – as beautiful as Sonia, beautiful hands he had,' Michael remembered.

Jill would have known from reading Indira's biography that in the spring of 1930, at the age of twelve, Indira had led a procession of 15,000 children and spoken before a crowd of 50,000 in support of Gandhi's nonviolent campaign to make India independent. Indeed, Indira was part of the 'avalanche of women' who took an active role in securing their country's freedom. Jill would also have known that Gandhi himself had been inspired by the British suffragettes, who had a genius for public demonstrations that forced authorities to deal with the denial of basic rights. Like Jill, who had dreamed of becoming a dancer as a young girl, Indira had early on been fascinated with dance as an art form. Indira had a strong aesthetic sense which, like Jill's, seemed to come

---

* After her experience in Dubrovnik and her support of Croatian independence (see chapters 28 and 29), Jill asked Michael if he did not think the Kashmiris had a right to their independence. But he believed the two cases were different, and he supported the Indian claims, noting that many Muslims felt their rights would be better protected in an Indian state.

† 'We met the Prime Minister briefly & told her how much you enjoyed your visit to India & especially your evening spent with her. She too said that it was a pleasure for her to meet you,' Choti wrote to Jill on 19 January 1974. Jill was delighted when Mrs Gandhi followed up with an invitation to visit India again.

out of nowhere, since her family, especially her father, focused almost exclusively on politics. As Elizabeth Frank reports in *Indira: The Life of Indira Nehru Gandhi* (2001), she had a 'heightened sensitivity to colour and the texture and feel of cloth'. Jill saw the simply dressed Indira, but in Vienna as a young woman she would dress like a European – or like an Indian in beautiful saris, depending on her political purpose. Later, for Lyndon Johnson, she would arrive in Washington with an exquisite bouffant hairdo. In India, Indira's saris, 'their colour, material and style – evolved into a sophisticated form of personal expression and political communication', Frank observes. Indira had been in England during the war and experienced the Blitz. She had volunteered as a canteen worker. She had experienced blackouts and used food rationing coupons. In 1941 she lived at 20 Abbey Road in St John's Wood. 'Indifferent to social conventions', she had lived in London with her man before marrying him. Indira had experienced the same freedom and exhilaration Jill had cherished. And like Jill, Indira had lived in the shadow of a great man, whom she served as hostess. At her father's official residence she 'personally checked every light bulb in the lamps and every tap in the bathrooms. She made sure tall guests had high-back chairs and small ones footrests.' In fact, Indira's rise to power had been abetted by men who thought of her as only her father's malleable servant whom they could control.*

At the very time when Jill was expressing her disappointment in Jennie Lee, she had encountered a woman whose 'emergence as Prime Minister coincided with the burgeoning women's movement in the West'. While Indira, like Mrs Thatcher, would strenuously object to any ties to feminism – desiring to be judged solely in terms of her political role – there is no question that Jill's interest in her came at a time when public interest in woman leaders had been aroused.† When Jill and Michael met Indira, she was at the height of her power, having won a landslide election victory in 1971 and triumphed over Pakistan in a war of liberation that had created a new country, Bangladesh, out of the much abused land of East Pakistan. At this point her prestige exceeded even Margaret Thatcher's after the Falklands War (1982).‡ 'Indira was now

* It would be good to know what Indira thought of Jill and Michael as a couple. Her own marriage to Feroze Gandhi had been unhappy and acrimonious. Indira wrote to her friend Dorothy Norman: 'I am sorry… to have missed the most wonderful thing in life, having a complete and perfect relationship with another human being; for only thus, I feel, can one's personality fully develop and blossom.' See Elizabeth Frank's *Indira*.

† Golda Meir (1898–1978) was prime minister of Israel from 1969 to 1974 and provided yet another example of what it was now possible for women to do.

‡ 'Some people are very eager to say,' Michael points out, 'that Mrs Gandhi got on with Mrs Thatcher. I don't think she did. I knew her a damn sight better than Mrs Thatcher did. She was bored with Mrs Thatcher, who didn't have any ideas about the world, apart from anything else. Mrs Gandhi, whatever her faults, and she maybe had terrible ones, she was fascinated by what was happening in the world.'

elevated to god-like stature. She was praised in Parliament as a new *Durga*, the Hindu goddess of war, and likened to *Shakti*, who represents female energy and power.' The Gallup poll of 1971 reported that Indira was the 'most admired person in the world', Frank notes. Jill, Michael and Indira would meet again – in India and in London – solidifying a bond that was as strong as their love for India itself.

Returning home, Jill could not get India out of her mind. 'I should get down to my book,' she wrote; her work was now several hundred pages long and had expanded beyond just an account of the suffragettes and into a full scale epic narrative of the forces, institutions and personalities that shaped the Votes for Women drive from the mid-nineteenth century to the post-World War I era. 'Perhaps now that I've got this off my chest I can make some head-way. Only I dare say …'. Her journal stops here, as if once again she had been interrupted. In short order, she would become a Cabinet Minister's wife,* and in that capacity return to India in the autumn of 1976.

By then Indira Gandhi's triumphalist phase had ended. In June 1975 she invoked Article 352 of the Indian constitution, which declared that if the country was endangered by 'war or external aggression or by armed rebellion', then the President of India – Indira's hand-picked man – could declare a state of emergency. Under fierce criticism inside and outside India, Indira justified the Emergency by noting that the leader of the opposition, J.P. Narayan, had called on the police and the army not to obey government orders. In other words, there had been an '*incitement* to "armed rebellion"'.[1] Sceptics noted that before the Emergency, her administration had enacted a series of measures eroding the independence and the power of the judiciary, and that Gandhi had ruled so as to concentrate more and more power in the executive branch of government. Unquestionably, she had less tolerance of dissent than her father had exhibited. Khilnani quotes this revealing exchange between father and daughter in 1959:

> Reporter: Are you going to fight the communists or throw them out?
> Nehru: Throw them out? How? What do you mean? They have also been elected.
> Indira Gandhi: Papu, what are you telling them? You are talking as prime minister. As Congress president I intend to fight them and throw them out.

Now the courts and parliament were suspended, and on 10 June, George Fernandes, leader of India's Socialist Party, had been arrested for organizing the underground resistance to Gandhi. With Fernandes facing a death

---

* See Chapter 23.

sentence for treason and the press censored, Michael's reluctance to condemn Mrs Gandhi outraged the left.

What did Jill and Michael make of this anti-democratic development? Mervyn Jones notes that Indira Gandhi had become Michael's friend, and he was deeply loyal to friends. True enough, but to Michael – and to Jill – what mattered, in the end, was that to them the Emergency was just that, a temporary measure – even a deplorable deed – but not an irreparable injury to Indian democracy.

Members of the Socialist International, including Willy Brandt of Germany and Olof Palme of Sweden, expressed their concern to British Cabinet members. Michael said to Callaghan, 'I would like to go to India and raise these concerns with Mrs Gandhi because I know her quite well and see what she's got to say. It would be much better than just raising a row with her.' He did not want an 'estrangement'. The Foreign Office gave Michael 'some kind of briefing, but I don't think they liked the idea', he recalled. Mervyn Jones quotes a statement of Tony Crosland, then Foreign Secretary: 'We must clearly approach the Indians with great caution.' Crosland did not want to involve the Socialist International in India's affairs, an intervention he saw as only exacerbating Mrs Gandhi's 'sensitive' state of mind. But Michael believed Crosland was worried that he might say something that implied support for the Emergency.

Sir Michael Walker, the High Commissioner, met Michael and Jill at the New Delhi airport at 2.00 or 3.00 in the morning. 'I don't know what you've come here for,' Walker said, 'You're not going to be able to do much with Mrs Gandhi. We don't want a breach with her.' Michael replied, 'I don't want a breach, either. I've come to raise a number of issues with her.' When Michael began to enumerate his concerns, including the question as to why Mark Tully, one of the finest British reporters on India, had been expelled from the country, Walker said: 'You can't do that. If you say that to her, she will throw you out' – or words to that effect. 'He had a false idea of what I could say to her,' Michael observed. Walker advised him to go home.

But Michael was scheduled to meet with Mrs Gandhi that day and he carried on, raising every subject on his list, including Fernandes. She made no comment, except to say that she could not interfere with the judicial process.* 'I understand,' he told her, 'but you must understand how strong the feeling is about this member of the Socialist International. We would be doing the same for anyone in such circumstances, enquiring on his behalf.' To all his

---

* Fernandes was released from prison in 1977 and won a parliamentary seat in Bihar.

enquiries Michael received calm and reasoned replies – 'much calmer than any other political figure I've ever met'. She defended herself but admitted that there had been problems in the application of the Emergency powers. She told Michael of her fears that the CIA were plotting against her. She did not want to be another Allende.* Elections had been postponed, but she assured Michael they would go ahead.

During their week in India, Jill and Michael had lunch with Indira and spent a good part of the day with her watching the Dasera Festival. They saw her again at a dinner given by the High Commissioner. They also watched her venture out into crowds fearlessly without the kind of military protections dictators and even some democratically elected leaders regularly employ.

For Michael and Jill, what Indira did after the twenty-two-month Emergency was 'crucial to the whole salvation of India'. She lost the next election (1977), taking responsibility for the defeat, but in 1980 made her comeback appealing to the electorate, thus fulfilling, in Michael's view, her commitment to democracy. As to the Emergency itself, there is no record of what Jill thought about some of the more extreme measures, which would have surely clashed with her beliefs, although Michael freely conceded, 'There is a case for the other side.' In *Dr Strangelove, I Presume* (1999), he states that 'some terrible events had occurred' during the Emergency, and Mrs Gandhi's 'apologies for them were pitifully inadequate'. Indeed, her critics, such as Moni and James Cameron, argued with Jill and Michael about their excessive faith in Mrs Gandhi. And other friends, like Frank Cousins, also attacked Michael's position. In retrospect, Michael noted that Nehru had made huge miscalculations by following the planning models set out by the Soviet Union and building 'great big bloody dams' that made no sense economically or ecologically, as Khilnani points out. But India learned from its mistakes. In view of the entire history of the revolution that made India democratic, Mrs Gandhi's renewed commitment to the electoral process ranked, in Michael's and Jill's estimations, as one of the great democratic triumphs in history. 'Some people talk of her as though she were just an opportunist interested in her own survival. Jill saw her in action, and she was the least egotistical of leaders. Mrs Gandhi wanted India to play her part in the world,' Michael concluded, 'as of course Jill did.'

Jill could never understand, Moni remembered, why the Labour Party and

* Salvador Allende (1908–73), the Marxist President of Chile, was killed in a coup backed by the CIA. Gandhi had met Richard Nixon, then the US President, and the hostility between them was palpable, according to Elizabeth Frank's Gandhi biography. Mrs Gandhi's foreign policy tilt toward the Soviet Union (which abrogated her father's non-aligned policy) had angered Richard Nixon, making her a vulnerable Cold War target, she thought.

leaders like Neil Kinnock spent so much time on Africa 'at the expense of India'. Africa might look more socialist because India had such a hierarchical structure, but any educated woman could advance rapidly beyond her caste, because education itself proved to be the decisive factor and gave India a democratic dynamism many of Jill's fellow socialists failed to appreciate.

Jill and Michael continued to visit India and they would see Mrs Gandhi when she visited England. Mrs Gandhi visited Nye Bevan's memorial in Tredegar. It was pouring rain, Michael remembered, 'but she was not going to be put off' and climbed the steps to Bevan's stone monument. He pointed to the inscription that says 'Here Aneurin Bevan spoke to his constituents and to the world.' Michael noted that originally the sentence was to end at constituents. 'It was Jill who said they must add "and to the world".'

It was a terrible blow to Jill and Michael when Indira Gandhi's Sikh body-guards assassinated her in October 1984. But Jill and Michael's interest in Indira Gandhi's family extended to her successors, with Jill forming an especially close bond with Sonia Gandhi (a considerable collection of articles about Sonia remained in Jill's papers at her death). In her 1981 diary Jill wrote of Sonia's beauty, 'a little like Bridget Bardot … Sonia runs Indira's home, which is quite small & is taking a course in picture-restoring. She has promised to take me to the art galleries when we next go to India.'

Jill and Michael made their last visit to India in 1998. Both insisted on going to Kashmir in the depths of winter. For them it represented a kind of paradise and the locus of imagination for their dearest friends. They could not 'forgo another chance' of seeing the land for themselves – as they had done twenty years earlier, Michael recounted in *Dr Strangelove, I Presume*. To see the 'rivers and the mountains in all their radiant beauty' meant seeing 'why so many people treasured this as their homeland. Neither Jawaharlal Nehru's tryst with destiny nor Salman Rushdie's *Midnight's Children* would have been conceivable without Kashmir.' No one, not even the Prime Minister, felt able to deny their request, even though they would have no central heating in the freezing weather. 'The coldest place I've ever been to in my life,' Michael recalled, 'worse than Moscow.' He woke up in the middle of the night and said, 'God, let's go back.' 'Coward,' Jill said. 'Have some guts. You've come so far, you've got to go on.' She didn't feel any warmer than Michael. When they did fly back to New Delhi, Jill was running a temperature. The plane arrived six hours late, at 4.00 in the morning. 'Jill did not say anything,' Moni remembered, except that she did not feel like eating. She rested for a day, asking for nothing. 'We did not realize the extent of her heart condition.' She took a pounding, yet 'she did not impose herself. She was a very tough lady.'

India, Indira Gandhi, and the role women had played in the country's development inspired Jill to think of India in the grand terms that Khilnani later elaborated in *The Idea of India*. For all its failings, it was India – not Africa or China – that had built on the revolutions in America and France and that heralded the future.

23

Husbands and Wives
(1973–9)

Marriage is like democracy. It may not work, but no one has thought of a better system.

Jill Craigie, Odd Reflections

Jill returned from her first visit to India in a glow. Julie came for a visit and wrote afterwards on 8 November: 'You looked so well and seemed so happy. It's a long time since you have been something like your old self – the one I grew up with! So hats off to Michael's and your efforts. There is no concealing their success.' Jill's mood soured four days later when she received a 'nasty message from that wretched woman again and she also returned out of the blue the letter I wrote to her but she returned none of Michael's. What all that portends, I don't know. I wish to God she would jump in a lake. I suppose she is eager to let me know she is still fighting, at least that's how it seemed.'[*]

Julie then received a strange letter from her mother that made Julie think that Jill imagined she might die soon. The letter reads like a last will and testament. She wanted to make sure that Julie would inherit the house after Michael's death. Jill had put £5000 into the house (£2000 from her mother to do the upstairs flat and the rest from Jill's film money and from selling her paintings). After Michael's death, Julie was also to inherit most of the furniture Jill had bought: bookshelves, the dining-room table and chairs, a kitchen dresser, a chiffonier in the sitting room. Other items were destined for Laura (Julie's adopted daughter) and Damon, Julie's second son.

The letter provided a survey of Jill's domain and the acquired tastes of a lifetime: the library steps, the Wellington and in the drawing room the round Dutch marquetry table (for Esther, Julie's second daughter), the plush

---

[*] This may have been Lamia's last appearance in Jill's life. I have found no further record of her.

Victorian furniture. Michael had bought the dining-room table and chairs but Jill had had them reupholstered with needlework seats: 'I have such tender memories of Michael coming home in the early days of our marriage telling me with such pride how he had bought those chairs. I can remember so vividly the expression of his face, that for purely sentimental reasons, I very much want you to have.' She also wanted Julie to have the chair that Nye had smashed in his fight with Michael. It had been repaired and it was of 'historic value. I also remember rather ruefully having to pay to get it mended, seven pounds ten shillings when I was only getting £10 a week housekeeping money, and had not been earning any for some time.'

The 'antique china, pottery, Leeds, silver and copper lustre, paper weight etc.' all went to Julie, as well as all the paintings, except for one in Michael's library done by Dennis Matthews, which Michael might want to keep. She regretted selling her Renoir, a Henry Moore and other valuable paintings, but

> Michael has had their value in effect because it was often the case that I really couldn't manage on my housekeeping money and I was ultra-sensitive about asking. It is not so easy to earn regular money in a free-lance capacity especially this was the case after the car accident and when we had to fight elections and furnish houses. Anyway, I do feel by my earnings and the sale of my paintings and other economies I contributed to Michael's prosperity to a far greater degree than he ever realised. Of course, Michael has now put that side of our life on an entirely different basis which is far more satisfactory to me.

Julie was also to inherit her mother's library and ever-growing suffragette collection.

Julie never did figure out exactly why Jill went to all this trouble to set her house in order. Jill was not ill. Perhaps the letter from Lamia had contributed to Jill's mood, for she concluded her letter to Julie this way: 'I'm sure Michael will agree to these suggestions, but if he falls for somebody else and you have not settled these matters between you, there may well be difficulties.'

The letter said much about Jill's feeling for Julie as it did about her doubts about Michael. When Julie and Mike Randall were having money troubles, Jill wrote, 'I would always come to the rescue somehow if you were in dire trouble. You won't have to sacrifice your home, so don't think about that.'[1] When Julie had difficulty with her children, Jill wrote, 'In the end, I doubt if there is any satisfaction quite so great as launching children into the world, bad as the world is. Neither fame, success, money or anything else creates a greater feeling of achievement. You are by far my best achievement and then my relationship with Michael.'[2] Yet Julie never got over her earliest feelings about her mother and Michael: 'I wanted her to be fat and sit me on her lap. I didn't want this pretty, sought after woman with men after her and all the rest of it. I wanted her totally wrapped up in me. Which some mothers are, with husbands usually trailing behind them.'

'But you did have a friendship with your mother,' Sally Vincent pointed out to Julie.* 'Oh, Christ, yes,' Julie quickly responded. 'We could talk dirty, what Michael calls "chitter". He'd say, "Don't sit up too long chittering."' The talk ranged from sex to love to careers to Jill's book. 'You name it, we talked about it. We had so much to talk about. Always when Michael wasn't there. When he was, she was a different person.' Jill and Julie shared an intimacy that excluded Michael, an amity he respected and encouraged. This sisterhood paralleled the brotherhood Michael enjoyed with Mike Randall and Neil Kinnock. While the men drank and argued, shouting at each other, their voices getting louder and louder and louder as they thoroughly enjoyed themselves, Jill and Julie withdrew into the kitchen, washing up, still listening as the men went at each other, getting quite aggressive, stomping around and banging fists.

In the early morning hours mother and daughter would exchange confidences that most men do not vouchsafe to each other. 'Julie was a lot like Jill,' observed Philip Oakes. Both women 'loved gossip'. But it went much deeper than that – into the creation of a woman's world beyond the male ken. Julie wanted to see more of that Jill. Sometimes Jill would come alone to visit Julie at her country home after having seen an old suffragette friend, Grace Roe. 'We often had Saturday dinner parties and great Sunday lunch parties and played croquet on the lawn. Jill would drive down on Saturday and stay the night. You could not persuade her to stay an extra night. It used to upset me. We'd all beg her not to go.' But she would never leave Michael for more than a night.

On 28 February 1974 Labour returned to power with only a five-seat majority. Harold Wilson formed his second Labour government. In Ebbw Vale, Jill asked Tommy Evans, Michael's driver, to take her out in the car. Tommy asked where she wanted to go. 'Oh, just drive around,' Jill said. Presently, she asked Tommy what he thought of Michael joining the Cabinet. 'Depends on the job,' Tommy replied. 'Well, what about Secretary of State for Employment?' 'That's all right then, isn't it?' he said. Tommy had become a friend. He did not merely drive Jill and Michael around, he became a

* Both Sally and Julie were young professionals on Fleet Street in the 1950s but then lost track of each other until Sally interviewed Michael towards the end of Jill's life and considered doing a biography of Jill.

companion and remained at Michael's side after the car journey was over. He never got over the fact that Jill had consulted him. Jill and Michael were not like others in power he had driven to appointments.*

Michael Foot was a natural choice for Secretary of State for Employment. His ties to the unions were strong, and Wilson's first government had had considerable trouble when Barbara Castle, his Minister of Employment, published a White Paper, *In Place of Strife,* which included certain anti-strike provisions that Jack Jones, General Secretary of the TGWU, told her plainly would never be acceptable. Michael, too, opposed Barbara's programme and predicted in *Tribune* that it would significantly weaken Wilson's government. He advised her to withdraw her legislation until she could consult with the TUC. She refused and the TUC rejected her Industrial Relations Bill. She failed to get her proposals through Cabinet, ruining her chances of becoming Prime Minister. So it would be better to have Michael in the government and the unions along with him, Wilson concluded. A.J.P. Taylor, Michael's friend from his CND days, wrote to Michael: 'So Max was right after all. You have climbed to the top of the greasy pole or very near it.' Another friend, journalist Alan Brien, wrote: 'When was the last time there was a Labour tribune of the people in office who could be described, even by opponents, as "transparently honest"? … For the many young people coming up, you are our great hope for democratic Socialism.' On 18 March, Jill wrote to Julie: 'I think Michael could turn into a kind of Gladstonian figure and become Prime Minister at a late age, when I have departed from this world.'

Michael joined a Cabinet dominated by centre-right figures like James Callaghan, Denis Healey, Tony Crosland, Shirley Williams and Roy Jenkins. To their left stood Barbara Castle, Tony Benn, Peter Shore, Jon Silkin and Albert Booth[3] – all of whom were concerned to co-ordinate a position that sometimes diverged from the Cabinet consensus. Jill was present when Barbara 'declared that ministers in government become so obsessed with their own departments that they fail to take account of the difficulties encountered by like-minded colleagues. She suggested weekly dinners to rectify the neglect.'† Inviting the husbands and wives of cabinet ministers would make

---

* 'You wait here,' Margaret Thatcher told Tommy when they reached their destination. It would never occur to her – or to most politicians – to treat a driver as anything but a driver. David Owen was so unspeakably rude to his drivers (said Winnie, Michael's driver during his period in the Cabinet) that no one wanted to work for him.

† According to Mervyn Jones in *Michael Foot*, Judith Hart, Minister of Overseas Development (a non-Cabinet position), proposed that the group meet once a week for informal dinners. Michael says Tony Benn instigated the idea. In her 1981 diary Jill attributed the idea of husbands and wives to Barbara Castle and wrote to Jones on 26 May 1994 rejecting his version. Mervyn wrote to Jill on 31 May 1994 saying that Hart had told him the dinners were her idea. 'It's perfectly possible that the idea occurred simultaneously to Barbara.'

the meetings seem less political, Michael observed, and less likely to arouse Harold Wilson's suspicions of a 'cabal' or party within a party conspiring against him. 'Many of us thought,' Michael remembered, 'that the previous Wilson government had fallen apart partly because the people on the left didn't stick together.' The group began meeting in a restaurant and then in members' homes. 'The wives competed for the culinary honours, with Jill generally earning the warmest congratulations,' Mervyn Jones reported.*

Jill detested Mervyn's account, which she told him demeaned all of the wives:

> We wives felt most privileged to be privy to the cabinet secrets every week – a unique situation. We were all highly motivated politically. Liz Shore was a top civil servant at the Ministry of Health, also a doctor. Caroline Benn sat on influential Education Committees and had written standard books on the subject. Rosamond Silkin was a magistrate. Joan Booth looked after her husband's constituency and acted as his whole time secretary. We all contributed to the discussions.
>
> What a put-down to be relegated by you to the kitchen, competing in cookery and 'bickering' – well known anti-feminist term – among ourselves. The assumption that women in groups cannot get on together is a masculine myth which opponents of women's suffrage liked to throw at suffragettes before the first world war. In my experience it is usually the men who bicker. We wives invariably found ourselves in agreement, sometimes in opposition to the men including our own spouses. In your treatment of this unique political innovation, you present yourself as an inveterate male chauvinist, which I know you are not. Incidentally, if Liz Shore or any of the others read your biography, they will think that I put you up to give me the honours for cookery – most embarrassing. When it came to an attempt at the <u>haute cuisine</u>, there was nothing to choose between us.

Jill seems, in this instance, to have been hyper-sensitive, reading more into Mervyn's narrative than is there, perhaps because she did not like him or his biography of Michael.† In his reply (31 May 1994) to Jill's objections, Mervyn wrote:

> Judith [Hart] also told me that there was a sort of light-hearted contest as to who could put on the best dinner, and no one looked forward to the unappetising meals chez Benn – a comment, incidentally, also made by Barbara when I was talking to her recently. I am quite willing to cut out this reference if it offends you, but I really don't think there is any implication that the wives were only interested in cooking

* Jill had little contact with Cabinet wives outside the husbands-and-wives dinners. When I asked Denis Healey if his wife would come to the phone to say a few words about Jill, Edna Healey declined, saying she did not know Jill well enough to make a comment. Susan Crosland in *Tony Crosland* (1982) does not mention Jill.

† See Chapter 29 for more on Jill's reaction to Mervyn and his biography of Michael.

and not in political discussion, so I don't believe that it makes me look like a male chauvinist. After all, it is a fact that you are an excellent cook as I well know, and it is also a fact that cooking is a skill of which anyone (male or female) can be legitimately proud. I am of course aware that you, Liz Shore and Caroline Benn are persons of achievement, but if I had pointed this out, readers might get the impression that I find it surprising (and anyway what about Ted Castle and Tony Hart?) Re-reading the passage, I cannot find the word 'bicker'. I referred to 'acrimonious spats', but these were between participants in the dinners regardless of gender, and I suppose were most often between Michael and Tony.

At any rate, the dinners were far more ambivalent affairs than either Jill or Mervyn acknowledge in their letters to each other.

On 18 March, Jill wrote to Julie:

I must say these weekly dinners are a revelation. Both Judith and Barbara far more egotistical and pushing than the men, embarrassingly so. Barbara always tries to monopolise the conversation – we had several meetings here with them before the formation of the government – and she talks about herself incessantly.[4] Judith much changed since she shared your flat, also most tub-thumping. I can't think why British women politicians lose so much of their femininity, unlike the Indian women in public life… I greatly like Peter Shore who, in my view, grows in stature and could well become a Prime Minister.*

'Michael is very sweet to me but he's lost his old happy look which pierces me to the heart and I get the most awful depressions which I try to dispel with work, not always successfully,' Jill confessed to Julie. Jill struggled on with her book, *Daughters of Dissent*, which was now over 500 pages, far exceeding the length imposed by the Thames and Hudson picture book series. She had embarked on a full-scale historical/biographical narrative that would show the nineteenth-century conditions out of which the suffragettes arose. 'I'm getting on slowly with my book,' she wrote to Julie, 'but it progresses all the same and I think will be rather original. It's much more difficult writing sustained prose, if it can be called prose which I doubt, as it isn't really my metier, quite different from writing articles.'[5]

'Our life is a little too social,' Jill wrote to Julie, complaining about the interruptions of her work. 'Florence Nightingale wrote, "How can any woman achieve anything worthwhile if she has to do it in between whiles" or words to that effect. Well, some manage, God knows how,' Jill concluded. But she became fascinated with the new political arena Michael had entered:

---

* Michael had been impressed with Peter Shore's performance in the Cabinet, 'almost the very best of them'.

Had one of our husband-and-wives dinners at Tony W. Benn's last night. I like Tony's wife and she is most elegant, but Peter Shore describes her as Tony's Lady Macbeth![6] We all wore elegant casual long dresses or blouses and skirts, but dear, poor old verbose Barbara Castle had to be seen to be believed. She was wearing a tight, page-boy-type black velvet tunic of the shortest mini-length with black stockings and high heeled shoes! The tunic had rows of buttons, some in the most unlikely places. I suppose it was meant to look sexy, but somehow there is always a touch of the barmaid about Barbara — said she rather cattily.

Jill and Michael were now invited to parties and receptions that extended the range of Jill's interests:

At the Indian embassy, where we went the other night and received the invitation to visit that country, the Indian High Commissioner told me that Michael's voice was the only one in the Labour Party that counted in India, his admiration really is genuine and he just can't believe that Michael won't be leader of the Party. I rather enjoyed the Indians, especially the novelist, Napaul [V.S. Naipaul], if that's how it's spelt. He has a theory all women, or rather, most women are passive and turn into what their men make of them, but although I couldn't help thinking that may be true of myself, I wondered whether so broad a generalisation could be accepted. As he's about the most successful novelist of our time, it seemed to me amazing in view of the subject which engrosses my working hours and the strides made by women since then that such an attitude still exists.

Photographs of Jill from the mid-1970s show a radiant slim woman looking more like fifty than sixty. Paul Foot thought she quite liked Michael's Cabinet years. 'I remember saying, "I think you're going to get to Downing Street." I thought her eyes lit up a bit.' Men responded to her, Jill reported to Julie:

Went to dinner with Liam [MacQuitty], of all people, the other night. I have a very pretty blouse from Mexicana, all tucks, lace and embroidery, most feminine and becoming which you would approve of, worn with brown velvet skirt split open in the front and lined with white silk, gold belt, shoes and bag. The whole outfit most fetching judging by compliments from Liam who was just about as affectionate as he dare to be in front of Betty [his wife].

In spite of down days and frustrations, 'Michael can talk of nothing but his job and is enjoying every moment,' Jill assured Julie. For Jill the husbands-and-wives dinners had become high drama, high comedy and sometimes a soap opera, with Barbara as the *bête noir*:

She talks and talks and talks, it's almost a disease. Rosamund, John [*sic*] Silkin's wife,* groans audibly but I must say in my observer role I listen with fascinated curiosity marvelling at the way she seems impervious to the fact that she bores everyone to distraction. Yet what she says, I must admit, often makes good sense. The other night she had an outburst about 'feminine ethos'. 'We will never have a decent Government,' she said, 'until the feminine ethos prevails. Beautiful cities, sensible housing, education, all the questions of most concern to women, will never figure in any political programme so long as politics are dominated by men whose main passion is power, power, power!' All her male cabinet colleagues treat these outbursts with tolerant good humour.

The other bother was Brother Benn – as Michael calls him in *Loyalists and Loners*. In 1971 Tony had reported in his diary Jill's prediction that either he or Peter Shore would be the next Party leader. Such comments fed his missionary zeal, or as Tony Crosland, a student with Benn at Oxford, put it: 'No one doubts his sincerity in seeing himself as a Messiah.' Michael watched in dismay as Tony began to anoint himself as the left's standard bearer.† Michael could see no logical political reason for Tony's behaviour, and wrote in *Loyalists and Loners*: 'It was more, I believe, a psychoanalytical than a political problem.' Jill wrote to Julie: 'Michael thinks Tony Benn is cracked. He really is slightly mad. Michael often tells me quite seriously. Tony is also rather good fun in company and can be wildly humorous.' Part of Michael's irritation with Tony, Barbara recounted in her diary, had to do with Michael's feeling that Tony was jeopardizing party unity.‡ 'Mike is obsessed with the need to win the next election and is bitterly opposed to anything that might disrupt the party before then ... What interests me is how imperious Mike becomes in these discussions, getting positively irritable. But I don't object: I welcome the fact that Mike has developed such authoritativeness.'

At a husbands-and-wives dinner on 2 July 1974, Michael lashed out at several Cabinet ministers who were complaining about cuts. When Barbara 'chipped in' about hers, Michael 'almost shouted', she reported in her diary: 'Don't listen to her. Quash her.' A fascinated Barbara noted: 'He is so passionately dedicated to the success of the Government that it is as if his

---

* Silkin, Minister for Planning and Local Government, joined the Cabinet in October 1974.

† Barbara Castle felt the same, telling Tony (as he recorded in his diary 11 June 1974): 'You with your open government, with your facile speeches, getting all the publicity, pre-empting resources... trying to be holier than thou and more left-wing than me.' In *The Castle Diaries 1974–1976* (1980), Barbara confirms Tony's account. *Loyalists and Loners* sets out why Michael found Benn so undeserving as a Champion of the Left: he had been a moderate, middle-of-the road Cabinet minister and no Bevanite, no Tribunite, no CNDer – indeed, a member of no group on the left.

‡ Ben Pimlott in *Harold Wilson* reports that by 1973 Wilson 'began to regard Benn, not merely as a boat-rocker, but as a serious threat to the Party's electoral chances'.

nerves are on edge about it. (Mind you, he has bullied me affectionately all the time I have known him.)' The group worried about an election that would be coming soon. Something had to be done about Labour's precarious majority, but no one seemed confident of the Party's chances. Indeed, what had fuelled Michael's irritation was talk of a coalition government as the only way to stay in power. Just a week earlier (24 June), Jill had picked up this mood, writing to Julie: 'I'm a bit worried about the election, not only for political reasons, but now I have a personal interest in the victory. Michael is much happier in office, he really is born for it and it's tremendously good for our marriage. In many ways things have never been better between us, or at any rate, not for some time.'*

A land deal scandal involving Wilson's close associates damaged him, even though it became clear that he was not implicated. The press put out stories about how Wilson had become isolated from his cabinet ministers, and during this 'rough summer' for Wilson – as his biographer Ben Pimlott puts it – Jill disclosed the grousing to Julie:

> They all want to get Wilson out but they keep him there out of hatred of Callaghan who is two people, very very different in private than in public. In public he is the good humoured amenable Unkle [sic], in private he is surly, stubborn, reactionary and hellish. Neil Kinnock thinks that Michael would get the leadership in the unlikely event of a show-down over Wilson, but others fear Callaghan would get it.

Jill is harsh. Tony Benn – certainly no favourite of Callaghan's – reports instances when Callaghan was 'avuncular and agreeable' in private and in public,' although Callaghan's biographer, Kenneth O. Morgan, notes that Callaghan 'could be brutal in the extreme'. With professional women he seemed ill at ease. Barbara Castle hated him, especially because he had led the charge in Cabinet against *In Place of Strife*. Michael and Jim Callaghan had never been close personally or politically, although the two men had an amicable relationship in Wilson's cabinet, and Michael began to see Callaghan, virtually Wilson's co-partner according to Morgan, as the key figure in maintaining Party unity.†

---

* Ben Pimlott in *Harold Wilson* writes, 'a second election within a few months seemed inevitable'. But Wilson did not schedule polling until 10 October, and he ruled out joining forces with the Liberals.

† In February 1974, shortly after Labour won its slim majority, Edward Heath tried unsuccessfully to save his government by forming a coalition with the Liberals. Callaghan 'rather than Wilson took command during this tense interlude,' writes Kenneth O. Morgan in *Callaghan: A Life* (1997). 'The older man by four years, he seemed physically and mentally the more vigorous of the two... Harold Wilson, physically and emotionally weary and almost against his will, became Prime Minister. At his side as senior lieutenant was James Callaghan, the new Foreign Secretary and generally felt to be the decisive force.' Philip Ziegler in *Wilson: The Authorised Life* (1993) sees Wilson as merely more relaxed and willing to allow his experienced Cabinet ministers more latitude than in his 1964–70 government.

At another husbands-and-wives dinner on 22 July, Jill spoke up: 'We have got to win the election. We stuck by our principles for twenty years and where did it get us?' Michael joined in: 'We have got to dress up our vote-winning policies as principles and dress up our principles as vote-winning policies.' Tony Benn, reporting this conversation in his diary, added, 'Eric [Heffer] said he was deeply shocked by this. I think his view of Michael is completely shattered.'*

Jill was keenly aware that Michael's effectiveness as a cabinet minister depended on his shrewd assessment of his colleagues and union leaders and their commitment to the 'Social Contract', which he defined in Labour's 1974 election manifesto as

> the whole range of national policies. It is the agreed basis upon which the Labour Party and the trade unions define their common purpose... Naturally the trade unions see their clearest loyalty to their own members. But the Social Contract is the free acknowledgement that they have other loyalties – to the members of other trade unions too, to pensioners, to the lower-paid, to invalids, to the community as a whole... This is the Social Contract which can re-establish faith in the working of Britain's democracy in the years ahead.

In other words, behind the scenes Michael was urging union leaders to 'moderate their claims', as Jill put it in a letter to Julie. Demands for wage increases had to be considered in the context of what was best for the community as a whole, whereas it was natural for a union leader to wish to get the best possible deal. Far more diplomatic than Barbara Castle, Michael was nevertheless voicing the same concern she had shown in *In Place of Strife*, and he had even joked (everyone but Barbara Castle liked the joke) that his policy could be called *In Place of Barbara*.

Jill appreciated – indeed, she became fascinated – with Michael's exquisite balancing act, which included tolerating some wage increases that violated the Social Contract. 'The successes in this field far outweigh the breaches, but of course the former cannot be advertised or gloated over because it would make the union leaders look soft.' Michael was concerned because the increases he had negotiated with the unions would seem paltry and their members would feel they had been double-crossed if the 30 per cent rise in salaries for judges and civil servants recommended by the Top Salaries Review Board took effect. According to Jill, Michael had written Wilson three letters requesting that the

* Eric Heffer (1922–91), Labour MP from Liverpool (1964–91), served as an industry minister in 1974–5. On the far left, he wanted to hold the Party to its socialist principles by fostering working-class militancy.

Cabinet discuss the issue. Jill reported that Wilson and the Cabinet had so far treated Michael's 'interventions with the utmost contempt'. Tony Crosland, sitting next to Michael, had snidely dismissed his 'populist view'. Michael wrote Wilson that he would resign if the 30 per cent rise went through. 'We have thrashed the matter out,' Jill reported to Julie:

> Of course we well understand that it will be said that Michael has contracted out because he no longer believed in the Social contract, at least that would be said by his enemies. Others will say he was bound to resign anyway.[8] Then there are those in the Cabinet who would be pleased to see the back of Michael certainly. Callaghan, also Short and Prentice, Jenkins for certain.

Jill expected a showdown in the Cabinet that day (20 December 1973), she confided to Julie. 'Michael fears a blotch, blur and unsatisfactory compromise. He has no desire to harass the Government; at the same time there is much dissatisfaction with much of the programme.'

Jill's letters deplored the level of argument in the Commons:

> I was most ashamed of the poor attendance as several good points were made from both sides of the House. It is always the same. Poor attendances, no one eager to list, almost everyone thinking they have nothing to learn. As usual, the House only filled up when Carr* and Michael wound up at the end. Then, to add to the frustration, those who had not bothered to listen to the debate started interrupting the main speakers with questions that have been previously answered either by the Chancellor or Michael in other debates. Many M.P.s really are greatly corrupted by what I am now convinced is too easy a way of earning a living. They have no boss to tell them off every now and again. So long as they obey the whips and give the minimum time to the constituents, they are free to spend hours and hours in the bars, which are always full, to use the House as a Club in which to entertain their mistresses or haunt the strip-clubs of Soho. Of course, they are not all like that, but the more I learn about what goes on, the more surprised I become at what goes on. I could tell you some amazing stories, but I must not spend all the morning writing this letter.

Jill thought Michael paid too much attention to the interrupters; it made him look weak:

> Wives, I must say, are put in a most delicate and difficult position on these occasions. The sycophants, in which the House abounds, many of whom believe that Michael will become leader one day – there are quite a number of those – flatter him, insisting he is far too generous and would have made a wonderful speech but

---

* The former Conservative Secretary of State for Employment.

for the Tory interrupters. Peter Shore's wife, who sat next to me, asked me, on the other hand, whether Michael gave way so often because he really had nothing to say. And that was what it looked like. So when Michael asked me whether he had made a botch of the speech – as he often does – I neither liked to depress him nor bolster him to such a degree that he really believed that he did well to give way so often. Actually, I avoid criticising, I don't think husbands can take it very often from wives. But he knows when I am really enthusiastic and I think he likes it when I show it, and that way he can draw his own conclusions.

Jill liked Michael's chances of carrying the day in Cabinet, however.

As for the repercussions, if he is forced to resign, which could happen, I have said, watch Callaghan and if he looks pleased, BEWARE! But if Michael were to resign on this issue, he would carry with him the National Executive, the T.U.C., the Labour Party constituencies in the main and a fair proportion of the Parliamentary Labour Party. Because, of course, the correspondence I referred to would be published and believe me, Michael has worded his letters, as you would expect, most shrewdly and extremely effectively.

Michael's last words to Jill as he left Pilgrim's Lane for his Cabinet showdown were: 'You told me that Dick Crossman said that the only way to get the better of Harold is to stand up to him because he will then do anything to avoid a row. So you can't say I haven't taken your advice.' Jill said, 'You really are the most shocking flatterer, because, of course, nothing would have stopped you acting as you did.' Then to Julie, Jill added: 'I really feel most proud of him.'

Mervyn Jones prints Michael's third letter to Wilson, carefully worded after Michael consulted with Barbara Castle. She had objected to the harsh words 'the Social Contract would be in ruins' if the rise went ahead, telling Michael he was making her own job 'impossible'. So instead Michael expressed his concern about the 'timing of all these top salaries decisions', concluding: 'I still hope that we can have on Thursday [19 December] the kind of discussion I asked for. Otherwise I would feel that you made my job as Secretary of State for Employment impossible.' Michael got his Cabinet discussion but lost the argument.* He did not resign but he did register his dissent in the House, explaining that he could not approve the 30 per cent rise for civil servants when the TUC had agreed to accept less. He returned to the issue on 11 May 1975, telling the Cabinet, reports Barbara Castle in her diary, 'what we did about top salaries … was a fatal mistake'.

---

* In his diary Tony Benn reports his surprise that James Callaghan supported Michael to the extent of proposing the rise be deferred. This chain of events is a good example of why Michael thought he could work with Callaghan.

On 7 March the husbands and wives met at Pilgrim's Lane. 'There is a very strong rumour that Harold Wilson is about to retire,' Tony Benn noted in his diary. Nobody could pin down the source. 'Jill is very much in favour of Harold going,' Tony wrote, and has said at their previous meeting (29 February) that 'two or three people in the Ebbw Vale Party ... thought Michael should resign from the Government but none had the courage to tell him'.* On 16 March 1976 Harold Wilson delivered his shocking announcement to the Cabinet: he had submitted his resignation to the Queen. He was only sixty, and it had been expected he would carry on for another decade or more. Tony Benn, James Callaghan, Tony Crosland, Michael Foot, Denis Healey and Roy Jenkins all became candidates for the leadership. Michael did not win, but he came in second, with 133 votes to Callaghan's 141, fulfilling Jill's expectations. Callaghan immediately saw how much strength Michael had in the Party, and he consulted Michael about Cabinet appointments, making Michael himself Leader of the House, an appointment that gratified Michael. In spite of her earlier hostility to Callaghan, Jill quickly perceived that the going would be smooth and profitable for her husband, who would come to regard Callaghan as Wilson's superior in managing the Cabinet and the government. When Jill visited Chequers, Callaghan could see how much she would have enjoyed living there herself, and said with good humour, 'Nine more votes and you would be living here.'[9] Audrey, Callaghan's wife, welcomed Jill warmly, and Jill reciprocated. Callaghan did not remember seeing Jill very often, but the rapport between the two couples delighted Michael.

Writing to Julie on 27 July 1976, Jill confessed: 'I can't help feeling that the Government will fall before Christmas.' But Michael was 'fairly optimistic' and determined to sustain the minority Government. At another husbands-and-wives dinner, Tony Benn 'talked darkly of resignation and Caroline was in what Peter Shore calls, her Lady Macbeth mood. She kept urging Tony to act instead of talking about action.' But with Benn out of the Cabinet, some left-wing MPs might abstain, and then Mrs Thatcher would take over:

> I suggested that if there was to be action all five – Tony, Peter, Albert,† John [Jon] Silkin, and Michael – should act together because they would then be able to get their own way in Cabinet. Callaghan could not risk such a split. I was put in my place by talk of 'blackmail', 'holding a pistol at Jim's head' and so forth, so tender are politicians about the feelings of their leaders, strange to relate. Still, it must be

---

* It is characteristic of Jill to relay to Michael and to others political gossip that he would not otherwise notice or hear. As Glenys Kinnock said, in this sense Jill performed a kind of political intelligence operation.
† Albert Booth had succeeded Michael as Minister of State for Employment.

admitted that Michael tells me often how Jim is a changed man, so reasonable, quite
unlike his old self … He is doing his best under impossible circumstances.

If Callaghan went down to defeat, it would be a 'great upheaval in our life', Jill
admitted. She would miss Winnie, who was much in demand among cabinet
ministers for her driving skills. Like so many people who worked for Jill or
Michael, she became almost a family member, whom they continued to see
after she ceased working for them.

Jill's outburst at the husbands and wives' dinner was atypical. Tony Benn
remembered that she was usually an alert observer.[10] He sensed Jill's
frustration – that she had more to say – but she was 'immensely loyal' and
would say nothing to compromise Michael. Commenting on the Cabinet
wives, Tony remarked 'the wives are always much abler than the husbands'.
He put Jill in the same category with his wife and Edna Healey. Jill had a 'clear
mind' and convictions, he could see, although he did not believe that Jill was
absorbed in the details of Labour politics any more deeply than his own wife.
He saw her as quite a separate person from Michael the politician – not an
easy role to maintain for a political wife – or for a husband when the roles are
reversed and the woman has the dominant role, as in Barbara Castle's and
Margaret Thatcher's marriages.*

Tony remembered Jill as a 'marvellous hostess' who prepared 'marvellous
meals'. Only her 'detestation of Wilson came out and her dislike of Barbara',
he recalled. When Jill did voice her opinion, Barbara Castle put her in her
place. 'She did say one or two rude things to Jill,' Michael acknowledged, 'here
in this house.' 'You don't understand these things. You're not fully engaged in
this operation,' Barbara told Jill. 'Jill did understand. It was very stupid of
Barbara,' Michael commented, 'it didn't advance Barbara's cause. Jill wanted
to make that second government work.' To Michael, Jill had, in some ways, a
more complete political vision than Barbara. Michael reflected: 'Barbara had
no children and that made a difference.' Tony Benn suggested, 'Barbara was a
prima donna and would have seen Jill as a secondary figure.'

For another touch-and-go two years, the Callaghan/Foot team buoyed up
the Labour government, drowning in devastating cuts imposed after the
acceptance of an International Monetary Fund Loan and divided by
acrimonious debates within the Party on devolution (Neil Kinnock and Leo

---

* Tony Benn remembered that in 1964 at the Lord Mayor's banquet in Guildhall it was announced,
'"The Minister of International Development and Mrs Castle." Well, she was the Minister of International
Development. I thought poor old Ted. He's been excluded. You couldn't have a woman who was a Minister.
Therefore it must have been the Minister and his wife.'

Abse, for example, opposed the idea of home rule for Wales and Scotland, and thought Jill and Michael far too romantic and sentimental about the Welsh).* There were tensions in the husbands and wives group as well, although Jill drew great satisfaction from their dinners for both social and political reasons, writing to Julie on 1 March 1977 and giving the details that Julie, as a superb cook herself, would want to have:

> I gave a super dinner on Friday, Vichyçoise, Chilli Con Carne with a salad of crisp lettuce, grapefruit, Walnut and a special dressing of oil, vinegar, sugar, and Yoghourt, chocolate soufflé with rum, exotic fruits and cheese and some of your Italian wine. Tony Benn was most charming and witty quite unlike his public image. But he and Peter Shore can no longer abide each other, at least, Peter and his wife, can hardly bear to talk to Tony although I do not think such hatred is reciprocated... Michael is bearing up well and Tony says he is the first person he has known who has <u>psychosematic</u> health, if that's how it is spelt, since office makes him unreasonably healthy, more so than ever before, contrary to any other member of the Cabinet.

Jill's response to Tony is significant. Michael remembered how touched Jill was to see how Tony treated his wife Caroline, who fell asleep on the floor at Pilgrim's Lane while the political discussions raged. At the end of the evening Jill appreciated the way Tony tenderly woke his wife and took her home. Tony laughed when Jill's memory was brought to his attention, saying Caroline 'was not interested in the minutiae' of Cabinet politics, but 'it was an incredible thing to do at a political dinner'. Relations between Tony and Michael continued to deteriorate, with Michael at one point saying to Tony, 'You just want the Tories in.' Michael apologized and wrote Tony a note to say it would be a disaster if Tony resigned from the Cabinet, and Tony reciprocated with a generous note. But he wrote in his diary: 'My links with him are severed completely.'

Now reliant on the Liberals to stay in office, the Labour government struggled on. Jill wearied of her husband's efforts to stay afloat. 'Is it worth it?' she asked.† Of course it was, Michael thought, since the alternative was Mrs

---

* Kinnock put his case succinctly: 'I am here to represent working-class people irrespective of their nationality.' He and Michael had 'hellish rows' that usually ended in a convivial drinking session. As Mervyn Jones notes, the 'arguments never caused any personal bad feeling'. Jill told Gwynfor Evans, a Welsh nationalist, 'If I were a Welshwoman I'd be in Plaid Cymru.' See 'For the Sake of Wales', *The Western Mail*, 22 May 1996.

† Mervyn Jones quotes this question Jill put to Michael in Geoffrey Goodman's presence. Certainly Jill would have been proud of his part in the passage of the Public Lending Right Act (1979), which ensured that British authors received payment for the free lending of the books by public libraries. And she would have been very pleased to see his article, 'An Alliance of Women' in *Whose Loan Is It Anyway?*, published by the Registrar of Public Lending Right in 1999. He pays tribute to Brigid Brophy, Maureen Duffy and Elizabeth Thomas, who 'put the indispensable finishing touches to the legislative act'.

Thatcher. But even Michael's closest associates, like Neil Kinnock, wondered if the piecemeal, compromising policies of an almost powerless minority Labour government were doing anything to effect the 'fundamental and irreversible shift in the balance of power and wealth in favour of working people'. Jill often took Neil's side – when, that is, she could put in a word. The two men argued at such a high decibel range that no one else could be heard. Jill's friend Moni remembered one instance when Jill smashed her fist on the table and told the two men: 'LISTEN TO *ME*!' Glenys Kinnock would ask her husband after one of these huge back-and-forth harangues if perhaps he and Michael had gone too far. No, Neil did not think so. And sooner or later there would be another fight just as raucous as the last one.

Michael's willingness to sail ahead cost him support on the Tribunite left – now moving toward Tony Benn and his talk about open government. The polls in 1978 forecast a Tory victory, so Callaghan held on, betting that the economy would improve his prospects. Michael regarded Margaret Thatcher (elected Conservative leader on 12 February 1975) as 'quite formidable', Jill told Pat Romero, who was then researching a biography of Sylvia Pankhurst, on 4 April 1978. Jill took comfort, however, in pointing out Thatcher's 'synthetic' and 'artificial' manner – the result, Jill thought, of having taken elocution lessons.

'People have no idea how difficult it is for Michael to so arrange the business of the House,' Jill wrote on 27 April 1978 to Rebecca West, who had become a confidant after Jill had written to her about her book. Michael had

> to keep everyone sweet and in line and to cater for the outsize egos of so many parliamentary colleagues so that the P.M. can go to the country, as they say, at the most convenient time which, so far as I can tell, would be the last possible moment next year. But governing with a minority is hopeless and the worst of it falls on Michael. It is far more congenial to be in charge of a department. Not that he complains but he comes home looking terribly tired. And as vast numbers of his constituents are being thrown out of the steel works, things will be no easier for him in Ebbw Vale. Still he bears up and I think the Foots are born for public life.

Then there arrived the 'winter of discontent', with its lorry drivers' strike, followed by refuse collectors, hospital porters, ambulance drivers, street cleaners and other workers, all contributing to the appearance of a society breaking down. A Tory campaign advert provided a lugubrious litany, accompanied by suitably sombre music: 'The rubbish piled high in the streets, ambulances left unmanned, the dead unburied…'. Callaghan, returning to a cold England from an international conference in the Caribbean, was con-

Jill on the set of *Blue Scar* (1948), her documentary about the Welsh mining community. Jill filmed a meeting between the miners and the management about declining coal production; locals were astonished to see an actual row about poor working conditions captured word for word.

Filming a domestic scene for *Blue Scar*. Liam MacQuitty (third from right) had 'absolute faith in the film' and his new company Outlook Films financed it on a cash basis.

Michael Foot addresses a meeting in Devonport, Plymouth in 1950, with Jill in supporting role.

10 Morgan Street, Tredegar, Ebbw Valley. Jill and Michael's constituency home was a dilapidated miner's cottage on one of the town's main streets; Jill elaborately refurbished it with Victoriana.

Canvassing in Tredegar in 1960 in the run up to Michael's victory in Nye Bevan's old seat. An active campaigner alongside Michael, Jill occasionally expanded on his statements, so that when he declared the Soviet Union spent more on education than Britain, she quickly added 'per capita'.

Jill and Michael in a tender moment, with Vanessa at their feet, at Paddock Cottage in Leatherhead in May 1959. This 'writer's hideout' was offered for use by their friend and benefactor Lord Beaverbrook. (*Michael Ward*)

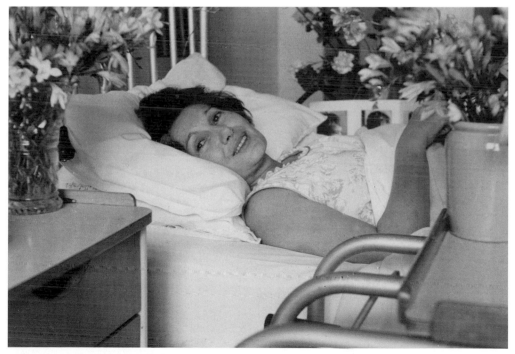

Jill in hospital after the near-fatal car crash in 1963. She would spend five weeks in hospital and undergo several painful operations on a crushed hand. (*Julie Hamilton*)

Jill and Michael in the garden at Keepers, Julie's country home in Sussex (1974). Their visits were always an event. 'She was a wonderful, loving grandmother,' said her grandson Damon. *(Julie Hamilton)*

Jill, Michael and Dizzy in Pilgrim's Lane, 1983. Jill and Michael bought this Hampstead house in 1964 and it reflected, in the words of the *Evening Standard*, her 'uncluttered taste – white walls, burnished sanded floors, plenty of books and pictures'. *(Julie Hamilton)*

Campaigning for the 1983 election as Labour Party leader. Jill and Michael with Tony Benn.

Michael speaking after the results are announced in Tredegar in the 1983 election. Michael's seat was safe, but Labour was comprehensively beaten. (*Julie Hamilton*)

Christmas 1985. Jill with all her family around her. From l to r (back row): Amanda Donohoe (then girl-friend of Jill's eldest grandson Jason), Jill, Michael, Julie, Julie's husband Myron Bloom and Mike Randall; (front row): Jill's grandchildren Esther, Damon, Laura and Jason.

Jill and Michael with Paul Foot and Paul's youngest daughter, Kate. Jill and Michael were extremely proud of Paul, who drew on Jill's knowledge of the film industry for his book on Harold Wilson. Paul also took an avid interest in Jill's suffragette research.

Jill, Michael and Dizzy in the garden at Pilgrim's Lane. Sunday was always gardening day and Jill would say: 'Well, I know I'm going to stay alive because I'm always thinking about what I'm going to do next year in the garden.' *(Julie Hamilton)*

Michael with Stevan Dedijer in Dubrovnik, Croatia. Jill and Michael were regular visitors to the city and had friends in the arts and politics, including Stevan, whose brother Vladimir had defended Yugoslav dissident Milovan Djilas. Jill's final film *Two Hours from London* (1998), based in Dubrovnik, was a stinging indictment of the West's failure to intervene in the wars in the Balkans.

Jill with Michael and Barbara Castle in 1999, shortly before Jill's death. The two women had a difficult relationship, and Barbara never took Jill seriously as a political player. She did, however, hail Jill's 'guts and beauty' at her memorial service.

Jill at home in 1983 with a sample of her suffragette archive material behind her. She began collecting in the 1940s, and gradually amassed an enormous quantity of material, on which she drew for her epic history of the forces, institutions and personalities behind the suffrage cause. *(Julie Hamilton)*

fronted by the *Sun* headline 'Crisis – what crisis?'; although Callaghan never actually said these damaging words, he was tagged with them nonetheless.

The Liberals, like the Conservatives, were eager for an election and disappointed that one had not been called in the autumn of 1978. On 28 March 1979 the minority Labour government lost a vote of confidence by one vote (311 to 310). Jill was there and left this record of what transpired in her papers:

> It was a most emotional evening, but not as depressing as it might have been as Michael's masterly speech, witty and serious by turn, elated everyone including those in the galleries, the press and the opposition. We both expected him to be howled down as Ministers often are at the end of a controversial debate when Members have obviously dined and, by 10 P.M. more obviously have imbibed rather too well. I loathe hearing anyone howled down. Conscious of foreigners in the gallery who have come to study the ways of our Parliament, the spectacle of Members letting themselves go like unruly school boys fills me with shame. Winnie... said that her mother remarked after listening to a debate on the radio, that M.P.'s seemed to behave like maniacs; an impression they often create; but nothing would induce them to moderate their conduct for the sake of the media. There are those who prefer not to have the debates broadcast, just as, way back in history, there was also opposition to admittance into the House of the press. The day will come, no doubt, when lighting difficulties have been overcome, that parliamentary proceedings will be televised; in my view, the sooner the better.
>
> If the scene of high drama had been televised last night, the public would have been so amazed that it might well have influenced the result of the polls, all of which indicated at present a forthcoming Tory victory. Winding up for the opposition, William Whitelaw, the most agreeable of Tories, read his speech in the manner of a sixth form prefect with the result that when Michael stood up after him and spoke, as he usually does, impromptu, without notes and in a more conversational tone, he transformed the atmosphere. There is all the difference between reading a carefully prepared speech without regard to the main points made in the course of the debate and actually replying to Members who have already spoken. Those in the gallery must often wonder, like myself, what is the answer to some particularly important point made in one of the speeches, but only Enoch Powell and Michael have sufficient mastery of the language and can think quickly enough to do this, though how they can remember who has said what and which constituency he or she (usually he) represents is a cause of wonderment in itself.

A page is missing from Jill's account, so if she wrote more about that momentous evening, it has been lost. But she did tell Pat Romero about Michael's visit to the Queen. He 'thanked her for all she had done to make everything work so smoothly and then told me that the queen looked so astonished that he assumed no one had ever thanked her before. They got on awfully well together, partly because they chatted about dogs and constitutional history, both being singularly well informed on all the unusual nuances and details connected with the subject.'

Although Jill would not miss the formal state banquets and the ridiculous protocol, she had had her fun. She had sat across from a huge tapestry of the Rape of the Sabines. The 'wonderful detail' provided her with a start to a 'lively conversation with a sticky partner'. Jill created her own comedy one evening when 'strolling around with dukes and duchesses, the latter glistening like Christmas trees with their tiaras, diamond ear-rings, bracelets and so forth'. Jill gazed at a Gainsborough. A gentleman inquired whether she had a special interest in painting. 'Well, I'm wondering whether that particular Gainsborough isn't really a fake. The trees are not at all his style.' Soon the talk was about how Mrs Foot had questioned the authenticity of a painting. 'I believe Mrs Foot is right. That Gainsborough is a fake,' said one spectator. 'Well, it helped to make the party go,' Jill confided to Pat. 'Fortunately, Michael was not within ear-shot.'

Jill often wondered what she had contributed to Michael's period in office. They argued over everything – that seemed to be the way they expressed their profound engagement with each other, Patricia Hollis observed when she later interviewed them for her biography of Jennie Lee. A television documentary captured Jill taunting Michael:

> 'I know you call yourself a feminist.
> 'Indeed.'
> 'And I think you are a great feminist in theory. But in fact in practice I don't think you are.'
> 'All these charges – saying that I'm not a feminist. They're absolutely monstrous. I'm strongly in favour of women's rights. When I had a chance, we went ahead with equal pay and all these other things – maternity grants, all done under your influence.'
> 'It wasn't mine.'
> 'Of course it was.'
> 'That's another thing about you. You're a terrible flatterer.'
> 'Yes.'
> 'You say things purely for pleasure. You don't believe a word of what you're saying. You don't really believe I had any influence at all.'
> 'Some people deserve to be flattered, including you at the head of the list. You think all women are to be treated equal. You think that's a good way to treat them? What if I went and treated other women the same way I treated you? Barbara Castle, for example. There you are. You're on the defensive now.'

As edited, the exchange gives Michael the last word. Hollis remembered that especially at Pilgrim's Lane the last word would be Jill's, even when Hollis thought Michael had the stronger case.

By 1 April, Jill and Michael had returned from a brief but memorable trip to Malta, which Jill wrote up:

> Who would have imagined that we would be treated to the spectacle of a Prime Minister and two other men cooking and serving our luncheon, then washing up while their womenfolk remained seated without lifting a finger to help. Such is the custom practiced by Mintoff* every week-end, at Christmas and on fete days. The men cooked a marvellous lunch, on a gas stove which I would have regarded as too small in view of the fact that there must have been 10 to 12 people. The luncheon was excellent, consisting of a, to me, nameless Mediterranean baked fish, saute potatoes, a delicious salad of raw vegetable with a French dressing into which Maltese home-grown olives had been inserted, and a special Maltese ragout, cheese, coffee. We eat in his homely farm-house kitchen-dining room in which a number of decorative objects adorned the walls. Naturally, in such surroundings and circumstances, the repast was thoroughly informal and for that reason all the more enjoyable.

It was almost, in fact, like a meal at Pilgrim's Lane. Jill went on to discuss Mintoff's proposal to make the Mediterranean a neutral zone, which reminded her of a promising Polish proposal many years earlier to create a neutral zone in Europe, an idea that the American administration, she regretted to say, rebuffed. Mintoff's style suited her own, a feminine, intimate ethos that Barbara Castle, too, longed to see in political life. For all their disagreements, Jill and Barbara were both William Morris socialists and did not believe aesthetics and politics should be kept separate.† But most men did make the separation. They would not notice – Michael would not notice – much about the nature of decor, or think to make a note of what he had eaten or how it had been presented to him, or what that style of presentation said about his hosts.

Writing to Pat Romero on 13 April 1979, Jill confessed: 'Mrs Thatcher is not to be underrated. I very much doubt if we can win an election under Callaghan if only because he does not inspire much confidence in the active workers in the party. He voted for the expulsion of Aneurin Bevan and there are many who will not forgive him for that.' Labour lost the May election.

* Dominic Mintoff (1916–), Labour Prime Minister of Malta in 1955, 1956–7, 1971–84.

† Would Tony Benn or Dick Crossman or any of the male diarists be able to create the kind of entry found in *The Castle Diaries 1974–76*? For 5 March 1974 Castle writes: 'Our first Cabinet at 5pm. The first shock was the sight of the inside of No. 10. Heath must have spent a bomb on having it done up. Gone was the familiar, functional shabbiness. Instead someone with appalling taste had had it tarted up. New old gold carpeting everywhere; white and silver patterned wallpaper, gold moiré curtains of distressing vulgarity; "nice" sideboards with bowls of flowers on top. It looked like a boudoir.'

On 28 May, Jill wrote to Pat Romero that Margaret Thatcher was no feminist and had 'no intention of introducing feminine values into politics, into housing and planning, for example, which the men have made a mess of, but alas, her general outlook is rather more masculine than that of some of her Cabinet colleagues'.* Jill catalogued Thatcher's 'qualities':

> Guts, determination, assiduity, shrewdness, efficiency, ruthlessness, political conviction – she has far more genuine faith in conservative theories than many of her colleagues and faith can be rather impressive – stamina, and high academic qualifications in science. I don't think she knows any history to speak of, certainly not women's history and I doubt if she has much of a sense of humour.

Watching Mrs Thatcher undo Michael's work was painful, of course, but Jill looked forward to 'more time for theatres, operas, films and dinner parties. In short, we can now lead a civilised life.' In September she enjoyed a wonderful holiday in Cyprus with all four of her grandchildren – 'my first full family holiday,' she reported to Pat Romero (24 September), and 'surprise surprise, dancing with Michael most nights. I astonished my grandchildren with my up-to-date antics on the dance floor while Michael jiggled more discreetly in rhythm.' This happy episode, however, could not obliterate the depressing fact that the heady days of high political office were over. If it was a relief to see Michael less on edge, it was a devastating loss not to see her husband in power. If the Labour government had staggered through its last two years, there was also something heroic in Michael's efforts and, for Jill, the hope at least that a new election would put the government in a solid position. Now all that sense of expectation had evaporated.

Now Jill had been freed – so she thought – to finally complete *Daughters of Dissent*. But an attack of shingles had left Michael blind in one eye, and now 'Michael requires me as chauffeur.'† She would drive him to the Labour Party

---

* When Thatcher was elected Conservative leader in early 1975, Barbara Castle had written in her diary: 'She is so clearly the best man among them and she will, in my view, have an enormous advantage in being a woman too. I can't help feeling a thrill, even though I believe her election will make things much more difficult for us. I have been saying for a long time that this country is ready – even more than ready – for a woman Prime Minister... After all, men have been running the show as long as anyone can remember and they don't seem to have made much of a job of it... I believe Margaret Thatcher's election will force our ['male-dominated'] party to think again: and a jolly good thing too. To me, socialism isn't just militant trade unionism. It is the gentle society, in which every producer remembers he is a consumer, too.'

† Jill's wording is significant. Julie often wondered why it was Jill who was always the *required* one. In 'Jill Craigie aims to put the record straight on the Suffragettes', *South Wales Argus*, 22 February 1978, one finds this comment: 'She believes she could have made a contribution to planning and housing in this country, but she turned down requests to stand as a Labour candidate because she felt it would not have suited her husband.' Referring to her work, Michael often said, 'Jill was interrupted', and so she was – 'I have spent my time in and out of the hospital reading to him,' Jill wrote to Pat on 25 October 1976 during the shingles attack.

conference the following week – sure to be an unhappy affair since the party was 'going through one of its periodic suicidal phases', arguing about its own constitution rather than the vital issues of 'unemployment, cuts in social welfare, education and so forth'. She saw the trouble then as not a left/right split, but a 'battle of egos'.

Focused now on writing his book, *Debts of Honour*, a collection of essays on fourteen men who had shaped his sensibility, Michael showed Jill the initial table of contents. 'What!' she exclaimed. 'A book without a woman!'*

---

* Michael rectified the omission, including an essay on the Duchess of Marlborough.

24

Daughters of Dissent 1
(1975–82)

How do you like DAUGHTERS OF DISSENT for a title? You see, I am not only writing about the Pankhursts. They are used for the purpose of giving my story a narrative since in one way or another they were in on the fight from the earliest times – Peterloo etc.

Jill Craigie to Patricia Romero, 12 March 1978*

Grace Roe had died while Jill was away in Cyprus and to Jill's dismay the *Guardian* had truncated the obituary Jill had written. Late in life, Grace had become a star by appearing in the BBC documentary about the suffragettes, *Shoulder to Shoulder* (1974), directed by Midge Mackenzie. A generation younger than Jill, Midge had replicated Jill's own experience – looking up and interviewing the surviving suffragettes and confronting a male-dominated film industry. Midge worked not knowing who would buy her film or distribute it. But she had the benefit of good timing – working first in New York in the late 1960s and early 1970s as the woman's movement heated up, then taking an American aggressiveness with her back to London. Although Jill and Midge never became friends, Midge met Jill several times and sensed Jill's admiration – an admiration mixed perhaps with some regret and even envy (although Jill was apparently gracious enough never to reveal it to Midge). Jill, after all, had given up the kind of independence Midge exuded. 'Have just finished reading Mary Soames' book on her mother, Clementine Churchill,' Jill reported to Pat Romero. 'It is quite absorbing and an account with which any woman married to a man in public life can identify herself, up to a point.' To what point? Jill did not say.

In her obituary of Grace Roe, Jill wrote beautifully about that day in 1908

---

* Peterloo Massacre (1819). This mass meeting held at St Peter's Fields, Manchester, to demand parliamentary reform ended in the deaths of eleven people when the Manchester Yeomanry charged the crowd. The name Peterloo was a pun on the Waterloo victory of 1815.

when Grace had spotted a member of the 'screaming sisterhood' selling the WSPU periodical *Votes for Women*. Grace followed the woman to Hyde Park, where she witnessed a spectacular demonstration on a glorious summer day. Grace saw Mrs Pankhurst's panoply of women in 'long white muslin dresses and picture hats, gliding behind silken embroidered banners'. They were the brides of a movement that bore no resemblance to press caricatures of drab spinsters. Speakers appeared on twenty platforms. The sight of Christabel, 'invariably graceful', Grace told Jill, turned Grace into a suffragette then and there. In Jill's prose, women's suffrage became not only a politics, but also an aesthetics of emancipation.

Jill reprised Grace's career as a WSPU organizer – how she prepared for demonstrations by putting on underwear suitable for a hockey match. According to Jill, women's suffrage revealed the brutal comedy of public life. Grace travelled in disguise as a chorus girl in a black wig, black satin costume and high-heeled shoes supplied by the Actresses Franchise League. She was force fed 167 times, suffering permanent damage to her throat and digestive system. Yet she lived to the age of ninety-one and led a full life as a social worker. One of Grace's most vivid memories had been her confrontation with that great statesman, Lloyd George. She had disturbed one of his meetings with a megaphone. Jill ended her obituary with a scene in which she and Grace were going through Grace's papers. 'You wouldn't want this, would you?' Grace asked. 'Never have I read so eulogistic a tribute,' wrote Jill. The tribute referred to Grace's magnificent success at engaging women during World War I to work in factories in order to overcome a serious shortage of munitions. 'The tribute,' Jill concluded, 'was signed by Lloyd George.'

'Unhappily, my researches into the women's movement – 1867 to 1918 – have made me feel much the same as a woman shut in an asylum with the conviction that everyone but herself is insane,' Jill wrote to the writer and historian Kenneth Morgan on 15 September 1976.[1] Feminist scholar Sheila Rowbotham regarded Jill as part of a 'lost generation… To be an independent Socialist woman interested in feminism must have been quite lonely, really. All the other ones would be older like Vera Brittain who would remember that earlier time.' 'I am quite sure I would have been a suffragette. What about you?' Jill Craigie asked Pat Romero (20 September 1977).

Jill's sense of isolation – one might almost call it a justifiable paranoia – when it came to the historiography of Votes for Women stemmed from years of reading book after book, each repeating certain fundamental misconceptions:

1. Women got the vote because of their service in World War I.
2. The militant suffragettes destroyed any possibility that women would have got the vote before World War I.
3. Sylvia, not Emmeline or Christabel, was the key figure in the suffragette movement.
4. Acquiring the vote made no significant difference in women's lives.

Taken together, these fallacies had demeaned a profoundly important social and political movement and skewed the history of the Liberal Party, not to mention countless biographies and studies of the male politicians in this period.

As Jill's book increased in scope in the late 1970s and on into the 1980s and 1990s, she would delay completing her work and instead engage in a series of what she called 'holding actions': shrewd and provocative newspaper articles and book reviews in various newspapers aimed at transforming the public's awareness of what Votes for Women meant. Like any plucky polemicist, she gave no quarter. In the *Observer Magazine* (16 January 1977) she began: 'No great political and social movement in British history has been more maligned and misunderstood by male historians than the women's campaign for the vote.'* She then arraigned Peter Rowland, Roger Fulford, Roy Jenkins, Kenneth Morgan, Andrew Rosen and Brian Harrison for committing errors and perpetuating misunderstandings that showed, she concluded, 'Asquithianism still prevails within the academic walls.' In effect, her language suggested she was breaching a rather hermetic world of historians who had not troubled to re-examine the conventional wisdom. These historians had treated Herbert Asquith (1852–1928), the Liberal Prime Minister (1908–16) during much of the suffragette period, as more of a victim than a villain, leaving the impression that the suffragettes were hysterics who damaged their own movement: 'Legend has it that militancy retarded the cause. Yet for 22 months during 1910 and 1911 the militant wings joined forces with the constitutionalists to mount the most intensive campaign of *peaceful* propaganda seen in Britain for constitutional reform.' Unable to withstand the pressure, Asquith finally consented to meet with a group of non-militants who warned him that if he blocked two upcoming bills giving women the vote, they would 'have to go to the country' and say the Government had, in effect, vetoed votes for women. Both bills passed second readings with overwhelming majorities, but Asquith annihilated the first by abruptly adjourning Parliament and disabled the second by proposing a Reform Bill extending

* Jill's opening sentence and her article are a revision and condensation of her longer article/proposal, 'The Suffragettes', discussed in Chapter 21.

voting rights to more men with the promise of amendments to include women. As Jill observed, no suffragette was deceived: 'Women had been taken in by that trick before.' In fact, the peaceful campaign in 1910–11 was the culmination of more than fifty years of agitation for the right to vote. Four times before 1906, majorities in Parliament had been in favour of enfranchising women, but Liberal governments – chiefly under the leadership of William Gladstone – had blocked the final passage of legislation enabling women to vote. How then could Roger Fulford write: 'The most ingenious mortal living could not devise a Bill for the enfranchisement of women which would command in the year 1906 a majority in Parliament'? Fulford was not a historian, Jill implied, but merely an Asquithian apologist.

Jill had copies of Christabel Pankhurst's correspondence concerning Fulford's book, and Jill noted that Christabel had wished Fulford to know that after the war Lord Crewe, the staunch anti-suffragist, had entreated the House of Lords to grant women the vote so as to avoid another suffragette campaign. The vote, in other words, came not as a reward for war work, but as an acknowledgement of the social and political costs of denying women the vote.

As to Brian Harrison's suggestion that acquiring the vote changed little, Jill showed that within a decade twenty-nine acts of Parliament had benefited women enormously, including the Married Woman Act, the Matrimonial Causes Act, the Infanticide Act and the Guardianship of Infants Legitimacy Act. 'Last year's Sex Discrimination Act would not have been passed if women had been without the vote.'

Jill spared a paragraph for men like Edward Thompson, John Grigg and F.S.L. Lyons, who 'write about women with feeling and perception'. To Kenneth Morgan, a historian she criticized for 'perpetuating the conventional view of suffragettes', she had written earlier: 'I am not of that species who think their own criticism of greater importance than the general merit of a book, besides I am too well aware of how much of oneself goes into the writing. I was gripped by your Keir Hardie [biography] from beginning to end.'[2]

The day after Jill's *Observer* article appeared, the paper published a letter from Fenner Brockway:* 'I was fascinated by Jill Craigie's description of how women got the vote. I am glad she debunked the myth that it was because of their services in the First World War.' He explained that a large majority of MPs were pledged to votes for women, and had the war not intervened, an election would have resulted in an enfranchisement bill. Of course, the war had done the women's cause good, Brockway noted, but speaker after speaker

---

* Fenner Brockway (1888–1988), a Labour MP (ILP before 1914) and a pacifist who served a twenty-eight-month prison term, supported votes for women, although he opposed the militants' arson campaign.

in the House of Commons had 'emphasized that their support had nothing to do with the war'. In fact, many of the women who had served in the war were under thirty and would not have benefited from the limited enfranchisement law of 1918. 'The war-work tale was little more than a useful government face-saver,' Jill wrote in 'How Women Finally Got the Vote' (*The Times*, 16 January 1978).

But it was not just the work of male historians that made Jill feel that 'everyone but herself was insane'. In 'Unshackled – but not yet free' (*Socialist Worker*, 10 June 1978), her nephew, Paul Foot, sympathetic to the cause of women and steeped in hours of talk with Jill about her project,[3] wrote:

> It is fashionable today among socialists and revolutionaries to denounce the suffrage movement. Did not Christabel Pankhurst support the war? Did she not career off into crackpottery about the Second Coming of Christ? Did not Emmeline Pankhurst, in a ridiculous protest against the Labour government to enact votes for women, join the Conservative Party?
>
> *Yes, all these things happened – and worse.* But those who concentrate upon them cannot see the trees for the bark. For the suffrage agitation beckoned a whole generation of women out of the gloom of Victorian servility. It inspired to self-activity hundreds of thousands of women who had been taught from birth to be seen and not be heard, women without birth control, without tampons, without anything but the most degrading education.
>
> These women showed more imagination, more courage, and more ingenuity than any other mass movement in all our history. And they *won* the vote from a reluctant ruling class and government.

The words could have been Jill's, except for the denigration of Mrs Pankhurst, whose disappointment in the Labour Party's record on votes for women Jill shared.[4] Where Jill parted company not only with Paul, an international socialist, but with many of her other socialist friends, was her evolving perception that Emmeline Pankhurst was the true mother not only of Votes for Women but of the women's movement. That Emmeline became a conservative and Christabel a fundamentalist took nothing whatsoever away from their tremendous contribution to a democratic society. For Paul, getting the vote was not enough because the fundamental nature of society had not changed; the system had not been overthrown. For socialists, it was inconceivable that Sylvia, who remained faithful to socialism, should not be seen as the key Pankhurst.

How much work Jill had to do and how far she had to go, personally and politically, to make an impact on the consensus against Emmeline and Christabel is apparent in the fact that she had to start at home. In the *Evening Standard* (8 March 1966), Michael had published a tribute to Sylvia as 'THE woman of the century' while reviewing David Mitchell's book on the suffragettes, *Women on the Warpath*. Jill said, 'You've got it wrong.' Michael had taken Mitchell too seriously. 'I hadn't really understood the case,' Michael admitted. 'We hadn't had all these discussions about that.' In his review, Michael supposed that because Christabel had become 'royal and respectable' (she had been made a Dame), only 'our Sylvia' (Emmeline Pankhurst is not even mentioned) gets the accolade. It was Sylvia who triumphed over the Conservative Lady Astor, who inquired whether she was teaching the East End working women to be good: 'I do not consider that my province,' Sylvia replied, 'They know as much of goodness as I do. I try to spur them to revolt against the hideous conditions in which they live.'

By the mid-1970s, however, Michael had joined Jill in her effort to resurrect Mrs Pankhurst's reputation.[5] He continued to affirm Jill's view in spite of an almost uniformly socialist pro-Sylvia bias among his friends. Jill began to show Michael drafts of her work and her ideas began to percolate through his later reviews and essays. Not only did he admire the singularity of her views, he also saw in them a feminism that he wished had pervaded the early Labour movement. Today he remains the best single source on how Jill developed her book.

Jill did not publish her findings against Sylvia until 1 May 1982 in an article for *The Times*, 'Sylvia, the revolutionary who ended in a feudal palace'.* Jill described Sylvia's Leninist phase, when she gave speeches calling for the Navy to bombard Westminster Palace. She thought the 'new Jerusalem could be built overnight on the ashes of established institutions, forgetting that forced growths fail to put down deep roots'. Disenchanted with revolutionary Communism, Sylvia returned to a defence of parliamentary democracy. Then Jill addressed Sylvia's grievances against her mother, who had favoured Christabel, and quoted an impeccable source – one that did not belong to the Pankhurst/WSPU fold – to show why Sylvia's account was not reliable:

> In a carefully considered review of *The Suffragette Movement*, the constitutionalist, Ray Strachey, wrote: 'There is much bitterness in its pages, much inaccuracy and misstatement and an evident and undisguised animus against Mrs Pankhurst and Christabel which is almost tragic in its intensity... As a historical document, indeed, this book is invaluable; but as a contribution to history it is valueless.'†

---

* The title goads those who try to discredit Emmeline or Christabel by concentrating on their later politics and religious beliefs. The article praises Sylvia's work in Ethiopia but it contains a reference to her living in a 'grace-and-favour villa as the family friend and adviser to the only surviving feudal monarch, Emperor Haile Selassie'.

† June Purvis's biography is studded with corrections of Sylvia. A glance at the index reveals numerous instances where Purvis believes Sylvia is inaccurate or misinterpreting events.

A brilliant writer, Sylvia makes herself out to be 'heroine, martyr, and a great healer', Jill added. So vivid is Sylvia's writing that she had virtually swept the field against her mother's and sister's less riveting accounts. 'Sylvia's prejudices, coupled with her inability to consider two sides of an argument, warped her judgement, making her an erratic guide on the subject of politics and people. She misrepresents by omission.' Indeed, the refrain of Jill's article is 'a fact omitted in *The Suffragette Movement*'. Sylvia 'never lost sight of her objective – human welfare and progress', Jill affirmed, but in her 'need to prove her worth … in feathering her nest for posterity, she laid a trap into which several historians have fallen'.

Jill's keen evocation of the pitfalls of historical study accounts in large measure for the aura of authority she began to display in the 1970s. Not only did her articles attack traditions of scholarship, they also alluded to a trove of evidence only accessible at Pilgrim's Lane. Biographer Michael Holroyd, investigating George Bernard Shaw's writing on the women's movement, sought and secured entrance to Jill's archive. 'You work upstairs,' she said, inviting him into her study. Then they would have lunch in the garden. 'I came away thinking it a magic place,' Holroyd testified.

One of Jill's undated letters to Holroyd shows how steeped she was in Shaw. She discusses *Mrs Warren's Profession* (1898) and explains how bold Shaw had been in giving his feminist heroine, Vivey, a first class degree in mathematics. It had been a 'long haul' for women to obtain admission to universities, Jill pointed out: 'In 1890, Philippa Fawcett,' daughter of Mrs Fawcett, leader of the National Union of Women's Suffrage Societies (NUWSS), 'came above the Senior Wrangler [top-ranking male student] when she took her Mathematical Tripos.' Her success, especially in mathematics, inspired women but provoked some men to call her a 'freak' and 'unfeminine'. A woman with a degree, some men maintained, would not find a husband. Thus Jill concluded: 'In taking it as a matter of course that a woman could succeed quite easily in winning a degree, especially for mathematics, Shaw was carrying on the argument; another example of the way he came up to scratch in his support of the women at moments of crisis or at peak points during the campaign.' Holroyd rememberd that Jill 'venerated' Shaw's *Intelligent Woman's Guide to Socialism and Capitalism* and thought of it as part of her education. 'She was extremely helpful on that and put my understanding of the early feminists in the proper context so that I did not make too many anachronisms.'

'I greatly enjoyed your working here,' Jill wrote in the same letter. Holroyd kept another short letter, 'a note of encouragement', he emphasized. She expressed her pleasure over an article he had just published. 'She would know, being what you call a self-doubter, and having had such a difficult time over her career, how a bit of encouragement gave one energy and made one get on with the next article or anything else.'

Jill was well aware of the risks she ran: 'I have not written in a vindictive spirit,' she assured Kenneth Morgan. Referring to her *Observer* essay, she added: 'All the same, as such an article, coming from one without an academic training, who is not an intellectual and who has not as yet published a book, is extremely presumptuous, I expect to be attacked and if you should join in there would, of course, be no hard feelings.'*

Understanding that more weight had to be given to texts that challenged Sylvia's story, Jill persuaded Virago Press to re-issue *My Own Story: The Autobiography of Emmeline Pankhurst* in 1979, with an introduction by Jill. Historians had dismissed this book – produced 'hurriedly, in 1914,' wrote Andrew Rosen in *Rise Up Women!*, 'when Mrs Pankhurst was at the height of her fame'. After quoting Rosen's statement that the autobiography is 'virtually useless to the historian' because it is 'so replete with errors and glossings over', Jill responded, 'No historian would dismiss, for instance, the *Memories and Reflections* of the Earl of Oxford and Asquith on account of their glossings-over or, for that matter, their errors.' Jill then gave a very careful account of how the book was produced, noting many of its errors but also showing how it contained Mrs Pankhurst's characteristic expressions revealing both her ideas and her personality.

Heretofore, Jill's support had come from the suffragettes themselves: 'I know you are going to produce something quite unusual – I've known it for a long time,' Grace Roe wrote to Jill on 15 September 1973. These were sentiments shared by many other suffragette survivors. Roe came to regard Jill as the movement's historian, handing over all of her papers to Jill and making Jill her literary executor.

Jill had been working under the assumption that the passion for women's issues aroused in her in 1940 would never again seize the imagination of masses of women. It came as something of a shock, a pleasure and eventually a burden when a new generation of women scholars began finding their way to Pilgrim's Lane in the mid-1970s. Patricia Romero, an Africanist writing a biography of Sylvia Pankhurst, was one of the first to write to Jill. Not conversant with suffrage history or British politics, Romero sought out Jill's expertise, and Jill, in turn, put Romero to work for her.

---

* The letter is signed Jill Foot (a relatively rare use of Michael's name) and dated 15 September (1976).

They would correspond over more than a decade, producing well over a hundred letters, exchanging sources of information, advice and support. Jill enfolded these women into her personal life, making them – in varying degrees – her confidants, even as they regarded her as a touchstone upon which to test not only their scholarly perceptions, but also their sense of themselves as women.

Pat Romero, in her forties when she contacted Jill in 1975, wrote to a woman now in her sixties who looked and acted much younger. When friends of Romero's gave a glowing description of a meeting with Jill, she wrote to Pat:

> Your friends have given you an entirely false picture of me. I am not beautiful but old and nor am I particularly smart although I was poshed up on the occasion when we met having just come from Westminster Hall following the Magna Carta ceremony. I feel thirty, which is rather irritating in a way, as it sometimes comes as a shock when I see myself and realise that I am nothing like thirty. I am just as healthy as I ever was, no less energetic and generally enjoy life if I am not in a mood of depression, as we all are at times...[6]

In other letters Jill explained her frustrated efforts to film the suffragette story, her success in getting the then Home Secretary Roy Jenkins to open the suffragette records for her,* her plans to have the ailing Grace Roe (now approaching ninety) stay at Pilgrim's Lane until Jill found a suitable nursing home and Jill's slowly progressing book. Jill exhorted Pat not to present Sylvia as the 'saint she makes herself out to be... Bring out her jealousy of Christabel... Not like Christabel herself who, whatever her faults, had been far more magnanimous in print.'[7]

Over the years as friends and scholars watched Jill chip away at Sylvia, it seemed to some as though she had developed a mania. Jill could get carried away by her missionary zeal, to be sure, but as she wrote to Pat Romero (22 November 1977), 'I do think it dangerous in all family feuds to pay attention to only one side of the argument.' Both Christabel and her mother were 'autocratic', and so were all the Pankhursts. 'Sylvia herself was dictatorial and did her best work, after all, under a feudal regime,' Jill observed. Christabel had expelled Sylvia from the WSPU because Sylvia had violated the organization's rule of not working for any political party. 'Sylvia may have been right,' Jill wrote. 'Maybe it was a silly rule. But given the rule, Christabel

---

* Jenkins had given Jill access to records not due to be released until 2025, with the proviso that she not reveal her source of information. Among the gems Jill found was Winston Churchill's instruction to a prisoner governor: 'Do not be too squeamish in forcibly feeding the women.'

could not do other than throw her out.' And Jill did not shy away from criticizing Mrs Pankhurst when responding to another female scholar's work: 'Incorrect to suggest that the majority of suffragettes remained loyal to Mrs P. The WSPU lost the most influential and the most intelligent of their supporters.'*

Jill and Michael met Pat and her husband Philip in Venice during the summer of 1976. Jill and Michael stayed at the posh Danieli, an accommodation they could now afford because he was a Cabinet minister. Pat thought they disliked the hotel and were more comfortable in the 'working class area, in a small boarding house'. Pat remembered that 'Michael did not approve of gondolas (capitalistic) and hence he always insisted that Jill (and others in their party) ride the large public boats. I vividly recall Jill bemoaning not being able to go in a gondola. But she absolutely adored Michael and certainly did not make a fuss about the mode of transportation he chose. We did eat at very good restaurants.'[8] After the trip, Pat wrote to Jill: 'You are not old and you are truly beautiful. I thought you would be a rather scholarly type, and reserved. To find you a beautiful free spirit was great fun. I can't think of anyone with a better personality to be working on the Pankhurst women.'

As Jill followed up leads Pat suggested, her goal seemed to recede: 'Oh Pat, where does all this research end?' Jill found it hard to concentrate on more than 'one thing at a time'. The husbands-and-wives dinners became occasions when she cooked for twelve, and she found 'that alone occupies my mind to a disproportionate degree'. How did Pat do it? Jill wanted to know how she wrote her book, performed her professorial duties and functioned as a mother.[9]

Jill claimed that the 'genius of modern woman derives from her capacity to fragment her energy! Given the necessary ability, the specialist can always succeed! That, at any rate, is my rationalisation.'[10] Appreciative of the praise Pat had lavished on her own son, Jill wrote (24 October 1977):

My daughter, brought up to be independent, had a brilliant career in newspapers but threw it all up for domesticity in a big way. She is a great home-maker, has four children, grows all her own fruit and vegetables, keeps chicks and is almost self-supporting in food and loves every minute of it. I am very proud of her as she does all that work with extreme elegance, but I doubt if she would have enjoyed it so much if she had not had a choice.

---

* Jill made this comment in connection with her vetting of the introduction Jane Marcus was writing to *The Young Rebecca*. See the discussion later in this chapter.

Like so many guests who came to stay with Jill and Michael, Pat felt cosseted. Michael brought her hot tea in bed every morning, even though he would come in quite late and on occasion 'stumbling drunk (!) from Parliament'. Pat never heard an objection from Jill. She mentioned it in passing but seemed to take it all in her stride. Pat never saw Jill attempt to curb his drinking. Jill cooked all the meals and treated Pat to a peek at her enormous collection of suffragette material crammed into drawers and bookshelves and in no particular order.* 'She would haul out a paper or a letter, show it to me and take it back assuming I could remember the contents.' Pat felt Jill was 'not very generous in sharing her own store of material'. Others might say Jill was all too generous, giving far too much of her time to academic scavengers. But their mutually supportive letters reflect few tensions between the two women. 'Jill held forth with her opinions and on the material in those papers she had squirreled away in the big drawer,' Pat remembered. 'I was rather intimidated by Jill's superior knowledge. Keep in mind that I am an Africanist and was over my head in all of that suffrage stuff.'[11]

According to Pat, the other side of Jill – her sense of vulnerability – came out when she used to trade on Michael's name. She would invite Pat and historian Steven Koss to Michael's Parliament office for drinks. Pat thought Jill felt insecure without academic credentials, and Michael's position helped to bolster her. 'Jill was no intellectual but she was clever (in the best sense) and had a lot of flair,' Pat concluded.[12]

Jill invited Pat to the fiftieth anniversary celebration of the parliamentary act that fully enfranchised women, an event that Jill helped to organize under the auspices of the Callaghan government.[13] 'One of the most endearing qualities that Jill possessed was her total lack of class consciousness. Here I was, a PhD professor representing (keeping in mind the choice was Jill's alone) American women at that event and she also had her longtime housekeeper [Kathy Seery] in attendance – we all went together in the limo Michael then had available to him.' Although Michael praises Jill's achievement in helping to organize the celebration, Jill was characteristically low-key about it and left very little in her papers to reflect her work in raising public consciousness about an important part of history.

Through scholars like Patricia Romero, word of Jill's work began to circulate in the academic world, especially among 'Fem-Lib women', as Pat called them. Pat wrote to Gloria Steinem, for example, telling her about Jill

---

* This is exactly how I found Jill's study when I began work on this biography.

and asking Steinem if she had met any of the surviving suffragettes. Steinem had relayed via Pat the whereabouts of Alice Paul, an important link between British and American suffragettes.[14] Through Pat and other scholars, Jill launched a campaign against historians like David Mitchell, whose book reviews in the *New Statesman* continued to skew, in Jill's view, the history of the suffragette movement. 'I wrote a long letter to the Editor per your request,' wrote Pat on 17 February 1976. 'I will write Roger Fulford tomorrow.'

The swirl of activity relating to Jill's work rejuvenated her. 'I am getting on quite fast with my own book now,' she wrote to Pat Romero on 12 March 1978. By 16 May 1978, Jill had built up such an aura of authority that Pat asked her to write a letter of recommendation. It proved awkward, though. Jill had not written a book. She had no academic credentials. Wanting to place Jill somehow, Pat put in parentheses after Jill's name Mrs Michael Foot. Jill thought it disgraceful that anyone could secure a fellowship based on the recommendation of Michael Foot's wife, and Pat apologized for not making her intentions clearer.

When Jill first began corresponding with Pat Romero in 1975 and 1976, she also struck up a relationship with a feminist scholar, Jane Marcus, then thirty-seven. Unlike Romero, however, Marcus had already assimilated suffragette history and quickly supplied Jill with pointers: 'Have you looked at Rebecca West's piece on the Pankhursts in *Eminent Edwardians*? What do you think of it?' Jane wrote sometime in 1976. Rebecca's vivid early feminist writings had captured Jane's imagination, and Jill took note. Jane also directed Jill's attention to the Ray Strachey review that had called into question Sylvia's history of the movement. Jane confirmed many of Jill's most cherished convictions, insisting, for example, that the 'Pankhursts forged an alliance between working-class and upper-class women'. Jill had been troubled that so many socialists had branded the Pankhursts, save for Sylvia, as middle-class types whose movement turned Conservative. Jane wrote on 20 January 1976: 'I think it could be argued that the left, by excluding women (except Keir Hardie) and choosing "adult suffrage" forced women into their difficult position, that it was the I.L.P. and Fabian avoidance of "the woman question" which is responsible for what seems to be the swing to the right of the W.S.P.U. just before and during the war.' In another letter (1 March 1976) Jane wrote, 'It's no use complaining after the fact that the Pankhursts ended up deriving most of their support from upper middle class women without looking at the bitter struggle labour demanded of its own women, forcing them to choose between the I.L.P. and the W.S.P.U.' Reading a draft of June Purvis's essay on Mrs Pankhurst, Jill commented: 'It is a pity there are no examples in your piece of anti-votes for women in the Labour Party and other forms of sex discrimination on the part of working men.'*

Like Pat, Jane confided in Jill about family and personal matters, and Jane's robust temperament and galvanizing letters stimulated Jill. 'I like Jane very much,' Jill wrote to Pat on 24 October 1977:

> and if I give her a lot, as she seems to think, I must admit she gives me even more which she denies. Jane is very <u>feminist</u>, perhaps a little too suspicious of male attitudes, but has an excellent marriage to a scholarly chap and has 3 children and like you, somehow manages to cope with her writing and domestic responsibilities.

Jane was doing even more than that, since she had no permanent academic employment and would go through a terrible time when her husband was diagnosed with testicular cancer.

During a break in her husband's cancer treatments, Jane went to see Jill:

> She was so kind to me in every imaginable way, helping me through the worst crisis of my life. Not only was she my intellectual mentor, I came over with my own set of prejudices and we fought and we argued. We'd go from a conversation about suffrage to Jill's stories about raising her daughter to problems with my daughter. I discussed the most intimate details of my life – not as if she were my mother, but I guess she was what I wish my mother to be: she was so liberal in her ideas about sexuality and raising children. When I arrived, I was desperately exhausted, and she said to me, 'Well, it must have been really hard to go without sex for all those months.' To just lay it on the line like that!

Jane spoke of her husband's suffering and that somehow he seemed to blame her. Jill said, 'He's probably scared out of his wits. You have to go back and return him to pleasure.' Jane remarked, 'This was such a good woman! You could see she was very generous to Michael, maybe too much so.' Alone, with her husband in the hospital and her terrified kids, Jane got through her ordeal with Jill's help.

'Because I was a socialist, I assumed Sylvia Pankhurst was the best,' Jane said. 'I thought only in terms of class', a posture which set her apart from her

---

* Not that Jill treated the entire Labour Party record as anti-votes for women. It all depended on which period, which Labour figures are in question and whether Jill was thinking of the leaders or the rank-and-file. On 23 September 1978 she wrote a letter to *The Times* objecting to Brian Harrison's statement that 'the arms of the Labour Party conference and of many Labour leaders were open only for adult suffrage…'. She pointed out that not only Keir Hardie but [Philip] Snowden and [George] Lansbury 'consistently supported the women's bills' and that the Labour Conference of 1912 'resolved to reject any extension of the franchise for men which excluded women and was the only party to make votes for women part of its official policy'. As late as 3 September 1985, however, Dora Russell wrote to Jill: 'The men in the Labour Party are making it very difficult by repeatedly turning down women's demands, and not accepting that politics must be seen as a two sex activity.'

American colleagues but bound her to the Brits. 'Christabel was some kind of maniac. I argued and I argued with Jill. She had a view of the whole movement, and she really thought that in a social movement you had to understand what motivated various groups. And I couldn't see anything except who was right.' Jane equated Sylvia's side with the New Left, the anti-war movement in the US. 'Jill had a much broader historical perspective.' It is very exciting, Jane noted, that a self-made woman had such breadth of imagination. 'She did not condemn.' Jill took Jane into the Fawcett Library, which held valuable sources on the votes for women movement, introduced her to everyone there and showed her some of Sylvia's letters which disabused her of 'my, I suppose, idolatry'. They discussed every aspect of Sylvia's life and then continued their argument by phone and letter.

Jane's courage and joy in argument won Jill's heart. Jane also took up a lot of space: 'Had Jane Marcus here for a week which stopped me working,' Jill wrote to Pat on 12 March 1978. In her thank you note, Jane wrote (2 March 1978): 'I can't begin to thank you for all your pampering, good food, snowdrops by the bed and Sydney Smith in the toilet, mostly your stimulating conversation, after all these months of silent anxiety... I loved meeting your Michael and imagine, from the way he looks at you, that he does know how lucky he is... You've certainly been a great inspiration to me.'

Jane sent her articles: 'All very sound but terrifyingly erudite by my standards,' Jill wrote to Pat on 13 April 1979. 'But she seems to have very good ideas.' Jane brought Jill out of the 'asylum' of her own convictions – or perhaps more properly speaking, Jane had moved into the same garrison with Jill: 'So far there is not a single serious historical study of English feminism and judging from the favourable response to Rosen's irresponsible book, there doesn't seem to be an audience of scholars to demand both accuracy and intelligence.' George Dangerfield had written a brilliant book, Jane conceded, but his interpretation of the suffragettes was wrong – an opinion Jill shared and which troubled Paul Foot, who revered *The Strange Death of Liberal England* as a classic. When Jill's *Observer* article appeared, Jane wrote on 8 March 1977: 'I so agreed with you that it was like reading myself.' Jane asked Jill to write a letter of recommendation, but Jane finessed the question of Jill's credentials by emphasizing the unique strength of Jill's suffrage collection.

Jill was keen to learn Jane's experience in the anti-Vietnam War movement. Did she leaflet? Did she ever get a chance to write position papers? Jane explained that both she and her husband had been active in the Peace and Freedom Party in California and in supporting draft resisters. Jane told Jill about the misogyny of male leftists, and that became a subject of many conversations: what do you do with men on the left? Jane's impression is that it had been worse for Jill than it had been for activist American women like Jane. Feminism in the 1970s America was all about 'out of the kitchen, girls', Jane remembered. But she liked making jam and planting a garden and painting her house and creating a home. 'Jill laughed with me over all these things.' Jane said to Jill: 'I can't give it up. It makes me feel closer to my mother.' Jane observed that for Jill, 'a dinner party used all of that creativity'. Jill was a 'natural' and yet 'super sharp intellectually. She was opinionated, but she wasn't mean. She didn't hold a grudge.' For Jane, Jill was a link to that earlier generation of women Jane studied, and Jill had a fund of knowledge that simply was not available in the academy. 'She was not trained. That's where her genius was. She did not put things in an academic box.' Meeting Rebecca West was rather like an audience with the Pope, but Jill was so 'warm and so sisterly'. She was also 'so unEnglish. She could have been French or Italian. Her love of life, her sensuality …'.

Jill got along just as well with Jane's husband, and the two couples spent comfortable evenings together talking about wine and food and travel. Lots of Jane's left-wing friends thought it was 'wicked and bad' to value pleasure so much. Jane developed a kind of craving for Jill born of gratitude and respect. On 21 March 1979 she wrote that she would 'give a good deal for six hours straight conversation with you'. She longed for Jill to visit her: 'I could fuss over you the way you've always fussed over me & brought me back to sanity.' Jane thought of Jill as an 'experimenter with life, with a new role for women, which is difficult to live if you do not have any models'. This isolation is why, Jane pointed out, Jill was so drawn to Rebecca West, a single mother with an only child. Jane's interest in Rebecca West had stimulated Jill to read Rebecca and to look her up.

Jill first wrote to Rebecca on 22 February 1976, explaining that she was writing a book on the 'struggle for women's political emancipation with particular emphasis on the history of Governmental and, especially, Asquithian opposition'. In the *Clarion* (25 July 1913, collected in *The Young Rebecca*), Rebecca had written: 'Is not the idea of letting Mr Asquith decide anything on earth, not enough to blot out the sun in heaven? He would make an excellent butler. I can imagine that owlish solemnity quite good and happy polishing the plate or settling a question of etiquette in the servants hall.'

Jill wanted to talk over such matters with Rebecca as well as meet a writer whose work she greatly admired. She realized that Rebecca received many 'similar requests', but Jill thought it a 'sin of omission' not to learn what

Rebecca had to say on the subject. Rebecca's undated reply – her choice of words – make their rendezvous seem destined to happen:

> Dear Miss Craigie
>
> I would think it a great pleasure to meet you and certainly would be delighted to do anything I could to help you in your work. I have always thought of you as a valiant pilgrim.

Less than a month later not only had Jill seen Rebecca, they were also now in league with each other, Rebecca having confirmed Jill's view of Sylvia. Jill had said, 'I know why I disliked her, why did you?' Rebecca replied that while she did not know Sylvia well, she found her 'hasty and perfunctory' when Rebecca had worked in the WSPU office.[15]

Both Jill and Rebecca attacked David Mitchell's biography *Queen Christabel*. In 'A sexist approach' (*Observer*, 16 October 1977), Jill pointed out numerous errors and provided this excerpt of Mitchell's powers of eloquence and analysis: 'A Bitch occupies a lot of psychological space. You always know she is around. A Bitch takes shit from no one. You may not like her, but you cannot ignore her.' Jill observed: 'Surely the point in writing her biography should have been to discover how it was that some of the most respected women in the land, women of high intellectual, professional, and creative attainment, alongside those in humble walks of life, resorted to militant action on the incitement of this inexperienced young woman?' In 'All in a Good Cause' (*Sunday Telegraph*, 16 October 1977), Rebecca identified more errors and deplored Mitchell's utter lack of historical context. She wondered why he discounted the social and political ideas of suffragettes and concentrated on their 'overt or latent homosexuality'. Doubtless the movement had lesbians in it, but they did not constitute a significant segment. 'It is my impression that most members of the Women's Social and Political Union, if approached by Lesbians, would not have known what was at risk until they had attended a course of half-a-dozen lectures with magic lantern slides.' Rebecca supported Jill's view that militancy 'can justly take the credit for enfranchisement'. She then took on the other issue that had troubled Jill: the widespread feeling that getting the vote had accomplished nothing. Rebecca replied that getting the vote finally depended on wearing down the opposing politicians, but the wearing down had a

> painful corollary; the enfranchised women stepped out into a world which was dominated by the fact of fatigue. They had to co-operate with men for the simple reason that the structure of society was, if not under male control, at least occupied by legions of the male; and they were dead tired with a fatigue honourably acquired.

Rebecca's explanation is worth quoting because it articulated for Jill the devastated post-war world in which she had to function as a young woman: 'The reason feminism did not make any marked progress in the 20s and 30s was that at that time nothing was making much progress,' Rebecca concluded, encapsulating a critique of British society she had brilliantly explored in the epilogue to her masterpiece, *Black Lamb and Grey Falcon* (1941). Thus it was that Jill's pilgrimage had led her to Rebecca, a generation older, who could explain whence Jill had come.[16]

Jill regaled Rebecca with inside gossip, knowing Rebecca's fascination with the royals:

> We have been to Windsor Castle for a visit… The queen is highly intelligent, steeped in constitutional history, but Princess Margaret is unashamedly ignorant and her smile switches off like an electric light in the most disconcerting fashion. The queen is rather interested in our exhibition* and will probably come during the second week and it gave me something to talk about, although she herself is at no loss for words.

If Jill was the mother Jane wanted, it soon became clear to Jane, Michael and Julie that Rebecca fulfilled Jill's 'mother-want', to use Elizabeth Barrett Browning's phrase in *Aurora Leigh*,† which Jill read and heavily underlined during a holiday in 1978. The poem confirmed Jill's own radical feminism in lines that brand

> all the ignorance of men
> And how God laughs in heaven when any man
> Says 'Here I am learned; this I understand;
> In that I am never caught at fault or doubt.'

Men *per se* were not the problem, but rather the patriarchal society that fostered their false sense of superiority. Browning wrote to a friend that 'a happy marriage was the happiest of conditions', but *'where were the happy marriages?'*[17]

Jill would write several pieces about Rebecca West, a twentieth-century Aurora Leigh always looking for happiness in love, always disappointed in the men she nevertheless found so attractive. Michael responded keenly to the

---

* The fiftieth anniversary celebration of the parliamentary act that fully enfranchised women.
† In the poem Aurora announces:
    I felt a mother-want about the world,
    And still went seeking, like a bleating lamb
    Left out at night in a shutting up the fold,
    As restless as a nest-deserted bird.

affinity between these two women. Reading J.R. Hammond's fine study *H.G. Wells and Rebecca West* (1991), Michael spotted sentences that reminded him of Jill and Rebecca, both of whom shared an interest in the 'intelligent woman with time on her hands who is resolved to make a success of married life'. Hammond quotes Rebecca's observation that she had been 'exposed throughout my childhood to every disadvantageous influence' and was therefore 'driven through life by an insatiable craving for goodness'. Both women, in fact, rejected the patriarchal picture of God the Father in Heaven, the obsession with sin, punishment and expiation – the sadistic version of Christianity that they believed blighted the lives of women and men. Both women made almost a religion out of their acute aesthetic perceptions. Michael thought of Joan in H.G. Wells' novel *Joan and Peter* (1918), a character modelled after Rebecca but also evocative of Jill. 'She would discover the intensest delight in little, hitherto disregarded details, in the colour of a leaf held up to the light, or the rhythms of ripples on a pond, or the touch of a bird's feather.' This power to perceive, this union of the intellectual and the aesthetic, is what united Jill and Rebecca.

In the reciprocity of their friendship, both Jill and Rebecca experienced a rebirth. As Jill wrote to Rebecca on 3 April 1978, Rebecca had 'fired my imagination and... impressed upon me the extreme importance of the project proposed by Jane, that is the republication of your early feminist writing, a subject to which previously I gave little thought.' Rebecca had not given work written sixty years earlier much thought either, but, Jill assured her, 'For all those now busily engaged in reinterpreting history, and there is quite an army of us, your early writing is of a value which I believe to be beyond even your imagination...'. Jill provided Jane with Rebecca's scrapbook, and Jane worked at Pilgrim's Lane on her collection of Rebecca West's writings, *The Young Rebecca*.

As part of Jill's continuing campaign to persuade Rebecca to republish her early work, she wrote: 'All kinds of organisations are springing to life, offshoots of Women's Lib. Just like the off-shoots of the WSPU.' Jill mentioned 'the Virago girls – a lively lot whom I think have been in touch with you...'. 'The Virago girls' were not feminist separatists – that is, they did not abjure men. Late in life, in other words, Jill had found a group that saw no contradiction between socialism and feminism and, indeed, wanted to wed the two.

Ursula Owen, then an editor at Virago, explained what Jill had done for Rebecca, for Virago and for herself. Virago, a progressive publisher was reissuing classic works by women writers, rediscovering forgotten texts of historic importance in the women's movement, and adding yet another dynamic to the second wave of feminism that peaked in the 1970s. Only two years old, the firm was publishing about twenty books a year, at a one-room office in one of the 'seedier parts of Soho', Ursula recalled. In the spring of 1977 Jill phoned the publisher, announcing she wanted to talk to them (the three women who made up the entire staff). 'I remember my first impression of her very clearly,' Ursula wrote in a memoir:[18]

> partly because she was always a very vivid presence. She arrived looking exquisitely elegant, quite unphased by having to climb the four flights of stairs that left most people breathless, and apparently utterly at ease in what was a cluttered and noisy office. She observed us all – everything – with the closest attention, with those extraordinary piercing clear eyes, and talked immediately with her characteristic directness – no beating around the bush, no bullshit – about politics, publishing, the women's movement. She invited me to see her handsome collection of feminist books and memorabilia, and later lent us some of her wonderful suffragette posters to display in our office.

Like Jane Marcus, Ursula was impressed with the breadth of Jill's vision:

> I have always thought that her interest in the Pankhursts reflected her interest in political and emotional complexities. The Pankhursts were extraordinarily different from each other, as well as from other suffrage campaigners, both in their tempera- ments and their political views: Emmeline Pankhurst, the elegant and charismatic 'reed of steel', Christabel the campaigner for chastity, and Sylvia, the socialist who eventually broke with her mother and sister, represented some of the *kinds* of divisions that women's movements have always embodied. Jill saw the need to understand these divisions and to tolerate passions in others which she didn't necessarily share. It made the task of writing about them enormously more difficult, but she was too scrupulous to gloss over problems.

Ursula Owen's words are almost a précis of the book Jill was writing. To hear Jill talk was to become subsumed in that great project. Like Jane Marcus, Ursula thought of her generation of women as getting on with changing the world as fast as possible. 'Tolerance was not always our greatest talent.' Jill wanted to be part of that action, to connect with the second wave of women's liberation, but she said 'no great thing happens suddenly'. Indeed, the 'great thing' had been suspended in Jill's life since 1940.

It was characteristic of Jill to put forward her agenda on her first visit to Virago:

1. Mrs Pankhurst's memoir, *My Own Story*, should be republished, as should other classics about women's suffrage.
2. Reprint Rebecca West. Jill had brought along Jane Marcus to help make the case.

The second suggestion struck Ursula as particularly bold, since Rebecca was 'a deeply controversial figure' for both socialists and feminists. Like Rebecca herself, Jill refused to abide by any canons of 'political correctness'. Jill valued love and marriage – a combination that Ursula's generation found hard to reconcile because of conflicts between 'love and work' and the desire to be 'in the market place, in order to be properly part of the world'. Faced with a choice, Jill had chosen love, Ursula concluded, 'yet somehow she managed to be unequivocally independent-minded'.

Ursula became a friend and was invited to Pilgrim's Lane for supper. 'I don't think Michael found it easy to understand Jill's feminism,' Ursula said. 'I love him dearly, but he did find it difficult. I think she saw that – that he was never going to fully understand it. She looked after him. She thought that was important, and I think it was. It is what he needed.' Ursula later worked in the House of Commons and watched the way husbands' and wives' lives inter-meshed, and decided, 'Life as an MP often means that wives really have to do a lot of looking after of these guys.' Confronting Michael would do no good. Jill was outspoken – certainly taking issue with what he said – but not on the basic issue of their way of life.

Ursula also saw how much Michael contributed to Jill's love for Rebecca. A great fan of *Black Lamb and Grey Falcon*, which Michael had called a 'hymn to patriotism', he sent Rebecca charming notes and she responded in kind, having the same flirtatious spirit that made Jill so appealing. Invited to Pilgrim's Lane and asked who she might like to meet, Rebecca replied that 'any of the Virago girls would do, but if you want to broaden my horizons I would say anything [sic] but Barbara Castle – much as I love you, I couldn't take that!' Jill invited Ursula, who knew Rebecca could be a deeply daunting, even frightening figure. But Rebecca took a liking to Ursula and regarded with immense pleasure Virago's plan to reprint her work. Ursula knew that some people thought of Rebecca as having become a right-winger, but she herself was interested in Rebecca's remarkable and outspoken feminism. Rebecca held court all evening with Michael talking about what they had read. Later Rebecca told Ursula how much she loved Michael Foot. 'We could get Rebecca to talk about anything,' Michael remembered, except one sensitive point: H.G. Wells, with whom Rebecca had a son.

'I am a terrible blind old crock, but if you really want me to come on

Sunday, October 25th, nothing will stop me,' Rebecca wrote to Jill on 14 October 1981. By then, nearing ninety and just barely able with powerful magnifiers to read the books she was still reviewing, Rebecca could hardly walk and climbing steps was an agony. Jill usually served dinner downstairs. But after one dinner with Rebecca, when the guests had been invited upstairs to the sitting room, Rebecca had said to go ahead. She needed to rest a bit and she would join them shortly. After about ten minutes, Jill looked for Rebecca and saw her crawling up a set of steps on her hands and knees. She hated troubling Jill and Michael; she always insisted on obtaining her own transport (even when he had a government limousine at his disposal) and never wanted to show what suffering she endured to prepare herself for company.

Later Jill set up a dinner in the sitting room so the evening would be all on one level for Rebecca to meet her guests, Mike Bessie and his second wife Cornelia. Jill's diary gives the menu: 'Taramasalata with black olives, individual moussaka made with the best beef mince, plenty of fried aubergine, wine, herbs, etc, a delicious bean salad, & choice of creme brulée and lemon meringue pie. They rejected the cheese. Champagne & Othello wine.' Jill viewed the meal and the setting with great satisfaction: 'I must say that our sitting room is most comfortable & pleasing with plenty of flowers, a blazing log-fire lit for decorative purposes… The room has the effect of making all our guests look very relaxed and at home. Rebecca always expresses her admiration for the room.'

In good form, Rebecca railed against Tolstoy (in a review she once compared his mind to that of a member of one of the lower criminal classes). Cornelia remembered Jill that evening sitting at Rebecca's feet as Michael read to Rebecca Byron's great poem 'Darkness'. Cornelia watched Jill watching Rebecca and Michael. Rebecca flirted with Michael, and 'This brought out a vivacity in Jill,' Cornelia remembered. It was beautiful to watch these women and to see the sexual instinct in Rebecca still very much alive. Jill enjoyed watching Rebecca and Michael match wits and arguments, for Rebecca was no Byron lover – though if anyone could make her one, it would be that 'sweet woolly-wit' Michael Foot, as she fondly called him in a letter.[19] Jill wanted to lighten Rebecca's burdens: 'If you would like me to come and prepare a meal for you, do let me know. I really mean that.' And she did. Rebecca wrote to Jill: 'Do come and light up my evenings for me whenever you can.' Rebecca kept a diary that included a kind of running list of enemies (the 'odious') and friends (who sometimes could be odious, too). But of Jill, Rebecca simply said, 'I love her dearly.' A decade after Rebecca died, Jill said: 'I adored that woman. You don't make friends that affect you so emotionally late in life.'

The last year of Rebecca's life was one continuing illness, although she managed to keep writing until her collapse six months before her death. Fond of her food and drink, she found it a trial to observe doctors' diets and to be treated like an invalid by nurses. 'Jill was like a little girl,' Jane Marcus remembered, when she planned her manoeuvres against the 'nurse police'. Jill would send flowers and caviar and other goodies. She said, 'You know, Rebecca can't stand it, they're feeding her yogurt for lunch.' True enough, and Rebecca sent Jill profusely grateful thank-you notes. Jill would write back, sending along more drink with a note: 'When we were in hospital after a car accident, I found that a glass of Champagne taken regularly before dinner lifted my spirits.' In one of her last notes, Rebecca wrote: 'Thank you for the lovely, lovely violets, you lavish girl. I am so tired, but not tired when I think of you.'

Jill would see Rebecca for the last time in November 1982. 'I think I was one of the last to see her when she was fully compos mentis and then she was extremely affectionate, so much so that it seems as if she had begun to depend on my company,' Jill wrote to Jane Marcus on 12 January, two months before Rebecca died.

When Rebecca died in 1983, Jill wrote one of the most moving of her obituaries, emphasizing Rebecca's experience as a suffragette – already at the age of nineteen the equal of George Bernard Shaw as an original and very funny polemicist, as Shaw himself acknowledged. Born Cecily Fairfield, she changed her name as a writer to reflect her identification with 'Ibsen's dazzling and rebellious heroine, as if willing her whole life to become a defiance of what men thought women ought to be,'[20] Jill wrote the day after Rebecca died. Rebecca 'considered the public schoolboys, who made up the House of Commons during the suffrage agitation, as the greatest natural opponents of feminism, along with the parasitic woman of the upper or middle class whom she dubbed Our Lady of Loot'. But what finally bonded Rebecca to Jill was her broad historical view of the House of Commons, to which Michael had devoted so much of his life:

> There has developed there a system of government which bears witness to the extraordinary nature of the human soul and to the hopefulness of the prospects that are before human society. There again and again assemblies have gathered in all honesty, have matured to power, have fallen into corruption, have miraculously reassembled again, glorious with the honesty of a new generation and a new movement. There men of all sorts who seem utterly selfish and corrupt have to an extraordinary extent, that the most cynical interpretation of history cannot dispute, showed that they cared a little for the human good.

Jane Marcus troubled over the fact that Rebecca had seemed to turn Conservative after her early feminist days, but Jill and Michael saw a different Rebecca, one true to principles that overrode party affiliation.

Rebecca's radical phase, Jill pointed out in another article,[21] had been influenced by Christabel Pankhurst, but Rebecca's mature verdict on the locus of the suffragette movement came round to Emmeline Pankhurst in a resounding sentence Jill loved to quote: 'One felt, as she lifted up her hoarse, sweet voice on the platform, that she was trembling like a reed. Only the reed was steel, and it was tremendous.' Rebecca, like Jill, saw Emmeline as the mother of the movement, just as Jill saw Rebecca as the mother of her own aspirations. Emmeline stood like one of those eighteenth-century French effigies of liberty, firing both Jill's and Michael's political imaginations, branding them with Rebecca's vindication, her claim that Mrs Pankhurst had been 'the last popular leader to act on inspiration derived from the principles of the French Revolution'.

Rebecca's death would soon be followed by Grace Roe's. The duties Michael had taken up as Labour Party leader had put a full stop to work on *Daughters of Dissent*: 'I've done nothing to my book for months,' Jill wrote to Pat Romero. It would only get worse before it got better.

With the deaths of Rebecca West and Grace Roe, Jill's human links to the heroic suffragette era were severed. How deeply she felt these losses she never recorded. While they had inspired her work, she would now have to soldier on alone – supported, to be sure, by a new cadre of younger feminist women, and yet alone, nevertheless. A rather wistful figure, Jill Craigie, steeped in the past, attempted to bring to life and relevancy a robust vision of women in the ensuing Labour Party debacle and the rather dispiriting Thatcher years that were about to engulf her.

Defeat
(1980–83)

You, Jill, are the victim of your own competence. But at the present time in the language of priorities, sustaining Michael takes first place. You will never regret that, however hard sometimes. <u>I know</u>.

Jennie Lee to Jill Craigie, 1 April 1981*

In the summer of 1980, James Callaghan told Michael that he would retire after the Labour Party Conference in October. Dismayed, Michael tried to dissuade him, realizing that the Party had no other figure with as broad an appeal to the British public or one who could put together a better Labour Cabinet. Always ambivalent about a leadership position – since it had first been suggested to him at the time of Nye's death – Michael told Callaghan that he would not be a candidate. At the Party conference old friends and colleagues on *Tribune* urged Michael to join the competition. He told them he intended to support Peter Shore. Geoffrey Goodman, Ian Aitken and Dick Clements – all journalists whom Michael respected – told him Shore could not defeat Denis Healey (on Michael's right) in a leadership contest.

When Callaghan officially resigned on 15 October, the left, regarding Healey as too far to the right, began to organize a stop Healey campaign. On 16 October, Ian Mikardo, one of Michael's oldest backbencher comrades, told him that he would be 'letting us all down if he didn't run'.[1] Michael said he would 'think about it', and Mikardo sensed an opening. Union leaders also exhorted Michael to run. Jill remembered that 'every half-hour the doorbell rang and more telegrams arrived urging him to stand. We read them together and he finally wondered aloud whether he might be letting them all down by not participating. I agreed.'[2] Neil Kinnock (who advised Michael against

---

* Nye Bevan liked to say that socialist politics was the language of priorities.

running because winning the leadership would be such an 'endless trouble for you') remembered that Jill invited Michael's supporters to Pilgrim's Lane on Sunday, 19 October, when he was due back from a speaking engagement in Dublin. It was Jill's style to want her husband to make up his mind by arguing it out with his friends.

Jill received a warm, encouraging note from Audrey Callaghan. 'I should like to have had much more contact with wives,' Audrey wrote, but her husband had seemed to her in a 'constant state of crisis with so little time for contacts – wondering whether we would survive from one month to the next'. Audrey heaped praises on Michael. Time and again he kept the Commons 'at bay... always witty – good tempered. I have the greatest admiration & affection for him. He & Jim made a good team.' Audrey wondered whether she should 'congratulate or commiserate' with Jill if Michael won the leadership election. 'What I am sure of is that Michael is standing only because he thinks it is best for the party.'

Peter Shore did not attend the Pilgrim's Lane dinner. According to Mervyn Jones, 'Shore failed to contact' Michael that Sunday evening and was shocked to learn from Michael the next day that Michael had decided to enter the contest. Denis Healey could hear a 'bitterly disappointed' Shore 'plodding up and down the Shadow Cabinet corridor between his room and Michael's for anguished discussions.'[3] In *Who Goes Home? Scenes From a Political Life* (1995), Roy Hattersley writes of the 'cruelly abandoned Shore'. Michael did not believe that Shore resented his entry into the race – or did not resent it for long. John Cole in *As It Seemed To Me* (1996) reports that Shore 'took Foot's late change of mind with characteristic good humour'. But Neil Kinnock thought otherwise, saying that Shore 'took to his tent and sulked *for years!*' He had been Harold Wilson's protégé, Kinnock observed, and a 'rising star in the Labour Party'. With excellent academic qualifications, he started making assumptions about his own capabilities, Kinnock suggested. This confidence became a 'crack in his character that grew into a fissure'. A Shore coterie reinforced his pretensions. Jill watched with growing suspicion as Peter Shore later deserted Michael in his greatest hour of need. Glenys Kinnock remembered Jill's complaints. She would start to say, 'And that Peter Shore!', and Michael would cut her off with 'my dear child'.

How Michael entered the competition for leader – and won (securing 139 votes to Healey's 129) is important in Jill's biography because of his joke: 'My wife might divorce me if I don't.' She was cast as the pushy wife, 'as if I could ever make Michael do anything he objected to', she wrote to Pat Romero. 'Jill did not put me up to it,' Michael insisted. But 'she was as much interested in keeping the Labour Party together as I was'. After reading the deluge of telegrams and letters imploring Michael to stand, she had simply asked him 'how he could resist such appeals and whether it would not be insulting to the movement to ignore them. He, however, had come to the same conclusion.' But this misapprehension about Jill's influence persisted even among a few of Michael's friends, including Connie Bessie, who saw Jill, Mike Bessie recalled, as driving Michael into political roles unsuited to a nature better attuned to the writer's life. 'You will no doubt hear that Jill was the galvanizer,' Leo Abse remarked:

> That isn't quite right. I think she realized correctly that people like Benn and Shore – they weren't worthy. They weren't fit to clean Michael's shoes. She knew the value of her husband. Why should Michael play second fiddle to second class men? You could hardly call Healey second class, but there was no reason to feel that she didn't have someone of greater quality than the other contenders. She was not a power hungry woman wanting to be a prime minister's wife. She had different values.

But Michael Foot's task was formidable. He had to reconcile the left- and right-wing factions of the party – a task made almost impossible because Tony Benn, anointing himself as a leader of the left, began to directly challenge compromises Michael wished to enforce as leader, while Roy Jenkins, Shirley Williams and other senior Labour Party members began considering the creation of a new party that would represent more moderate, centrist values. Even more troubling were the efforts of a radical Trotskyist faction, calling itself the Militant Tendency, to gain power within local ward parties and impose a leftist agenda that would doom the party's efforts to win the next national election. Michael himself was burdened by his image as a unilateralist. His unwavering belief that Britain should destroy its nuclear arsenal struck many in the electorate as naïve and dangerous, making the country's position in world power politics very weak indeed. This terrible political stew became roiled by rising unemployment, the controversial Falkland War, and social tensions and rioting, especially among disaffected youth. The media made it all worse for Michael, since he could not make a move without being second-guessed and ridiculed for being a man past his prime and incapable of transforming Labour – still hamstrung by its links to the trade unions – as an effective countweight to Conservative rule. Thoughout these trials Jill remained a faithful ally, but she could only watch and support him.

Writing to Pat Romero on 6 January 1981, reporting the results of Michael's first Labour conference as leader, Jill conveyed his conviction that the impending formation of the SDP (from 1989 the Liberal Democrat Party) 'can do us real electoral damage, so don't count on that Christmas at Chequers!' Michael had met with Roy Jenkins and other Labour Party members said to be ready to shift to the SDP and was 'very annoyed because what they said to him is very different from what they say in public'. Indeed, Jenkins, along with Shirley Williams, David Owen and William Rodgers, defected from the Labour party and joined the newly formed party in March 1981. Knowing of Michael's concern that the Benn line would make the parliamentary party subservient to conference policies, Jill reminded her husband that Keir Hardie had 'threatened to resign if bound in the Commons by a conference decision to deny women their first instalment of the franchise and he used this in his speech to great effect'. Edna Healey overheard Jill and was 'so delighted with the precedent that she turned to me and said, "My God, get your book done. We need it."' But Jill no longer had long evenings to herself, since her grandson Jason was now living at Pilgrim's Lane. She was fond of him and liked to take him around to the Commons. Julie thought that her mother rather enjoyed creating the impression that Jason was her son. Now in his early twenties, Jason was Jill's oldest grandson. He had escaped unharmed from the terrible 1963 car crash, and he showed an interest in film-making. 'I do think Jason is growing into rather a splendid boy, loads of charm, a winning smile and most agreeable to me,' Jill wrote to Julie on 21 May 1975.

Jill had bought Michael an electric trouser press and reported to Pat that 'I am now very strict with him about his clothes... He looks really well turned out these days, much better than most M.P.s, most of whom look like seedy bank-clerks.' But she could do nothing, of course, about misreporting in the press:

> He gets quite irritated with me – and you know how irritated he can get – when I ask him some questions such as, 'So why did you say you would compromise on nuclear disarmament.' Or why did you say, 'that we would make Britain more socialist than ever before conveying the impression that everything would be nationalized?' On each occasion he has had to reply, 'That is a complete distortion of what I said.'

Michael remained, however, in 'good fighting form'.

By June 1981 Jill was writing to Rebecca about Michael's 'gruelling time' with Tony Benn, who kept calling for a more democratic party but whose proposals, in Michael's view, meant disturbing the delicate balance between the parliamentary Labour Party, the National Executive Committee (NEC), and the constituency parties. Anticipating the autumn Party conference, Michael had decided to have a 'show-down' with Tony, Jill reported to

Rebecca. Denis Healey, elected Deputy Leader at the last conference, had not been helpful, since he continually urged Michael to speak out more strongly against Tony, who had decided to contest the deputy leadership.* Michael thought that would be counter-productive because it would alienate Tony's supporters on the NEC and in the constituency parties, and both would be sorely needed in the next election campaign. 'In short,' Jill concluded, 'Michael is under continual pressure from the right to fight the left and from the left to fight the right, while, on the executive, he is treated for all the world as if he were a political crook, and that is no exaggeration.'

Jill's diary begins on 9 October and concludes on 14 December 1981. It is the record of a reluctant diarist. Her role – more observer than participant in her husband's career – also provides fascinating insight into the workings of a political marriage. This diary is not a political document in the way that Barbara Castle's or Tony Benn's diaries are, although virtually every page is suffused with politics. Jill conveys doubts about diary keeping, about making oneself a media object, so to speak, a hero on one's own page. Commenting on Barbara Castle's diaries in *Loyalists and Loners*, Michael observes, 'Blessed are the diarists; for they shall inherit the earth.' After that review, 'Barbara did not speak to me for three years,' Michael recalled.

Jill's diary begins:

> Judy & Jason have urged me to keep a diary from now onwards. I have always thought this rather a sneaky thing to do. But looking back at our husbands-and-wives dinners, mentioned in Barbara Castle's diaries and, no doubt, recorded by Tony Benn, it is clear to me that individual impressions of events differ and therefore in any given situation the account of no more than one or two witnesses lacks balance. For instance, no one reading Barbara's version of those dinners could imagine how all of us wives, Rosamond Silkin, Caroline Benn, Liz Shore, Catherine Balogh, and others who may have been present were absolutely united in regarding Barbara's presence as absolutely intolerable.

Why did Jill persist with her diary? It was, of course, to add another witness, especially since she went on to remark, 'Michael's much misrepresented these days.' Virtually from the beginning of his term as leader the media derided him as a hapless, unkempt, unrealistic choice, doomed to take his factionalized party to defeat with policies supporting unilateral disarmament, a 'little Englander approach' to the Common Market and world affairs and an economy dictated by union bosses.

---

* In *Michael Foot*, Mervyn Jones suggests that Benn was disappointed that he had not been chosen for Deputy Leader when Michael assumed the party leadership.

Is Jill's diary any more authoritative than others who viewed the same events? To begin with, it is the view inside a marriage, and it is also the confession of a wife who is not able to change the course of events or to make even the slightest alteration in her husband's behaviour. It is not Castle in command or Benn on the attack. It is a record of failure without self-pity, and it is a valuable political document precisely because it is not merely political. Jill is also not a hardened, disciplined diary keeper. The diary is sporadic, the product of an overwhelming impulse to have her say for the record (her words). Yet she left the diary unfinished, unrevised, with crossed out lines and no sign of re-shaping it as a self-justifying document.

Jill's diary begins on a hopeful note in the autumn of 1981, after the Labour Party conference at Brighton. Denis Healey defeated Tony Benn, Michael's scourge, for the Deputy Leadership, by less than 1 per cent and Michael received, in Jill's words, a 'tremendous ovation for his speech', cleverly creating the 'feeling that only by unity could Labour win the next election. "I want to see a Labour government," he said in effect, "in which both Denis & Tony play an honourable part,"' Jill reported with delight. At the conference Jim Callaghan gave Michael high marks and told Jill that for the first time he thought Labour would win the next general election

Michael restrained Denis Healey from going after Tony Benn by knocking him off important committees. Jill's diary makes it apparent that Michael wanted to defeat Tony Benn without humiliating him. Tony had a following in the rank and file, and Michael needed those people to work for him. Jill understood Michael to be following a policy of containment, not confrontation. Later she would question his policy: 'What would happen if he lashed out at length at a P.L.P. [Parliamentary Labour Party] meeting; if he spelt out just what they were doing to bring about the downfall of the party? Is he tough enough? Or would toughness exacerbate the situation?' She consoled herself with thinking, 'give him enough rope & Tony will hang himself in time. Michael agrees.'

Jill did not have high hopes for Tony's co-operation with Michael. She could not understand why after losing the deputy leadership contest, Tony did not renounce any further interest in the post and make a speech allying himself with Michael's efforts to defeat Thatcher. 'Had Tony made such an announcement he would have received a tremendous ovation and thus greatly increased his chances of winning the leadership in the future,' Jill confided to her diary.

Jill recognized Healey as a valuable partner beside Michael when the two men visited the Soviet leader Leonid Brezhnev in September 1981, at the height of East–West tensions, just a few weeks before the Labour Party conference. Healey's background as Defence Secretary in Wilson's first government put the Labour team on a par with Soviet military experts. Brezhnev indicated a willingness to negotiate missile reductions in Europe, and the Western press gave Foot and Healey good reports. Jill reported in her diary Michael's dismay when the Foreign Office and other members of Thatcher's government dismissed the Russian offer 'as of no consequence'. Healey – no unilateralist – and Michael spotted an opening, which the Reagan administration took up half-heartedly two months later.[4]

In the week following the Labour Party conference, Jill began to wonder about Peter Shore. Although a 'good humanist & most human in his personal dealings, as is his wife, Liz', he was 'inclined to be rigid & right wing'. She now doubted his qualifications to be leader, since he could not separate the problem of Tony Benn from his followers, many of whom were 'sincere, decent, and dedicated socialists'. She believed in Peter's reasonableness and honesty and thought, given the opportunity, the well-spoken Shore might make a popular leader, although by 2 November she was deploring his public speeches accusing the party of 'looking inwards'. She thought he was 'one of the worst culprits'.

Jill did what she could – going to Croydon on 21 October to help with a by-election – 'the crowd very stodgy compared with the Welsh'. She worried that the SDP candidate would eat into the Labour vote. On 23 October she recorded a 'black, black day. SDP has won at Croydon' and the Labour man had come in third. Jill realized the result would put additional right-wing pressure on Michael to 'knock Tony off of committees'. But she had seen how well Tony's supporters had treated Michael in Croydon and how hard they had worked in the election.

On 27 October 1981 Jill and Michael had dinner with Indira Gandhi at Les Ambassadeurs at Swraj Paul's expense.* Jill noted that the expensive meal averaged £17 for the main dish 'exclusive of vegetable'. Mrs Gandhi 'remarked on the price & carefully selected the least expensive items. Thus she set us all an example.' The meal must have cost at least £500, Jill thought. Indira had two questions for Michael: 'Why do you think the prospects for your party have improved? Why is the British press so eager to promote Shirley Williams?'† Jill did not record Michael's answers, but instead reported Mrs

---

* Now Lord Paul, he opened a factory in Michael's constituency and became a good friend of Michael's, as well as a staunch supporter of Mrs Gandhi.

† (Baroness) Shirley Williams (1930–), a Labour MP and Cabinet member (1974–9), a moderate who switched to the SDP and created a sensation in November 1981 when she won a supposedly safe Tory seat in the Crosby by-election.

Gandhi's continuing fears about CIA interference in her country and her concern that her defence chief's increasing budgets made it difficult to improve the lot of her people. 'She looked strangely attractive – slimmer & younger than when we last saw her in 1978... almost ethereal. She is calorie conscious without being heavy handed about it. Like so many Indian women she has a low attractive voice...'. She visited Jill and Michael at Pilgrim's Lane on 13 January 1983 for a lunch with the Kinnocks and the Camerons.

Musing on the Croydon defeat, Jill wrote: 'Sometimes I hate politics. It plays havoc with emotions.' She reserved most of her sympathy for the 'workers who devote so much of their spare time – or whole time if unemployed – striving for victory & then seeing them let down'. Her heart went out to those who 'were not working for themselves, who sought no personal advantage or glory, but who were concerned only to advance the cause of socialism for idealistic motives'.

There were days when Jill had a hard time holding her home together – walking Dizzy, a Tibetan terrier whom Jill and Michael had acquired after Vanessa's death at the age of seventeen, in the morning on the Heath, putting her garden in shape and planning a dinner for union leader Clive Jenkins: 'Unfortunately, I made a mess of the dinner, not that Michael thought so.' The basil and mushroom soup was not hot enough, the roast beef and vegetables overcooked, the creme brulée 'not sufficiently brulée', with only the salad 'crisp & excellent'. Jill's verdict: 'absolutely shameful... quite humiliating'. And she loved Clive. He always brought a 'delicious French wine'. Dinner dealt with rumours that Tony Benn was not well – indeed rather unstable. Jill scoffed, thinking the gossip about Tony 'wicked wishful thinking'.

Early on in her diary Jill identifies Michael's media problem: how to give the voters en masse a sense of his own personality in place of the media-created caricature. At Croydon she had observed how well he spoke, yet she regretted that the 'microphone is the curse of modern politics. None of the speakers needed the mike, least of all Michael. It cuts the speaker off from the audience diminishing all chance of intimacy.' Michael Foot was a great stage performer. He was like an actor who could not make the transition to movies. Until recently, most politicians did not know how to suit themselves to the media – it took Margaret Thatcher a good half decade to do so – and in the media's early days – as Michael's biographer Mervyn Jones points out – Michael could be a media star because the media adapted to politicians, presenting them as they were, so to speak, just as the earliest films often shot stage plays without exploiting any of the unique visual and aural qualities of cinema. Today, of course, politicians are prisoners of sound bites.

During Michael's period as leader, Jill herself did a series of commentaries on Capital Radio that influenced her assessment of his performance. Citing polls in late October 1981 that gave Michael only a 28 per cent approval rating, Jill commented:

He is greatly loved – far more so than Callaghan – by Labour activists & those who know him, but not by the public at large. I believe it is because on the box he lacks the cozy, avuncular, reassuring style of Callaghan & Healey & also because, when filmed speaking in front of the microphone at a public meeting he is too inclined to shout, which gives the impression that he is haranguing the audience. I don't quite know how to cure him of this without deflating him & making him feel all the more nervous & self-conscious, so I have not tried.

In a later passage, she complains about Michael's reading of his speeches:

It never works. However brilliantly they read, they are not written as he speaks. He is quite irritated with me when I show signs of anxiety about the prospect of him reading these speeches, which are prepared in the office; but I think now he will be more prepared to change his tactics. These prepared speeches could be useful if they were entirely rewritten, translated, as it were, into the *spoken* word. I have to do this for all my talks on Capital Radio & though I read them, they could no more be used as an article than ordinary conversations for dialogue in a play. Arrogant though it may seem, I could rewrite those speeches putting the same facts in with Michael's way of speaking – excluding the wit however – than he can himself. They read so well that he is deceived by them.

As the observations of a film director, screenwriter, playwright and journalist, Jill Craigie's remarks carry considerable authority, but she did not attempt to enforce that authority on her husband and he made no effort to be guided by her direction. In retrospect, however, he conceded the justness of her criticism.

Why in a successful marriage did it prove impossible to collaborate? The answer is suggested in this diary passage, written after Michael's reply on 5 November 1981 to the Queen's speech:

He did well, but was depressed afterwards thinking he had done badly. Having to read on previous occasions the speeches written out for him in the office – written not in the spoken word – has slightly weakened his confidence... Michael is beginning to lose faith in his own instincts. They will have to be rebuilt up.

Jill did not regard Michael as a fragile husband or politician. A typical passage in her diary reads:

I should add that I am far more depressed about the press reports and Michael's standing than he is himself. 'I am not giving in,' he told me cheerfully... He has always had a knack for living in the present & can always laugh, as he did at breakfast, at anything he reads which appeals to his sense of humour.

But how could Jill criticize Michael when 'so many journalists write about him maliciously'? How to be a wife and a media critic at the same time?

On Armistice (Remembrance) Day, 8 November 1981, Michael Foot, dressed in a short, dark green coat, placed a wreath at the Cenotaph in a ceremony that included the Queen, the Prime Minister and other high officials. Soon the Tory papers took up the cry that Michael had disgraced the event in his unfashionable coat, misnamed a 'donkey-jacket'. On the printed programme for that day Jill wrote, 'Never to be forgotten. The terrible onslaught & abuse over Michael's innocuous bottle-green overcoat.' Neil Kinnock recalls how he and Michael used to trade elaborate mock insults about the way each other dressed. After 8 November 1981 they never made such jokes again.

In her diary Jill wrote:

> I must say it is such a struggle to get Michael to wear decent clothes that I get fed up when he refuses to take any notice of my advice. He foolishly imagines that he can get away with wearing anything he likes. His shoes are *dreadful*. Why won't he wear ordinary shoes like other men? Michael's have huge rubber soles that are made of some extraordinary ersatz material which bears no relation to rubber or suede & are very clumsy.

'The very next day,' Kathy Seery remembered, 'Jill said, '"Now we're going to John Lewis's to buy Michael a coat." We brought home a lovely navy blue coat. But he looked dreadful in it. It was a longer coat, and it just didn't suit him at all. He looked far better in a shorter coat.' Michael did not like the new purchase, 'said he wouldn't wear it', Kathy reported. Jill took it back to the shop.

Jill told an amused television audience years later that it was 'not a duffle coat, not a donkey-jacket, it's a very good British coat made in Britain, very respectable! By the time that they [the media] had finished with it, he was wearing white socks, brown shoes, tartan tie, and it snowballed... I listened to *Stop the Week* and the whole of that programme was on this damned duffle coat.' The television interviewer suggested that 'there's a school of thought that perhaps Michael Foot can make anything look like a duffle coat. You obviously sent him out looking tidy and some miraculous thing happened after that, didn't it?' Jill conceded that the jacket should have been properly buttoned up. The audience laughed when she added, 'Well, the Queen Mother said it looked ever so nice.' Jill did not say what she had written in her diary on 9 November: 'I did tell him not to wear it, but he said it was too cold not to.'

Jill spent most of the day after the donkey jacket uproar avoiding the press parked outside her Hampstead house. When she returned home in her car and found them still there she managed to drive away without their noticing her. She recorded that she did not dare answer their questions and then added: 'Even no comment would be commented upon, probably with suggestions that I looked furious, worried, unconcerned or whatever interpretation the reporter thought most likely to please the editor.'

In the last analysis, however, Jill's diary does not blame the media for Michael's defeat or blame Michael for not adapting to the media. If he had made Jill his sartorial, political and media adviser and done as well as Thatcher and the Conservatives in fashioning a modern media campaign, it still seems likely that he would have lost. For the other story in Jill Craigie's diary is the dynamics of the Labour Party, the jockeying for position by Benn and the anti-Bennites, and worst of all, the failure of Michael's longtime associates – with the exception of Neil Kinnock – to provide him with the level of personal and political support that might have bolstered the Party if not brought it to victory.

On the issue of the Trotskyist group within the party, the Militant Tendency, Jill wrote: 'Over and over Michael has asked members of the right wing to draw up a plan for dealing with them. Are they to be expelled, he asks, for selling the paper *Militant*? What is supposed to be the exact nature of a militant's offence.' Michael feared that the ambiguity and publicity of an expulsion effort would be counterproductive. He was not against expulsion, but it could not be done overnight. Even worse, 'Michael's so-called friends and supporters,' Jill confided in a letter to Julie (11 November 1981), 'dissolve away when he's in trouble. You'd think Peter Shore or Silkin would rally round and try to boost his morale. Not a bit of it, though Michael denies that they are unfriendly.' In her diary (11 November) she concluded, 'Our party goes at a Niagara pace down into the abyss.' Tony Benn had just given a speech declaring the party's policy was nationalization without compensation. 'Now poor Michael is under an obligation to repudiate Tony Benn's assertion.' The next day Michael 'delivered an ultimatum to Tony to abide by the rules of collective responsibility'. Jill doubted Tony would agree. 'Michael is like Solomon and the baby. Both the right & the left would be happy to cut the Labour Party in half.'

Jill attacked Peter Shore again, and Michael excused him 'on the grounds that they differ on policy'. So did Michael and Jim Callaghan, Jill recalled, but Michael 'suppressed many of his own disagreements'. Jill noted that Peter 'doesn't stroll into Michael's office & have chats with him or suggest that they meet for dinner, as in the old days. Peter's eyes, I believe, are on the succession. He may, for all I know, be pleased if he thinks Michael's doing badly.'

Jill took apart a leader in the *Guardian*. She marked this passage:

> Mr Foot's admirers are now in doubt about his motive for repeatedly offering the hand of friendship to Mr Benn when he only gets bitten for his pains. Some nurse the suspicion that Mr Foot might have invited Mr Benn to speak for the very purpose of demonstrating how he would use this opportunity [Jill wrote 'correct']. With many political leaders that would be a credible suspicion, but it is not in the nature of Mr Foot [Jill wrote 'incorrect']. The Labour Leader seems not for the first time to have been the victim of his own good nature, and his overwhelming thirst for party unity regardless of the obstacles in its way [Jill wrote 'ridiculous'].
>
> Last night, under pressure... [Jill wrote 'ridiculous, under no pressure, had made up his own mind, but Neil Kinnock backed him to word the ultimatum strongly'] Mr Foot issued an ultimatum. Either Mr Benn promised to conform, or he would be denied both Mr Foot's vote and his endorsement in the Shadow Cabinet elections.

Jill suspected the leader had been written by an SDP sympathizer.

Jill was picking up rumours that Labour right wingers were denigrating Michael at the BBC. Who was it? she wondered. Healey? Peter Shore? Hattersley? During dinner at Il Paradiso on Friday, 13 November, Roy Hattersley interrupted Jill, Michael, Neil and Stan Orme (one of the few left wingers Jill trusted)* to say that 'there was great criticism & anxiety over Michael's dithering. They wanted him to act there & then.' Jill watched Michael's mood change as he told Hattersley the right was usually wrong in the advice it gave him. But Jill acknowledged that Michael had shown at least the appearance of weakness in dealing with Benn. 'Neil would have been much tougher,' she admitted, and predicted greatness for Kinnock, another Lloyd George, she thought: he combined 'a strong radical streak with an acute sense of realities'. Neil told Michael to shift priorities: put the problem of unemployment first, the nuclear arms race second. Back at Michael's office from Il Paradiso, Jill was pleased that Silkin turned up and then noted: 'Peter Shore did not come near Michael.' She took it as a sign that the worst was

---

* Orme, a Cabinet minister in the Wilson/Callaghan government, had been one of the first friends Michael called when he decided to stand for leader.

over. 'Little by little,' she believed, Michael would 'edge Tony right out of his present position in the Labour Party as a whole'.

Headlines the next day confirmed Jill's feeling that Michael had come out of this crisis well, with even Roy Hattersley approving his strategy in a television appearance. But there was only a brief respite before the return to the usual press criticism of Michael's stumbling leadership. Peter Shore continued to make 'depressing speeches', which Jill thought drove people into the SDP. At dinner on 23 November, Peter offered to take up the unilateralist line as Foreign Secretary or Defence Secretary. An astonished Michael said, 'But don't you realise that you are regarded as the greatest hard-liner of them all?' Would Peter ever resort to nuclear weapons? Jill asked. Yes, he said, if Britain were invaded. To Jill it was an immoral answer, since like Michael, she did not believe anyone could survive a nuclear exchange. Jill found his behaviour so puzzling that she

> could not help feeling that if there were a putsch against Michael from the right of the party, Peter would not hold himself aloof, nor give Michael any warning. Peter would probably tell him outright, 'I think it's time for you to go.' Liz, whom we all like immensely, usually prefers to gossip with another woman while the chaps are discussing politics, but I noticed that she remained very quiet & listened with deep interest whenever the topic turned on Peter's own position.

Jill also began to see signs that the impartial BBC was slanting reports against Michael. But Donald Dewar, an MP who lived in the upstairs flat at Pilgrim's Lane, told Jill he did not believe there was any effort to dump Michael within the PLP.

Relief from internecine Labour Party politics came at a Speaker's dinner (5 December) for the Prince and Princess of Wales. Jill met Denis Thatcher, a 'deadly and quite cheerless' man who managed to make even gardening – a subject Jill loved to talk about – boring. Michael recalls that she laughed when they met Denis Thatcher. *Private Eye* had satirized Denis calling for just a 'tincture' when he wanted a drink. Offered a drink, Jill said 'just a tincture, please'. She quite liked Prince Charles, whom she thought 'highly gifted' and wasted in his royal role. 'He makes a witty speech & certainly keeps up to date on political matters.' Michael bet Prince Charles a bottle of claret that the SDP 'would not hold the balance after the next election'. But the show stopper, of course, was Princess Diana, arriving 'resplendent in a low cut off the shoulder evening dress in blue taffetta. She has lovely shoulders & arms & looked quite beautiful & talked to everyone with animation, charm & apparent enjoyment. It was easy to see why people go mad about her.'

Afterwards Jill and Michael went out to dinner with Spike Milligan, who told Jill that *Finnegans Wake* had inspired the Goon show. Spike worshipped James Joyce and also William Butler Yeats and Yeats' artist brother Jack. 'I wonder how many people realise just what a scholar Spike really is,' Jill wrote. Only Spike, when he visited Pilgrim's Lane, had 'immediately recognized that a huge portrait we possess is of Oliver Cromwell's son, Tumbledown Dick. I ought to set down the jokes Spike made that evening. They pour out of him making Michael roar with laughter. No one watching, as many did in the restaurant, could have believed how heavy is the burden he carries.' Spike asked Michael: 'What's so good about being the opposition leader? What's the best part?' Michael said, 'The cars, Spike.' Did Michael make use of opportunities? 'Oh yes,' Michael said, 'we go to the Lake District.'[5]

Jill's diary ends abruptly on 14 December 1981. She gives no reason for stopping her account. Then, in January 1982, she broke her right hand. Her writing hand and wrist encased in plaster 'put me right out of action' for twelve weeks, Jill wrote to Pat Romero on 13 May 1982. 'Life is very full, perhaps too full. I get terribly involved in politics, in women's meetings, C.N.D., and so forth, for what use I sometimes wonder.'

With Britain's victory in the Falklands War, Mrs Thatcher began the May 1983 election in a triumphal mood. Michael had supported the war (I have no evidence to suggest Jill disagreed with his position), to the dismay of many on the left, and seemed unprepared to counter the awesome Tory media campaign.

Jill's one lapse during the 1983 election – if that is what it was – came when the press quoted her as suggesting Michael would step down as Prime Minister after a few years. Neil Kinnock could not believe she said any such thing. She was working too hard to get her man elected to give it all up in a year or two. In *Another Heart & Other Pulses*, Michael calls the report a 'considerable misapprehension'. According to Mervyn Jones, Jill did not realize that her casual conversation with Labour supporters had been witnessed by a journalist. Whatever happened, what she said brought the attention back to his age and made him seem a man of the past, a caretaker.

About the 1983 election Michael remarked:

> Jill got it in the neck. She had to go round the country. It was much worse for her than for me. She wasn't with me at crowded meetings. She was campaigning almost every day and was greeted wherever she went with people saying, 'Your husband wants to leave this country defenceless.' She stood up to it pretty well, I must say. She didn't make any reproof to me about it. We faced terrible defeat. But it wasn't dull. To some extent, she blamed the people running the campaign. But it wasn't fair. It was my own bloody fault.

'The organization of the Labour party was terrible; no one was really prepared for an early June election,' Jill wrote to Pat Romero on 29 June 1983.

That terrible election night Jill and Michael watched their friends suffer a defeat from which many would not recover. To the last, Neil Kinnock thought Michael might have won had he confronted a self-indulgent Labour left and the traitors on the right. In the early hours of the next day 'we just looked at each other without saying anything'. They were 'shattered', Jill told Robert Harris, Neil Kinnock's biographer.

In the *Guardian* (14 June 1983) James Cameron summed up what had happened to the public effigy of Michael Foot. He had 'changed overnight from being the Marxist Menace, the Dangerous Disarmer, and became with hypocritical compassion, the pitiful Lear of Labour, the ailing dotard of democracy, the senile socialist, the unhappy has-been, to be patted sympathetically on the back and sent back to the shadows.' But the letters Jill and Michael received both from ordinary voters and from the prominent strengthened his determination to remain in public life and her devotion to him. The words in the countless letters spoke of his honesty, fairness and integrity, and of faith and trust. 'We are ordinary people,' wrote Mrs Sally Cheadle of Shrewsbury to Jill. 'It seems to me we've had our noses rubbed in it, we now have to have our backsides slapped as well. Only then do I think we shall be ready for a man like your husband. I would be so proud of him, he is a gentle giant.' Four days later Barbara Castle wrote to Michael:

> You conducted your campaign with great courage and dignity and whatever the press may say, you increased your stature in the eyes of our movement. The memory I shall carry of you is of indomitable guts and stamina. The débacle was certainly not your fault. Don't be downhearted. The contrast between you and Mrs T will become increasingly obvious – to her detriment.
>
> Please tell Jill for me that she was a great asset to you – unflaggingly smiling and unruffled when she must have been going through hell. My love to both of you – and my respect.

Jill admired Michael's resilience and his sense of humour. During one of his speeches, their dog Dizzy suddenly emerged from beneath the platform cloth and set off a group of hecklers. Michael silenced the jeers and roused his audience: 'Don't you say a word against my dog, or my wife, or there'll be trouble.'[6] The election revivified Jill's and Michael's love for each other. 'It only got better and better,' he said, as they entered the final, triumphant phase of their marriage.

House and Garden

(1976–91)

The weather has been ghastly except today when it is so lovely that England and my garden seem the best place in the world.

Jill Craigie to Julie Hamilton, 4 August 1990

'What a very happy evening we spent with you both on Tuesday, & how lovely to dine with you in the garden on an absolutely perfect summer evening. We also had a real feast of courses, all delicious,' wrote Enoch Powell's wife, Pamela, to Jill. The date was 11 August 1983 but it could have been 1973 or 1993, because there was something timeless about Pilgrim's Lane – or rather perennial, since house and garden and dinners and lunches and parties and meetings and celebrations went on year after year with unfailing panache. The thank-you notes were stuffed in drawers, in a chest in Jill's bedroom and in odd places around the house – perhaps close to where she read them.

Each guest's thank-you note contributes to a picture of a Pilgrim's Lane affair: 'And what a scrummy dinner you gave us – remaining yourself, cool, calm & conversational throughout its final stages & delivery-to-table! There can't be too many London gardens boasting beans & vines. It was delectable sitting in the gloaming before dinner with vines trailing around & a delightful prospect.'[1] On another occasion Jill assembled a stellar list of guests to give Gloria Steinem – founder of *Ms.* magazine and one of the driving forces of feminism's second wave – a nice send-off for the publication of *Outrageous Acts and Everyday Rebellions* (1984). Fay Weldon called the evening 'historic … as well as fun'. Gloria wrote in her book, 'To Jill, with gratitude for my first dinner – and with thanks for rescuing women of the past – and future.'

An invitation to Pilgrim's Lane meant a lunch or dinner. Jill hated cocktail parties, 'crammed with everyone shouting to make themselves heard', she wrote in her diary, describing one she attended at a local Hampstead book-shop, Norrie's, 'standing up all the time. It struck me that the Hampstead intellectual, whom one hears so much about but never meets, must all have been there. But it's strange that intelligent, sensitive people attend these barbaric rituals… We have never, never given a cocktail party; nor will we.' Some of Jill's dinner parties were ambitious indeed:

> We were twenty-eight to a sit down meal and rather a fabulous meal though I say it myself. Company consisted of a few politicians, not many, including Neil and Glenys. Several academics, including Ken and Jane Morgan, also an American philosopher of the name of Broderick, several journalists and some show biz characters including Pete Townshend, rock star of some years ago… It was a very good party. But the strain of preparing for so many is a bit much.[2]

For a large party Jill would squeeze twelve people around the dining-room table, to which she could join a long, thin, collapsible trestle table that would seat another eight – and tables would be put in the garden. Jill did the cooking, though occasionally in her later years she had help from Julie, a superb cook who published several books on the subject and wrote a news-paper cookery column. Binh, a Vietnamese restaurateur, catered a dinner once; her food was delicious. Mrs Seery would come in to wash and clean up.

Neil and Glenys Kinnock were frequent guests. Jill called Glenys 'an enormous asset to the Labour party, beautiful, mother of two and teacher, daughter of a railway signal-man and sophisticated. I cannot imagine a better combination. By sophisticated I mean that she can hold her own with anyone anywhere and remains charming, natural, tactful, sincere and holds fast to her political convictions.' It troubled Jill that the 'extreme feminists' attacked Neil. 'We were delighted that he won the leadership contest and both did our best to ensure the result,' Jill wrote to Pat Romero on 4 November 1983.* Kinnock had succeeded Michael as leader in October at the party conference, easily defeating Roy Hattersley, Peter Shore and Eric Heffer.

Jill told Robert Harris, then writing a biography of Kinnock, that she had watched Neil mature from a somewhat 'glib' young man to a courageous and mature thinker. To Pat Romero she wrote: 'He will be, I think, less scrupulous and more wily and devious than Michael, which is just what we need in view of the amount of brain-washing and throat-cutting which dominates British

---

* Clive Jenkins, *All Against the Collar: Struggles of a White Collar Union Worker* (1990) reports that Michael asked, 'What if I were to decide not to accept the nomination.' Jill, 'a percipient and shrewd observer said, "I know what he will do." She paused and our eyes met. "He will go for Neil." Michael looked at me and I nodded. He thought for awhile and said in that case he would gratefully decline the nomination.' Michael then rang Neil.

politics at this period.' Neil clearly enjoyed Jill's direct, even raw expression of feeling:

June 15th 1983

Jill my lovely

You really are some woman – and some friend. I can't live up to what you say – but I'll try and then you can come to gloomy old No. 10 and tell me again!!

Love,

Neil

Neil remembers a party for Michael in the early 1980s – politicians, theatre people, arts people, journalists (one who got so drunk that instead of eating the nuts he ate the potpourri). Jill Tweedie and Alan Brien were there. The subject of Tony Benn came up, and Alan defended him. Michael came over and listened and said to him, 'You bloody fathead!' The argument raged. Jill listened and then said quietly to Alan: 'You could only say such poppycock with such enthusiasm with the confidence of ignorance.' The remark brought the argument to an abrupt halt.

For the guests, a good part of the fun involved watching Jill and Michael. Michael Holroyd saw a Jill immensely supportive of Michael, very fond of him and yet a tease. 'She did not agree with everything he said by any means,' adds Holroyd's wife, Margaret Drabble, who admired the 'colourful texture' of their lives. 'Does he still have that little silver tankard for his drink?* There were little touches like that that made you feel at home.' Holroyd notes that 'everything took on an aesthetic quality'. Thinking about the range of friends Jill and Michael invited into their home, Holroyd observes: 'We are more segregated now, vacuum packed.'

'If you didn't know them well and watched them in a room together, you would think that Jill was very dominant, because what you wouldn't necessarily observe is that he would allow that to seem so. It didn't deter him from doing what he had to do. He just didn't fight back,' Mike Bessie commented. 'Jill was quite brusque with Michael sometimes,' Margaret Drabble remembered: 'Don't sit there. Don't get in everyone's way!' Holroyd added: 'She was not edited.' Perhaps this is what Mike Bessie meant when he said:

Jill was not long on grace. You knew she was being truthful and sincere. She wouldn't say something she didn't mean, and you knew jolly well she would say something that she meant. I think this was one of her troubles, especially with other

* The answer is yes.

women. I think this affected my first wife Connie quite a lot. Jill just didn't make those obeisances to grace. Not only did she not fudge, but she didn't find graceful ways into and out of awkward situations.

Cornelia Bessie intervened to say, 'except that Jill had charm, and charm covers over a lack of grace'. 'I was not impressed with her sense of humour,' Mike ventured. 'Were you?' he asked Cornelia. 'It didn't occur to me,' she replied. 'She had gaiety, but not wit,' Mike asserted. Cornelia felt Jill's warmth and liked watching those moments when Jill disagreed with Michael. They were a 'peppy' couple. The feminist in Jill was 'all of a sudden up on her hind legs snarling – sweetly snarling'. In the house, 'Jill was very much playing wife – delicious meals and all that.' Cornelia did not see much of Jill apart from Michael, but when she did, Jill was different with no Michael around to defer to. Cornelia thought Jill was 'conflicted, playing the role of good wife to Michael and being a feminist. I must say occasionally at those dinners in that house I wondered who Jill really was. She was very good at role playing.' Cornelia also had the feeling that in certain respects Jill was 'out-of-date'. Jill would say something that did not seem 'with the times', but one rode over it because one loved her.

Another friend of Michael's remembers Jill calling with an invitation to dinner: 'It was always a royal command. If you were doing something else, she'd say "drop it."' 'A lot of Michael's friends didn't really like Jill,' Cornelia said. 'As so often happens to the wife of somebody who is so well known, there is a physical force that builds up and it explodes. And I have seen that in Jill. It got on people's nerves. This was a hindrance to Michael.' Others seemed far less troubled by Jill's outbursts and even found them diverting. Margaret Drabble remembered meeting Jill and her saying 'Oh, it's Michael's seventieth birthday [23 July 1983] and I'm not doing anything! And he's cross.' Drabble said, 'Why don't you come to supper with us?' This was very last minute and Drabble got a chocolate cake, but Michael seemed reluctant to Drabble. He didn't want to put her to any trouble. Melvyn Bragg came, and it turned out to be quite an amusing evening as impromptu evenings so often are.

Of course, an account of Pilgrim's Lane in later years would not be complete without a report on Dizzy. Like Vanessa, Dizzy also lived to seventeen and looked so much like her predecessor that, as Michael said, it seemed as though he had had the same dog for thirty-four years. Jill loved dogs, Michael emphasized: 'We took care of the dogs, and the dogs took care of us. It's not true that you can't teach an old dog new tricks,' Michael insisted.

'Dizzy learned new tricks all the time.' During Michael's busiest periods Jill would walk the dog on the heath and naturally Dizzy became quite attached to her. He would become 'almost unmanageable in my absence', Jill wrote in her diary (13 October 1981), 'I have got to find a way of making him a little less dependent on me for fear of what might happen to him when we are abroad.' There was no real solution. Jill and Michael could not bear to put the dog in a kennel, and so friends would usually look after Dizzy while the Foots were away.

Dizzy joined the Pilgrim's Lane parties. 'There was no difficulty about that,' Michael claimed. 'He misbehaved himself occasionally.' When Dizzy chewed up some stuffed toys the Goodman children had brought to Pilgrim's Lane, Jill was upset. 'Oh forget it,' they said. But a few weeks later she had a teddy bear and other toys delivered to the Goodman home.

The house and garden at Pilgrim's Lane became a place of refuge for Salman Rushdie, following Michael's favourable public comments about Rushdie's controversial novel, *The Satanic Verses* (1988). Indeed, Jill and Michael were among his chief defenders when a fatwa issued by Iran's revolutionary leader called for his death and the author was forced into hiding. As early as 26 October 1988, before they were his friends, Rushdie had written a letter:

> Dear Mr Foot:
>
> I just wanted to let you know that the generosity of your words at the Guildhall last night and on the radio this morning has meant a lot to me, not least because it contrasts so sharply with the patronising, mean-spirited rancour of some British critics of my book.

Rushdie was not exaggerating when he pointed out the remarkable difference between the British and American reception of *The Satanic Verses*.[3] Perhaps the most disgusting attack had come from Hugh Trevor-Roper:

> I wonder how Salman Rushdie is faring these days, under the benevolent protection of British law and the British police, about whom he has been so rude. Not too comfortably, I hope … I would not shed a tear if some British Muslims, deploring his manners, should waylay him in a dark street and seek to improve them. If that should cause him thereafter to control his pen, society would benefit and literature would not suffer. If caught, his correctors might, of course, be found guilty of assault; but they could then plead gross provocation and might merely, if juvenile, be bound over. Our prisons are, after all, overcrowded.[4]

The line-up (both right and left) against Rushdie included Norman Tebbitt, Paul Johnson, John Simpson, Julie Burchill, Roald Dahl, Germaine Greer and

John le Carré. Besides being rude, Rushdie stood convicted of being unpredictable, short-fused, arrogant and self-obsessed. He went to too many 'smart parties'. Melvyn Bragg, revolted by this 'brute philistinism' called forth by Rushdie's 'unwillingness to play the traditional victim', wrote in 'Whispering Assassins' (*Guardian,* 2 February 1993): 'I am pleased he refuses to curl up and accept his fate. His anger does him proud.'

Jill and Michael's support for Rushdie was emotional, intellectual and practical. At the urging of Leo Abse, early on Michael made representations to the Home Office urging that a security detail be assigned to Rushdie and that every effort be made to ensure his safety. Soon Rushdie and his second wife Marianne Wiggins began dining at Pilgrim's Lane. Jill wrote about one such evening to Julie (14 March 1989). She had served one of Julie's fish dishes

> served with garlic bread, as instructed, followed by cheese, and a choice of lemon tart and chocolate creams; it was quite a perfect dinner. Bodyguards also received food and drinks galore so that by the time the Rushdies left, about 12.45 A.M. I was up until nearly 2 a.m. clearing up and felt whacked out yesterday, aching all over with bad cramp in the legs at night. But today I am fine.

As to Salman (as she called him), he was 'fascinating in every sense and much perturbed, as you can imagine'. He told Jill that he had been surprised that his book would cause such a storm. Jill found the novel's use of Islamic mythology heavy-going, but she liked the 'touching scene at the end of the book when the son is reconciled to his Moslem father'. She had no doubt that Salman was a genius. 'Even the parts which are difficult to understand are interesting to read because of his use of words. In every sentence there is some word which makes the whole glow like a diamond.' The man himself was 'most attractive in a funny kind of way, extremely well informed about everything – art, music, etc, etc.'

Evenings with the Rushdies were usually soirées of six or so people, the newsman and regular guest Jon Snow remembers. Jill went out of her way to invite guests whom Salman wanted to meet or she thought he would find entertaining. 'We both felt our friend was badly in need of friendly company & it was very good to see him cheer up.' 'You have both been wonderful in an almost impossible situation,' wrote Margaret Drabble and Michael Holroyd (23 August 1989).

When Salman, estranged from his second wife, fell in love with the editor Elizabeth West, he brought his new wife to meet Jill and Michael. In a thank-you note (5 November 1990) Elizabeth expressed her pleasure in meeting Jill and the other guests and in the delightful meal. 'It's comforting to know that moves are being made to help Salman; last night gave him a great boost.' Ian Aitken wrote to Jill on behalf of himself and his wife Catherine to express their gratitude for 'letting us meet such an extraordinary person. It is utterly amazing that anyone in such an appalling situation manages to behave completely normally, and actually to take a sharp interest in other things than his own plight. What's more, he is also a thoroughly nice chap. My loathing of the people who sneer at him has increased exponentially.'

Michael reviewed all of Rushdie's books – striking a personal note by always referring to him as Salman. To Michael, he represented a tradition of satire and mockery originating with his heroes Swift and Sterne. It was rather thrilling to have his company, complete with rather tense, even paranoid, security guards, Jon Snow remembered.* 'The curtains would be very firmly closed. Jill relished it. It was full of drama, the covertness of it and the idea of battling some invisible enemy. It was the great defence of the word.' This support came with risks: Michael had received 'an avalanche and that is no exaggeration of abusive letters from Moslems when he praised Satanic Verses and made no secret of the fact that he wanted it to win the Booker Prize. Michael was chairman of the committee. Some of the letters were so awful that Una [his secretary] held them back,' Jill wrote to Julie on 14 March 1989. Another letter (24 July 1991) announced: '*The Sunday Times* has found out that we have had Salman Rushdie to dinner. I hope we don't get another brick through our window.' Jill and Michael were charmed by Salman's love for Elizabeth. Pilgrim's Lane became one of their havens. For Salman, 'the combination of the political and literary was just unbeatable', Elizabeth recalled.

Pilgrim's Lane, thanks to Jill, became both a social and a family institution. Paul Foot lived there for a time, as did John Foot, Michael's brother, and all four of Julie's children – Jason, Laura, Damon and Esther. Friends came for several days, even for weeks. Laura, who lived for about a year in the house while working at temporary jobs in London, remembered the excitement of entering Jill's study and hearing from her about the suffragettes and looking at her collection of old photographs. Like Jason, who had his own wicker chair when he visited Lala (the name all the grandchildren used for Jill), Laura had her own rocking chair. Her earliest memory is of Jill serving her and Jason their favourite foods and telling them stories. To Laura, Jill seemed to span all generations. Laura could join in Jill's parties whenever she liked.

---

* The security guards, an intelligent lot, said Elizabeth, were impressed with Michael's library.

Jason had a feistier relationship with Jill, arguing with her about his film scripts when he decided to make film-making a career. She could be dictatorial, telling him a screenplay had to be written in such and such a way. Like his mother, Jason would go through periods when he would not speak to Jill, 'but then Jason quarrelled with everyone in the family'. Laura pointed out. Jason never doubted that Jill loved him and was proud of him. She had given him his start by asking Ronnie Neame to employ him.

Damon became Jill's favourite; she would always find an excuse for his bad behaviour. She romanticized him, telling Michael that Damon reminded her of Julien Sorel in *Le Rouge et Le Noir*. Esther, the youngest, spent a very happy year at Pilgrim's Lane, although later, when she got married, there were 'tensions and disagreements' between granddaughter and grandmother. Damon remembered that Jill made provocative statements that set Esther off, such as 'you should never deny your husband sex'. But Esther believed that 'Jill and I had a mutual understanding. Underneath that was a lot of love. We were both very strong women who naturally sometimes did not see eye-to-eye.'

From the mid-1970s to the early 1980s, when Esther and Damon, Julie's two youngest children by her marriage to Mike Randall, were still quite young, Jill created at Christmas holidays a typed-up 'programme of events' covering several days (some of this was a joke, for Jill knew her grandchildren would not tolerate this much structured activity). On Monday, 20 December 1982, for example, they would arrive for lunch, then walk on the Heath with Dizzy, attend carol singing at Christ's Church, Hampstead, followed by supper and a 'quiet evening' at Pilgrim's Lane listening to music. Subsequent days included visits to the House of Commons, shopping and excursions to the Victoria and Albert museum, the theatre and the cinema. Until 1979, when the Callaghan government fell, Michael's driver Winnie would take the children to holiday events.

Jill spaced out her grandchildren's activities, building in time for play around the house. Damon remembers they had the run of Pilgrim's Lane and that his grandmother was never fussy about their behaviour. She would hide silver coins all over the house so that the children could hunt for them. She would buy them board games. For Damon it was an easy transition from his home to Jill's because mother and daughter had such similar tastes in furnishings and decor. Julie had absorbed Jill's taste for antiques, and Damon remembered mother and daughter going off to antique shops in Tunbridge Wells.

Damon and Esther's earliest memories of Jill date from the mid-1970s and involve her visits to Julie's country home in Sussex. Jill and Michael would drive down in their old red Hillman. She was not 'the best of drivers', Esther said. 'To the end she drove and never got any better.' Jill did not come often, so her arrival was always an event. Damon would watch his mother tidying up the toys on the floor. There was a build-up around Jill's and Michael's arrival, and much later Damon realized that 'Mum was always wanting to impress. It created a barrier, even a fear, in us. I hate to say it, but Jill came across as something of a snob. I think Mum felt Jill looked down on her. To this day I don't understand it.' But as soon as Jill appeared, the tension of preparation vanished. 'She was a wonderful, loving grandmother.' Esther and Damon remember her stories about the adventures of two children. 'It was ongoing. Every time we saw her we'd get another story,' Damon says.

Julie remembered an incident in Cyprus in 1979 during a family holiday when her children were 'a little short on saying thank you to the waiters'. Jill suddenly blurted out, 'You have the most badly brought up, badly mannered children I've ever come across.' Esther got up and left and didn't speak to Jill for a week.

Julie's thirteen-year idyll in the country came to an end in 1983 when her marriage to Mike Randall disintegrated. Later, she fell in love with Myron Bloom, a world-class horn player and an unhappily married man. These dramatic changes in Julie's life upset Jill, who had worked so hard on her third marriage and did not like the fact that both Mike and Myron had been married at the time of Julie's first involvements with them.

Julie found her mother's disapproval unbearable. After a confrontation between mother and daughter at Pilgrim's Lane, Julie appealed to Michael, who had often helped her out, emotionally and financially. 'I am very sorry to have caused such a scene while celebrating Jill's birthday,' she wrote to Michael on 8 March 1984. 'Now I know Jill blames Myron for everything – She is wrong … It is not a very helpful way of demonstrating love by showing dislike of someone I love, both to me and to him.' Even worse, she told Michael, her son Jason had sided with Jill. 'I do not want any more criticism however constructive and well intentioned. I want to sort things out alone please – that does not mean I don't love you … I know you think I have made an awful mess of my life. Well I <u>do not</u> think that, and it would be very bad if I did …'. She wanted her mother's support, but she also wanted now to work on her problems by herself.

Jill wrote back: 'Darling, I really do hope things go well for you with Myron if you are truly convinced that you can make a good life for yourself with him.' But Jill worried about Julie's tendency to have high hopes. Jill suggested that Myron might return to his wife. After all, he had been married thirty years. Jill also asked Julie to consider the impact on her children. They were feeling unloved because Julie spent so much time with Myron. Jill thought Julie had narrowed her conception of happiness to living with Myron. 'But after a year or so, that is, if your present plans fall through, you would suddenly discover how many joys and excitements and opportunities are still open to you and you would begin to wonder how you could have got yourself into such a state of despair.' This undated letter (*c.*1986) ended: 'Anyway, darling, take heart, do not despair, and do not underestimate yourself. You are the only one to do so.'

Julie began an entirely new life in the United States, living in Bloomington, Indiana, where Myron had a teaching appointment in the outstanding music department at the University of Indiana. For part of Julie's period away from England, Laura stayed with Jill, and mother and daughter exchanged confidences on how they viewed Laura's progress to adulthood. In effect, Jill had become, Julie acknowledged, 'mother' to Laura.

Jill loved gardens. Most of her homes had gardens, and she had always been a passionate gardener. In April, at the beginning of the season, she loved to go to the garden market on Columbia Road, East London, early on Sunday morning. 'We'd set off at about 6.00,' recalled Jillian Lehel, who lived on Pilgrim's Lane and had married Julie's first husband, Victor. Arriving at the market early meant securing a good parking spot. But the sky would often look leaden, and the two would sit in the car gloomily, saying little, wondering whether it would rain. 'But when we got there, it was just like being in an art gallery.' Jill loved it, looking here, looking there, comparing prices. Flowers were sold by the dozen on trays. Jill would buy hundreds of annuals, tray after tray. 'She insisted on going up and down the market, up and down,' Jillian emphasized. Jillian would say, 'That's enough now, come on.' Jill loved to bargain. She said, 'No, no, just one more. I see something I like. Oh, I see something there I like. Ah, that will fill in a gap.' Sometimes Jillian would lose Jill, a short woman who disappeared into the crowd saying, 'Just one more darling. While I'm here, I might as well have another tray.'

'Michael would sometimes be utterly dismayed when we came home with all the trays,' Jillian remembered. 'Oh, my child, my child, my God,' he would moan, knowing that she would disappear into the garden for two days to plant the whole lot. 'You never can say that,' Michael objected. 'I never protested about flowers coming into this house.' Like a little girl, Jill would ignore Michael. 'It was sort of like being told off by Daddy,' Jillian suggested.

They would have their coffee and croissants,* even while Jill was outside, mentally planting. Jill, just shy of eighty, wrote to Julie on 4 August 1990:

> Now I am going to boast. You cannot imagine what feats of strength I achieved in my garden last Sunday, lugging great tubs of soil all over the place, sacks of peat, scrubbing, cleaning, pruning and doing so much heavy work that it would have exhausted a strapping great adolescent. And though I felt absolutely limp in the evening – this work went on all day – I suffered not a single twinge the next day. So how's that for a grandmother?

Sunday was *always* gardening day, Julie remembered. Jill might have a dinner party that night (dinner parties were often on Sundays), but no matter what, she gardened. At the end of the season Jill would have a clear out and do it all over again. She loved pansies, dahlias, and loads and loads of geraniums, lobelia and bedding plants. Jenny Stringer argued with Jill about her choices – too much impatiens and bursts of colour to the point of vulgarity. Jill called Jenny a snob.

Before the Columbia Road days, Jillian had had a 'nodding acquaintance' with Jill, but after being invited to a dinner with Jason and talking more to Jill and finding her so supportive and encouraging, they became good friends. Jill talked to Jillian about Jillian's interest in textile art. 'As long as you didn't interrupt her during the day, when she was writing her book, she was very generous.'

Jillian loved to have a drink with Jill late in the day or a whisky with Michael, and watch the news at 7 p.m. 'Sitting in the garden with Jill was always a pleasure. It was cosy there, like an outdoor room. Jill had it arranged so that there were lovely places to sit – under a pergola or on a bench beneath an arbour.' Michael described her plans for a fountain, which she somehow never got round to. 'It was a swamp when we first came. It was all done according to Jill's design.' Jill liked to say, 'Well I know I'm going to stay alive because I'm always thinking about what I'm going to do next year in the garden.' She would say to Jillian, 'Oh, look at that, it's coming out.'

---

* The croissants were a tradition, and when Jillian and I returned from Columbia Road on an April Sunday, Michael had the croissants ready for us.

Daughters of Dissent 2
(1983–99)

It is so long since I have looked at my own manuscript that, judging by past experience, when I do open it again I fear I will be overcome with a desire to rewrite the whole thing.

Jill Craigie to Pat Romero, 29 June 1983

In a way, her book takes you to the twentieth century; her life takes you through it.

Michael Holroyd to Carl Rollyson in conversation about Jill Craigie

Jill did start over again and again. She typed until a page was perfect. Her letters show that each time she resumed work on her book, the structure changed. In itself, this was no sign of weakness. Indeed, Pat Romero praised Jill for the courage – a real writer's courage – to scrap her work and begin again. 'I read through my last five chapters and was about to deliver them to my publisher when I suddenly felt an irresistible compulsion to rewrite them all in a slightly different way and from a different angle,' Jill wrote to Pat in a letter from the late 1980s.

Jill's dramatic breakthrough occurred some time shortly after Michael's election defeat in 1983 – when she shifted away from making the Pankhursts *the story*, and turned her attention to the individual human dramas that made up the Votes for Women cause. The desire to invoke the sweep of history, and its incremental movement from the nineteenth to the twentieth century, now constituted the architecture of the book. Nowhere does she mention Rebecca West as an influence, but it is hard not to see West at work here – particularly in the desire to bring history home, to see it functioning in the everyday lives of people, to seek in the psychology of individuals the forces of history. And like Rebecca, Jill attacked the way history had been told – in this case in Ray Strachey's biography of suffragist Millicent Fawcett:

The biographer wrote under manifest inhibitions, as if obliged to submit her manuscript for Millicent's approval. The ordinary worries of everyday life, the state of her income, the odd domestic upset, find no place at all in her narrative. 'An unshaken reasonableness was evident in everything she did, whether great or small, and consequently her biography contains nothing sensational' Ray Strachey explained. Similarly, in the *Life of Henry Fawcett*, Sir Leslie Stephen admitted: 'I write under conditions which compel a certain reserve.' He too wrote the life at Millicent's request; she read it, and would not countenance any personal or intimate revelations. Consequently, we are left with the impression that the Fawcetts were rare specimens who knew nothing of personal tests and fluctuating emotions. Clearly much more was happening beneath this artificial surface.

Jill now had a contract with Jonathan Cape, and on 29 July 1985 she received an encouraging letter from her editor, Liz Calder:

> I've just read your first chapters with the greatest pleasure. They are so wonderfully readable and I very much like the way you tell the story as a continuous narrative... Your great knowledge and research is so smoothly assimilated that one feels utterly at ease with your telling – the research is never lumpy and I think you've hit exactly the level and tone to reach the widest readership.

Jill missed her Christmas 1985 deadline but she wrote with confidence, sending in three more chapters of a book which had grown from 90,000 words to one that would be about 'three times longer'. At Cape, Graham Greene, the novelist's nephew, responded: 'You have gathered some marvellous material and it is exciting and satisfying to have the story so fully told. I continue to be confident that it is going to be a tremendous book. Clearly there is going to be a problem about length, but I don't think you need think about that too much at this stage.'

Jill's introduction to *Daughters of Dissent* begins with an epigraph from Barbara Taylor's *Eve and the New Jerusalem* (1983): 'The historical ear, at least until recently, has been tuned almost exclusively to the male voice.' Jill embellishes this conceit by reminding us of what happened when Virginia Woolf turned the pages of G.M. Trevelyan's classic *History of England*. Trevelyan had nothing to say about the part women played, except that wife-beating had been a customary and acceptable practice as late as 1470. Trevelyan recognized remarkable women in Elizabethan England, but 'it did not strike him as curious that no feminine voices were raised in protest at a state of affairs in which women could be beaten and locked up with impunity and flung about rooms'. Surely a sense of injustice is 'innate', Jill argues: 'The lament "it's not fair" comes almost as readily to a small child as "I want".'

Of course, women did protest, but only 'during the past two decades' did a 'new breed of historians' question the standard works of history. 'Never in any period did the female sex lack rebels and rebel leaders. They played their part, in all, yes all great agitations for reform; for example, in the anti-slavery movement, as Chartists, in the anti-Corn Law agitation, as agricultural labourers, trade unionists or Owenites.' Jill cites specific women and specific events, putting the lie to the legend that women had not spoken on public platforms before the advent of the Pankhursts:

> In August 1819 over a hundred Female Reformers assembled at the outskirts of Manchester behind a white silk banner embroidered with the demand for universal suffrage and parliamentary reform. They took their place at the head of a great procession, a peaceful procession, with children mounted on men's shoulders, with colourful banners and music from many bands. Everyone wore their best clothes: one reporter noted that even the destitute looked tidy.

Spectators (men and women) jeered at the marching women dressed in white ('forerunners of suffragettes in their interest in pageantry', Jill notes). These women should be home cooking, cleaning and taking care of their families. William Cobbett (1763–1835), the uncompromising radical and author of the incomparable *Rural Rides* (1830), referred to these women and other Female Reform societies 'usually with enthusiasm, yet in none of the latest books on his life and times, even in one published in two large volumes, do the authors mention the Female Reformers'.

Jill's introduction is studded with the names of forgotten women like Catharine Sawbridge Macaulay, who had a profound impact on the French revolutionary leaders, on George Washington and Mary Wollstonecraft (Wollstonecraft did not become a major figure in the college curriculum until the 1970s). 'The failure to take account of what women were doing robs history of much of its life and colour,' she contends. 'How often have we heard the tale repeated that the women's suffrage campaign was an upper and middle class affair, unrepresentative of the sex as a whole? Not until 1978, when Jill Liddington and Jill Morris published *One Hand Tied Behind Us* was that particular lie exposed,' Jill points out, citing numerous examples of working-class women suffragists. Jill gave Virago its due for resurrecting the women's texts she had brought to them. These texts showed that Votes for Women was not a sporadic, haphazard or exclusively female cause:

> In fact, after 1869, debates on women's enfranchisement took place in the Commons in 1870 (twice), 1871, 1872, 1873, 1875, 1876, 1877, 1879, 1884,

1892, 1897. A majority of the Commons favoured votes for women from 1886 onwards. The women's bills passed their Second Readings three times, in 1870, 1886, 1897. The list of dates is surely remarkable; the reality behind them even more so.

Then Jill wheeled about to face the retrograde feminist side of the opposition to her argument. She wanted to demolish the myth, repeated by many 1970s women's liberationists, that an earlier generation, hung up by the fight for the vote, had actually set back the cause of women:

> So far from fighting for the vote for the vote's sake or for its symbolical value, suffragists drew up lists of reforms unlikely to be carried into effect until M.P.'s had to appeal to women for votes. These reforms – such as alleviation of poverty, a rise in women's wages, and a variety of health measures – were not passed until after women secured the vote. 'If the electoral franchise were considered to be so trifling a concession, tyrannical governments would not resist its introduction with the might at their command.'

Jill dismissed Kate Millett and Germaine Greer, two of the presiding authorities of women's liberation, for their ignorance of history, for thinking the suffragists were a genteel lot and that women today could only be revolutionary by resorting to extra-parliamentary action: 'Feminists who think and speak only in terms of revolution usually scorn real revolutionary tactics. At the same time, they often refuse to engage in normal political practices, in pursuits and electioneering, for which they express contempt.' But what did radical feminists have to offer? Consciousness raising! Only by getting away from men, these separatists argued, could women make the 'painful decisions' to 'positively change their way of life'. Jill commended the radical's 'intellectual abilities', but she found a 'less attractive aspect' to calling men the enemy and setting out to alter the male psyche: 'If the test is, as it should be, political change over the whole field, feminists must think afresh.' For the feminists had performed

> unwitting services for their opponents. By giving the impression that they are more concerned with long-term ideology than immediate needs, they may alienate women of the working classes; they may even tend to put them off both feminism <u>and</u> socialism. A young mother trapped in a flat, struggling to cope with a couple of toddlers, is more likely to respond to a policy devised to give her a degree of control over the way she is housed and a chance to say what she most needs in the way of amenities than the suggestion to liberate herself which is, of course, or at least may be, a middle class idea.

Jill could have added that she had given these women a voice in *Who Are the Vandals?* Instead, she described the wives and mothers living in council estates:

> In a number of general and by-elections, I have found total incomprehension as to what feminism is about. The most amusing example came in a factory producing bras and pantie-girdles. When I asked whether anyone was interested in Women's Lib, I met with a chorus of NOES. 'They want to do us out of our jobs', they told me. Feminism to them meant nothing more than burning bras.

Jill concludes her introduction with her memoir of meeting the suffragettes. She had 'long conversations' with Sylvia Pankhurst, Mrs Pankhurst's closest friends and Emmeline Pethick-Lawrence. They 'talked about the campaign for hours on end'. Then Jill met the constitutional suffragists and 'found their reminiscences no less fascinating'. The antagonists – the militants and the nonmilitant – were, in the final analysis, interdependent in Jill's vision. 'No suffragist that I met ever looked back on the campaign with regret.' Their story constituted the 'real struggle for human freedom… worth retelling and sure to be reinterpreted from age to age. No one can tell it in full, to pursue all its ramifications, all its side-issues and to bring to life that great company of leading characters.' Jill presents this drama as the story of two families, the Pankhursts and the Fawcetts. She had thought about them 'so often throughout my adult political life that I feel I know them almost as if they were close relations … If not for the myths and misconceptions still surrounding the campaign, I would not have decided to write this book.'

Jill begins her book with 'The Well-To-Do Garretts' and Millicent Fawcett's 'rare moment of indiscretion' at a women's meeting in 1906, when she remarked that she would 'rather be shut up in a cage of Bengal tigers' than sit on a committee with Mrs Pankhurst. Whatever their disagreements, however:

> They had both resolved to reserve their artillery for their opponents, the anti-suffragists known as the Antis… Millicent Fawcett, the older of the two by eleven years, conducted her life cautiously with the subtle restraint of a Bach fugue. The younger woman conducted hers with the passion of the *Eroica*. The one appealed to reason, the other to emotion. While they each kept a wary eye on the other's defects and tactical errors – rarely on their own – they could not see that they were complementary, equally vital to the cause they served.

Both women claimed to have been suffragists all their lives. 'But how they arrived at these opinions,' Jill announces, 'what shaped their general outlook, would be impossible to understand without knowledge of their backgrounds, and of the mighty events which engulfed their families during the nineteenth century.'

Daughters of Dissent then plunges into a depiction of nineteenth-century family life:

> Imagine a father, an ordinary businessman, surprising his children at breakfast by bursting into the room with a sergeant-major's bark: 'Head up and shoulders down! Sebastopol is taken.' Those were the words of Newson Garrett, Millicent's father. Though no more than eight at the time, she could exactly remember him urging some seamen to join the navy and fight in the Crimea.

This passage inevitably leads to Newson Garrett's biography – his birth in 1812, his support for the Reform Bill of 1832, and then back to the Crimean War, in which Florence Nightingale astounded the world with what a woman could do. 'The music of her enormous prestige mingled with the fantasies of thousand of restless young women, sounding a call as if from some magical Pied Piper. One of these restless young women was Elizabeth Garrett, aged nineteen, Newson's second eldest daughter.'*

Elizabeth Garrett Anderson (1836–1917), Millicent Fawcett's sister, becomes the focal point of Chapter 1, embodying in her person the sly, even manipulative, approach to social change that Jill herself practiced. The story of Elizabeth (as Jill calls her) becomes the best example of the mini-biographies of nineteenth-century women-rebels that appear as vignettes and grace the stories of the book's main characters. If Florence Nightingale had turned nursing into a woman's profession, then why not do the same with doctors? This thought had occurred to Elizabeth's friend, Emily Davies, who became Elizabeth's mentor. Both women had taken their cue, in turn, from Dr Elizabeth Blackwell, the first women to practise medicine in Britain after obtaining her degree at a small US college. Elizabeth's wish to become a doctor horrified her parents. In a characteristic aside, Jill observes:

> Millicent in her memoir and Elizabeth's daughter in her biography of her mother tended to gloss over the terrible scenes which ensued. In their hagiographic accounts of family life, they might not have mentioned the scenes at all, but for their desire to show Newson in a favourable light. They admitted that his wife shut herself in her bedroom and cried and cried, making herself ill. And that Newson wrote to Elizabeth to say, 'You will kill your mother if you go on with this.'

Secretly Millicent sided with her sister, and Elizabeth herself unbent only so

---

* The music of history is such a pervasive metaphor in Jill's book that it is difficult not to see it as the symphonic screenplay she had always wanted to write about the women's cause.

far as to accompany her father to London so that he could show her what opposition she would face in the medical community. But when one of the medical men laughed at Elizabeth and then 'turned to insults', Newson Garrett declared: 'If she wished to become a doctor, a doctor she would be.' Her cause became his.

After almost eighty well-documented pages (including footnotes and bibliography), the reader has a grasp of the tensions at war in a woman's psyche, of how the seemingly passive Millicent was, in fact, in league with her aggressive sister, and how Millicent, with her 'singularly happy childhood', nevertheless saw herself as an advocate of women's rights 'from the cradle'. Indeed, Jill shows Millicent's radicalism arising right out of watching her capable mother: 'The sight of this neat little woman, with piquante features and tiny hands, bustling about in long voluminous petticoats and a crinolined skirt, supervising work in the laundry, dairy, and kitchen, often churning her own butter, producing cheese, pastries and cakes in between feeding and nursing her babies to the last, led Millicent to believe, when looking back on her childhood, that in another era, her mother might have proved a most capable manager of a big business.'

In 'The Struggling Gouldens', the Garretts' gradualism gives way to the Pankhursts' radicalism. Emmeline Goulden Pankhurst read Carlyle's *French Revolution* at the age of eleven or twelve and never forgot it – providing 'one of many examples of nature imitating art', writes Jill in the wake of Oscar Wilde. Emmeline's father, Robert Goulden, blessed her revolutionary mission by claiming she had been born on 14 July 1858, the anniversary of the day the Bastille fell, although he gave the correct date, 15 July, on her birth certificate. Jill deftly describes how Emmeline spent her precocious childhood and youth hearing about the Peterloo massacre of 1819 (Emmeline's grandfather had been present) and no doubt, Jill speculates, asking: 'Why did the cavalry charge?' Emmeline grew up with the deeds and names of radicals like Richard Cobden (1804–65) and John Bright (1811–89) ringing throughout her home. Both men were members of the anti-Corn Law League and known as apostles of free trade. High duties (protective tariffs on grain) made it difficult for the poor to feed themselves. 'It has often been suggested that the Anti-Corn Law League was the primary school for the women's suffrage campaign,' Jill notes, for women came out in numbers to hear radicals denounce the Corn Laws. Added to this uproar were the anti-slavery sentiments of American abolitionists who travelled to England enlisting the support of radicals in the Union cause against Southern secessionists. On 20 May 1867, when Emmeline was nine, John Stuart Mill moved an amendment to include women in the proposed Reform Bill. On polling day Emmeline expressed her hope that a Liberal victory 'would do the most wonderful good to the country'.

Jill ties this steady drive for reform to Emmeline's own dynamic Carlylean notion that history has to be led and commanded. Jill imagines that Emmeline's father, who favoured her, could not resist this 'little doll with her pale complexion, flawless as porcelain and mop of jet black curls'. Then Jill abruptly halts her story of Emmeline's energetic education in radicalism by remarking that Emmeline saw the futility of passing resolutions: 'Men, it seemed to her, did an awful lot of talking which came to nothing.' In Emmeline's ambivalence about her father Jill located the root of Emmeline's militant suffragism. Her inheritance of his very English liberal moderation gave way, during her youth in Paris, to a fondness for both fashion and radical politics. As Jill puts it, 'Fond of clothes, she was eager to make the most of her appearance, and soon learned how to do so in ideal circumstances.'

In 'Trials and Triumphs of the Garrett Sisters' and 'The Women's Best Friend' (Chapters 3 and 4), *Daughters of Dissent* continues to oscillate between the two families, always putting the Garretts first, showing how among the more temperate women the recognition of injustice and craving for reform ignited an outrage that formed a continuum with radicals like the Pankhursts.

The hero of these chapters, however, is John Stuart Mill, campaigning for Parliament. His demeanour as well as his ideas are conveyed through the impressions of Millicent Fawcett:

> For anyone interested in politics, to hear a long admired and famous man address the public arouses the kind of excited anticipation felt by Shakespearean lovers to hear a celebrated actor playing *Hamlet*. In the small, densely packed room, she had the good fortune to witness one of the most sensational events of the campaign. At question time a man rose from the back and read a passage from a pamphlet: *Thoughts on Parliamentary Reform*. This stated bluntly, 'the working classes, though different from those of most other countries in being ashamed of lying, are yet generally liars.' This comment, printed on a placard by an opponent was handed up to Mill. 'The question I would like to ask' said the fellow, 'is, did you write this?' 'I did', said Mill and promptly sat down.
>
> After a gasp of astonishment, the audience burst into a thunderous and a seemingly endless roar of cheering and applause. They had expected, of course, the equivocations common to politicians and had been bowled over by his honesty. A shoe-maker, George Odger, rose when the noise finally subsided to say that the working classes wanted friends not flatterers and felt under an obligation to those who stated what they sincerely believed, even if critical of themselves. Millicent heard it said afterwards that those two words, 'I did', won Mill the election. She

claimed later that his ascetic, chiselled features and delicate physique combined, as it was, with an unusual degree of moral courage, kindled her enthusiasm for women's enfranchisement tenfold.

This story of Mill's reply has often been told, but has it ever been framed so as to show how political consciousness is animated?

Mill's *The Subjection of Women* 'had a greater influence on educated women all over the world than any other secular publication', Jill states, providing copious evidence for her claim.* Jill describes a passage from Mill that he said had been inspired by his wife, Harriet Taylor:

> He pointed to the difference between the sexes in the way women had to live their lives. Whatever their creative work, they still had to attend to the multitudinous details of everyday life, which steal time. They did much of their thinking in circumstances which, 'almost any man would make an excuse for not attempting it...'. A woman's mind was so continually occupied with small things that it 'can rarely permit itself to be vacant, as man's is so often when not engaged in what he chooses to consider the business of his life.' It was just in those vacant hours when, suddenly some unbidden thought or fresh idea springs magically to mind and assists in the creative process. The emotional and mundane demands made continually on women, the persistent interruptions cheated them of the concentrated effort extending over hours which was essential to the creation of art at its most sublime.

Sigmund Freud, Jill reports, feared that such passages would upset his fiancée.

In 'Fame and Infamy, 1870' (Chapter 5), the writer/director of *The Way We Live* draws a picture of how the architecture of society impeded social progress:

> Once in the old market towns, the homes of lawyers and other professional people were customarily set in the same streets as labourer's cottages, work-places, shops and centres of social activity, the whole tending to create integrated communities. Women and children were not cut off from their menfolk during the day. By contrast, the Victorians expanded the urban environment on a massive scale, building with imported materials row after row of monotonous houses; and this same method might be applied to the meanest of habitations for low paid workers to the most pretentious for the well-to-do. In this expansion of towns and cities for the sole purpose of residence, to meet the incomes of various owners, women were increasingly confined to the home and the social classes more rigidly segregated than ever.

---

* In her copy of Christabel Pankhurst's *Unshackled: The Story of How We Won the Vote* (1959) Jill wrote, 'why no mention of John Stuart Mill?'

But another innovation of Victorian life, the railway, put women in touch with each other and facilitated the lecture tours sponsored by suffrage societies, many of them inspired by Mill. 'Never before in British history had so many women taken part in a campaign, not only as equal partners with men, in itself a novelty in secular life, but often as the leading elements.'

The first six chapters show that not only did women's interests range far beyond the vote itself, they were also involved in the day-to-day tactics of trying to figure out the best strategy of securing women's freedom in every sense of the word. This was the story that Jill could tell by fleshing out the innumerable stories of individual women and hence the submerged history of suffragism.

It is difficult to read *Daughters of Dissent* without seeing it as a disguised autobiography. How could Jill not be thinking of herself when she wrote sentences like, 'The perpetual search for favours from men could be a most wearisome treadmill; how many male egos and prejudices had to be pandered to, how many contrived countenances might be needed to cancel an inward fury while being patronised.' (Chapter 6) When Elizabeth Garrett expresses her fear that marriage will blunt her ambition and blur her commitment to success in public life, her husband replies that she must sink her ego into her cause. Jill comments: 'But most women are softened by love and she was no exception.' Few women like Millicent Fawcett – or Jane Eyre – had blind husbands who become, in Jill's words, 'totally dependent upon the love of the heroine'.*

If *Daughters of Dissent* never really emerges from the nineteenth century, if Jill herself became entirely enmeshed in that century's tensions, it may be because the twentieth century did not resolve – indeed, it perpetuated – the same dilemmas even as women did progress. As Jill writes of the suffragists in Chapter 6:

> These women indeed had wills of iron. Nothing could deflect them from pursuing their objectives, even if they could also be unclear about where their chosen paths might lead. Their conception of emancipation was shrouded in mist. They professed to believe in equality between the sexes, that is, in equal rights for women to all privileges and opportunities granted to men, but they could not define what would be the further relationship between the sexes, or women's relationship to society, once equality had been achieved.

* Mike Bessie commented that as Michael grew older, he became more dependent on Jill. The dependence was there at the beginning, Mike suggested, but it was not so readily visible – or, indeed, so graphically apparent – until Michael became lame after the 1963 car accident and half-blind after his attack of shingles in the mid-1970s.

What would happen, these women wondered, when women could have both marriage and career?

In the first third of *Daughters of Dissent*, the Pankhursts do not fully emerge – they are a latent historical force gathering energy – as Jill dives into the lives of Millicent and Henry Fawcett, reading deeply into their actions and virtually crying out for more intimate detail. It is, as Jill put the case in her review of Patricia Romero's *Sylvia Pankhurst*, the 'biographer's determination to disinter the truth' – which in this case Millicent sought to bury. Jill wants life, not just issues; scenes, not just data; characters, not just effigies: 'When they sat in the tiny drawing room of their London home, Henry with his long legs stretched half way across the floor, Millicent in her crinolined skirt, reading the news-paper reports aloud, they must have vented feelings of exasperation when so few journalists understood or cared about the true reasons for defeating the Bill.' There it is: the 'must have' that desperate locution biographers always resort to when they do not know. And like biographers – whether they admit it or not – Jill generates her own evidence and becomes her own authority:*
'She [Millicent] was deeply involved in her husband's erratic parliamentary career, but in pursuing her other interests – educating her daughter, writing, making speeches, attending committees and keeping social engagements – she gave the impression that no one aspect of life was of greater concern than another' (Chapter 7, 'Braving the Storm').

Jill thought of herself as writing a revisionist history. In her letters to various scholars she often complained that professional historians had not read *Hansard*. A case in point: her treatment of Disraeli in Chapter 8, 'Victorian Values'. Jill notes that in 1875 and 1876 Disraeli voted for a bill that would have partially enfranchised women at the very time that Gladstone adamantly exposed any extension of the vote for women. 'Disraeli had nothing to gain by this vote,' she observes, 'it might have been more expedient for him to have stayed away from the House that night.' She then makes a plausible case for Disraeli's intention to enfranchise women in the Reform Bill of 1867. She chides his biographers: 'None of them has mentioned it even in a foot-note, neither the leading biographers of the last century, Monypenny and Buckle, nor Lord Blake in this one. And the latest biography, Sarah Bradford, in her substantial volume published in 1982, is content to repeat the omis-sion. The neglect of these votes strikes me as an injustice to both the women and Disraeli.'†

* This statement will be familiar to readers of R.G. Collingwood's *The Idea of History* (1946).

† Michael Foot, taking a cue from V.S. Pritchett, has argued for Disraeli's feminism, particularly in novels that present a vivid and diverse array of women characters. See 'The Good Tory', *Debts of Honour* (1980).

Jill finds it disturbing that in no biography of Gladstone could she find the analysis she herself was forced to write:

> If only Gladstone had applied his mind to the Woman Question with the same imagination [as he had applied to Ireland], women might have been enfranchised in 1884. It was not as if there had been any manifestations of public hostility to the demand. No woman's suffrage meeting had been broken up, no one had been forcibly ejected. Suffragists, though ridiculed in the early days, had never had to contend with the persecution suffered by Elizabeth Garrett and Sophia Jex-Blake in their attempts to enter the medical profession, nor with the violence inflicted on Josephine Butler and her friends in their crusade against the Contagious Diseases Act. The public had grown accustomed to women voting at local elections and standing for elections to the School Boards. Nor was there any evidence that women would all vote in the same way; a fear constantly expressed in parliamentary debates. The voting patterns at local elections revealed that women, like the men, generally voted Liberal in Liberal constituencies, Conservative elsewhere.

Jill does not dismiss Gladstone's greatness, but she does offer it up at a deep discount. In Gladstone's hands, on so many occasions, the fate of reform rested.

While writing *Daughters of Dissent*, Jill realized that notwithstanding the male hysteria surrounding the suffragettes, men had done as much as women for the cause of the vote and that their contribution had gone uncelebrated, if not unnoticed. Striking figures were Richard Pankhurst, Benjamin Disraeli, MP Henry Fawcett (Millicent's husband) and W.T. Stead (editor of the *Pall Mall Gazette*), but MP Charles Dilke (1843–1911) – towards whom the trajectory of Chapter 11, 'A Fit of Mortality', turns – steps forward as the man most likely to subdue opposition to women's rights among men of 'all political colours'. A public figure with impressive contacts abroad, a legislator who had mastered parliamentary procedure, he had attempted to employ women as factory inspectors and generally proposed putting them into positions of authority. He was a proponent of strong republican views who battled for extensions of the franchise, but he was accused of 'ruining' an eighteen-year-old girl and making her his mistress. During a sensational divorce trial the charge against Dilke could not be proved. Afterwards, W.T. Stead, considering himself the arbiter of public morality, Jill observes, went for Dilke. 'By the time the press had finished with him he appeared to be a monster of depravity. When the wolves are out for a politician's blood they can hunt in packs.' Dilke was ostracized from public life.

Dilke's calamitous story eclipses all others in this book. As Jill concludes:

The tragedy of his life was no less tragic for the suffrage campaign. He, of all the potential leaders of the Liberal Party, would never have opposed the will of the majority in the Commons by blocking a women's suffrage bill. He might even have overcome resistance to the measure in the House of Lords. Sir Charles Dilke was the suffragists' lost leader, the one who might have saved them two extra decades of wearisome labour and suffering; the one and only man who might have transformed women's history.

This evocation of Charles Dilke's doom and the delay in the women's cause it occasioned ends the second third of Jill's epic book.

Beginning with Chapter 12, 'The Subjection of Suffragists', Jill begins to dismantle Sylvia's harsh view of her mother during these years. Jill notes that Sylvia suffered from headaches and weak eyes (preventing her from reading properly until she was eight) and succumbed to morbid spells and crying fits. In short, she did not have her sister Christabel's charming good looks or winning ways. 'Sylvia did not receive her fair share of attention,' Jill states flatly. 'She must often have felt hurt and neglected,' Jill surmises. 'A competitive spirit is often born in the nursery.' No doubt, Jill implies, Mrs Pankhurst did neglect Sylvia, 'but little was then known about psychological science. The discoveries of Freud had not as yet been widely studied in England. Such knowledge today makes it easier to understand the causes of maladjustments and to take appropriate remedies.' This exculpation of Mrs Pankhurst is complemented by Jill's nod to Sylvia: 'She saw herself, no doubt with some justice on her side, as a victim of injustice, even as a martyr.' She knew, however, that her father adored her, and she came to see herself as the sole, true inheritor of his principles. In effect, then, Jill provides a kind of subtext, a family romance/conflict that plays in the background of Sylvia's *The Suffragette Movement*. Historians who simply absorb the book as history have been duped, Jill implies. Her psychological/biographical demolition of Sylvia is worthy of the psychological/biographical excavations of Rebecca West in *The Meaning of Treason* and *A Train of Powder*. But like Rebecca's books, Jill's is founded not only on fact, but also on intuition, a reading of human character that is only as persuasive as Jill's imagination can make it – which is very good indeed – but which is also liable to attack from others equally adept at extracting other inferences from the evidence.

Why all this matters – that is, what kind of homemaker and mother Mrs Pankhurst was – is evident when Jill turns to what happened when Mrs Pankhurst almost died from a severe haemorrhage after giving birth to a boy, Henry Francis. 'It did not occur to Emmeline,' Jill writes, 'that there might be something wrong with a system which permitted incompetent midwives to care for women in labour.' A few suffragists had been aware of the problem, however, and Chapter 12 explores the careers of those like Josephine Butler who were responsible for creating a Midwives Institute. Their efforts show how Emmeline, like millions of other women, still had much to think through about their roles as mothers and independent persons. In effect, then, Jill transforms the family drama of the Pankhursts – as Sylvia depicts it – into the broader social canvas of late-nineteenth-century British society.

The next three chapters evince an extraordinary grasp of the nexus between changing social attitudes and the intricacies of legislation designed to enforce change. To what extent can radical programmes be enacted piecemeal? 'Reformers,' Jill observes, 'especially those who pride themselves on being truly radical, frequently fail to understand that their quarrel with politicians is not necessarily one between right and wrong, but between two rights. Compromise, however regrettable, may not be the last word in betrayal.'

Buttressing the narrative of parliamentary manoeuvres is a presentation of the social canvas, a panoramic portrayal of the labouring classes. We learn not only how many women were employed, but also how much they made and what they did with their money.

> The textile industries of the north, northern Ireland and Scotland accounted for 794,349 female employees. They maintained, on the whole, though not in every area, a higher than average standard of living. Many a mother continued to work in the Lancashire mills, not so much from necessity, but to take home extras and enjoy a measure of financial independence, for which she might be willing to pay a baby-minder five shillings a week; that could be as much as home workers could earn in a week making army uniforms under government contract. Male workers had grown terrified of being ousted from the textile industries by the cheap labour of women.

Of course a question arises: what would have happened if these women had the vote? Women like Emilia, Lady Dilke (1840–1904), Jill reports, organized these female workers into unions. Along with her husband Sir Charles, she struggled to establish a minimum wage and decent working hours for women. The impact of such details is apparent when the parliamentary debates begin and anti-suffrage opponents speak of women as a sex apart, a sex that does not know the way of the world, a sex that needs to be sheltered (Jill takes aim at Asquith's speeches). Jill lets the irony sink in without comment: this is a society that affords women very little protection – in the home or outside it.

As a counterpoint to the lives of working-class women, Jill continues the story of Elizabeth Garrett Anderson, who begins transforming the medical education of women when she is appointed Dean of the London School of

Medicine in 1883. She had triumphantly proven that she could sustain a good marriage and remain a professional, public woman. Jill clinches the point by noting that 'even as early as 1880, when most people still believed that a wife's career would be incompatible with marriage, out of twenty-one feminine names entered into the Medical Register nine were those of wives'.

Daughters of Dissent, for all its use of biography, statistical reports and historical narrative is, in the end, a great drama. Jill creates great scenes, climaxes that achieve their impact by drawing together several characters, each of whom has already been the focus of an earlier story or anecdote, so that the impact of the book comes as a crescendo. We are put on the stage of history, witnessing in Chapter 13, for example, the triumph of Millicent's daughter, Philippa Fawcett:

> Millicent had occasions for frequent visits to Cambridge. Not only was she on the council for Newnham, but her daughter was the college's most promising student. Philippa had won a scholarship, having obtained a first class with distinction in Latin, a first class with distinction in Algebra and Euclid and a third class with distinction in logic. She was about to sit for her tripos papers and so highly did her tutors rate her chance of achieving an outstanding result that they could not conceal their excitement. Millicent herself, in a rare state of nervous tension, dared not attend the reading ceremony. 'I have made up my mind not to be too anxious about it,' she informed a friend, 'there are a great many better things in the world than beating other people in examinations.' Agnes, the interior decorator, who was also a member of Millicent's suffrage society, shared her sister's anxiety. On the actual day of the ceremony the sisters stayed at home keeping themselves busy and probably glancing anxiously at the clock from time to time. They awaited a telegram to inform them of the result. The Senate house itself was packed with visitors and university personnel. Old Newson Garrett sat between two grand-daughters, Philippa in the gallery ... The person appointed to read the results began with the men; the name 'Mr Bennet' announced as senior wrangler produced prolonged cheers. When the reader had got through the men, he announced: 'Women.' 'Ladies' roared the male undergraduates; 'women' the announcer repeated. 'Ladies', roared the undergraduates, still louder. This exchange continued increasing the suspense. When at last he came to the name of Miss Fawcett, he announced that she was <u>above</u> the senior wrangler, 'thus winning the most famous mathematical honour in the world' wrote Ray Strachey. A gasp of astonishment; then it seemed the cheering and the waving of hats and the surge toward Philippa would never end. Josephine Butler was among the first to shake her hand. The announcer wished to proceed with his list, but when he attempted to read the name of another woman, the undergraduates yelled: 'Miss Fawcett's. Read hers again.' The students of Newnham and Girton anxiously awaiting their own results could not hear above the pandemonium ...

Leading articles appeared in *The Times* and most other papers on Miss Fawcett's amazing academic achievement. The news flashed round the world. Telegrams deluged the [Fawcett] home in Gower Street.

Such scenes increase in number as the book surges towards the momentous, crucial debates in the House of Commons between Asquith and Balfour,* towards the passionate women's advocate, Keir Hardie, and the exuberant and engaging Robert Blatchford (1851–1943), whose *Clarion* gave women like Rebecca West a platform,† and towards Christabel Pankhurst's realization that patient women would not secure the vote. Some disappointed suffragists gave up the political battle and turned to mysticism and spiritualism. In this atmosphere of discouragement and disillusionment, the story of the Pankhurst family emerges and begins to overtake the earlier emphasis on the Fawcetts. Indeed, history almost seems to demand the Pankhursts:

> Millicent had now been working for the Franchise for thirty years; but she could think of no way of breaking the deadlock … She had her convictions but they lacked intensity. Neither she nor her biographer left any indication that she distressed herself over, for instance, the fate of the victims of sexual abuse or about the appalling poverty so prevalent in Victorian times. Here, as in many other respects, the contrast with Emmeline Pankhurst was sharp and profound.

As usual, Jill is acute about what her sources leave out and which other sources can fill the gap.

The last three chapters form, along with two unwritten ones, the final third of *Daughters of Dissent*, which in uncut form approaches 300,000 words, a work sixty years in the making. It is a pyramid of a book, with Emmeline Pankhurst, the mother of the movement, at its pinnacle. She is never the only important character in the narrative – in fact, Christabel's activism and intellectual capacities eclipse her mother's – but Emmeline's *presence* as leader and symbol, as a comprehensive human being with children and a love of dress and of politics and of art, would have made her the cynosure of a completed *Daughters of Dissent*.

Christabel Pankhurst brought her mother into the twentieth century,

---

* Arthur Balfour (1848–1930), Conservative Prime Minister (1902–5).

† Blatchford organized all sorts of activities for socialists, including cycling clubs. Jill devotes wonderful pages to how the bicycle, like the railway, put women on wheels and contributed to their liberation. It was Blatchford, Jill notes, who realized that Christabel was a good dancer. This kind of detail is not trivial; it contributes to Jill's comprehensively aesthetic view of socialism. Without such aesthetic perceptions – and Blatchford had many of them – socialism, in Jill's view, is a mean thing and hardly worth struggling for. The socialist tower blocks oppressed her not because of their exalted aim, but because of their awkward execution.

showing with searing insight how every delay in getting the vote for women demeaned them in every aspect of their lives. By providing the historical backdrop for all such insights, *Daughters of Dissent* serves as the engine for understanding why Mrs Pankhurst, called back to her roots in the French Revolution, sanctioned Christabel's militant campaigns. As Jill writes of Christabel: 'She loathed the false dignity earned by subservience and extolled as feminine or womanly. For her, true dignity lay in revolt.'

Christabel's vehemence is placed in a context provided by other radicals like Keir Hardie, Annie Kenney and Hannah Mitchell, and in the context of Mrs Pankhurst's growing realization that the ILP – notwithstanding Keir Hardie – would never mobilize to get women the vote. Eager to discount historians who have argued that advocacy of votes for women (or even a limited franchise bill for men) would have hampered the vote-getting power of the labour movement, Jill provides a list of successful candidates, including John Stuart Mill and Charles Dilke, adding:

> One particular item in a manifesto, liked or disliked, may make little difference to the intentions of voters unless the reform is so contentious at the time as to dwarf all other considerations, such as its effect on peace and war, taxation or, as in Gladstone's days, Home Rule, disliked by many electors on account of Fenian violence and loss of life. The dominating issues of most concern to the electorate were free trade, fear of a taxation on food, the rise in the cost of living and disillusionment with Balfour's administration. The Conservatives had been in power for too long; the public was deeply weary of them and ready for reform.

Jill then gives a meticulous version of what happened at the Free Trade Hall on 13 October 1905 when Sir Edward Grey, the prospective Liberal Foreign Secretary, introduced Winston Churchill, a future candidate for North West Manchester. Historians have presented contradictory versions of the scene in which Christabel and Annie Kenney are said to have interrupted the meeting with cries of votes for women. 'Curiously, two highly relevant, indeed governing factors in the situation have generally been ignored or glossed over,' Jill argues. As a student of law, Christabel knew how important it was to follow 'normal procedures'. In this instance, she sent a 'courteous note' to Grey requesting a meeting on votes for women. She received no reply, although, Jill reports, it was not unusual for politicians to receive 'deputations of suffragists at election time'. She did not interrupt the meeting but rather waited to see what the speakers might say about suffrage. Christabel's tactics were innovative. She was not asking, as previous suffragists had done, whether a member of Parliament would support votes for women, but whether a government would commit itself to the cause. Undoubtedly (although Jill does not say as much) this is why Grey did not reply to Christabel's note.

Jill sets the scene deftly, describing the women coming into the hall and sitting in the rear in a 'high state of tension. Election fever is like war fever; heaven protect anyone out of tune with the mass sentiment.' An enthusiastic crowd cheered Grey, applauded his policies on Japan, France and South Africa. Then a heckler questioned him about unemployment. An unruffled Grey obligingly dealt with the problem. 'His tolerance of the male heckler interested Christabel.' The women waited for someone to say something about suffrage while the meeting now moved into question time. After a few more questions about unemployment, Annie Kenney rose and said, 'Will the Liberal Government give women the vote?' In the 'awesome silence', the chairman ignored the question. Then Christabel rose to put the question again. Then the hall broke out in roars as Annie unfurled her votes for women banner. Men tried to push her down in her seat. Christabel wrapped her arms around Annie and handed a note to the Chief Constable of Manchester, asking Grey once again to answer the question put by Kenney, 'as one of 96,000 organised women textile workers'. Grey read the note, smiled and handed it around to his associates. When the meeting was about to end without any acknowledgment of the note, Christabel rose again as 'men roared abuse, shook their fists, matrons screamed their indignation'. Jill emphasizes: 'Christabel and Annie were petite, seemingly frail, certainly feminine, most unlike the Amazonian fighters for women's rights of people's imagination.' Some audience members now looked on aghast as stewards roughly handled these two women. Cries of 'shame, shame' could be heard. Some left the hall in disgust. After the two women were ejected from the meeting, Grey said suffrage would not be a party question in the election and he did not propose to speak about it. Jill observes: 'A number of suffragists must have been present, yet not one had the courage to ask, why not? Grey had always pro-fessed himself in favour of women's suffrage and in the past ... had voted for franchise bills. Why could he not have told the simple truth?'

Jill's question might, in one sense, sound naive, for how could Grey commit his Liberal government to the question? But it is her concentration on the suffragists in the audience that compels admiration. What were they doing to put the kind of pressure on Grey that would eventually make suffrage a party and a government question? Christabel was offering all sides in the suffrage struggle an opportunity to change the terms of the debate, and they failed her. This is why militancy then seemed to Christabel the only course of action available to her and the WSPU. When the policeman holding her hands behind her back did not arrest her, she realized that the 'only alternative would be to spit, much as it went against the grain. So she spat.' Christabel's arrest succeeded in gaining press attention, confirming her view that only acts of militancy brought attention and won the movement new followers. More importantly, however, in terms of the scene Jill describes, Christabel's action shattered the stalemate that had stymied an earlier generation of suffragists. The other consequence of Christabel's actions, Jill shows, is to turn her mother more and more away from the labour movement as the women's hope. Women would have to act for themselves.

Jill's narrative does not go much beyond 1906. By 1992 she apparently had the bulk of her book – these eighteen chapters – in draft form.* Throughout the early 1990s Jill continued to work on *Daughters of Dissent* and to attract young scholars to Pilgrim's Lane. On 11 September 1990 she received a letter from June Purvis, describing herself as a 'sociologist by training' who had become 'hooked' on women's history. June wanted to write a biography of Christabel. AT LAST! For decades women had been coming to Jill to discuss Sylvia, pro and con, and then Jill had to deploy all her resources to explain why Sylvia was not the starting point. June later wrote, 'I arrived at similar conclusions to Jill about the current historiography about the Pankhursts quite independently, without having read Jill's work.'[1] But Jill 'sharpened' June's awareness of the gaps in her sources. When June founded her own journal, *Women's History Review*, she put Jill on the editorial board.

Trips to Paris, Venice, Dubrovnik and then to Indiana to see Julie and her children, coupled with looking after Michael and working in the 1992 general election, kept delaying Jill's work on *Daughters of Dissent* even as June sent encouraging messages. An almost three-year gap in their correspondence (May 1992 to February 1995) reflects Jill's absorption in making her final documentary, *Two Hours From London* (1994). Then she got involved in selling 10 Morgan Street (after Michael retired from Parliament in 1992), and she embarked on an ambitious programme of home improvements: ceramic black-and-white tiles for the front path and steps, new curtains and other fabrics for a settee and armchair, cleaning various carpets, a new sink in the utility room, improvements to the central heating system, several plumbing jobs and best of all a brand new kitchen – the last paid for, Michael liked to point out, by the libel judgement against Rupert Murdoch's *Sunday Times* following its publication of an outrageous article naming Michael as a KGB

* She said as much to me when I interviewed her about Rebecca West.

spy. On 27 August 1996 Jill wrote to June: 'I have got back to my book on the movement with much rewriting, but it is quite difficult with Michael home so much of the time these days. What a lot men eat! All the preparations for meals and clearing away afterwards goes on, which we women would never do for ourselves. All the same, despite much scepticism, I do intend to complete my ms by the end of next spring.' Jill was quite aware that friends like Jill Tweedie had become increasingly critical of her for locking up so much original suffragette material for such a long period. They also had serious doubts that Jill would ever finish her work. On 2 September 1996 Jill replied to a David Mitchell letter inquiring about her book: 'I can only say that it remains to be seen whether I ever succeed in getting through my opus.'

On 4 October 1998 Jill wrote to June about her

> strong feeling of claustrophobia for which I have been inflicted during the past year or two; a feeling that life is no longer my own to live as I wish. That is not to say that I am discontented with my lot, far from it, but it may have something to do with feeling obliged to serve three meals a day, unless we happen to be going out, and what it entails.

Jill was buoyed by the appearance of Maxine Willett: 'A young woman has walked into my life as if sent from heaven.' Maxine, a student recommended to Jill by biographer Brian Brivati, wanted to be an archivist, and she was now starting on Jill's collection as 'work experience'. Maxine, in turn, found Jill inspiring to work for – so lively, so approachable, so interested in Maxine's own career.* 'She never talked down to me. We had wonderful conversations about my attitudes. It would never have occurred to me that I couldn't have gone to university.'

Jill never relinquished hope of finishing her book, but she also dreaded the reaction. She often mentioned that she would be attacked by the male historians she criticized. She also knew that her view of Sylvia would not go down well with her socialist friends. She would endure scepticism, if not censure, in her own party for putting one of Britain's socialist icons on the rack. Barbara Castle, in *Sylvia and Christabel Pankhurst* (1987), had taken the Sylvia line, and Jill had called her up, threatening to 'flatten her'. Glenys Kinnock added to Jill's anger by telling her that Castle had accepted the commission in order to pay for a new roof. Jill 'snorted and gasped with horror', saying that 'Barbara would sell her soul for a new roof.'

Jill also attacked Glenys's partiality for Sylvia, and Glenys replied: 'At least

---

* Maxine now works as an archivist at the Women's Library in London. She kindly sent me a spreadsheet of the detailed record she made of Jill's suffragette materials.

I'm not a turncoat like you. I've stuck with Sylvia, the only one [Pankhurst] who remained a Socialist.' Jill told Glenys she did not know what she was talking about and that she had vastly overestimated Sylvia. 'But I'm not just talking about Sylvia's contribution to Votes for Women. It's much broader than that – the fact that she remained loyal to the values she always had.' Glenys told Jill she had gone to Ethiopia and put flowers on Sylvia's grave. 'Pfft!' said Jill. 'The world was divided between Sylvias and the rest,' Glenys said.

Paul Foot's *Red Shelley* (1980) provides a context for measuring how Jill stood out from her socialist peers:

> The Left has often inclined to the view that 'working class struggle' is far too serious a matter for 'women's issues'; that 'women's issues' arise from 'personal politics' which have nothing to do with the 'real struggle' to change society in a socialist direction. The absurdity of this hardly requires explanation. The oppression of women, in Shelley's day as now, eats away at the unity of working people. Among working men it promotes the bully; among working women obsequiousness and subservience. Among both men and women it militates against political involvement and in favour of the status quo. If society is to be transformed from below – a view normally associated with the Left – the fight against the values and priorities of male domination is inescapable.

To withstand the opposition, Jill wanted to produce a definitive book, a dream of a book, the *only* book she would ever write.

Jill worried as well about being up to date. There was always another monograph to consult, another fact to be documented, another Sylvia assertion to be investigated. Then the book got so long. 'Jill always said she needed a good editor,' Jenny Stringer remembered. Michael looked at the early chapters and made editorial suggestions. Jill worried about the tone of her book. In her diary for 9 March 1998 she wrote: 'Trying to put over the story in a more light-hearted vein, but with jokes at the expense of the politicians rather than the women.'

After Jill's death in 1999, Michael expressed doubts about Jill's ability to master the book form, suggesting she was more visual than verbal. Mike Bessie, speaking from a lifetime of observing authors he edited, never thought Jill would finish. The book could never be as perfect or as comprehensive as she wished. Julie remembered Jill discussing her book about a year or two before she became ill.

> 'I wish Michael would go and take a good month in Jamaica so I could finish my book. I need an uninterrupted month. But you know he wouldn't go alone. He couldn't possibly manage without me.'

'Well, I'll go with him.'
'No, no, no, I couldn't have that.'

Julie thought her mother did not want Michael to manage without her: 'I daresay he might have gone – particularly if she had said go to Jamaica or somewhere like that.'

With Michael around, Jill could not pursue her 'ideal way of working'. She liked to wake up with the book on her mind, make a cup of coffee and, dressed or not, go into her study and write. Periodically she would get up and wander about, making another cup of coffee, thinking about the book without any thought of meals. Perhaps feeling peckish at lunch or teatime, she would wander back down to the kitchen, make a sandwich, still thinking about the book, and work until 3.00 or 4.00 in the morning. A month on that schedule – without even the interruption of a cleaning lady coming in – and she would have completed the book, Jill claimed. 'Can't you take yourself somewhere?' Julie asked. No, because Jill had so much material in her study that she had to consult.

In the end, however, it was not the interruptions that thwarted the completion of *Daughters of Dissent*. Michael's view that Jill was 'blocked' has to be definitive, since he intently watched her decades-long struggle with how to construct the denouement of her epic. He draws a parallel here with Rebecca West, whose brilliant but incomplete epic, *Survivors in Mexico*, was published posthumously in 2003. If a writer vastly more experienced than Jill had so much trouble organizing the final third of her book, it is not surprising that Jill should have been similarly balked. In the end, she could not quite come to grips with how to *write* her vision. For Michael there is great sadness that she became stuck on the page in a way she would not have been on the screen.

Paul thought of Jill as the Casaubon character in George Eliot's *Middlemarch,* unable to complete his *Key to All Mythologies*. Jill never did show Paul her book. For all their discussions on the subject, Paul was nonetheless surprised to learn that Jill had written so much. After so many years, June Purvis observes, Jill's book had become 'a way of life'.

28

Two Hours From London
(1962–95)

Whatever went wrong, we had wonderful holidays.

Michael Foot

It was born out of our anger about what has happened, about Western leaders deceiving us about the war, and we made it to change the West's policy.

Jill Craigie's description of *Two Hours From London*,
unidentified newspaper clipping, Jill Craigie Papers

Jill and Michael were pilgrims – seekers of the sun, good food, leisure to read and art to treasure. They travelled often, as far as India, Morocco, the US (to visit Julie in Indiana), Prague, Malta, Spain, Amsterdam (where Jill examined Sylvia Pankhurst's papers), the south of France and Paris, Rome, most often to Venice and later Dubrovnik. In France, Jill read the newspapers to Michael (her command of French was much better than his). In Rouen they read Proust for the first time. They visited Montaigne's tower, and over a period of two or three years read all his essays in the vicinity of the sites where he had written them. Montaigne presented, Michael avowed, the 'whole humanist case of the way you should look at the world'. When they returned home from a trip, they would often go almost immediately to the theatre, which became a way of prolonging their holiday feeling.

From 1962 onwards, Michael recorded in his copy of Hazlitt's travel writings every significant holiday he and Jill took and what they read while abroad. They read Ruskin, Mary McCarthy, Gore Vidal and James (Jan) Morris, whom they met in Venice. Morris's *Venice* (1963, revised 1983) had a special appeal because it presented the romantic Venice, 'very grand and bent-backed … a gnarled but gorgeous city'. Morris, a resident of Wales, wrote that Venetians reminded him of the Welsh; they had the 'melancholy pride of people on their own, excluded from the fold of ordinary nations'. Such words appealed to Jill and Michael, especially when Morris spoke of Venetians as homely and provincial – positive terms to Jill – and of the city as a 'collection of villages'. 'Venice is the happiest place on the planet', Michael affirmed. 'That's why I can't stand Thomas Mann [*Death in Venice*]. Venice is not like that at all. Stendhal stayed in Venice throughout the one hundred days of Napoleon's return from Elba, which is the proof of Stendhal's love of Venice.' The city was for Jill a visual delight, and she loved to walk and wander there. If Venice had any fault, it would seem apparent only in later years when Jill said it became 'too crowded'. For a change they went to a little island, Burano, but only, Jill insisted, 'when the sun was shining'. In the early 1950s Jill and Michael had read *Young Melbourne*, a classic biography by David Cecil, Michael's tutor at Oxford. They had been persuaded by the author's anti-Byron portrait. So Venice became part of the rehabilitation campaign that eventually resulted in *The Politics of Paradise: A Vindication of Byron* (1988). Only Michael's Bevan biography receives a better blessing in Jill's letters.

Only one city, from Jill's point of view, equalled and in some respects surpassed Venice, and that was Dubrovnik in Croatia. The Yugoslav Communist Party had invited Michael to Belgrade shortly after he became leader of the Labour Party. The Yugoslavs asked him, 'Why do the Tories treat us better than you do?' Michael answered, 'It's all because of Djilas.'* Michael agreed to visit Belgrade only after the Central Committee granted his request to question the restrictions put on Tito's chief critic. On that trip Michael was taken to Dubrovnik. Enchanted, he walked the length of the ancient city wall with its fine views of the city, the hillsides and the sea. On his return home, he said to Jill: 'Here, you want a new place to go for your holidays …'.

Jill and Michael found Dubrovnik more intimate than Venice. It is such a compact city. As she departed and looked back at Dubrovnik, Rebecca West called it 'a city on a coin'. 'Dubrovnik has a dramatic beauty, Venice is a playground,' suggested Vesna Gamulin, who would befriend Jill and Michael in Dubrovnik.

Jill and Michael nearly always stayed at the Villa Dubrovnik – usually in September. Throughout their stays, before and after the 1991 war, the hotel's manager, Nada Marić, the only woman manager of such an establishment in the city, took care of them. From the villa, seated on a hill, the city shines in the distance, a fairy-tale kingdom complete with an old encompassing city

---

* Milovan Djilas (1911–95) had stayed at Pilgrim's Lane for a week during a trip to London. Michael had reviewed his books and regarded him as one of the finest Marxist thinkers and historians of the twentieth century.

wall and streets with small Renaissance palaces. Walking down the hill and into the charming streets, Jill and Michael visited galleries and ate in restaurants. They gathered about them a group of friends in the arts and in politics, including Stevan Dedijer, a Serb who remained a fervent citizen of Dubrovnik and an adamant opponent of Slobodan Milošević's regime in Belgrade (1988–2000). Stevan's brother, Vladimir, a journalist (one of the few brave Communists to support Djilas at his trial in 1955), had also befriended Jill and Michael. Family members and friends also began to come to this Craigie and Foot rendezvous.

In one of the public art galleries Jill saw a painting by Duro Pulitika. She said to Michael: 'I want to meet that chap.' They quickly found their way to the artist's studio, and Jill began to collect a significant collection of his work. The 'liquid mass of colour' made the interior of Pilgrim's Lane another garden.

Here was the artist for her, a man of her own romantic, exuberant and erotic sensibility. Michael thought the rapport between his wife and the artist was almost instantaneous. Jill used to flirt with Duro, Julie remembered. 'She found him very attractive.' Vesna noticed it but wasn't sure that Duro did. He did not speak English, but his wife Mira did, and the couples, along with Vesna, would go out together. Seeing Duro, Michael remembers, became the highlight of Jill's holiday. To Julie (6 September 1987) Jill wrote: 'The Yugoslavs are painting so superbly that I am convinced there will be as big an interest in the artists here in some twenty years time as there was in the French impressionists.'

When Jill and Michael began their yearly pilgrimages to Dubrovnik, Tito, the architect of post World War II Yugoslavia, had been dead for about a year* and the city was still part of the former Yugoslavia. In March and April 1981 Kosovo erupted in riots and demonstrations against the central government's repressive measures. Students demanded autonomy, if not outright independence, for the overwhelming Albanian majority. The central government, however, continued Tito's policy of a centralized state and refused to negotiate. A new 'collective presidency' now ruled the country, with the leaders of the six republics and two autonomous provinces serving rotating one-year terms. By 1987 Slobodan Milošević, then President of the League of Communists of Serbia, had become the focal point of Serbian nationalism by exploiting Serbian fears that the Kosovo Albanians intended to suppress or even drive out the Serbian minority. With the break up of the Soviet bloc at the end of the 1980s, the individual countries within Yugoslavia, long forced

---

* He died on 4 May 1980, just three days short of his eighty-eighth birthday.

together, began to break away. Slovenia quickly established its independence in July 1991, and managed to avoid the bloody conflict that spread from Croatia, through Bosnia-Herzegovina into Kosovo. In late July 1991, the Yugoslav air force attacked central Croatia and began invading and occupying parts of the Dalmatian coast.

Jill and Michael were in Dubrovnik in early September 1991. For the first time Michael heard the words 'ethnic cleansing', spoken by a man from Belgrade. 'They are going to claim every territory that has Serbs.' Well, there were not that many Serbs in Dubrovnik, Michael replied. 'They don't mean just areas with Serb majorities but any area where there are Serbs.' Jill and Michael were not then aware of the scale of the Serbian attack to the north, but they soon discovered the dire situation: instead of flying home directly from Dubrovnik, they had to go first to Montenegro, then they flew to Belgrade and on to London. By the end of September, Dubrovnik was blockaded.

Jill and Michael watched the month-by-month disintegration of Yugoslavia with horror and outrage. They had not wanted to see Yugoslavia break up, but they were keenly aware of the country's failings and they supported the independence movements, especially in Croatia. As Stevan Dedijer told them, 'For Serbia to be free, Croatia must be free.' They were appalled that US and British government policy rejected the recognition of Slovenia and Croatia. Western governments from that point on would consistently underestimate the will to resist Serb advances in Croatia and Bosnia-Herzegovina. Jill and Michael believed that in spite of the Serb military superiority, the Croats and Bosnians could not be conquered without at least tacit Western support. In October the Yugoslav Air Force attacked Zagreb. On 17 October the 120-day siege of Dubrovnik began. The Yugoslav navy bombarded the heart of old Dubrovnik, which dates back to Roman times. Heavy shelling continued into November. On 18 November the city of Vukovar was destroyed. On 6 December shelling of Dubrovnik continued for ten straight hours. Three days later the Yugoslav navy withdrew, leaving much of Dubrovnik in ruins. Finally, on 15 January 1992 the European Community recognized Slovenia and Croatia. Soon the violence would shift to Bosnia-Herzegovina.

On 26 August 1992, in the aftermath of Dubrovnik's devastation, Mira Pulitika wrote to Jill and Michael that she and Duro had remained in Dubrovnik because it was their home. She recalled their last meeting in Duro's studio, drinking champagne and toasting their new country. They never imagined that such a brutal 'crucifying' war would try to rob them of their city and their history. 'To attack Dubrovnik means to attack the very foundations of western civilization,' Mira wrote. Dubrovnik had suffered catastrophic damage – thousands of shells had fallen on the city and its suburbs, killing and maiming people. Duro and Mira had lived for five months without electricity and running water. His native village, Bosanka, 'doesn't exist any-more', she informed Jill and Michael. Much of the surrounding area had been burned. Virtually every hotel except the Villa Dubrovnik had been destroyed. The shelling had stopped; now the hell they had suffered seemed an 'ugly dream'. She ended her letter: 'But, we know we are going to reach freedom and peace. And see you again in eternal Dubrovnik. Thank you again for your taking part in our tragedy… We know you did everything you could.'

The day before, Michael had published in the *Guardian* an attack on British diplomacy, which in the past twelve months had pursued a 'policy of appease-ment: a constant misjudgement about what was actually happening, and a persistently pusillanimous response to it. And it is these two features of our policy which have fed the ambitions of the aggressor.' Virtually every observer on the ground – as well as common sense – corroborated correspondent Mark Thompson's eyewitness reports in *Tribune*: 'Along with the rest of the outside world, I watched Serbia destroy Yugoslavia in the name of Yugoslavia while stirring up disaster for itself in the name of its own future.' Thompson's book, *A Paper House: The Ending of Yugoslavia*, published three months earlier, presented an irrefutable case. It made nonsense of Lord Blake's comment, 'No one can stop these tribes slaughtering each other.' These 'tribes', Michael pointed out, had combined to throw out their imperial masters; these 'tribes', in the past, had earned British backing. Writing at the time of a London conference on the wars in Yugoslavia, Michael concluded: 'It is our business to ensure that the London conference is not turned into another Munich.'

It took the Balkan wars to revive the film career of Jill Craigie, now eighty-one, and it became as much her war as the Blitz had been. Searching for a way to arouse public opinion about the desolation of Dubrovnik and about a war spreading to Bosnia and beyond, Jill attended meetings of the Croatian Peace Forum and met Branka Magas, author of *The Destruction of Yugoslavia: Tracking the Break-Up 1980–92* (1993) and editor of *The War in Croatia and Bosnia-Herzegovina 1991–1995* (2001). Branka and her husband, Quintin Hoare, became frequent guests at Pilgrim's Lane. 'I doubt whether Jill would have had the energy to make the film if she had not met Branka, a great driving force,' Michael believed. Jill was thrilled to have this support from someone who knew the history of the region and had witnessed Yugoslavia's break-up. For Michael, Branka was now added to the list of Jill's mentors – 'enthusiasts like Charles Reilly and all the great ones who had a zest for their own jobs'.

Branka and Quintin especially valued Jill's and Michael's support on letters to the British newspapers, because much of the old left either opposed intervention to stop the wars or ignored the issue. A kind of sisterhood with Branka emboldened Jill and encouraged her to build on her simple, instinctive feeling that the stories filling British newspapers about Croatia as some kind of dark, tribal, blood-lusting, fascist land were ludicrous. Jill saw that Branka and Quintin shared the confidence she had placed in Stevan Dedijer, a pivotal figure who had seen it all, so to speak, from inside Tito's Belgrade to the new Croatia emerging under the new president Franjo Tudjman.

'Jill was fearless, absolutely fearless,' Branka asserted. 'She never thought anything was too difficult or any person too difficult to take on.' Quintin remembered that she had 'real stand-up arguments with people like Denis Healey'. Michael called him 'Denis the realist who makes these great pronouncements'. Denis said to Jill: 'What nonsense you people are talking about Yugoslavia. Milošević is going to stay. You needn't think you can get rid of him.' Jill would ring Branka up and say, 'Have you seen… Someone ought to write a letter!' Branka established connections for Jill in Zagreb, where she gathered material for her proposed film.

When Jill first proposed making a film, Michael balked. Walking with him on Hampstead Heath, Julie said, 'Listen. Jill *wants to go.*'

'Oh, it's a bad idea.'

'She wants to go and there's talk of me taking a camera and going with her.'

'No, ridiculous, my child, ridiculous.'

Initially Michael had 'the same doubts we all had', broadcaster Jon Snow remembered. Could Jill translate her passion into a viable film? Then Julie phoned her son Jason, now an experienced cinematographer: 'Where do I get … and how do I use …'. She had never touched a video camera but thought she could learn. Jason told her what to do, but eventually – like Michael – he got involved. 'She got Michael so fired up about it that he was going to do what she told him to do,' Snow said.

Snow was shopping at Sainsbury's in Camden Town when she accosted him about the film that '*had to happen.* She was *obsessed with it, absolutely obsessed*': '*You* have got to get *me* a meeting with Michael Grade [the head of Channel 4]. You've got to get it commissioned, paid for…'. Jon told her that people were fed up with Bosnia and were telling Channel 4 not to do so much on the subject, and Snow felt the pressure to do less. So to Jon the idea of ringing up the head of Channel 4 and saying: 'Hey, you know Michael Foot's wife, Jill Craigie, wants you to commission her,' was likely to get the reply: 'Jon, you can bring me many things, but do not bring me another documentary, least of all one made by two octogenarians.' Jon said to Jill: 'You've got to make it. The idea of you and Michael going into this war-torn country and making the film, I have absolutely no doubt that if you ever do it, it will get placed.' Jon admitted that his 'heart was in his boots'. He could not imagine Michael with his expansive all-over-the shop kind of political presentation harnessed to deliver a narrative track for a film made in the middle of Dubrovnik. 'It just isn't his skill. He has always been inapplicable to the television age.'

Jill would call up Jon regularly, giving progress reports: 'I've done this. I've managed to get that.' Jason had agreed to be the cameraman and co-producer; Michael had sunk a part of his pension (£12,000) into the film. But their efforts to raise money from wealthy friends proved fruitless. Harold Lever (1914–95), a financial genius and a Labour MP (1945–79), turned Michael down. Sidney Bernstein (1899–1993), a British film producer and founder of Granada, 'was awful,' Michael said, 'I had to pay for the bloody lunch in the end.'

Channel 4, the BBC and others rejected the treatment Jill co-wrote with Jason. But Jon Snow could see the project coming together; if anything, Craigie & Co. became more determined with every rebuff. Now feeling responsible for encouraging Jill, Jon had a talk with Channel 4 before Jill and Michael embarked for Dubrovnik. 'Let's see what happens' came the sceptical response. Even if the film got made, though, Jon feared they would bankrupt themselves.

Without Jason, it is hard to see how Jill could have made a film. He became intrigued with the idea of going into a war zone with Jill and Michael. Jason's film company, Open Eye, put up almost as much money as Michael had. Every other service performed for the film, including the work of the crew, came gratis with the promise of payment if the film ever made any money. But everyone concerned went ahead knowing they might never even make back their expenses.

Jason's contribution to *Two Hours From London* grew out of Jill's encouragement, years earlier, when he had expressed an interest in film. She introduced him to Oswald Morris, who had been Kubrick's cinematographer for *Lolita* (1962). And Jason made his way up from assistant editor to cameraman to director, learning his craft as Jill had once wanted to do.

Jason's strongest memory is of the December 1993 trip to Dubrovnik. Jill had angina exacerbated by sudden changes in temperature. They arrived in a freezing Zagreb a week before Christmas. A fog grounded all planes to Dubrovnik. But they had to be in the city the next day in order to start the shooting schedule. Jason found an old Croatian bus. Jill hated buses and would have relapses as the bus climbed up and over the mountains, with Jason and another crew member holding her up in the cramped vehicle as she tried to catch her breath. Jason remembered a moment in that numbing fourteen-hour bus expedition when the vehicle slowed and all the lights inside and out were turned off. They were now in the war zone. Jason looked out and could see burning embers. Frightened, they broke out a bottle of duty-free brandy. Jason looked across at Jill. She was beaming, 'a HUGE smile', he said, 'absolutely enjoying every moment of it'. Later Jill told Jason that she had been reminded of the war, the greatest part of her life.

They arrived two days before Christmas with the sun shining. 'I never saw it looking so beautiful,' Michael remembered. Stevan Dedijer met them. Jill had sent him questions in preparation for her film. The Villa Dubrovnik housed refugees. Duro Pulitika's studio had been changed into a command centre during the siege because he had such a good view of the harbour. During seven intense days of shooting, Vesna watched Jill and Jason row. 'She *had her ways with him!* He had to listen to her, although sometimes he rebelled. It was two professionals arguing, not a grandmother and grandson.' Jill gave no ground. Jason got fed up with retakes. 'No,' Jill said, 'we have to do it again.' And they would do it again. 'Jill was magnetic,' Vesna emphasized. 'We wanted to be part of whatever she decided.'

All this activity cloaked Jill's fragility. Only from a distance, when you could watch her coming towards you, did you notice she was old. 'In her company, you forgot everything except her eyes and what she said.' Vesna recalled. Vesna never saw Jill and Michael quarrel. On the contrary, the bond between them seemed absolute, personally and politically. They were on the same mission together, with Jill in charge. Vesna introduced Jill to Kathy Wilkes, a don at St Hilda's College, Oxford, who had become, through two decades of visits to Dubrovnik, an honorary citizen, and who brought medical supplies into her beloved city during the siege in a twenty-year-old British ambulance.

Vesna and Kathy provided the essential contacts and the facilities for the making of Jill's film. Vesna, who acted as their interpreter, working as Chief of Protocol in the Dubrovnik City Hall, organized meetings with the Mayor and took Jill and Michael to the sites they wanted to film. Kathy also got access to places that would have been forbidden to anyone else. Kathy, a great admirer of Michael Foot, watched in dismay as Jill dictated to Michael where he should stand, what he should do and so on. She had him standing in a cold, raging wind and crouching next to a concrete pillar where a Serb sniper would have been. But she didn't like the angle of the shot and tried another. 'Jill ruled us all and Michael took orders,' Kathy said.

Returning home in early 1994, Jill and Jason had much work to do yet to complete the film.* It had started out almost as a home movie, but in order to present an overwhelming indictment of the West – and most especially of John Major's government – which had stood by while a designated world heritage site was decimated, the outraged protests of Conservative MPs such as Patrick Cormack, as well as of Margaret Thatcher, were included. Their words would be intercut with scenes of carnage, political testimony punctuated by Michael's on-the-spot interviews with Dubrovnik's defenders. Jill wanted Michael to speak her narrative in intense but subdued tones – quite the opposite of the oratory he had employed in the Commons. But Michael found it difficult to adjust to the kind of intimate voice the medium demanded. Jason wanted to sack him. Jill took Michael into the studio and with infinite patience went over every word with him. There were arguments. Jill always won. 'Say it this way,' she told Michael. In the *Daily Telegraph* (4 January 1995), she said: 'If he didn't do it properly, he went back to the top.' She wanted the emotion, but she wanted it in practically a whisper. 'He has never had to speak so quietly or so slowly.'

Jill did not appear on camera but in fact she did most of the interviews. Michael was not good on his feet; he did not know what questions to ask. 'He didn't know what the film needed,' Jason concluded. 'He would get stuck. He didn't know how to improvise because he didn't know his objective, really. It was not a failing of his. The film simply wasn't his vision.'

The film also needed a finale, a break away from the action to a higher ground. Jason wanted a big name to make the film sellable, but also someone who could speak authoritatively about ethnic cleansing and religious fundamentalism. Over dinner in Dubrovnik while shooting the film, Jason proposed that Jill bring in Salman Rushdie. Jill balked. It was her film – and Michael's. 'It came across to me that she did not want to be overwhelmed by the greatness of other people. That argument went on for a long time.' Eventually Jill agreed, and during one of Salman's visits to Pilgrim's Lane she put questions to him. Jason saw her treating Salman with 'kid gloves', and persevered with some questions of his own. 'It was interesting because she took it very personally,' Jason said. He was thinking of the film, and Jill (Jason

---

* Jill received a good deal of information and encouragement from Bill Tribe, an English teacher who had taught in Dubrovnik for twenty-six years, who wrote her a long letter on 8 March 1994: 'When I arrived in Britain in late August 1992 I was shocked at the media reportage of the war. The Bosnian government for which I had worked and whose cause was so obviously just, reduced to merely "the Muslims", a "warring faction"!'

thought) was thinking of Michael. She did not want Salman to overshadow him.*

In the event, Jill had no cause for worry. *Two Hours From London* turns on the axis between Michael Foot and Salman Rushdie. These two great figures stretch across cultures and political arguments and provide the human rights argument on which the film is founded. Of all the commentators (public and private), two of Jill's friends, the broadcaster and novelist Melvyn Bragg and the philosopher Ted Honderich (28 December 1994) came closest to articulating Jill's aesthetic in their letters of appreciation. Bragg (30 January 1995) noticed how beautifully the sound track had been synchronized with the images and the narrative. Honderich noticed that the film was not a collection of arguments, but *an argument*, a cohesive whole.

The film opens with a siren and images of tanks, a suffering woman and burning buildings superimposed on Dubrovnik's Renaissance architecture. Labour MP Malcolm Wicks describes a 3 a.m. session in Parliament when Edward Heath, that great European, that staunch promoter of the Common Market, pleaded with the Conservative Prime Minister John Major to promise not to intervene in Bosnia. 'A huge murmur arose in the House of Commons – mainly on the government benches, but I'm sorry to say partly on the opposition benches too. And I thought that's it, that's the murmur of Munich.'

Accompanied by the sounds of shelling, Conservative MP Sir Patrick Cormack observes that the failure to come to the aid of the Bosnian Muslims, a minority in the heart of Europe, sets off 'awful echoes of the Holocaust.' One Croat historian notes that Dubrovnik was a 'test case'. The Serbs knew that if they could shell Dubrovnik with impunity, then there was no reason to suppose the project of establishing a greater Serbia could be stopped. 'This was not and never was a Civil War,' Michael observes, 'it was mainly an unprovoked attack on civilians by a heavily armed military force. It was genocide. How is it possible that we should have allowed such sights as these again in this century?' In the editing, Jill carefully integrated Salman Rushdie's concluding words into the action of the film. He begins: 'Europe has betrayed an idea of itself. What you have is a Bosnian government that claimed to wish to uphold European values – pluralism and tolerance and multiethnicity, and against this government has been ranged a nationalistic, racist and murderous aggressive force.'

Salman Rushdie concludes: 'What does one say to growing up children of murdered parents?... What does one do to persuade these children to accept

---

* Hearing her son Jason tell the story, Julie broke in: 'She never let on. I never knew that.'

European values?… What does one say ten years from now, fifteen years from now … and we find ourselves with a Hamas or Hizbullah sitting on the edge of Western Europe and launching revenge attacks?' 'As for ourselves', Michael adds, 'how can we live with the shame of looking the other way?'

Then the full images of horror flash on the screen. After watching the film, Jon Snow wrote to Jill on 14 December 1994: 'I will not forget for a long time the final image of the child with arms aloft.'

Jon Snow admitted later that he had been quite nervous about coming to see the film.* What would he say if the film wasn't any good? Gerald Isaaman, former editor of *Ham & High* and a friend, wrote to Jill and Michael:

> The film … tells the whole horrific story in a chronological and comprehensive way, something which all the media, not to mention the awful politicians have failed to do so far. It is a confused and confusing story, but the public in general has been unable to grasp the true significance of each new development because, basically, nobody explained fully how the whole jigsaw goes together. That is your great achievement, and also that of Jason.

Denis Forman thought it a marvellous film, but it was 'too biased. You'll never get it on the BBC.' Jill thought BBC rules about bias were nonsense. The whole point about a political film is that it has a point of view. Jill had attacked the BBC fairness doctrine as early as 6 July 1962 in a *Tribune* article, 'Pilkington: A Second Chance for Television', arguing: 'Every democrat would agree that a fair hearing should be given to all and that the BBC itself be neutral. But why always in each programme?… On television, nobody is allowed to win, they can only cancel each other out.'

By 16 December the film had been acclaimed in Zagreb, but neither Channel 4 nor the BBC seemed prepared to broadcast *Two Hours From London*. In a letter dated 20 December 1994 that David Lloyd of Channel 4 sent to Richard Tindle, Jason's colleague at Open Eye, Lloyd worried that Tudjman 'gets off <u>extremely</u> lightly – to put it mildly'. He professed not to object to the film as a polemic, but rather because 'no Serb or Western government viewpoints are included or sought out in the film, it is clearly not an impartial piece of work, as the Broadcasting Act … defines such things'. To show the film would necessitate a discussion afterwards that was as long as the film itself. Lloyd did not reject the film but his response was not encouraging.

Then on 1 January 1995 a huge spread in the *Observer* headlined 'Foot

---

* 'Not as nervous as we were showing it for the first time,' Michael said.

Names Guilty Men of Bosnia' told the story of the making of *Two Hours From London*. The article's title carried an illusion to the famous pamphlet *Guilty Men* that Michael and others had written, denouncing the appeasers who had left England unprepared for World War II. The dramatic story of how the film was made, together with spirited comments from Michael and Jill and descriptions of the film's techniques, made fascinating and provocative reading:

> Craigie uses the type of shots you see in any documentary of the rise of Nazism: Nuremberg-style rallies, parading soldiers, Milošević in slow motion summoning the demons of nationalism from the crowds. The maps, with their encroaching flood of Serbian conquests, are shown in colours reminiscent of the maps of the spread of Germany: rich yellow, purple, and red.

Ultimately, the publicity about the film, along with Jason's deft playing off of the contending parties against each other, eventually produced a sale for £50,000 to the BBC, making just enough to pay everyone for their services. Broadcast in the spring of 1995, *Two Hours From London* received fine reviews, most of which emphasized its lucidity, passion and 'homemade sincerity'. John Naughton in the *Observer* (2 April 1995) wrote:

> Here is an elderly couple, one of them in frail health, who should be spending their twilight years enjoying the quiet, bookish celebrity to which they are richly entitled. And yet they are so moved and outraged by what they see happening in the heart of Europe, and so enraged by the dishonesty and moral cowardice of their governments that they sink their savings and a year of their lives in a magnificent attempt to counter some of the lies and equivocations which have underpinned the betrayal of the Bosnian people. And what do they get?
>
>   Why, they get a 'balancing' discussion, chaired by Michael Ignatieff on *The Late Show* (BBC 2) later the same evening. Round the table are: Alan Clark, tumescent diarist; Edward Pearce, moral maze-dweller; Fred Halliday, omniscient don; Norman Stone, street-fightin' historian; and Mary Kaldor, who serves as both token female and statutory liberal.

Salman Rushdie came in for mixed reactions: 'Nor, sadly, if you want to get your point across to the British people, is the controversial figure of Salman Rushdie the most obvious of witnesses to call,' wrote Peter Patterson in the *Daily Mail* (30 March 1995). Tim Lusher, *Western Morning News* (30 March 1995), praised Rushdie's eloquence and the appropriateness of including him in the film. A few other critics carped at the film's one-sidedness or still thought Britain should stay out of the Balkans. But most critics found

Rushdie's account of Europe's self-betrayal compelling. 'In more than 15 years of reporting on TV programmes I've never seen a more moving or a more shaming film,' wrote Graham Keal in the *Northern Echo* (29 March 1995).

The fiercest attack came from Professor Tobias Abse (Leo's son). He wrote to the *Ham & High* (1 September 1995) to express his astonishment that Jill and Michael had been able to 'swallow, without reservations, the official Croatian government line ...'. Abse was not pro-Serb. He insisted the conflict was a religious civil war and pointed out that Serbs, Croats and Bosnians are all ethnically the same. There was also no distinct Croatian language. Tudjman was an anti-Semite. Croatia was undemocratic. Only the former Yugoslavia, with all its faults, had provided a structure for a pluralistic society. Jill's reply noted that Abse's picture simply did not square with what she had observed and had absorbed from her Serb friend Stevan Dedijer, a longtime resident of Dubrovnik. Michael's reply did not seek to exonerate Tudjman, but none of Abse's points could deflect Michael from seeing that from the start the aggression had been 'organised and directed by Milošević in Belgrade'.[1]

A more disturbing response came from Paul Foot. 'It was the only time I've had harsh words with Jill,' Paul said. 'On that one she just baited me. She rang me up and just went on and on and on,' telling him that his position was 'unacceptable. Why do you take such a ridiculous line?' Finally, Paul remembered, 'I just snapped – let loose what I thought – she shut up at once.' He did not think that she had 'thought it through in the terms I was arguing. I'm not pro-Serb or pro-Croat or anything. To take either side was to damage the internationalist position.' He could not support the 'bloody reactionary nationalists on either side'. Paul had other political differences with Jill and Michael, but only his stance on the break-up of Yugoslavia upset her.

The reviews of the film mentioned Jill but often focused on Michael, as if he had authored the film, whereas in fact every word he spoke had been Jill's. 'It *sounds* as if it is made by me, but it's not mine. It was all shaped by her. She understood what would happen on the street before I set foot on it,' Michael said. She changed the script and improvised and kept shaping the documentary as she discovered new film clips.

It hurt Jill to be overshadowed. Jason and Julie could see how much she wanted recognition. 'She was two people,' Julie suggested. 'The public face she wanted people to see was taking a backseat. It isn't really what she wanted at all.'

Shortly after making *Two Hours From London*, Jill and Michael attended a birthday party for Neil Kinnock, hosted by their mutual friend Lord Paul. Robin Cook, then shadow foreign secretary, was there. 'And she went for him!' Michael recalled with relish. She upbraided him for not really applying his mind to what was happening in the former Yugoslavia. The party needed to take a firm stance on Serb aggression. 'You are just very arrogant.' Jill went on – 'so much so,' Michael added, that James Callaghan came up to her and said, 'Jill, you should let him off now.' But Jill continued. 'She wasn't going to let him off,' Branka concluded.

Jill was quite aware that *Two Hours From London* had defects, as she wrote to David Lloyd of Channel 4 on 4 January 1995. In a new film, *Our Legacy*, she wanted to address the central weakness of *Two Hours From London*: 'an excess of commentary over pauses and the failure to forestall obvious criticisms, i.e. no interviews with Serbs, no indictment of Tudjman'. The film would be set in Kosovo and would centre on key Albanian characters living in a police state. As in her previous film, there would have to be a narrative – a kind of potted history of Milošević and how he achieved power – but the emphasis would shift to the implications for the rest of Europe. What were the consequences of Serbian aggression and what resulted from the destruction of cities like Vukovar? What happened to the refugees? Would the United Nations punish war criminals? One of her guides would be Noel Malcolm's book, *Kosovo*. As to the dangers involved in filming once again in the Balkans, Jill concluded: 'I note that Maggie O'Kane, renowned for her anti-Serb articles, is now working in Belgrade, apparently in safety. What she can do so can we.' Alas, the film did not get made, and it took its place among many other projects Jill might have completed had she been able to live to a biblical old age.

29

Wife and Mother
(1994–9)

At a Pilgrim's Lane dinner in late 1994 or early 1995 for Salman Rushdie and Elizabeth West, Jill told the story of her rape. Jon and Madeleine Snow were also there. She had held this secret for more than forty years, telling only a few friends, including Ronnie Neame, Julie, Anne Robinson and June Purvis. Jill's frustration increased over the years when she heard that Koestler had tried to rape Dick Crossman's second wife and learned that Anthony Crosland (1918–77), who served with Michael in Harold Wilson's Cabinet, said 'You know he's a rapist.' 'It was an enormously charged evening,' Jon remembered. Somebody at the table had just said something about Koestler. Jill had been drinking and without any sort of inhibition proceeded to tell the story. 'I don't think she meant to,' Jon said, 'but she had been waiting a long time to tell it. It was as if somebody had pulled the plug out of the dam and it came gushing out. We were pole-axed. Michael sat, silent. You could see she was absolutely contorted about it – right to that day.' Her confession led to some discussion of Koestler's influence and how he had manipulated people. 'I was very, very surprised that it ever came out in print. I don't think she ever wanted it to come out in print,' Jon noted.

On 8 April 1995, in a review in the *Financial Times* of a book on espionage, Michael commented briefly on his relationship with Koestler and mentioned their quarrels – adding, by way of conclusion: 'My quarrels with him were not solely political. I discovered, years after the attempt, that he had tried to rape my wife.' The wording is curious, of course, since Jill had made graphically clear that the 'attempt' had succeeded. 'I didn't spell out the whole thing then,' Michael said afterwards. Julie thought it was the journalist in Michael. He knew it was a good story.*

* There is merit in Julie's remark, since Michael's review is written as a cliffhanger, beginning with the intimation that he has a personal matter to discuss and then concludes with the bombshell sentence about the rape.

The next day, Barry Hugill, in 'Koestler tried to rape my wife claims Foot' (*Guardian*, 9 April 1995), called Koestler a 'serial harasser of women who had attempted at least two rapes'. In addition to Jill, he had accosted Inezita Baker, Richard Crossman's second wife. Hugill had called Jill and she said, 'I really don't want to talk about it, but it is absolutely true.' Then Hugill quoted a senior Labour figure (unnamed) in the Wilson and Callaghan government who said, 'He was a terrible man. He made advances to my wife. He was quite blatant. I knew about the attack on Jill Craigie and it is quite possible there were many more.'

'Jill did NOT know that Michael was going to mention the rape,' Julie insisted:[1] 'I was round at Pilgrim's Lane having morning coffee with Jill when the phone never stopped ringing, and Jill was getting very annoyed and upset to say the least, the press would not leave her alone.' Julie and Elizabeth West remembered that Jill was quite angry with Michael.

Michael Scammell, Koestler's authorised biographer, wrote to the *Observer* (23 April 1995) to point out that rape is a 'highly charged word and needs to be used with precision'. A few years earlier he had interviewed Michael Foot, who had declined to comment on Koestler's relations with women. Jill had refused to speak to Scammell. Scammell speculated that Koestler's 'unaccustomed vigour and physicality' had shocked her 'sense of decorum' and made her think he was 'bent on rape'. If Jill had only been more firm – more physical – Koestler would have 'grinned and walked away'. The cosmopolitan Koestler, who grew up in Budapest and Vienna and lived in Paris and Berlin in the 1930s was the product of a time that had a more 'casual attitude to sex and romantic liaisons than that prevailing in Britain'.

Scammell's presumptions require comment since they impugn Jill's story. In 1952 Jill Craigie was forty-one years old and had enjoyed a rather full and varied sexual life. She was hardly a British provincial unaware of sexual practices on the Continent or likely to confuse an aggressive come-on with a rape. As to Jill's not seeing Scammell, it is clear that she had not intended her story for print. Indeed, without more from Jill, the story faded – until another Koestler biographer, David Cesarini, came calling. Jill gave Cesarini, for the first time, a full account of the rape. The biographer treated her account with great care, sending the proofs to Jill for her review. Michael later praised Cesarini for 'absolute accuracy'.

The serialization of Cesarini's *Arthur Koestler: The Homeless Mind* (1998) in the *Daily Telegraph* suddenly made Jill's rape a matter of public controversy. In contrast to Scammell, Frederic Raphael argued that Jill was not a naive young woman and should have known that Koestler was a reckless man. In effect, he accused her of living dangerously and then crying about the consequences.[2] Raphael attacked Cesarini for making Koestler's 'phallocentric behaviour' the main issue, rather than his contributions to literary and political history. Jill replied in 'I was worried about my life, not my honour', an interview with Libby Brooks and Stephen Moss (*Guardian*, 25 February 1999):

> I never expected to be believed, you see. It was bound to happen. There is always suspicion. They always think that the woman did something... But I did expect Arthur Koestler to be had up. I used to look through the Sunday papers waiting for it. I thought that some woman was bound to report him to the police. I thought that he wouldn't get away with it, but I was wrong.

On 5 March 1999 Catherine Peters wrote to the *Guardian* describing her own narrow escape from Koestler. In 1950 she spent a summer in Paris. Then just nineteen, she was introduced by her father to Koestler, 'one of the most interesting and stimulating people I have ever met'. A few days later he telephoned her and invited her to a restaurant. Afterwards, he suggested they go to a hotel for the afternoon:

> I declined, repeatedly and with increasing vehemence. He seemed to accept this; the conversation reverted to general matters, and I foolishly accepted a lift to my lodgings. Once in the car the attack became physical and violent, and I have no doubt that if I had not leapt out in a traffic jam I should have been abducted and raped.

Peters told her father and he made Koestler apologize to her. They remained friends, although she never permitted herself to be alone with him again. 'I don't know whether this fascinating man was "a serial rapist". I do know he was capable of a totally unexpected and unprovoked attack on a woman, and I believe every word of Jill Craigie's story.' Jill received many consoling letters from women – some with their own stories of male abuse and rape, stories that they also had never dared to tell.

The burgeoning story agitated the authorised biographer, who wrote to *The Times Literary Supplement* (23 April 1999), attacking Cesarani for misleading the librarian in charge of the Koestler Collection at Edinburgh University. Cesarani had said he was making a study of Koestler's Jewish identity and not attempting a full-scale biography. The aggrieved Scammell noted: 'I was granted exclusive use of the archive for biographical purposes by the literary executor of the Koestler estate, and Cesarani has not only destroyed that exclusivity, but also pre-empted an enormous body of material including photographs that I would have been the first to publish.' This accusation of bad faith drove Scammell on to animadversions on Cesarani's 'overheated' biography and to casting further doubt on Jill's story. He listed his many interviews with the women in Koestler's life and concluded: 'Not once did I hear the accusation that Koestler raped, or attempted to rape, any of these women or their friends.' Then he tried to push Jill right off the pages of any Koestler biography: 'She revealed her story to Cesarani at literally the eleventh hour, barely two months before his book was published, so that there was no time for reflections on the part of Cesarani, nor, apparently, any desire for it.'

As Scammell explained in a letter to Michael Foot (15 June 2000), he came to London in search of women who knew Jill and perhaps knew about the rape or were in a position to assess her truthfulness. He assumed that Jill and Michael had chosen Cesarani to tell the full story because Scammell might 'conceal or play down this incident'. He supposed that Michael realized that many of Jill's friends did not believe her story – or at best thought she had exaggerated or garbled her memory of what happened – 'particularly since she made it public only at the very end of her life. My goal was to test these theories finding women that your wife had confided in many years earlier, much closer to the time when the incident happened and in this I was successful.'[3] But Jill had not revealed the story in her dying days – which is just one of the hasty Scammell's erroneous impressions.

Michael replied to Scammell's letter on 26 June, noting that he had proposed a meeting with Scammell on his last trip to London. He stood by the integrity of Jill's story and Cesarani's biography. On 19 July, Scammell wrote to apologize for his previous 'unduly sharp' letter. He was not aware of Michael's earlier proposal for a meeting. But Scammell was most interested in attacking Cesarani, a 'pirate-biographer'. He again repeated that Jill's story was 'widely disbelieved, especially by members of your and her generation, including many who knew her personally though not necessarily very well'.

The correspondence ended with Michael's reply on 18 August 2000:

> I have received your letter of July 19 and I have read it, as I believe any normal person would, with a rising resentment. It should disqualify you altogether from being regarded in any quarter as a reputable biographer. If you are making any reference to Jill Craigie in your own book… I trust that you will invite your publisher to print the whole of our correspondence … it is evident from what you have written me that you are not to be trusted to report faithfully on the matter.

Michael concluded by noting that Jenny Stringer suggested to Scammell that he interview Michael 'weeks before you interviewed her or Anne Robinson'.

Neither Jenny nor Anne were among those Scammell sources who disbelieved Jill. Indeed, when I sent an e-mail to Scammell asking if he still doubted Jill's story, he replied (3 February 2002) that the 'balance of evidence' confirmed Jill's story. He did not say why he had changed his mind. But in the end, as Michael Sheldon, biographer of George Orwell and Graham Greene, put the case in *The Times Literary Supplement* (15 January 1999): 'One cannot ignore the disturbing testimony of Jill Craigie.'

In the spring of 1994 Michael told Mervyn Jones that Jill was unhappy with the proofs of his biography of Michael. After Mervyn wrote a conciliatory note, Jill rang him up:

> 'I'm furious with you. I will not allow the book to go through in this shape. I will not allow this.'
> 'What are you talking about?'
> 'You're calling me a bad mother.'
> 'No, not at all.'

Mervyn took Jill out to a very good restaurant. 'It was a failure,' he confessed. At the end of their conversation Jill said, 'I hate you. And I will always hate you.' Mervyn shrugged. What could he do? He asked for the bill.

On 26 May, Jill followed up with a twelve-page double-spaced letter. After sparing a few sentences of praise for Mervyn's handling of *Tribune*, CND and related matters, she reiterated what had really soured her: 'the accusations you made against me in my capacity as a mother'. The final six pages constitute an item-by-item defence of the schools Julie attended and of the care Jill took of her only child. Mervyn stood by the account Julie had given him of her upbringing. Jill called Julie and ended up screaming at her. 'How could you speak to Mervyn like that?' Julie replied that Mervyn had not been careful to distinguish between Jill's upbringing and Julie's. 'How could he get it wrong?' Jill asked, 'He took notes.' When Julie explained to her mother that all she had told Mervyn was she did not like her boarding schools, Jill replied: 'Now I know what you said to Mervyn is true.' Julie felt, 'She never really believed me,' and it was 'impossible to erase it. She was too old ... the hurt was too great.'

Responding to Jill's anger, Michael put Jill's case to Mervyn, who said, 'All I've done is what Julie reported to me.' But he agreed to make changes in the paperback. Michael stuck by Mervyn, however, even helping to launch the book at various gatherings. Jill stayed away.* 'She did always hate me. She

---

* She could not have been pleased to see the references to her as Jill Foot in the text and in the index, which cites only about half the number of pages on which Jill appears in the narrative.

never forgave me. I was crossed off the dinner list. When I greeted her at a public meeting, she turned her back. She never spoke to me again.'

'I didn't read the biography at all carefully,' Michael admitted, suggesting he could have at least mitigated some of the quarrels. 'I was engaged then on my book about H.G. Wells.' But even if Michael had read Mervyn's biography more attentively, it is not certain he would have seen Jill's cause for grievance. He is not inclined to view human effort with suspicion.

Julie returned to this volatile atmosphere in December 1994 after her marriage to Myron Bloom had failed, despite her decade-long effort to acclimatize herself to America.* She had also lost a good deal of the money she had put into her American house, and re-entry into British life for a woman in her sixties was difficult. As journalist Martha Gellhorn said of herself at a similar age, she had lost her place in the queue.

On 21 June 1996 Julie wrote to Jill and Michael:

> It is not because I am unable to speak my thoughts that I am writing to you; it is because I want you to have it in writing to refer to should you ever forget how I feel.
>
> I am completely aware of the immense sacrifice you will be making for me in enabling me to buy this flat. I am also aware that it is not the first time you have helped me out financially. I think I have probably been quite a burden to you over the years to say the least. I am not proud of my record at all. And above all I am appalled at the situation I am now in. As you know it depresses me more than I can reasonably put into words. I really did not expect to find myself in such a situation at any point in my life. I seem to have made so many mistakes and am quite at a loss as to how I have failed so much. I dislike the situation I am now in more than perhaps you realise; and no way did I or do I take it for granted that you would help me in this way. My emotions overwhelm me when I think about it. I do realise that that may not appear to be the case when we talk, but I assure it is.

On 5 May 1998 Anne Robinson wrote to Jill: 'It would be wrong of you to think you have failed Judy. I think you have been wonderfully supportive and generous. As you have always been to all your women friends.' Anne remembered 'how wonderful you were to me when Penrose [Anne's husband] and I were going through that dreadful time. I bored you for hours every afternoon and you patiently listened. Also you were a fantastic source of ideas and I have learnt so much from you over the years.' Anne wrote candidly about her battle with alcoholism, her up-and-down career, and her troubles with her daughter in *Memoirs of an Unfit Mother* (2001): 'Alas, a mother's best is rarely enough. A mother's best can result in shocking damage and the

* Julie has written an absorbing account of this period in the unpublished *Aaron & Charlie: A Mother's Tale.*

second half of a child's life spent recovering from the first. A mother's place is in the wrong.' Jill had done her best, and only in retrospect did she realize (like other wartime parents) that it would have been better not to send Julie away to school during the war. The trauma of being sent away was worse than the danger of staying in London. Jill confessed as much in her long letter to Mervyn Jones.

There were truces and even happy reunions. Jill and Michael agreed to take some of the equity out of their house so that Julie could buy a flat in London. Julie accompanied them on a happy holiday to Dubrovnik in September 1995. Jill sent a postcard to a friend enthusing about a 'truly idyllic holiday without a tourist – alas for the locals – perfect unpolluted seas, perfect exotic blossoms, perfect fresh fish and shell fish, etc, etc, etc, this is the place, plus music, culture.'[4] Jill had not done much swimming since the onset of angina, but Julie, a strong swimmer, took her mother into the water with her. Julie suddenly felt an overwhelming joy and liberation. In the water her mother was vulnerable and childlike. 'It was so beautiful. That brought back the relationship I had with her when I was young', when they had been like girlfriends who 'told each other secrets that nobody knows'.

When You Grow Old

(1997–9)

In her last years Jill seemed as sharp as ever. Fiona Millar, then in Cherie Blair's office, remembers a dinner in March 1999 with Jill, Michael, the Goodmans, the Kinnocks and their daughter Rachel, and Matthew Lewin (then editor of the *Ham & High*) at which Jill was in good form and full of gossip about the current political scene. As old Labour, Jill and Michael had their reservations about Tony Blair & Co. Francis Wheen remembered Jill delivering a 'lengthy philippic' on the government's 'bullying of single mothers'. Then she leaned across the table and asked Michael loudly: 'Isn't that right?' Michael responded, 'What? What? Sorry, can't hear you.'[1] As Lord Paul said, 'You were never in doubt about Jill's opinions. If Michael did not want to answer a question, he remained silent.' 'It was very convenient for Michael that she could say all the things he couldn't say,' Anne Robinson observed. 'Yes,' John Penrose added, 'they balanced each other out.' Melvyn Bragg remembered how Michael would listen to Jill's arguments with 'incredible graciousness' and take her ideas seriously, but 'It did not change his mind if he disagreed with her: "You're right, Jill, very sensible. There is another point of view" and away he would go; "I happen to hold the other point of view. I know Jill will be angry. But I hold the other point of view."' In private, Bragg suspected, they were much the same.

Michael's characterization of his hero in *H.G.: The History of Mr Wells* (1995) might as well be a self-portrait: a man with 'a happy, guileless, infectious gift of high spirits'. Critics, including Jill, noted Michael's desire to exculpate H.G., to absolve him of charges of womanizing, racism and excessive optimism about the human capacity to reason its way to progress. A two-part BBC *Bookmark* documentary on H.G. in 1994 gives three vivid clips of the kind of dialogue that went on between Jill and Michael as he worked on his Wells book:

'What I say is if a man is going to behave like a bastard he'd better be a genius. Is he a genius?'

'Of course he was.'

'Is he?'

'Yes.'

'Are you sure about that?'

'I'm absolutely sure.'

'They were real love affairs, you know.'

'I'm not disputing they were love affairs.'

'Then they weren't just such casual affairs.'

'If he really loved them, he'd have taken more trouble to protect them. He was a naughty boy in many ways.'

Jill did not think much of H.G.'s feminism:

'Wells was a kind of feminist. The feminists today hold it strongly against him because he was opposed to the women's vote. The reason for that was that he had little faith in parliamentary democracy. At the time he didn't think it mattered all that much. And I regard this as a black mark against him. Michael, I am sure, will find excuses.'

'When she says I'll find excuses, what she means is I'll find good reasons... He did understand the growing strength of the women's movement and wrote very powerfully about that.'

'The suffragettes made such a splash you couldn't ignore them. He used them, but he didn't praise them.'

'He was saying what a tremendous influence they had at the time.'

'He didn't say that.'

'Well ...'.

In *H.G.: The History of Mr Wells*, Michael reveals an instance of Jill reading over his shoulder, so to speak, as he quotes H.G. reminiscing about his working-class mother's hard life: 'Bearing a child was not the jolly wholesome process we know today.' Michael inserted a footnote: 'When did HG imagine the process ever became so jolly? So Jill enquired when she read this sentence.' One can almost see Michael glancing sideways at Jill in certain sentences: 'Some of the most prominent suffrage campaign leaders are presented as caricatures in his pages [in *Ann Veronica*]* whereas some of the real ones were raging beauties who could have held their own in any normal Wellsian gallery ... Sometimes HG was accused of a weakness or a wavering of his allegiance to the feminist cause; and sometimes, alas, as we shall see the accusation was true.'

---

* 'Jill wasn't as thrilled about the novel as I was,' Michael said to me. 'Jill didn't need Wells to liberate her, but I did.'

Jill is the critical conscience of *H.G.: The History of Mr. Wells*. She made Michael work hard to justify his defence of H.G. During the documentary he was obliged once again to answer her attack:

> 'He had to conquer a girl with a mind like that, and a body like that.'
> 'Yes.'
> 'There couldn't have been anything in the whole of his life and in his other affairs that are comparable, I don't believe. But you see he got tired of women and he always wanted to experiment with new women. Very poor on that basis, you know.'
> 'The first part of your answer is much better than the second part.'
> [Jill laughing] 'Yes.'

The 'yes' is said in amusement. Sometimes Jill would stop arguing and Michael *thought* he had won, Julie observed. But Jill remained convinced that whatever his virtues, H.G. was a deeply selfish man.*

According to Michael, one of the strongest points in H.G.'s favour is that he learned from his lovers all the time, especially from Rebecca West – a magnificent woman of so many qualities that the novelist deployed her in a gorgeous display of different female characters. If Michael is more enthusiastic about H.G.'s novel *Joan and Peter* (1918) than most critics are, it is because the hero and heroine are engaged in a 'two-way education… He said he was blind until she opened his eyes, and at every turn they were learning afresh.' Michael said as much – and often – about Jill: 'She was teaching me all the time.' Michael felt keenly H.G.'s loss of Jane. The inconsolable H.G. put together a book of his wife's writing and wrote a memoir of her, the woman who had made a home for him. And Michael understood how disadvantaged even brilliant women like Rebecca were: they could have their H.G., but not their Jane – the person who tied it all together for the man and enabled him to write. H.G., after all, was a man after Michael's own mind: 'The colour of life is largely a matter of homes.'

It is doubtful, Michael pointed out, that he would have written *Dr Strangelove, I Presume* without Jill's encouragement. She was 'very keen' on the book, Jill wrote to June Purvis on 4 October 1998, 'besides feeling thrilled that he has found the energy to complete it, about which he had entertained serious doubts'. Michael remembered that the 'spark of the book' came from a visit to India in the autumn of 1997. At the Sixth Indira Gandhi Conference (19–22 November), they met with Robert McNamara, the former US Secretary of Defense. They drank and talked freely late into the night. McNamara told

---

* Patricia Hollis, who observed this sort of disputation, privately thought of it as a kind of foreplay, although she could never quite separate Jill the wife from Jill the feminist from just Jill.

Jill that no amount of precautions could make nuclear weapons safe. 'There's going to be another accident,' he said. 'And that's what Jill had been saying all along,' Michael emphasized. Indeed, 'McNamara talked just like Jill. She was constantly demanding I do more about it.' Nuclear weapons had to be abolished, McNamara argued, with full-scale schemes of inspection.

In his book's dedication Michael wrote that all his books since 1945 had been dedicated to Jill, but 'this one especially. She was the most passionate CNDer of the lot, who saw from the start that man's invention of radioactive tortures for the future was the worst ever invasion of women's rights.' In my own copy of the book Michael wrote: 'Carl, this was more truly Jill's book than mine, as readers can see for themselves. She wanted to tell the world with an even more potent instrument than Byron's poetry.' Michael reprints Byron's great poem, 'Darkness', the same one he recited to Rebecca West, to demonstrate how the poet foresaw a world devastated by a holocaust resembling a nuclear catastrophe.* As McNamara said to Jill and Michael, the idea of a 'nuclear shield' is a chimera. What kind of shield is provided by weapons that ensure the destruction of everyone? Jill wanted to include even more in the book about issues concerning depleted uranium and the possible radioactive fallout from weapons used in Iraq and Kosovo.

It was not just Jill's ideas but her spirit that kept Michael going. She kept him agile and aware. 'Something happens to Michael Foot when he's in his wife's company,' Sally Vincent wrote in 'Here's Hoping' (*Guardian Weekend Magazine*, 2 January 1999):

> He sheds about 30 years for a start, and his spectacles go quite twinkly when he watches her. Jill Craigie is a dishy octogenarian and clearly deserves his devotion. She is sure he has given me a hard time. I am to have some tea, he is to go shopping. There is a shopping list on the kitchen table, writ large and clear. He picks it up and looks at it, 'Good God!' he shouts. 'You want all this? Sausages? Eggs? Cheese? Good God! All this, then!' He zips himself with some difficulty into a waterproof bomber jacket, to not very smart effect, and exits as to a front line.

Peter Thorburn, who began helping Jill with her gardening in the mid-1990s, observed how Michael deferred to Jill in her house. But she could not get him to do anything he did not want to do and she would become quite

---

* In his book Michael mentions that Shelley was H.G.'s favourite poet. Reading Paul Foot's *Red Shelley* made me realize that H.G. and Michael shared with Shelley the same erotic sensibility: 'He believed and acted quite consistently by the "love principle" he laid down in *Epipsychidion*: "That to divide is not to take away."'... Shelley was not in the least upset that his best friend should make love to his wife... He was willing to learn from his women friends and lovers, and in the process all his ideas were enriched and strengthened.'

exasperated. She'd say, 'You know, Michael has disappeared. He's trying to avoid laying the table.' She sent him to the shop to get some potatoes. He came back with some kiwi fruit. 'That's Michael,' Jill said affectionately.

She complained about Michael to Julie: 'Oh, Michael does nothing! Other husbands do ... He does nothing!' So she said to Michael: 'Pick up the coffee cups, put them on this tray and take them upstairs.' He did so and then she asked him if he had done the glasses. 'No, no, my child, I'll do it.' She went up to look and on the way up she found two broken coffee cups on the stairs and fragments in the bookshelves behind some books. 'It was a sort of ritual that Michael did the coffee,' Anne Robinson remembered. 'He'd walk over to the sink like this was a completely new adventure, mumbling and bumbling – no two parts of Michael seem to co-ordinate – and we'd wait hours for it.' Any man like the writer Brian Brivati who carried off with aplomb household chores like lighting a fire became an object of intense fascination, as Jill cast sidelong glances at Michael.

There were other incidents – like the mirror that somehow just happened to fall off the wall in Michael's vicinity. 'He never dared tell her,' Julie said. Listening to Julie's account, Ian Aitken added: 'One wouldn't dare to tell Jill many things.' He compared her to that other 'natural Duchess', Jennie Lee. Jill was not quite in that league, Ian observed, but close to it.

Jill enjoyed a visit to Chequers, and there was much to admire in the new government's performance, which she would compare to her days as a Cabinet spouse. At the party for *Dr Strangelove*, Jill sat next to historian Peter Hennessy who attacked Blair's lack of principle. Jill asked him – as Michael and Brian Brivati remembered it – 'a few questions':

> 'Have you ever argued with him?'
> 'No.'
> 'Have you ever tested his ideas?'
> 'No.'

Question by question she made an impressed Hennessy think through glib assumptions.

Fiona Millar marvelled at Jill 'still going strong at 1.30 in the morning when frankly the younger ones amongst us were dying to get to bed'. Fiona admired the way Jill picked up interesting points of conversation and made sure the whole table savoured them. Feminist and historian Cate Haste described Jill's prodding technique: 'I don't agree with that ... Now, I think you're completely wrong there ... What about such and such?' No assertion remained unchallenged. This combative mode might seem abrasive on paper but in company it was 'delightfully intense and terrifically warm', Cate noted. If the men went off on a tangent and ignored the women, Jill spoke up, memorably silencing Michael and philosopher Ted Honderich on one occasion.[2]

Fiona appreciated the way Jill could spot talent in its early stages, like the journalist Jonathan Freedland before he became a big name. Fiona lent Jill her daughter's Spice Girls CD because Jill was 'fascinated by the phenomenon but had never heard them'. Fiona's last memory of Jill was of her 'reeling off into the night with her *joie de vivre* and youthful spirit'.[3]

People easily got the impression that Michael was older and frailer than Jill. That was Bonnie Scott's impression when she called on Jill and Michael in the course of editing an edition of Rebecca West's letters. Michael told his friend Ted Honderich that he might look like the weaker vessel, but he expected Jill to die before he did. 'Jill always said she would die before Michael,' Jenny Stringer remembered. 'Michael is as tough as old boots,' Jill once told Mervyn Jones.

It would not have been surprising if Michael had fallen on the uneven Hampstead pavement. But in May 1999 it was Jill who took the fall, and in her own home. Upstairs, getting out of her bath, Jill heard the door knocker. She went to the window to see who it was, slipped and fell.* Peter Thorburn, who had a key, had simply wanted to alert Jill he was in the house. When he entered, he heard her cries. He could not help smiling when she greeted him with: 'You were probably expecting to see a naked woman on the floor.' She apparently had put on her nightgown before her accident. He got her to bed where she could phone for an ambulance. As she was wheeled out, she made some comment about Peter looking after the pots and window boxes. 'It's you I'm worried about, not the plants,' he said.

Jill had fractured her hip and would need a small plate put in. Her heart had weakened and over the course of the next few months she would experience several attacks. Michael spoke to June Purvis about two weeks after the fall. 'How is she?' June asked. 'Not too good,' Michael replied. But he never lost hope that she would recover. She could no longer walk the stairs and remained on the second (street level) floor. Since she could not climb to her study, she could not work on her book. 'I must finish my book,' she told Julie.

Julie doubted the competence of her mother's medical care at the Royal Free Hospital in Hampstead. She watched the orthopaedic surgeon come in with an entourage after the operation and say, 'Oh, aren't we doing well.' Julie said to him:

---

* Later it was discovered that the water on the floor came from a leaking ceiling pipe.

'Are you joking? My mother's *dying*.'
'She was a very sick woman when she came in.'
'No she wasn't.'
'Are you accusing us?'
'If you think I am. I want a heart specialist *now*. I want your top heart specialist in here *now*.'

Shortly afterwards Julie got a call from the nurses relaying the heart specialist's message: 'Your mother's in crisis.' Jill's heart had sustained more damage after a hip operation that had gone on too long, and she had trouble recovering from the anaesthetic. Julie 'quite rightly kicked up a row in the hospital', Michael said. Another of Jill's friends, Celine La Freniere, remembers Jill's own anger at the Royal Free about the infection that set in after her hip operation.

Jill worsened in August. Michael, ever the optimist, thought she would recover one more time; they would have a few more years. There were 'swift departures to nearby Royal Free Hospital, but the return trips to the garden … repeatedly restored her sanity & her courage, the fighting spirit which was always the truest inspiration of her feminism,' Michael wrote in an unpublished manuscript. As late as September or October, Maxine continued to visit and help Jill put her papers in order. Jill did not seem any different to Maxine: 'She was just lying on a daybed and said it was going to take a little longer to recover, and then they would start on the next phase.'

Jill had days when Julie heard her say, 'I don't think I'm going to survive this.' Peter Thorburn saw her in a depressed mood: 'I might as well kill myself if I'm going to carry on feeling like this.' This surprised Peter because Jill was such a strong woman. But her medication debilitated her, and she did not want to be an invalid. She had certain requirements: she must be able to garden and give dinner parties. She liked to look her best, so she saw few visitors towards the end. To those she did see, she never complained about health. Whenever Celine enquired, Jill always brushed her off, saying that she and Michael were quite well.

In retrospect, Julie felt Jill knew she was dying, and 'we denied it and that left her alone'. Once Julie did turn on Michael, saying, 'Give her her peace, tell her it is all right to go now.' Julie thought Michael was frightened at the prospect of losing Jill and could not confront it. He would say, 'It will be all right, my child.' Michael slept on a small sofa near Jill in their sitting room. Jenny Stringer remembered that Michael put together breakfast trays for Jill.

Lizzie Parker, Julie's old friend who had lived at 33 Rosslyn Hill, visited Jill and found her unwilling to talk about her illness. Michael began talking and Jill interrupted: 'I don't want to hear about Byron. I want to hear what Lizzie has been doing.' Lizzie loved Jill's calm air of command. 'I just adored her.'

Friends of Jill and Michael began to help them sort out their affairs.* Jill had always thought that eventually she and Michael would require a live-in couple to help them manage. Their main asset was the house, and on that they needed to build a financial plan – one that Moni and Denis Forman, Anne Robinson and her husband John Penrose, and Jenny Stringer spent many hours putting in place. His friends were 'making a really big effort', Michael remembered gratefully, one which enabled him to take equity out of the house to supplement his retirement income.

As Jill grew worse, she also grew angry with those who insisted on telling her she was looking well. Michael, however, did not believe Jill ever gave up her lust for life. Just a week before her last hospital stay, she had talked brilliantly to Michael and Jenny for nearly two hours straight about her book. 'She had so much energy that I just didn't believe she was going to die,' Damon said. Jenny thought Jill might still pull through, although a very tired Jill said she had had enough.

Jill left no record of her feelings during this final period of her life, except for the underlinings in the last book she read, Francis Wheen's biography of Karl Marx. She noted Marx's estrangement from his parents and how little he had to do with them later in life. He never enquired about their health and did not attend his father's funeral. She clearly took an interest in Marx's wife's declaration: 'the girl must find her complete satisfaction in the man's love, she must forget everything in love'. Marx's pronouncement that 'Our task must be unsparing criticism, directed even more against our self-styled friends than against our declared enemies' struck a chord. It is obvious why the author of *Daughters of Dissent* found this passage riveting:

> [Marx] found an exact description of his anxieties in Balzac's novel *The Unknown Masterpiece*, the story of a brilliant artist so obsessive in his perfectionism that he spends many years refining and retouching the portrait of a courtesan to achieve 'the most complete representation of reality'. When he shows the masterpiece to his friends, all they can see is a formless mass of colour and random lines: 'Nothing! Nothing! After ten years of work ....' He hurls the worthless canvas on to the flames – 'the fire of Prometheus' – and dies that very night.

---

* Any number of friends like Peter Cuming and Celine La Freniere and the philosopher Ted Honderich had offered to do tasks of all kinds for Jill and Michael. 'Please remember that I can be called on to come round and put in a lightbulb or whatever, and for any other comradeliness,' Honderich wrote (27 May 1998). Much earlier he had walked Dizzy for a few weeks when Michael was away.

Jill worried about Michael. Who would take care of him? She wanted Julie to move in, but Julie refused. Julie spent her evenings cooking for Jill and Michael most days, after working from 10 a.m. to 6 p.m. for a film producer. She thought her mother was now asking her to take over the role Jill had played in Michael's life. Julie proposed hiring a woman to help out, but a problem arose when she could not work weekends. Julie said to Jill:

> 'I can't give up every weekend.'
> 'After all I've done for you! You can't do that for me.'
> 'I'd be doing this for you if you hadn't given me a penny. It's not related. It's because I'm your daughter.'

Hearing Jill's and Julie's argument escalate, Michael came into the room and shouted: 'Get out of the house and don't ever come back.' He then called Kathy Seery and asked her if she could come and make a meal. Kathy remembers the tensions that had built up to this explosive scene. 'I was doing far more than anybody realized I was doing,' Julie noted. 'I had no life. But the others thought I was shirking my duties.'

A few days later, Jill went into hospital. Esther visited her nearly every day. Jill would say to Esther, 'Darling, don't waste your time coming to see me here.' But then they would sit and chat for hours. Michael would get up from the corner chair where he had been reading and go out, returning when Esther had departed. Then Esther's visits stopped when she found out that her father, Mike Randall, was himself dying in hospital. Michael's secretary Una phoned to tell Julie about Jill. Julie wanted to be with her children and their father. 'You've only got one mother,' Una urged. Then Michael called, and Julie went to see Jill. Julie, ill with flu, was talking to Jill when Esther phoned on Friday 10 December to say that her father had just died. Julie said, 'Mike's died,' and then she fled from the room to comfort Esther.

Esther visited Jill on Saturday and Sunday. Jill said: 'I'm dying. I just want to die. I've had enough. I only get better so that I can get worse.' Michael spoke up, 'No, no, my dear child, you're getting better. You're much better today.' Jill's kidneys had failed and she was attached to a heart monitor. Yet Esther sensed an 'amazing amount of fight and energy still there'. Esther believed Jill was angry with Michael for not allowing her to let go. She took Julie's hand and said, 'Please let me go.' She still worried about Michael. Jenny Stringer told her that no matter what, Michael would be looked after.

One of Jill's doctors told Michael that he thought Jill had lost the will to live. Michael was sceptical. The day before she died, they had a long discussion. 'There's good news from Scotland,' Michael told her. A woman had been appointed Minister of Health in Scotland under the new arrangements for devolution, which their former lodger, Donald Dewar, had helped to accomplish. 'They're doing what you want in Scotland,' Michael said. 'They've got a woman in charge.' She was in great pain, but it did not stop her or Michael from discussing what went on in the world. On her better days Jill certainly did want to live, Jenny emphasized.

The next day, 13 December, Jenny Stringer and Michael left the hospital for dinner. But as they approached Pilgrim's Lane, Michael said: 'Do you mind if we return to the hospital.' 'Of course not,' Jenny said. In the meanwhile, Julie got a call to come immediately to the hospital. Her mother was sleeping as she entered the room with Esther. Julie watched the heart monitor and asked her mother if she wanted anything. 'No, thank you,' Jill said, her eyes still closed. Then, just as Michael and Jenny entered the room, Jill opened her eyes and died. Jenny said to Michael, 'Jill's going. She's going. Michael, speak to her!' Jenny saw the heart monitor slowing down and pressed the bell for the nurse. Michael held Jill's hand, stroked her forehead, and said: 'Oh my dear child, you're going to wake up and tell me off any minute now.'

Damon arrived about fifteen minutes after Jill died. 'Look at her,' Michael said to him. 'Look at how beautiful she is.' He did not look sad. To Damon he looked brave.

A few days later Michael burst into tears – a rare show of grief after months of anxiety and fear. He began almost immediately to plan what would later be called a 'celebration' of Jill's life and work. In a state of shock, he talked non-stop about Jill. 'When Jill died, the light went out of my life,' he told Peter Cuming. Damon heard him on the steps going to bed talking to Jill. Michael called Alan and Megan Fox in Tredegar: 'My Jill has died,' he sobbed. Over and over again Michael played the Mozart piece Jill had introduced him to when they first met. Neither Michael nor Jill believed in an afterlife. He cared nothing about a religious ceremony. He did not even want to know where Jill's ashes were scattered. Esther asked him: 'Don't you wonder if Jill is still with us somewhere, that she might send a sign that she is okay?' He scoffed. Later, however, he told Esther about going to a football match with his old friend Peter Jones, who had a new stereo system in his car. When Peter turned it on, Michael heard Jill's Mozart.

Julie was deeply troubled by her mother's final days: 'I never made it up with her. It was shocking.' Michael told her not to be upset: 'No, no, that was over in half an hour. Your mother and I had some fearful rows. She loved you very much. Don't think anything of it.' But Julie did. 'We parted on bad terms. I never got that hug and kiss.'

Michael received many letters of condolence that evoked Jill's presence better than the obituaries.

> I think how you would address Jill as 'my child' and grasp her hand and she would look up, and smile and flirt with you! I understand completely when you say the charm has gone out of life. – Anne Robinson

> She had such drive and commitment and a fantastic sense of fun. – Tony Blair

> She had a wonderful way of making you feel welcome and making the most ordinary thing intensely agreeable. – Sheila Rowbotham

> Whenever I was in her company I couldn't take my eyes off her, wondering what she was going to say next! She had that marvellous & total independence which so very few people have... she was such a light. – Melvyn Bragg

> I felt so sad for you when I read Jill is no longer here. You will feel bereft because after almost a lifetime together you have gained so much from one another that two personalities have mingled into a matchless harmony. – Margaret Thatcher

Michael treasured most of all a letter from Francis Wheen, which praised Jill's 'charm, kindness and *joie de vivre*'. Wheen recalled the 'marvellous romantic adventure you embarked upon together all those years ago. It is a most inspiriting love story, a true partnership of equals (Dare one also use the unfashionable word "comradeship"?) which gave joy and delight to your many friends. For me, as for countless others, Pilgrim's Lane was a haven of warmth and light. Such a lively, life-giving spirit cannot, I think, be extinguished: we shall all cherish and enjoy her memory for as long as we live.'

On 17 January 2000 Jill's friends gathered at 2.30 p.m. at the Conway Hall, Red Lion Square. There were ten speakers – four men and six women – a proper proportion for Jill, Michael thought.* An exuberant Michael spoke of Jill on CND marches and of her William Morris socialism. Clare Short, who had stoutly supported Jill during the making of *Two Hours From London*, paid tribute to her feminism – as did Ursula Owen, who recounted Jill's dealings with Virago Press. To everyone's surprise, Barbara Castle spoke, regaling the gathering with an amusing rendition of her disagreements with Jill but also hailing her guts and beauty. Surprised at Barbara's candour about her disagreements with Jill, Michael nevertheless arose and said: 'Was I right to let her loose?' It had been a success. Paul Foot, however, put it best when he spoke of Jill's 'forthright nature'. A conviction meant nothing if you did not

---

* They were Margaret Beckett, Clare Short, Glenys Kinnock, Barbara Castle, Ursula Owen, Julie Hamilton, Michael Foot, Bruce Kent, Jon Snow and Paul Foot.

'come out with it. Until a problem was debated, it couldn't be solved.' Paul lauded Jill's democratic temperament. He had once asked her if it would be all right to refer to her as his 'illustrious aunt'. 'Yes, illustrious would be fine,' she said.

A very nervous Julie also spoke. She found the situation difficult because she had no experience as a public speaker, and she was distressed because the tributes had said little about the mother and grandmother who meant most to Julie. She spoke of a powerful, exciting mother who had taught her about art and antiques and homemaking and cooking and giving parties and gardening. Amidst such a formidable gathering she did not speak of the mother–daughter anguish or the grief still pent up in her that had not yet found an outlet. She read an e. e. cummings poem, 'in time of daffodils', which beautifully captured Jill's spirit, especially the line 'our now and here with paradise'. For Jill tried to make a paradise of every moment – a sentiment she shared with her beloved Rebecca West, who shared with William Blake the belief that there is in 'no Jerusalem but this'.

A little more than a year after Jill died, Michael perched once again in the sitting room where she had spent her last days. 'She was lying over there – see' (he pointed to a sofa). He recited from a small collection of Yeats' poems edited by Seamus Heaney.

When You Are Old
When you are old and grey and full of sleep,
And nodding by the fire, take down this book,
And slowly read, and dream of the soft look
Your eyes had once, and of their shadows deep;

How many loved your moments of glad grace,
And loved your beauty with love false or true,
But one man loved the pilgrim soul in you,
And loved the sorrows of your changing face;

And bending down beside the glowing bars,
Murmur, a little sadly, how Love fled
And paced upon the mountains overhead
And hid his face amid a crowd of stars.

'I'm in favour of the pilgrim, you see.' He thought of the lane whose name Jill had changed, of course, but also of Plymouth. He loved the second stanza and read it again. His voice rose as he said 'glad grace'.

Jill Craigie and the Documentary Tradition

When Jill Craigie decided to become a documentary film-maker, she had few options. As Ernest Betts observes:

> The documentary film movement as a movement was founded on the conception of a non-theatrical audience that is today a vast array of specialised audiences, and we used to say at the time that there was more seating capacity outside the theatres than there was inside the theatres, and that was true enough, and it was founded on the expectation of financial support from governmental and other authorities concerned with the use of film, or logically likely to be concerned with the use of film for public enlightenment of one kind or another.

Jill respected John Grierson (1898–1972), the founding father of the British documentary, but he played no direct or supportive role in her evolving sense of the genre. Grierson had established his reputation on the strength of one film, *Drifters* (1929), a 'vigorously paced and imaginatively edited' film about herring fisheries, which vividly built up the lives of the working class into 'an epic of steam and steel,' writes Eric Barnouw in *Documentary: A History of the Non-Fiction Film* (1993). It is a film in which the men are as heroic as the machines are powerful, the two working as one to haul the 'harvest of the sea'. Barnouw adds that it 'meant a new career for Grierson', who continued work not as a director, but as a 'creative organizer', promoting his conception of the documentary and the men he deemed best able to consummate it.

Film historian David Thomson has called Grierson 'a harsh, restrictive enthusiast', who brought to his conception of the documentary a Calvinist fervour. A purist, Grierson forever attacked 'the studio mind' and the 'shim-sham mechanics of the studio', suggesting that feature film-making was artificial, corrupt and effete.[1] He wanted to show real people, not actors; he favoured explorations of working class, everyday life, not glamorized melo-dramas about the middle and upper classes. The rigid, simplistic distinctions did not appeal to Jill, whose work on *The Flemish Farm* (1943), her last collaboration with Jeffrey Dell, demonstrates how honourably and authentically a studio film can portray 'real people' and 'everyday life'.

Grierson's pro-Labour convictions coincided with Jill's, but he delivered them dogmatically: 'I look upon cinema as a pulpit,' he said.[2] Jill resented Grierson's rather controlling personality and empire-building mentality. By 1937 Grierson had become a bureaucrat, a powerful man who could obtain government funding for those he deemed worthy. In *London's Burning: Life, Death and Art in the Second World War* (1994), Peter Stansky and William Abrahams note that the Ministry of Information, which produced 1887 films during the war, 'formed the model' for Orwell's Ministry of Truth in *1984*. Jill said: 'The Ministry of Information – Grierson and all that lot. I met them. The films weren't subject to criticism, so they could get away with anything.' Jill saw Grierson & co. at The Highlander, a Soho public house where documentary film-makers tended to gather.[3] She 'so disapproved of their films' that they were hostile to her. An outspoken woman would not have been eligible to go through his mill.' Jill could not imagine a place for herself in the Grierson school. Jack Beddington, head of the film division at the Ministry of Information between 1940 and 1946, a 'big figure in the documentary world' and 'very cultured, very smooth... very good influence altogether', as Jill told film historian Charles Drazin, 'wouldn't give me a job. In any capacity.' She found 'no sort of camaraderie... no little group that one could get to and say, "what can we do about this male-dominated industry?"'

It troubled Jill that Grierson depreciated the aesthetic. '"Poet," in Grierson's vocabulary, was not a term of praise,' remark Stansky and Abrahams. Jill had much more in common with the greatest documentary film-maker of the period, Humphrey Jennings (1907–50), whose classic *Fires Were Started* (1943), a powerful depiction of firemen during the Blitz, was shot both on location and, for certain crucial sequences, in a studio. Jennings, a fine painter and impressive scholar of modern art, combined in his documentaries a passion for high art with a dedication to depicting ordinary people. Jill often spoke fondly of her meeting with him (he was one of the regulars at The Highlander) and with Paul Rotha (1907–84), whose work, especially *World of Plenty* (1943) and *Land of Promise* (1945), paralleled her own fusion of socialist and aesthetic principles.

When Jennings died, Jill wrote his obituary in *Tribune* (29 October 1950), lauding his concern with 'aesthetic detail'. She might have been speaking of herself when she wrote, 'He was more often than not out of work and when he was working there were few who knew how to use his talents. If the industry were not held in shackles by formula programmes and a rigid commercialism, if there had been more room for experiment, Humphrey with his abundance of ideas would have risen to heights beyond anything he had hitherto achieved.'

Unlike Grierson and co., Jill did not reject the commercial world of film-making; rather, she would use the studio story-telling style to her advantage and fuse the methods of feature film and documentary in ways that later mainstream and avant-garde film-makers would readily adopt, realizing that all film is an artifice, a construct, and that our sense of actuality in art is always a product of art – not a hefting of reality into art.

Among documentary film-makers – mostly men – Jill did not count. Of Paul Rotha, one of the few male documentary film-makers she befriended, Jill said: 'Both Paul and I were in bad for our socialism.' But there is an edge even in her fondness for Rotha: 'Jolly pompous he was,' Jill remembered. Humphrey Jennings alluded to the clubbish atmosphere around 'Rotha and other of Grierson's little boys who are still talking as loudly as possible about "pure documentary" and "realism" and other such systems of self-advertisement'.[4] Rotha was the reigning authority on documentary films at the time. Writing *Documentary Film* (1939), which was prefaced by Grierson, he commented that the genre is the 'creative dramatisation of actuality and the expression of social analysis'. Certainly *Out of Chaos* fulfils his desire for the voice-over narrator to be more informal, becoming a 'part of the film rather than the detached "Voice of God".' Yet neither Rotha nor any other critic commented on the friendly female voice Jill used for her art film, a voice sorely needed to balance Eric Newton's lugubrious delivery, but a voice evidently commanding little authority in a male-dominated society. Jill also followed Rotha's suggestion to let the workers – or in the case of Henry Moore, the artist – speak for themselves in 'simpler, more humble, and more honest speech' than the 'professional commentator'. She saw Rotha's *World of Plenty* (shot in 1942 and released in 1943) and found its treatment of the problem of feeding the world 'absolutely brilliant'. As Rotha said of his own work in *Documentary Film*, 'It caught all that was best in the determination of its time to make something better of the postwar world.' Like his *Land of Promise* (1945), which employed a 'full multi-voiced commentary, personalised in different characters' and a star actor, John Mills, *The Way We Live* blends together a central figure, a writer played by a professional actor, and his encounter with the broad range of people and professions representing themselves in post-war Plymouth. Like him, she was making 'argument films'. Yet Rotha does not acknowledge their affinity in *Documentary Film* or acknowledge that *The Way We Live*, like *Land of Promise* (which Jill saw in Rotha's company in a Leicester Square cinema), is 'an argument on homes and houses'.[5] Asked nearly forty years later about the fraternity of documentary film-makers, Jill replied: 'A woman didn't get any help from any of these people, you know, except the ones who made passes.'

Clyde Jeavons, a consultant curator at the British Film Institute, wrote a letter to the *Guardian* (17 December 1999) in response to obituaries that called Jill Craigie the first woman director in Britain. He pointed out that Aubrey Le Blond made skiing documentaries as early as 1900. Ethyle Batley, 'probably Britain's very first accredited woman film director of fiction subjects', according to Jeavons, made 'nearly 70 films between 1912 and her early death in 1917'. Jessica Borthwick filmed the Balkan War in 1913. Dinah Shurey directed silent feature films in the 1920s. Margaret Thomson, active in the late 1940s, receives honourable mention in Rotha's *Documentary Film*.

But a mere scattered score of women hardly constituted a tradition Jill could draw on. In an oral history interview, Jill mentioned Mary Field (1896–1968), a pioneering documentary film-maker best known for her *Secrets of Nature* series (1923–33) for children. Jill's closest match is Kay Mander (1915–), who also found it difficult to find a niche in a male-dominated industry, and partnered with her husband. She got a job working in continuity in the mid-1930s and by 1937 had become the first woman member of the Association of Cinematograph Technicians. She directed her first documentary short, *How to File*, in 1940 and joined Paul Rotha's production company in 1943, directing two films, *Highland Doctor* (1943) and *New Builders* (1945). At a screening of the former, Mander remembered Rotha being asked about who made the film: 'Right,' he said, 'I'll see you outside.' Mander is not even mentioned in Rotha's *Documentary Film*. When I asked Mander about Rotha, she had one word for him: 'Horrible.'

Like Jill, Kay Mander worked with ordinary people and 'married documentary techniques with a dramatic narrative'. Her *Homes for the People* (1945), which concentrates on working-class housing, invites comparison with *The Way We Live,* although Mander's film seeks only to present the woman's point of view and to present a vision of town planning.[6]

Appendix B

Ending *Daughters of Dissent*

After finishing Chapter 18 of her book, Jill had to deal with the way militancy divided the suffragette movement and with the still fiercely controversial debates about the roles each of the Pankhursts played in the great struggle, the legacy of their leadership and the legislation that finally gave women the vote. Paul Foot believed that Jill 'changed in the course of her conversations with me. Almost the last time I saw her she did say that after 1912, when Emmeline and Christabel had the split-up with the Pethick-Lawrences, the Christabel wing did go down the drain.' This would have been a view Jill shared with Rebecca West, who, in spite of her great admiration for Emmeline and Christabel, believed that the split weakened the WSPU and isolated it from other suffrage groups. 'I hung on her every word,' Paul said, 'because I had been worried about her [pro-Emmeline/anti-Sylvia] line.'

Jill did not accept, however, Sylvia's socialist/pacifist opposition to World War I. Jill thought the criticism of Mrs Pankhurst for supporting the war and ending the suffragette movement was wrongheaded, Michael said. Mrs Pankhurst and Christabel did not suddenly change their views on the vote after the declaration of war. Defending their country advanced the women's cause. Jill knew that Mrs Pankhurst's own education in France and her devotion to the legacy of the French Revolution made it all the more justifiable that she should side with Britain in coming to the aid of France against Germany, which had invaded France in the Franco-Prussian War (1870–71) when Mrs Pankhurst was a young woman. In other words, Mrs Pankhurst never ceased being a revolutionary. The defeat of France would have been a defeat for progressive Europe and certainly for its women. She would also have shown, Michael suggests, that even between 1918 and 1928, during the period of limited suffrage for women, Parliament passed significant legislation benefiting women. The whole temper of the House of Commons changed –

not enough, Jill would have conceded, but certainly things changed for the better, since women's legislation was no longer considered a joking matter.

Endnotes

Chapter 1 *On Her Own* (1911–28)

1. Unless otherwise noted, Jill's statements throughout this book are from an interview recorded November 1994, on deposit at the Imperial War Museum.
2. Jerry White, *London in the Twentieth Century: A City and Its People* (2001).
3. Simon Hoggart and David Leigh, *Michael Foot: A Portrait* (1981).
4. See Hilary Spurling, *The Girl From the Fiction Department: A Portrait of Sonia Orwell* (2002).
5. Charlotte Franklin, introduction to Margit Kaffka, *The Ant Heap: A Novel* (1995).
6. June Aberdeen to Carl Rollyson, 15 July 2002 and interview 23 July 2002.
7. I am indebted to Bob Thomson in the reference department of the Civic Centre Library, London Borough of Harrow Education Services, for identifying Southlands and for sending me the information about it included in *Harrow and Harrow School: A New Guide* (1929). The school closed in 1968 and left no records.
8. Michael Holroyd, *Bernard Shaw: The One-Volume Definitive Edition* (1998).
9. Quoted in Carole Klein, *Doris Lessing: A Biography* (2000).

Chapter 2 *The Death of the Heart* (1928–36)

1. Mervyn Jones, *Michael Foot* (1994).
2. Quoted in White.

Chapter 3 *At Sea* (1936–9)

1. 'Mr Jeffrey Dell', *The Times*, 20 March 1985. Obituaries also appeared in *Screen International*, 16 March 1985, and *Film and Television Technician*, May 1985. All are on file at the British Film Institute. Additional information provided by Barbara Dell.
2. *The Film Business: A History of British Cinema 1896–1972* (1973).

Chapter 4 *Free* (1939–43)

1. Interview with Barbara Dell.
2. Unless otherwise noted, the details of Malcolm MacDonald's career derive from Clyde Sanger, *Malcolm MacDonald: Bridging an End to Empire* (1995).
3. All references to MacDonald's unpublished autobiography and letters are derived from the Malcolm MacDonald Papers, Durham University Library.
4. For details about De Gaulle's treatment of his daughter, who died at the age of twenty, see Alden Hatch, *The De Gaulle Nobody Knows* (1960). Jill confided her memory of De Gaulle to Michael.
5. Interview with William MacQuitty.
6. See Frances Thorpe and Nicholas Pronay, *British Official Films in the Second World War: A Descriptive Catalogue* (1980).

Chapter 5 *Out of Chaos* (1942–3)

1. Peter Stansky and William Abrahams, *London's Burning: Life, Death, and Art in the Second World War* (1994).
2. All quotations from Morris are from Norman Kelvin, ed., *William Morris on Art and Socialism* (1999).
3. The essay is in two parts, and I quote from the text in Linda Dowling, ed., *The Soul of Man Under Socialism & Selected Critical Prose* (2001).
4. 'Fifties Features: The Woman Behind the Pictures: Jill Craigie.' Transcript of interview conducted 2 January 1986, courtesy of the British Film Institute. Charles Drazin interview with Jill Craigie 14 January 1994, courtesy of Charles Drazin.
5. Charles Drazin, *The Finest Years: British Cinema of the 1940s* (1998).
6. Quoted in Geoffrey Macnab, *J. Arthur Rank and the British Film Industry* (1993).
7. Fifties Features.
8. Charles Drazin interview with Jill Craigie, 11 November 1994.
9. For a brief description of quota quickies, see Michael Powell, *A Life in the Movies* (1986).
10. Jill Craigie, 'Underground Artists', *Sunday Times Magazine*, 9 November 1986.
11. 'Start of a Wonderful Adventure', *Electronic Telegraph*, 11 November 1998, www.telegraph.co.uk.
12. Ian Chilvers, Harold Osborn, Dennis Far, ed., *The Oxford Dictionary of Art* (1988).
13. Jill told this story to Michael and to Anne Robinson, although Robinson remembers the artist was Augustus John and the charge was ten guineas.
14. *Oxford Dictionary of Art*.
15. 'No trace of undercover pyjamas', *Guardian*, 21 November 1997.
16. *Stanley Spencer: An English Vision* (1997).
17. Maurice Collis, *Stanley Spencer: A Biography* (1962).
18. Quoted in McCarthy.
19. *Oxford Dictionary of Art*.
20. Jill's comment on Moore appears in 'Underground Artists', *The Times*, 9 November 1986.
21. Quoted in Roger Berthoud, *The Life of Henry Moore* (1987).
22. Quoted in Stansky and Abrahams.
23. For a much more detailed analysis of the film, especially of its soundtracks, see Carl Rollyson: *Documentary Film: A Primer* (2004).
24. *A Life to Remember*.

Chapter 6 *Revelation* (1940–44)

1. June Purvis discovered drafts of this unpublished memoir in Jill Craigie's papers. Unless otherwise noted, Jill's comments in this chapter are taken from this memoir.
2. No trace of this play survives in Jill Craigie's papers.
3. Rebecca West's essay on Mrs Pankhurst, 'A Reed of Steel', appeared in *The Post-Victorians* (1933) and was reprinted in *The Young Rebecca*, ed. Jane Marcus (1982).
4. Unidentified clipping in Jill Craigie's papers.

Chapter 7 *The Way We Live* (1944–6)

1. 'First there was fun – the ulcers came later', *Evening Standard*, 12 December 1967.
2. See Frances Thorpe and Nicholas Pronay, *British Official Films in the Second World War: A Descriptive Catalogue* (1980).
3. J. Paton-Watson and Patrick Abercrombie, *A Plan for Plymouth* (1943).
4. These details about Reilly's career are drawn from Joseph Sharples, Alan Powers, Michael Shippobottom, *Charles Reilly & The Liverpool School of Architecture 1904–1933* (1996), a copy of which Jill had in her study.
5. See Reilly's introduction to Lawrence Wolfe, *The Reilly Plan* (1945).
6. Channel 4 interview with Jill Craigie 10 November 1994, Imperial War Museum..

7. Interview with Barbara Dell.
8. On the radio programme *Quote… Unquote*, BBC Radio 4, 4 October 1981, Jill correctly identified Lady Astor's remark: 'I married beneath me. All women do.' Programme tape courtesy of Nigel Rees.
9. Channel 4 interview with Jill Craigie, 10 November 1994, Imperial War Museum.
10. For a more detailed analysis of the film, see Carl Rollyson, *Documentary Film: A Primer* (2004).
11. The critic is quoted in William MacQuitty's scrapbook on the film.
12. *Fifties Features.*
13. Charles Drazin interview with Jill Craigie, 14 November 1994.
14. *The Women's Companion to International Film* (1990).
15. 'Jill Craigie', in *Women Filmmakers and Their Films.*

Chapter 8 *Adventures and Amours* (1944–7)

1. Channel 4 interview with Jill Craigie 10 November 1994, Imperial War Museum.
2. See Mervyn Jones, *Michael Foot* (1994) for an account of Michael's early love life.
3. Jill Craigie, 'Political Bloodsport', in *The State of the Nation: The Political Legacy of Aneurin Bevan* (1997).
4. Charles Drazin interview with Jill Craigie, courtesy of Charles Drazin.

Chapter 9 *Blue Scar* (1946–9)

1. Charles Drazin, *The Finest Years: British Cinema of the 1940s* (1998).
2. Geoffrey Macnab, *J. Arthur Rank and the British Film Industry* (1993).
3. The *News Chronicle* (11 April 1949) praised MacQuitty's 'almost suicidal courage'.
4. David Berry, *Wales & Cinema: The First Hundred Years* (1994).
5. Terry Witts, *A Time of Tears: Llanharan and Brynna: the story of two mining villages where coal reigned supreme at the turn of the century* (2000).
6. Jill Craigie's preface to Witts's book.
7. Interview with Terry Witts.

Chapter 10 *My Dear Child* (1947–9)

1. Jill's letter appeared on 25 September under the heading 'Films and Fashions':

    'In an effort to prevent women from making do with the clothes they have got, fashion designers have gone all out to revolutionize fashion. We read that Miss Mae West will be appearing in the new long dresses in her play to be produced in Manchester. Actresses of my acquaintance are already arranging to have their entire wardrobes altered. To try to change fashion so drastically at such a period is, surely, one of the most anti-social moves to have been made for some time.

    To counteract this, I should like to suggest that there is a great opportunity for the British film industry. There is hardly a greater influence on fashion than the film. If British directors refuse to dress their stars in the new styles, I believe there is some chance that this wasteful move will die a natural death. If they do follow the fashion, it will certainly have a bad effect on our economies. I am sure that even film distributors will appreciate that a heroine in a murder story will look no less alluring if we can see her legs.'
2. *Quote . . . Unquote* (BBC Radio 4, 4 October 1989) courtesy of Nigel Rees.

Chapter 11 *33 Rosslyn Hill* (1949–52)

1. See Ellen Emerson, Ruth Harrison, and Diana Thomson, *Hampstead Memories* (2000).
2. Quoted in Leah Martin, 'House and Home: New Bohemia rises in the East End', *Sunday Telegraph*, 31 August 1997.
3. Jill Craigie, 'I call This a National Calamity', *Tribune*, 28 October 1955.
4. 'Love and Socialism', *Guardian*, 20 November 1997. In *Odd Reflections* Jill wrote: 'Jenny Lee said of her marriage to Nye, "God! What it did to my ego!" But she made up for it afterwards.' See

Michael's essay, 'Jennie Lee', in *Loyalists and Loners*.
5. My view of Jennie Lee is drawn from Patricia Hollis's superb *Jennie Lee: A Life* (London: Oxford University Press, 1997) and from interviews with Michael Foot.
6. Jill reminiscences appear in 'Political Bloodsport', *The State of the Nation: The Political Legacy of Aneurin Bevan*, edited by Geoffrey Goodman (1997).
7. Michael Foot, *Aneurin Bevin: A Biography, Volume Two: 1945–1960* (1973).

Chapter 12 *To Be a Woman* (1948–51)
1. Interview with Ronald Neame. See also Charles Drazin, *The Finest Years: British Cinema of the 1940s* (London: André Deutsch, 1998) and the discussion of documentaries as smelling of 'dust and boredom'. Michael Powell, *A Life in the Movies: An Autobiography* (New York: Knopf, 1987): 'I don't want to make a documentary. Documentaries are for disappointed feature film-makers or out-of-work poets.'
2. See Ben Pimlott, *Harold Wilson* (London: Harper Collins, 1992); Philip Ziegler, *Wilson: The Authorized Life* (London: Weidenfeld & Nicolson, 1993); Paul Foot, *The Politics of Harold Wilson* (London: Penguin, 1968). Foot's commentary on Wilson's treatment of the film industry, he told me, derives from his discussions with Jill. He wrote the book while living with Jill and Michael: 'Everything I wrote was taken down in dictation from her, and it's a pretty substantial section. I never heard a word that any of this was wrong.'
3. Charles Drazin interview with Jill Craigie (recorded 14 November 1994), courtesy of Charles Drazin. See also his *The Finest Years*.
4. Ernest Betts, *The Film Business: A History of British Cinema 1896–1972* (1973).
5. 'Fifties Features: The Woman Behind the Pictures: Jill Craigie.' Transcript of interview conducted 24/1/86, courtesy of The British Film Institute.

Chapter 13 *Rape* (1952)
1. My description of the rape closely follows the account Jill gave to David Cesarani, *Arthur Koestler: The Homeless Mind* (New York: The Free Press, 1998), which Jill and Michael reviewed for accuracy. I have also drawn a few details from interviews with Michael Foot and from Katharine Whitehorn, 'Inside Story: Man behaving badly', *Guardian*, 22 October 1998; David Lister, 'Storm as Raphael defends Koestler', *Independent*, 23 February 1999; Libby Brooks and Stephen Moss, 'I was worried about my life, not my honour', *Guardian*, 25 February 1999.
2. 'Secret Service, Private Passions', *Financial Times*, 8 April 1995.

Chapter 14 *Screenwriter* (1952–8)
1. Jill told this story in several interviews, including one recorded 27 March 1995 and sent to me by film historian Philip Kemp.
2. Gregory Peck to Carl Rollyson, 21 August 2000.
3. 'A new future for history', review of Sheila Rowbotham's *A Century of Women*, *Ham & High*, 18 July 1997.
4. 'Fifties Features: The Woman Behind the Pictures: Jill Craigie', recorded 24 January 1986, courtesy of the British Film Institute.
5. The galley in Jill's papers does not have a date on it.
6. Balcon's correspondence with Jill is in his collection at the British Film Institute. In a draft of her article, Jill protested the 'petty restrictions' that had produced a 'frustrating list of still-born stories in British studios'. Public relations officers vetted scripts. A film on the railways had to 'show everything working to perfection', for example. 'The Bank of England recently requested the withdrawal of posters showing a facsimile of a million-pound note.'
7. Jill Craigie to Philip Kemp, 13 April 1992; Philip Kemp interview with Jill Craigie, 7 May 1992, courtesy of Philip Kemp.

Chapter 15 *32A Abbey Road* (1954–9)

1. Jill's correspondence with Beaverbrook is available in the House of Lords Record Office.
2. I'm grateful to Julie Hamilton for consulting her diary and pinning down these dates.
3. For Julie's involvement with Sean Connery, I draw on interviews with Julie, Michael Foot, Kathy Seery and Lizzie Parker, as well as on Julie's account in a two-part series for the *Daily Mirror* (16 February 1983); Geoffrey Wansell, 'Connery The Monster, *Daily Mail* (13 May 2000); 'As Sean Connery Celebrates His 70th Birthday', *Hello!* (5 September 2000).
4. Jennie's letter to Jill is undated and can be found in her papers at the Open University Library.
5. Jill was quoted on a Channel 4 documentary, recorded 10 November 1994.
6. See Michael's essay, 'Brother Frank', in *Loyalists and Loners*, and the standard source, Geoffrey Goodman, *The Awkward Warrior: Frank Cousins, His Life and Times* (1979).
7. See Gayle Greene, *The Woman Who Knew Too Much: Alice Stewart and the Secrets of Radiation* (1999).
8. See Michael's brief memoir in Maxine Ventham, *Spike Milligan: His Part In Our Lives* (2002).
9. Quoted in Mervyn Jones, *Michael Foot* (1994).
10. Simon Hoggart and David Lee, *Michael Foot* (1981).
11. Patricia Hollis, *Jennie Lee: A Life* (1977)
12. Jennie Lee, *My Life with Nye* (1980).

Chapter 16 *10 Morgan Street* (1959–63)

1. See Michael's essay on Jennie in *Loyalists and Loners*.
2. Lady Beaverbrook to Jill Craigie, 22 December 1967.
3. Jill told this story about herself on the programme *Quote… Unquote*, BBC Radio 4, 29 December 1981, courtesy of Nigel Rees.
4. I'm indebted to Mark Seddon, who spent his honeymoon in 10 Morgan Street, for these details.
5. Interview with Glenys Kinnock.
6. I interviewed the Kinnocks separately.

Chapter 17 *Facing It* (1963–4)

1. See Richard Crossman, *The Diaries of a Cabinet Minister Volume Two 1966–1968* (1976).

Chapter 18 *Pilgrim's Lane* (1964–70)

1. Ben Pimlott, *Harold Wilson* (1992).
2. Michael Foot, *Harold Wilson: A Pictorial Biography* (1964).
3. Leo Abse, *Private Member* (1973).
4. Sonia Orwell to Jill Craigie, 23 May 1967.
5. Benn Levy to Jill Craigie, 15 May 1967.
6. Inge Weisz to Michael and Jill, 1 August 1969.
7. I made two attempts to contact Victor, but he did not respond to my inquiries.

Chapter 19 *Who Are the Vandals?* (1964–72)

1. *The Peterborough Effect: Reshaping a City* (1988).
2. Tom Hancock to Carl Rollyson, 3 June 2003.
3. *The Peterborough Effect* gives a detailed account of Hancock's role.
4. Jill had already reviewed Fulford's book in 'Still no justice for the suffragettes', *Tribune* (19 April 1957).

Chapter 20 *Obsession* (1970–72)

1. The term is Stendahl's, as elaborated in *De l'Amour*, one of Michael Foot's favourite texts. Quotations from the book in this chapter are from Gilbert and Suzanne Sale's translation, *Love* (1957).

2. Jill did not date her letters from this period, and Michael does not have an exact recollection, but Jill's Venice trip took place in the second week of April 1971. On 1 April a friend wrote to her to say he had been told she would come to Venice 'next Thursday'.

3. Kathy Seery said as much in an interview, and Julie added: 'I should think that she was privy to a lot of my mother's feelings at certain times when nobody else was around.'

4. All references to Paul Foot are contained in Jill's letters. Paul refused to be interviewed about this chapter of Jill's life, and he strenuously objected to the inclusion of this account in her biography. Unless otherwise noted, the rest of this chapter is based on Jill's correspondence to Julie and Mike Randall, and on Julie's corroboration of her mother's version of events.

Chapter 21 *Recovery* (1972)

1. In a letter dated 23 October (no year is given) and sent to Jill at Abbey Road, Beaverbrook writes: 'Give my love to Michael. He will precede Tony Greenwood at 10 Downing Street. And that will be a bad day for all the monied men who live in idleness on labours of their forefathers.'

Chapter 22 *The Idea of India* (1973–98)

1. Quoted in Frank.

Chapter 23 *Husbands and Wives* (1973–9)

1. The letter is dated Saturday the 12th and was probably written in 1973 when Jill was still at work on her play and sending drafts to Mike Randall.

2. The letter is dated February 17th and was written in the mid-1970s.

3. The late Peter Shore was ailing when I began work on this book, and I did not have the opportunity to interview him. His wife did not respond to my letters or phone messages.

4. I wanted to get Barbara Castle's side of the story, and Michael assured me that she would speak with me. He had just been interviewed by her authorised biographer, and he had refused to see her unauthorised biographer (per Castle's request). In an undated letter responding to my request for an interview she wrote, 'Of course I would be glad to see you about Jill Craigie.' I called her to arrange an appointment, and after setting a date she asked, 'And what are you going to do for me?' Startled, I said, 'I'm afraid I don't know what you mean.' 'Oh, a fee,' she replied. I explained that I was not in the habit of paying for information and did not want to set such a precedent. She answered that she had given her 'heart's blood' in interviews and did not receive anything in return. 'It does not have to be a large fee. You think about it.' I said I would, and then I wrote to Michael explaining why I felt I could not see her. Later Michael told me that she had approached him in some embarrassment about her treatment of me, but in the end he waved away her apology, not wanting to have any ill feeling between them. 'Of course, you must explain in your biography why you did not see her,' Michael said. When I told journalist Jon Snow about my dealings with Barbara Castle, he said she was just having me on. She liked a good fight. I should call her up and give her one – say something like 'You know I need to talk to you and payment is just not on.' I tried a more oblique approach, writing two more times to ask her if she had a copy of her remarks at Jill's memorial celebration and if I could have permission to quote one of her letters to Jill and Michael. She replied both times, saying she did not have a copy of her talk and that I could have permission to quote. She did not re-open, as I hoped, the issue of an interview. Then Barbara Castle died before I had the opportunity to attempt the Jon Snow approach. I do not honestly know if I would have tried.

5. Many of Jill's letters to Julie are undated, but I have been able to determine their approximate chronological order based on internal evidence.

6. Perhaps this comment is what prompted Tony Benn to send me the following response to this chapter: 'I notice there are some very unpleasant references to my late wife Caroline and whether you will include them or not is a decision for you as author and not for me but obviously I found them distressing and inaccurate.'

7. Tony Benn, *Against the Tide: Diaries 1973–76* (1989).

8.   In the *Financial Times* (11 February 1976), John Elliott wrote of a 'Ministerial career which has already lasted far longer had seemed likely . . . it has for some time been rumoured that he had been on the brink of resigning.'

9.   This is one of Michael's favourite stories. Callaghan told me he could not remember what he said, but he saw no reason to dispute Michael's version.

10. His first vivid memory of Jill dates back to the 1959 general election when he was responsible for the election broadcasts. 'Nye refused to be interviewed by anyone other than Jill.' A nervous performer on radio and television, Bevan found it hard to sit down for questions. 'She was so skilful with Nye, and he was able to be himself.'

Chapter 24 *Daughters of Dissent 1* (1975–82)

1.   Courtesy of Kenneth Morgan. Morgan added the year 1975 to this letter, but given Jill's reference to her *Observer* article which appeared early in 1977, the 1975 date is unlikely, especially since Jill's papers include a letter from Morgan dated 27 August 1976 in which he refers to a party a friend of his attended at which Jill made certain criticisms of his Keir Hardie biography. Morgan wanted Jill to specify his errors so he could correct them in a subsequent edition. Morgan says that she never did spell out her objections.

2.   Jill Craigie to Kenneth Morgan 15 September 1976. Jill always made Keir Hardie an honorable exception in her attacks on male politicians since Hardie had always been a staunch supporter of the Pankhursts and of votes for women.

3.   'There were at least five occasions – I'm not exaggerating at all – when I rang Jill to talk about the subject and go so absorbed that I got into the car and drove all across London and through the jams to bloody Hampstead for another hour of conversation,' Paul recalled. It was better not to have Michael there – 'not because he was obstructive but because he would change the subject. But she was single-minded about it and really interested to talk about it.'

4.   As June Purvis shows in *Emmeline Pankhurst: A Biography*, Mrs. Pankhurst's turn toward the Conservatives was anything but 'silly'. It is important to understand that during this crucial period – between 1908 and the outbreak of war in 1914 – Emmeline became increasingly disenchanted with the Labour Party and with the trade unions, even as her daughter Sylvia intensified her commitment to socialism and saw Votes for Women as a socialist issue. Emmeline, on the other hand, observed that socialist men no less than their capitalist counterparts worried about losing jobs to women if women had equal rights. A socialist, no less than a capitalist, disliked the idea of giving his woman property rights. Jill understood this well. She had no faith in a socialist revolution securing women's rights since she knew full well that so many male socialists were also male chauvinists. In Cora Kaplan's introduction to Elizabeth Barrett Browning, *Aurora Leigh and Other Poems* (1978), Jill underlined the statement: 'Both liberal and radical feminism insist that patriarchal domination is *the* problem of human cultures. It tends to ignore or diminish the importance of class conflict, race and the operations of capital, and to make small distinction between the oppressions of middle-class women and working-class or Third World Women.' When Jill disagreed with a statement, she wrote in the margin 'No!' or 'Wrong.' To Pat Romero (1 June 1979) Jill wrote that Kaplan had written a 'dazzling preface'.

5.   June Purvis, who became Jill's friend, has carried on this mission admirably in her biography of Mrs Pankhurst. See Michael's review of it: 'The Stronger Vessel', *Guardian*, 3 August 2002. Martin Pugh's entry on Mrs Pankhurst in *The Blackwell Biographical Dictionary of British Political Life in the Twentieth Century* (1990) presents the judgement Jill battled to overturn: 'Though Emmeline remains a heroine to many feminists, her role in the women's movement has been much diminished by modern scholarship.'

6.   The letter is dated 3 August and the year is probably 1976, when Jill would have been sixty-five. Of the Magna Carta ceremony she wrote in another letter: 'Receiving hundreds of guests in some of the most historic palaces in London makes me feel as if I am taking part in one of the satires we used to make at Pinewood studios in my film days. But I get a good view of the women's dresses

– some of them most weird – as they come swanning up the stairs.'

7. 'Neither Christabel nor her mother ever repeated the compliments paid to them, perhaps because they had no need of such reassurance being the recipients of so much flattery' – Jill Craigie to Patricia Romero, 20 September 1977.

8. Patricia Romero e-mail to Carl Rollyson, 10 July 2001. Michael's memories of the Danieli are quite different from Romero's. See Chapter 28. One can be a great lover of Venice – like Jan Morris, whose book *Venice* (1963) provided one of the guides to the city for Michael and Jill – and still write: 'The hotels are expensive, the gondolas and water-taxis ruinous, the porters, shouldering your fibre-glass bag from one alley-way to the next, extortionate.'

9. Jill Craigie to Pat Romero, 1 December, 1976.

10. Jill Craigie to Patricia Romero, 13 April (probably 1976).

11. Patricia Romero e-mail to Carl Rollyson, 14 July 2001.

12. Patricia Romero e-mail to Carl Rollyson, 10 July 2001.

13. 'I proposed to Jim Callaghan… that the Government should make a big thing of July 2nd this year and, indeed, the whole month because that will be the golden jubilee of British democracy,' Jill wrote to Pat on 12 March 1978. Callaghan wrote Jill on 31 January and 9 March welcoming her suggestions and inviting her to serve on the steering committee.

14. Patricia Romero to Jill Craigie, 3 December 1975; 9 January 1976.

15. My account of Jill's relationship with Rebecca is drawn from interviews with Jill Craigie carried out for my biography of Rebecca West, with Jane Marcus, Ursula Owen and Michael Foot, and from the correspondence (much of it undated) between Jill and Rebecca in Jill's papers and in the Rebecca West collection at the University of Tulsa.

16. Jill would expound her own take on what happened in the 1920s and 1930s in 'Lib in Woolf's Clothing', *Observer*, 2 July 1978, where she made the distinction between a 'feminist-conformist' and a 'feminist-anarchist'. The former held Shaw's view that women should be liberated so as to compete with men on an equal basis. But that is as far as he could go. Virginia Woolf, on the other hand, argued that the ideal of equality could never be achieved unless patriarchal values were rejected. Woolf had lost the argument, Jill concluded: 'Men continue to parade themselves in their silly costumes and women, be they professors, mayoresses or judges, join the processions more or less similarly attired. Acceptance of men's terms was the price of their admittance.' Yet when Jill thought of how little impact women had had on the structures of society – just look at the tower blocks, she observed – she doubted Shaw's faith in women's ability to 'knock sense' into men if the structure of society remained the same. She found her sympathies swinging toward Virginia Woolf. Indeed, she resumed her attack on male architects in 'System that stifles a budding Lutyens', *Guardian* (31 January 1983) and in heading up in the early 1980s a Woman's Action Housing Group composed of architects and civil servants. In the minutes for 21 June 1982, for example, Jill reported on plans to put together a list of 'housing do's and don'ts to send to feminist groups all over the country'.

17. Quoted in Kaplan.

18. I have drawn on Ursula Owen's 'An Appreciation: Jill Craigie, 1914–1999', in *Women's History Review* 9 (2000), and on my email correspondence, and two interviews – one for my Rebecca West biography and the other for this book.

19. I describe the scene in *Rebecca West: A Saga of the Century* (1995). Jill said, 'Michael stole her away from me in a kind of way.'

20. 'Playing Against Loaded Dice', *Guardian*, 16 March 1983.

21. 'The Free Woman', a short piece in *Cosmopolitan* timed to coincide with the publication of *The Young Rebecca* in 1982.

Chapter 25 *Defeat* (1980–83)

1. Ian Mikardo, *Back-Bencher* (1988).

2. *Western Mail*, 23 May 1983, quoted in Mervyn Jones, *Michael Foot*.

3. Denis Healey, *The Time of My Life* (1989).
4. See Healey's discussion of the trip in *The Time of My Life* and Mervyn Jones, *Michael Foot*. Jill took heart from a huge CND rally on 26 October, at which Michael received a 'tremendous reception' and the cause of unilateralism was revived.
5. Jill's calendar notes trips to the Lakes and to Cornwall in mid-August 1983.
6. Michael quotes this *Guardian* report in *Another Heart & Other Pulses*.

Chapter 26 *House and Garden* (1976–91)
1. Unidentified signature, 17 August 1984.
2. An undated letter to Pat Romero.
3. For an account of the American treatment of Rushdie, see Carl Rollyson and Lisa Paddock, *Susan Sontag: The Making of an Icon* (2000).
4. Quoted in an extraordinary piece of journalism by Fred Halliday, 'The Fundamental Lesson of the Fatwa', *New Statesman,* 12 February 1993. Halliday point outs, 'hardly a single writer from any Muslim country and especially from any Middle Eastern country, has been found to denounce him'.

Chapter 27 *Daughters of Dissent 2* (1983–99)
1. June Purvis e-mail to Carl Rollyson, 4 May 2002. June's letters make clear that she had read Jill's introduction to the Virago Press edition of Emmeline Pankhurst's *My Own Story*.

Chapter 28 *Two Hours From London* (1962–95)
1. The Craigie/Foot analysis is confirmed in Brendan Simms, *Unfinest Hour: Britain and The Destruction of Bosnia* (2001).

Chapter 29 *Wife and Mother* (1994–9)
1. Julie Hamilton e-mail to Carl Rollyson, 10 January 2003.
2. See David Lister, 'Storm as Raphael defends rapist Koestler', 13 February 1999.
3. Scammell did not reveal his sources to Michael. To my query, he sent an email reply on 3 February 2002: 'No, I can't tell you about the people I interviewed.' Thus the Scammell doctrine of 'exclusivity' remains intact. I should declare an interest. Scammell tried to bar my access to the American PEN's board minutes when I was researching Susan Sontag's records as president of American PEN. See Carl Rollyson and Lisa Paddock, *Susan Sontag: The Making of an Icon* (2000).
4. Courtesy of Celine La Freniere.

Chapter 30 *When You Grow Old* (1997–9)
1. Francis Wheen, 'Together for a firebrand, celebrating Jill Craigie', *Guardian*, 19 January 2000.
2. Interview with Ted Honderich.
3. Fiona Millar email to Carl Rollyson, 1 February 2002.

Appendix A *Jill Craigie and the Documentary Tradition*
1. David Thomson, *A Biographical Dictionary of Film, Third Edition* (1996).
2. Quoted in Barnouw.
3. Interviews with William MacQuitty and Kay Mander.
4. Quoted in Stansky and Abrahams.
5. For a good overview of Rotha's career see John Wakeman, ed., *World Film Directors: Volume One 1890–1945* (1987).
6. I am grateful to film-maker Midge Mackenzie for first drawing my attention to Mander, to Sarah Easen, Cataloguer, British Universities Newsreel Database, for the programme notes on Mander (whose films were shown recently at the Imperial War Museum) and especially to Kay Mander who spoke with me at length about her career.

Index